CAPES/Agrégation ANGLAIS

Jane Eyre

Le roman de Charlotte Brontë et le film de Franco Zeffirelli

ouvrage dirigé par Laurent Bury et Dominique Sipière

Claire Bazin
Professeur l'Université de Paris X

Stéphanie Bernard
Maître de conférences à l'IUFM de Rouen

Laure Blanchemain
Maître de conférences à l'Université de Limoges

Charlotte Borie
Lectrice de français à St John's College, Cambridge

Laurent Bury
Professeur à l'Université de Lyon II

Nicole Cloarec
Maître de conférences à l'Université de Rennes I

Raphaëlle Costa de Beauregard
Professeur à l'Université Toulouse le Mirail

Pascale Denance
PRAG à l'Université de Nantes

Max Duperray
Professeur à l'Université d'Aix-Marseille

Christine Evain
Professeur à l'École Centrale de Nantes

Jacqueline Fromonot
Maître de conférences à l'Université de Paris VIII

Xavier Lachazette
Maître de conférences à l'Université du Maine

Catherine Lanone
Professeur à l'Université de Toulouse II

Laurent Mellet
Maître de conférences à l'Université de Bourgogne

Eithne O'Neill
Revue *Positif*

Elise Ouvrard
Maître de conférences à l'Université de Caen

Anne Paupe
Maître de conférences à l'Université Paris XIII

Gilbert Pham-Thanh
Maître de conférences à l'Université de Paris XIII

Dominique Sipière
Professeur à l'Université de Paris X

Laurence Talairach-Vielmas
Maître de conférences à l'Université de Toulouse II

Taïna Tuhkunen
Maître de conférences à l'Université de Versailles St Quentin

Isabelle Van Peteghem-Tréard
Professeur en Classes Préparatoires

Shannon Wells-Lassagne
Maître de conférences à l'Université de Bretagne Sud

ISBN 978-2-7298-4033-4
© Ellipses Édition Marketing S.A., 2008
32, rue Bargue 75740 Paris cedex 15

Le Code de la propriété intellectuelle n'autorisant, aux termes de l'article L. 122-5.2° et 3°a), d'une part, que les « copies ou reproductions strictement réservées à l'usage privé du copiste et non destinées à une utilisation collective », et d'autre part, que les analyses et les courtes citations dans un but d'exemple et d'illustration, « toute représentation ou reproduction intégrale ou partielle faite sans le consentement de l'auteur ou de ses ayants droit ou ayants cause est illicite » (art. L. 122-4).
Cette représentation ou reproduction, par quelque procédé que ce soit constituerait une contrefaçon sanctionnée par les articles L. 335-2 et suivants du Code de la propriété intellectuelle.

www.editions-ellipses.fr

Table des matières

Partie I – *Jane Eyre*, le roman 5

Elise Ouvrard	*Jane Eyre* : roman de formation ou roman de quête ? 6
Xavier Lachazette	Roles and Representations of Nature in *Jane Eyre* 26
Charlotte Borie	*Jane Eyre* : la picturalité et son inscription dans le texte 43
Laure Blanchemain	Charlotte Brontë's Mirthless Laughter: Comedy in *Jane Eyre* 63
Gilbert Pham-Thanh	*Jane Eyre*: Taking Men in and Writing out Patriarchy 74
Laurent Bury	*Clothes, their Origin and Influence*: *Jane Eyre* et la philosophie des vêtements ...82
Catherine Lanone	"I am not a liar": Interpellation and Counter-interpellation in *Jane Eyre* 99
Jacqueline Fromonot	Secrets, Lies, Concealment and the Quest for Truth in *Jane Eyre* 110
Laurence Talairach-Vielmas	Legacies of the Past: The Buried Stories of Thornfield Hall 120
Pascale Denance	La construction de l'ipséité textuelle dans *Jane Eyre* à partir de certaines figures archétypales de rebelles et de tyrans 133
Max Duperray	Le théâtre intérieur ou le sens caché de *Jane Eyre* : « *the secret voice* » (133), « *the still small voice* » (172) 145
Claire Bazin	"The red-room" (9-14) : Explication de texte 153
Stéphanie Bernard	*Jane Eyre* : l'œuvre en création 162

Partie II - *Jane Eyre* à l'écran 177

Dominique Sipière	*Jane Eyre* : quel usage faisons-nous des classiques à l'écran?	178
Nicole Cloarec	*Jane Eyre* de Franco Zeffirelli (1996) : la glace sans le feu. Lectures croisées de la première rencontre entre Jane et Rochester	190
R. Costa de Beauregard	Commodifying culture and the politically correct in the 1990s: Franco Zeffirelli's *Jane Eyre* (1847)	199
Christine Evain	Que devient la narration à la première personne lors de l'adaptation cinématographique de *Jane Eyre* par Franco Zeffirelli ?	212
Eithne O'Neill	Subject, sadness and portraiture in Franco Zeffirelli's *Jane Eyre*	227
Isabelle Van Peteghem-Tréard	Cet obscur objet du désir, jeux d'ombres et de lumière dans *Jane Eyre*	236
Anne Paupe	Place and Space in Franco Zeffirelli's *Jane Eyre* (1996)	251
Taïna Tuhkunen	The terror and enchantment of colours in Franco Zeffirelli's *Jane Eyre*	260
Laurent Mellet	Désir et monotonie dans *Jane Eyre*	274
Shannon Wells-Lassagne	Visualizing the Gothic in *Jane Eyre*	286

Jane Eyre, le film de Franco Zeffirelli (filmographie, bibliographie) 297

Les auteurs 301

Partie I –
Jane Eyre, le roman

Jane Eyre : roman de formation ou roman de quête ?

Elise Ouvrard

Contrairement au manuscrit de *The Professor* qui fut refusé par de nombreuses maisons d'édition et ne fut publié finalement que de manière posthume, celui de *Jane Eyre* reçut un accueil chaleureux dès qu'il fut proposé à l'éditeur George Smith : ce dernier le dévora en une seule journée en août 1847 et le roman sortait des imprimeries deux mois plus tard pour connaître un succès immédiat. Son auteur, Charlotte Brontë, avait décidé d'écrire un roman « plus imaginatif et poétique » (Alexander et Smith 268) que le premier et le changement de genre avait conquis les éditeurs.

De fait les critiques se sont intéressés tout particulièrement à la question du genre et à ce qui faisait la spécificité du second roman de Charlotte Brontë. De nombreux ouvrages et articles traitent donc de la dimension autobiographique de *Jane Eyre*, de l'influence du gothique, mais aussi des résonances féministes du roman ou encore des possibles comparaisons avec le roman social sans oublier le conte de fées. Ce qui nous intéresse tout particulièrement ici, c'est la manière dont Charlotte Brontë conçoit le parcours de son héroïne, parcours qui ne semble pas si éloigné de celui de William Crimsworth, héros de son premier manuscrit :

> I said to myself that my hero should work his way through life as I had seen real living men work theirs—that he should never get a shilling he had not earned [...] that before he could find so much as an arbour to sit down in—he should master at least half the ascent of the hill of Difficulty. *(The Professor, "Preface", 1)*

Dans cette intention qu'affiche l'auteur dès la préface de *The Professor*, on trouve déjà l'idée que la vie est une lutte et que le héros doit faire preuve d'endurance et de volonté pour tracer son chemin, avec cette idée de pèlerinage indiquée par la référence à *The Pilgrim's Progress* de John Bunyan. Dans *Jane Eyre*, comme dans *The Professor*, Charlotte Brontë se concentre sur l'itinéraire et l'évolution de son personnage principal ; selon Robert B. Martin « *action moves towards the maturity and self-knowledge of its two central characters. Jane's maturation is, of course, the more detailed and central of the two* » (Martin 58). En effet, contrairement au roman *The Professor* qui s'intéresse au personnage William Crimsworth alors qu'il est déjà adulte, dans *Jane Eyre*, on suit l'héroïne dès son enfance, ce qui a poussé certains critiques à établir des liens avec le Bildungsroman, à l'image de Delia da Sousa Correa qui indique que la notion est importante pour la lecture du roman[1] (Sousa Correa 98).

À partir de ce parcours de l'héroïne, deux notions apparaissent donc essentielles pour la question du genre : celle de « roman de formation » et celle de « roman de quête » avec cette dimension bunyanesque qu'insuffle Charlotte Brontë au roman. Nous verrons donc d'abord dans quelle mesure on peut associer *Jane Eyre* au Bildungsroman ainsi que les limites d'un tel rapprochement. La vision du monde qu'avait Charlotte Brontë nous amènera en effet à considérer le rôle de la quête et à proposer une étude comparative entre *Jane Eyre* et l'ouvrage de John Bunyan *The Pilgrim's Progress*. Contrairement à la plupart des critiques qui, comme nous le verrons, ont rapproché les romans de Charlotte Brontë du récit de Bunyan, nous montrerons que les objectifs et moteurs de la quête sont différents d'un ouvrage à l'autre, malgré une préoccupation centrale pour le salut dans les deux cas. Nous terminerons alors par l'analyse de l'esthétique providentielle du second roman de Charlotte Brontë puisque, contrairement à *The Professor* dans lequel le protagoniste devait se passer de l'aide du destin (« *I said to myself that [...] no sudden turns should lift him in a moment to wealth and high station* », *The Professor*, "Preface", 1), *Jane Eyre* se tourne vers la Providence pour qu'elle vienne au secours de son héroïne, comme l'illustre l'appel surnaturel de Rochester.

Un roman de formation ?

C'est en 1820 que le terme « Bildungsroman » fait son apparition pour la première fois dans une série de conférences que tient Karl Morgenstern à Dorpat sur plusieurs romans philosophiques. Il faut attendre 1870 pour que Wilhelm Dilthey[2] propose le concept de Bildungsroman, le définisse de manière précise et l'identifie au roman de Johann Wolfgang von Goethe *Les Années d'apprentissage de Wilhelm Meister* (1795-1796)[3]. Le concept

---

1. Bien que l'article de Jerome Beaty s'intitule, lui aussi, « Jane Eyre *and Genre* », il s'intéresse surtout aux différentes sources qui ont pu inspirer Charlotte Brontë, ce qui explique qu'il ne soit pas fait référence à son analyse ici.
2. Wilhelm Dilthey, *Das Erlebnis und die Dichtung: Lessing, Goethe, Novalis, Hölderlin* [1906], Göttingen: Vandenhoeck & Ruprecht, 1921. Guy Stern s'est intéressé, quant à lui, et ce beaucoup plus tard, aux sources d'inspiration de Goethe. Il a montré que Henry Fielding, et en particulier *Tom Jones*, avait fourni les traits essentiels du Bildungsroman et que Christoph Martin Wieland, avec *Die Geschichte des Agathon* (1767), avait constitué le chaînon manquant entre Fielding et Goethe (Guy Stern, *Fielding, Wieland, Goethe and the Rise of the novel*, Frankfort : Peter Lang, 2003). On notera que l'*Agathon* de Wieland est, quant à lui, souvent considéré comme un roman psychologique.
3. Il semble qu'il faille distinguer le Bildungsroman (roman de formation), du roman d'éducation qui lui est antérieur et auquel appartient *Émile, ou de l'éducation* (1762) de Jean-Jacques

de Bildungsroman est de fait plus ou moins réservé à ce livre ; Daniel Mortier, comparatiste germaniste, a souligné le caractère particulier de ce genre romanesque (l'auteur traduit ici « Bildungsroman » par « roman d'éducation ») :

> Curieux genre que le roman d'éducation. D'une part, en effet, la conclusion de la plupart des études est, sinon qu'il n'existe pas, du moins qu'il se réduirait pratiquement à son prototype, le roman de Goethe, jugé finalement « unique en son genre ». D'autre part, la critique allemande en est arrivée à estimer que *Les Années d'apprentissage de Wilhelm Meister* n'étaient pas un roman d'éducation (Mortier 121).

Si la notion est contestée[1], on ne peut nier son existence, d'autant plus qu'elle sert à la relecture de nombreux romans anglais[2] tels que *David Copperfield* ou *Great Expectations* de Charles Dickens ou encore *The Mill on the Floss* de George Eliot[3]. Or, lorsqu'on reprend les différentes caractéristiques du roman de formation, telles qu'elles sont admises dans les ouvrages de référence[4] ou les sources secondaires citées précédemment, on s'aperçoit que *Jane Eyre* se distingue profondément du modèle.

Contrairement à la plupart des romans de formation qui mettent en scène un protagoniste masculin, Charlotte Brontë choisit, elle, de dépeindre le parcours d'une héroïne. D'autre part, les différentes étapes qui ponctuent le Bildungsroman — la formation scolaire, le départ de la maison familiale et la découverte du monde — sont quelque peu bouleversées puisque la formation de Jane Eyre à Gateshead se transforme en auto-formation. En effet, le cercle familial qui a recueilli Jane Eyre l'a mise à l'écart sans lui assurer la formation intellectuelle et morale qu'elle était en droit d'attendre et qu'elle a donc entreprise d'acquérir par elle-même. Les livres sont alors

---

Rousseau, du roman pédagogique auquel Robert Granderoute a consacré un ouvrage (Robert Granderoute, *Le Roman pédagogique de Fénelon à Rousseau*, Paris : Slatkine, 1985) ainsi que du roman français d'apprentissage, qui recouvre *Le Rouge et le Noir*, *Le Père Goriot*, *Les Illusions perdues*, *L'Éducation sentimentale* ou encore *Bel-Ami*.

1. Pour un développement plus complet sur la remise en cause de la notion, on pourra se référer aux articles de Marcel de Grève et de Françoise Lartillot, sur le site du Dictionnaire International des Termes Littéraires : http://www.ditl.info/arttest/art17344.php; http://www.ditl.info/arttest/art1885.php. Ces articles sont également une aide précieuse pour comprendre ce que recouvre la notion de « Bildungsroman ».
2. On pourra à ce sujet consulter l'ouvrage du spécialiste Jerome Hamilton Buckley, *Season of Youth: The Bildungsroman from Dickens to Golding*, Cambridge : Harvard University Press, 1974.
3. Alain Jumeau a consacré un chapitre de son ouvrage sur *The Mill on the Floss* à la question du roman de formation, qui pose véritablement problème dans la mesure où les deux personnages, Tom et Maggie, ne suivent pas du tout le même parcours (Alain Jumeau, *The Mill on the Floss, George Eliot*, Paris : Armand Colin, 2002).
4. On peut, par exemple, se référer à la définition que donne M. H. Abrams dans son *Glossary of Literary Terms* (M. H. Abrams, *A Glossary of Literary Terms*, 5e édition, Holt : Rinehart and Winston Inc., 1981, 119-120).

un élément essentiel de l'éducation de l'orpheline. La première image que nous avons de Jane Eyre est celle d'une petite fille qui s'est réfugiée dans la lecture de *History of British Birds*, lecture qui suffit à son bonheur : « *with Bewick on my knee, I was then happy: happy at least in my way* » (7). Le thème de la nature renforce le côté également libérateur de l'ouvrage de Bewick qui offre à l'enfant l'occasion d'assouvir sa soif de liberté. Avec cet ouvrage, tout comme avec les contes de fées, et les contes tirés de *The Arabian Nights*, Jane Eyre se distrait et s'évade du cadre familial qui l'opprime. Si la lecture constitue un divertissement pour Jane Eyre, elle est aussi riche d'enseignements, comme le montre Anne Hiebert Alton :

> Jane also reads works which are intended to educate her in religious, spiritual, and moral matters. She is familiar with the Bible, and she refers specifically to parts of Revelations (sic), Daniel, Genesis, Samuel, "a little bit of Exodus", Kings, Chronicles, Job and Jonah. […] In addition she knows the story of Pamela because Bessie reads it to her. *(Alton 267)*

Cette passion pour les livres explique pourquoi, malgré le refus de Mrs Reed d'éduquer Jane Eyre, cette dernière arrive à Lowood avec un bagage intellectuel et moral non négligeable, mais cette auto-formation initiale offre un contraste saisissant face aux parcours des héros et héroïnes des romans de formation.

Par la suite, la part d'apprentissage occupe bien sûr une place importante : Lowood apparaît comme un lieu de formation fondamental pour Jane Eyre, grâce aux deux personnages qui l'influencent dans cet établissement : Miss Temple, d'une part, et Helen Burns, d'autre part. On peut se demander cependant si la formation n'est pas avant tout morale, qu'il s'agisse de la relation de Jane avec le professeur modèle ou avec sa jeune amie.

Helen Burns est la première à distinguer Miss Temple des autres professeurs : « *Miss Temple is very good, and very clever: she is above the rest, because she knows far more than they do* » (43). Ses capacités intellectuelles ne font aucun doute, et Helen Burns loue également les qualités de pédagogue de la formatrice, qui sait captiver l'esprit de l'enfant, pourtant souvent distraite. Les qualités de Miss Temple dépassent cependant le simple cadre de la formation académique ; Jane Eyre et Helen Burns insistent également sur la grandeur morale du personnage. Ainsi, Helen Burns souligne sa bonté, bonté confirmée par l'acte charitable que la directrice accomplit en ordonnant que pain et fromage soient distribués à l'ensemble des élèves, lorsque le petit-déjeuner de ces dernières est trop brûlé pour être mangeable. Contrairement à Mrs Reed qui n'a de mère adoptive que le titre, Miss Temple joue un rôle maternel auprès des orphelines. Miss Temple est non seulement celle qui instruit, mais encore celle qui encourage, qui console, qui soigne. Dans l'adversité, elle est manifestement la seule parmi les professeurs de Lowood à trouver la force de soutenir les élèves, lors de ces longs trajets vers l'église en plein hiver, par exemple :

> I can remember Miss Temple walking lightly and rapidly along our drooping line, [...] and encouraging us, by precept and example, to keep up our spirits, and march forward, as she said, "like stalwart soldiers." *(51)*

La directrice joue un grand rôle dans la progression morale de l'héroïne ainsi que dans son équilibre affectif[1], d'autant plus que son rôle dépasse largement celui de simple formatrice :

> to her [Miss Temple's] instruction I owed the best part of my acquirements; her friendship and society had been my continual solace: she had stood me in the stead of mother, governess, and, latterly, companion. *(71)*

Helen Burns inspire également le respect de la jeune Jane Eyre, tant sur le plan intellectuel que sur le plan moral. Lorsque l'héroïne fait la connaissance de son amie, celle-ci est plongée dans la lecture de *Rasselas* ; Helen Burns suscite l'admiration de Jane Eyre par l'ampleur de ses connaissances, comme c'est le cas lors de la conversation qu'elle a avec Miss Temple, et l'influence moralement. Helen Burns s'attache à inculquer à Jane Eyre certains principes moraux élémentaires ; dans un premier temps, elle s'efforce de la détourner de la loi du Talion que Jane professe et de calmer l'esprit de révolte qui gronde en elle[2]. Si Jane Eyre écoute avec attention Helen, elle ne suivra pas cette voie de la soumission, face à Rochester ou à St John (le contexte est certes différent), car ce moi que Helen réprime, Jane Eyre, elle, l'affirme ; dans la scène qui l'oppose à M. Brocklehurst, l'héroïne précise : « *I was no Helen Burns* » (55).

Les propos de Helen Burns ont malgré tout un impact sur sa jeune amie, d'autant plus que ses actes sont en accord avec les valeurs qu'elle défend. À l'opposé de M. Brocklehurst, dont l'idéal se voit contredit par la vie qu'il mène avec sa famille, Helen Burns incarne l'exemplarité d'un idéal vécu. Ainsi lors de la scène où, punie par Miss Scatcherd, elle se tient debout

---

1. Jane Eyre se caractérise en effet par une carence affective profonde, telle que l'a connue Charlotte Brontë, qui, après avoir perdu sa mère, a perdu ses deux sœurs aînées. Comme l'indique Bernadette Bertrandias, cet état d'orpheline est déterminant pour le devenir de l'héroïne : « C'est l'état d'orpheline qui, dans *Jane Eyre*, fonde la dynamique de cette conquête, qui est en même temps une quête identitaire, dans ses dimensions sociale, morale, affective et spirituelle » (Bertrandias 49).
2. *"It is far better to endure patiently a smart which nobody feels but yourself, than to commit a hasty action whose evil consequences will extend to all connected with you; and, besides, the Bible bids us return good for evil"* (47).

au milieu de la classe, met-elle en pratique la notion d'endurance qu'elle prône auprès de Jane Eyre : « *I expected she would show signs of great distress and shame; but to my surprise she neither wept nor blushed: composed, though grave, she stood, the central mark of all eyes* » (43). Afin d'apaiser l'esprit de Jane Eyre, Helen Burns fait référence aux mots mêmes du Christ et plus particulièrement à un extrait du Sermon sur la Montagne, d'où est tirée une grande partie des références bibliques du roman : « *Love your enemies; bless them that curse you; do good to them that hate you and despitefully use you* » (49). Dans un premier temps, Jane Eyre paraît hermétique au discours tenu par Helen Burns : « *Then I should love Mrs Reed, which I cannot do; I should bless her son John, which is impossible* » (49), mais il exerce une réelle influence sur l'évolution de Jane Eyre au sein de ce roman qui est loin de constituer une « composition anti-chrétienne » (Rigby, citée dans l'édition Norton 452).

Le parcours de Jane Eyre enfant est donc largement moral, avec une évolution psychologique certes, mais qui ne permet pas à elle seule de conclure à un roman de formation. Il s'agit, par la suite, pour l'héroïne adulte de faire face à une suite d'épreuves morales, lors de moments décisifs, mais Jane Eyre acquiert en fait très tôt les principes sur lesquels elle s'appuie pour faire ses choix : dans le roman de Charlotte Brontë, les éléments de formation entrent en réalité en tension avec la notion de résistance, dans la mesure où Jane Eyre entend défendre son intégrité morale.

Finalement, ce qui distingue profondément *Jane Eyre* du Bildungsroman, c'est la vision du monde à laquelle il se rattache. Le Bildungsroman repose à l'origine sur un parcours éducatif et psychologique lié aux idéaux éducatifs des Lumières, qui s'appuient sur une perception du monde agissant positivement sur l'individu. Or, la tradition évangélique dans laquelle se situe Charlotte Brontë l'amène à concevoir le monde comme déchu. Les microcosmes que décrit Charlotte Brontë, qu'il s'agisse de Gateshead ou de Lowood, sont manifestement dégradés. En ce qui concerne Lowood, dont la toponymie est révélatrice (Low-wood), la condamnation porte sur les conditions mêmes de vie. On entend s'élever les voix des jeunes élèves pour se plaindre de la cuisine (« *Disgusting! The porridge is burnt again!* », 38) ; on perçoit également le caractère douloureux de certains souvenirs évoqués par la narratrice, tels que les dimanches d'hiver :

> Sundays were dreary days in that wintry season. We had to walk two miles to Brocklebridge Church, where our patron officiated. We set out cold, we arrived at church colder: during the morning service we became almost paralysed. *(50-51)*

Le terme « *paralysed* » indique d'ores et déjà les effets néfastes du froid sur les corps, dont la vitalité se trouve fortement diminuée. À cela s'ajoute enfin la maladie qui découle en réalité des deux facteurs précédents, c'est-à-dire le manque de nourriture et le froid : « *Semi-starvation and neglected colds had predisposed most of the pupils to receive infection: forty-five out of the eighty girls lay ill at one time* » (65). À Gateshead, c'est une menace de mort qui pèse sur Jane Eyre, mais la situation mortifère reste symbolique ; en revanche, à Lowood, la mort est bel et bien présente. On sait que c'est à Cowan Bridge, l'école de filles du révérend Carus Wilson, que Maria et Elizabeth Brontë, sœurs aînées de Charlotte, sont tombées malades. Elles ne sont rentrées chez elles que pour y mourir. Charlotte Brontë s'est d'ailleurs inspirée de sa sœur Maria pour créer le personnage de Helen Burns[1]. L'enjeu s'avère alors vital pour Jane Eyre, qui voit sa meilleure amie partir pour toujours. Dans la mesure où c'est le salut de l'héroïne qui est en jeu, *Jane Eyre* semble plus proche de la quête de Christian dans *The Pilgrim's Progress* que des années d'apprentissage de Wilhelm.

Un roman de quête ?

Jane Eyre se présente comme un être en errance, ainsi qu'elle l'affirme elle-même lors de son retour à Gateshead où elle se rend au chevet de sa tante mourante : « *I still felt as a wanderer on the surface of the earth* » (194). Cette errance de l'héroïne pose la question centrale du salut personnel, comme l'exprime Peter Allan Dale :

> What I want to argue is that this question of what one must do to avoid damnation (or achieve salvation) is very much at the center of the novel, that it implies the narrative's essential structure of expectation, the end toward which the narrative is assumed to be headed. *(Dale 112)*

Cet aspect est d'autant plus mis en valeur que le parcours prend une dimension bunyanesque. Les étapes du chemin de l'héroïne sont clairement marquées par les différents lieux fréquentés, lieux dont les noms sont allégoriques. Ainsi, Gateshead qui s'apparente à la porte à guichet[2] (« *The Wicket Gate* ») marque le début du périple, Thornfield représenterait le mont Hardu (« *Difficulty Hill* »), Marsh End[3] et Whitcross ne seraient que

---

1 "*Charlotte herself suggested that her own sister, Maria, was the original of Helen Burns in Jane Eyre. She later told her editor, William Smith Williams: 'You are right in having faith in the reality of Helen Burns: she was real enough: I have exaggerated nothing there: I abstained from recording much that I remember respecting her, lest the narrative should sound incredible.*" (Barker 43).
2. Les expressions françaises sont reprises de la traduction du *Pilgrim's Progress* par Renée Métivet-Guillaume (John Bunyan, *Le voyage du pèlerin vers l'autre monde : sous la forme d'un songe*, Lausanne : l'Âge d'homme, 1992).
3. Dans le roman de Charlotte Brontë, le marais symbolise une étape, une étape qui est certes difficile physiquement et moralement : « *Only my damp and bemired apparel, in which I had slept on the ground and fallen in the marsh* » (289), mais que Jane Eyre parvient à franchir brillamment :

l'enchaînement de la vallée de l'Humiliation et de la vallée de l'Ombre de la Mort tandis que Ferndean pourrait représenter la Terre des Épousailles (« *Country of Beulah* »), qui est d'ailleurs mentionnée dans le roman :

> Till morning dawned I was tossed on a buoyant but unquiet sea, where billows of trouble rolled under surges of joy. I thought sometimes I saw beyond its wild waters a shore, sweet as the hills of Beulah [...] *(129)*

Charlotte Brontë structure donc son roman comme une quête, mais en réalité elle se réapproprie le récit de Bunyan et modifie l'objet de la quête, tout en gardant l'idée de la vie comme voyage. En effet, si les critiques se sont intéressés à la question de la structure bunyanesque de *Jane Eyre*, aucun n'a véritablement déterminé la différence profonde entre Charlotte Brontë et John Bunyan et la plupart ont repris le terme de « *progress* », comme s'il avait le même sens dans les deux contextes. Ainsi on peut lire dans l'article de Jane Millgate, intitulé « *Jane Eyre's Progress* » :

> The linear pattern [...] is emphasized in throughout the novel by the insistence on the idea of a journey. We have already seen how this idea is sustained in terms of repeated allusions to classic literary travels, and above all to *The Pilgrim's Progress*; but it is also implicit in the whole story of Jane's career, in the way in which her progress from the lonely, downtrodden orphan of the opening to the happy, confident wife of the close has been organized in terms of an actual physical journey. *(Millgate 23)*

Jane Millgate utilise ici le terme de « *progress* » dans son sens moderne de progression, ce qui annihile la profonde différence avec Bunyan qui l'emploie, lui, dans le sens de « voyage » puisque, comme nous le verrons plus tard, il ne peut y avoir de véritable progrès pour lui[1]. Par ailleurs, la progression qu'évoque Jane Millgate est essentiellement sociale et n'a donc rien à voir avec le voyage du pèlerin de Bunyan. Or, la seule différence, importante il est vrai, que Jane Millgate distingue entre les deux récits réside dans le fait que Jane trouve le paradis de ce côté-ci des portes de la Cité Céleste.

« *Having crossed the marsh, I saw a trace of white over the moor* » (282). « *Marsh End* », qui est le nom de la maison où Jane Eyre est recueillie par St John et ses sœurs, s'inscrit dans la progression linéaire de l'héroïne, pour laquelle l'espace a toute son importance : « *I left Marsh End for Morton* » (305) signale ainsi un nouveau départ. Mis à part une occurrence (où « *marsh* » est employé dans une expression : « *I'd as soon offer to take hold of a blue* ignis fatuus *light in a marsh* », 208), les utilisations du terme « marsh » se situent toutes dans le volume III, du chapitre 28 au chapitre 35, ce qui confirme que le marais correspond bien à une étape de la progression de l'héroïne.

1. En effet, s'il existe des changements positifs de la personne, ils sont uniquement provoqués par l'action de la grâce et non pas déclenchés par la personne elle-même.

Sandra M. Gilbert est, quant à elle, allée encore plus loin, puisque dans son article intitulé « *Plain Jane's Progress* », elle fait de *Jane Eyre* une parodie de Bunyan en montrant à quel point Jane Eyre rejette le sacrifice de soi impliqué par le chemin choisi par St John :

> For it was finally to repudiate such a crucifying denial
> of the self that Brontë's "hunger, rebellion, and rage" led
> her to write *Jane Eyre* in the first place and to make it
> an "irreligious" redefinition—almost a parody—of John
> Bunyan's vision. *(Gilbert 804)*

Selon elle, le roman de Charlotte Brontë se caractérise par la victoire du désir romantique d'affirmation de soi et par le rejet de la Loi de Dieu le Père. Elle fait donc de la maturité et de l'égalité entre Jane Eyre et Rochester le but du pèlerinage de l'héroïne en supprimant toute dimension religieuse du roman. C'est cette omission du religieux et de la quête spirituelle que reproche Bernadette Bertrandias aux lectures d'inspiration psychanalytique (54), omission que nous ne pouvons nous aussi que regretter[1].

Afin de mieux comprendre cette quête spirituelle et la manière dont Charlotte Brontë se réapproprie le schéma proposé par Bunyan, il convient de revenir sur le sens même du *Pilgrim's Progress*. Comme l'évoque Roger Sharrock, dans son introduction à l'ouvrage de Bunyan qu'il a édité en 1965 :

> His [Bunyan's] vivid imagination was possessed in a simple
> and terrible form by the Calvinist doctrine that all men were
> predestined either to salvation or to damnation; he battled with
> doubts of his own faith. *(Sharrock, "Introduction" 8-9)*

Le fait que Bunyan soit attaché à la doctrine calviniste explique pourquoi Charlotte Brontë, qui rejetait la double prédestination, ne pouvait que modifier le schéma proposé par *The Pilgrim's Progress*, même si elle en a gardé certaines caractéristiques comme la structure pour *Jane Eyre*.

The Pilgrim's Progress est une allégorie (c'est une première différence avec le roman de Charlotte Brontë), racontée sous la forme d'un rêve, qui relate la quête du salut effectuée par un homme, Christian, au cours d'un long et difficile voyage. C'est le récit d'une conversion qui s'apparente à celle vécue par Bunyan lui-même, comme l'a souligné Roger Sharrock en précisant les profondes analogies entre *The Pilgrim's Progress* publié en 1678 et l'ouvrage *Grace Abounding* publié douze ans plus tôt en 1666. Dans son article « *Spiritual Autobiography in* The Pilgrim's Progress », Sharrock insiste sur les différentes étapes du cheminement de l'âme repérables dans

---

1. Dans son ouvrage, Bernadette Bertrandias défend l'idée que « la question essentielle, lancinante jusqu'au terme du récit, est en fait celle du salut » (54), idée sur laquelle nous nous appuyons ici également.

les deux ouvrages, à savoir la conviction du péché, la sainteté selon la Loi[1] (« *legality* »), la justification, la sanctification ou croissance dans la grâce (« *growth in grace* »). Christian reçoit relativement tôt l'assurance de faire partie des élus, dans le passage de la Croix :

> So I saw in my Dream, that just as Christian came up with the Cross, his burden loosed from off his Shoulders, and fell from his back; and began to tumble; and so continued to do, till it came to the mouth of the Sepulcher, where it fell, and I saw it no more. *(Bunyan 41)*

Par la suite, Christian doit affronter le doute et le désespoir et n'en est donc qu'au début de son périple.

Jane Eyre ne présente aucun chemin similaire de conversion, bien que la quête centrale soit celle du salut de l'héroïne, mais aussi du bonheur terrestre. Ce serait de toute façon une conversion d'un autre type qui serait mise en scène. Dans *The Pilgrim's Progress*, nous assistons au passage de l'incroyance à la foi, ce qui n'est pas du tout l'objet du roman de Charlotte Brontë, dans lequel l'héroïne est croyante dès le début. La conversion qui aurait pu être mise en scène aurait été de type évangélique, l'héroïne faisant alors l'expérience de la grâce. Quelle que soit leur définition de la conversion, de nombreux critiques ont souligné l'absence d'un tel moment dans *Jane Eyre*. Si certains, comme Elizabeth Rigby, ont conclu à la thèse d'une « composition anti-chrétienne », d'autres n'ont pas remis en cause la trame religieuse si essentielle au roman et ont analysé cette omission de manière différente. Ainsi Barbara Hardy[2] considère que les lecteurs victoriens n'avaient pas besoin d'un moment explicite (Hardy 67) tandis que Peter Allan Dale[3] pense que l'omission est volontaire : « *it represents a*

---

1. Une fois que l'homme reconnaît qu'il est pécheur (première étape de conviction du péché), il tente de se conformer à la Loi hébraïque (c'est la première Alliance avec Moïse) et décide d'appliquer les Dix Commandements, d'où l'expression de « sainteté selon la Loi ». Mais selon Bunyan, il ne s'agit que d'un vernis, l'homme reste pécheur, car il lui faut s'habiller de la justice du Christ, qui est le seul à pouvoir le sauver lors de la justification (référence à la deuxième Alliance, Alliance avec le Christ).
2. Il convient de préciser que Barbara Hardy comprend le terme de « conversion » comme le passage de l'incroyance à la foi : « *What we do not come to see is exactly how Jane comes to accept Helen Burns' faith* » (66), ce qui ne respecte pas le contexte de *Jane Eyre*. On pourra notamment se référer à l'ouvrage de D. W. Bebbington, *Evangelicalism in Modern Britain: A History from the 1730s to the 1980s* [1989], Londres : Unwin Hyman, 2000, et en particulier aux pages 5-10.
3. Peter Allan Dale envisage, lui aussi, le terme de « conversion » selon sa définition bunyanesque : « *the novel is about Jane's providential journey from unbelief to belief* » (115), ce qui est contestable. Selon lui, les lecteurs victoriens habitués aux crises et fictions religieuses ne pouvaient qu'attendre la confession de foi de Jane, confession qui aurait pu s'exprimer lorsque Jane Eyre se rend compte que Rochester est bien à l'origine de l'appel qu'elle a entendu ou encore à la fin du roman lorsqu'elle affirme son bonheur. Pour Peter Allan Dale, la confession de foi se trouve déplacée dans la bouche de St John : « *What has happened is that the expected closure of conversion has been displaced. Instead of Jane's final confession of faith we have a conspicuous silence on her part while another character affirms the Christian ending* ». L'hypothèse de l'attente du lecteur

deliberate withholding of an expected satisfaction from the reader » (Dale 119). Notre propos s'inscrit plutôt dans la lignée de ces critiques qui, malgré l'absence de mise en scène de la conversion, s'attachent à analyser le parcours moral et spirituel de l'héroïne. Cette progression diffère fondamentalement de l'avancée du pèlerin, étant donné que pour Bunyan, comme pour tous les calvinistes, le moteur essentiel du progrès spirituel est l'action divine[1]. Sharrock rappelle en effet :

> There is a central principle in Calvinist theology which resolves the tension between the total depravity of fallen man and the transcendent goodness of God; the soul can achieve salvation through no merely human righteousness, only through the imputed righteousness of Christ displayed in his incarnate life and sacrifice, and "imputed" or given to man because of no individual merits but by free grace in election. *(Sharrock, "Spiritual Autobiography", 103)*

Dans ce contexte calviniste, il ne peut donc y avoir de progrès au sens moderne du terme. En privilégiant ce sens dans son article « *Progress in The Pilgrim's Progress* », Fish conclut logiquement à l'absence de progrès : « *the only consistent spatial pattern Christian's actions trace out is cyclical, for whenever a new opportunity to fall into an old error presents itself, he invariably seizes it* » (Fish 267). Philip Edwards insiste sur l'erreur de Fish et pense au contraire qu'il faut prendre le terme « *progress* » au sens de « voyage » et que ce voyage occupe une place centrale chez Bunyan[2]. Le voyage chez ce dernier se traduit par un cheminement à travers les différentes étapes de la

---

de même que celle de l'intention de l'auteur ne sont cependant pas prouvées véritablement, la démonstration étant d'ailleurs difficile.

1. Chez les calvinistes, la Chute aliène l'homme de la source de la grâce et le prive de son état originel d'intégrité, de pureté et de béatitude mais elle a également pour conséquence la corruption totale ou dépravation totale de l'homme, comme l'indique l'article 9 de la *Confession de la Rochelle* : « Quoique l'homme ait une volonté, par laquelle il est incité à faire ceci ou cela, nous croyons toutefois qu'elle est totalement prisonnière du péché, en sorte qu'il n'a de liberté à bien faire que celle que Dieu lui donne » (Calvin, article 9). Cependant, à la différence de Luther qui soutient l'idée d'une justification forensique, c'est-à-dire extérieure à la personne, Calvin admet une régénération intérieure sous l'effet de la grâce divine : « Étant asservis au péché de par notre nature corrompue, nous croyons que c'est par cette foi que nous sommes régénérés, afin que nous vivions d'une vie nouvelle. En effet, c'est en nous appropriant la promesse qui nous est faite par l'Évangile, à savoir que Dieu nous donnera son Saint-Esprit, que nous recevons par la foi la grâce de vivre saintement et dans la crainte de Dieu » (Calvin, article 22).
2. Bunyan exprime l'aspect essentiel du voyage dans un de ses écrits intitulé *The Heavenly Footman*: « *Because the way is long (I speak metaphorically) and there is many a dirty step, many a high hill, much work to do, a wicked heart, world, and devil, to overcome; I say, there are many steps to be taken by those that intend to be saved, by running or walking, in the steps of that faith of our father Abraham. Out of Egypt thou must go through the Red Sea; thou must run a long and tedious journey, through the vast howling wilderness, before thou come to the land of promise* » (cité par Knott 223).

vie spirituelle, cheminement qui apparaît plus clairement à certains endroits qu'à d'autres, bien qu'il reste hésitant tout au long du récit[1].

Dans son étude du *Pilgrim's Progress*, Philip Edwards montre comment le voyage est d'abord synonyme de fuite, puisqu'il faut s'échapper de la Cité de la Perdition afin de trouver un refuge. Très vite cette idée de fuite s'accompagne de la quête non pas d'un simple refuge, mais d'un lieu de vie permanent, et ce, avant même que Christian ne trouve la porte étroite (« *Wicket Gate* ») : « *So when Christian reaches the gate, the journey is seen as a balance between escape from and movement towards* » (Edwards 112). Enfin, au quart du récit, c'est une nouvelle notion qui est introduite, celle de pèlerinage qui donne une nouvelle perspective au voyage, puisque l'idée de fuite est oubliée et que l'accent est alors mis sur le fait de voyager vers une destination précise.

Or, dans *Jane Eyre*, le voyage est au début beaucoup plus lié à l'idée d'échappatoire qu'à celle de cheminement vers une destination. Dans la discussion entre Mr Lloyd et l'enfant qui a lieu au début du roman, Jane Eyre manifeste le souhait de quitter Gateshead : « *If I had anywhere else to go, I should be glad to leave it; but I can never get away from Gateshead till I am a woman* » (20). Lorsque Mr Lloyd lui suggère l'idée d'aller à l'école, elle envisage d'abord ce lieu comme un départ et une rupture avec Gateshead, avant d'évoquer la nouvelle étape qu'il implique : « *school would be complete change: it implied a long journey, an entire separation from Gateshead, an entrance into a new life* » (20). De même, lorsque Jane Eyre quitte Lowood, elle n'a aucun but précis, il s'agit là encore de s'échapper, comme le traduit la répétition du terme « liberté », que met en valeur la structure en chiasme : « *I desired liberty; for liberty I gasped; for liberty I uttered a prayer* » (72). Ainsi que le suggère Thomas Loe dans son article, la progression de Jane Eyre est très étroitement liée à l'expérience du refus :

> This less visible plot linked with character in *Jane Eyre* depends on choice, but has received little attention because it depends upon Jane's choosing not to do something, or, in other words, upon her rejection of the options being offered. *(Loe 355)*

Ce rejet actif caractérise également l'épisode de la fuite de Thornfield ; fuite qui correspond à une prise de décision, mais qui ne s'accompagne d'aucun but précis. C'est seulement dans le dernier mouvement du roman que le voyage change de nature et qu'il devient « destination vers ». Aux

---

1. John R. Knott met l'accent sur le doute de Christian, doute qu'il associe à la conception de la foi de Bunyan : « *Christian continues to be vulnerable to doubt throughout his pilgrimage because Bunyan believed that faith could never be completely secured in this world. But his doubts are prompted by very different kinds of trial, appropriate to different stages of the journey* » (Knott 227).

yeux de Jane Eyre, il faut quitter Morton et la menace que représente St John, pour rejoindre Rochester.

Le monde dans lequel évolue Jane Eyre est un monde où il faut tracer son chemin en évitant les pièges avec discernement. Le terme « *judgment* » est essentiel pour comprendre le roman et Jane Eyre érige le discernement en garde-fou à la fin du chapitre XV (« *judgment would warn passion* », 130 ; l'édition Norton, qui indique « *should warm passion* », est fautive), bien qu'il soit parfois en danger, comme on le pressent dans son appréciation de l'être aimé :

> It had formerly been my endeavour to study all sides of his character; to take the bad with the good; and from the just weighing of both, to form an equitable judgment. Now I saw no bad. *(160)*

Malgré tout, l'héroïne entend bien y avoir toujours recours :

> The passions may rage furiously, like true heatens, as they are; and the desires may imagine all sorts of vain things: but judgment shall still have the last word in every argument, and the casting vote in every decision. *(171)*

Bien qu'il s'agisse de l'être aimé, Rochester représente, à un moment donné, une menace pour l'intégrité morale de Jane Eyre qui emploie elle-même le terme « *snare* » lorsqu'elle revient sur le choix qu'il lui incombait de faire : « *Which is better?—To have surrendered to temptation; listened to passion; made no painful effort—no struggle;—but to have sunk down in the silken snare* » (306).

Le choix de l'héroïne qui s'oppose visiblement à son bonheur immédiat ainsi qu'à celui de Rochester prend la forme d'un carrefour. Jane Eyre fait face à deux directions : celle de Millcote, opposée à celle de Thornfield. Derrière la bifurcation spatiale se cache la bifurcation morale. Jane Eyre fuit la tentation de devenir la maîtresse de Rochester ; au contraire, Christian cède souvent à ceux qui veulent le détourner du droit chemin, comme, par exemple, à Mr Worldly-Wiseman qui retarde son arrivée à la porte étroite. Christian est séduit par les chemins qui apparaissent plus faciles, ainsi que l'illustre l'épisode de « *By-Path Meadow* »[1]. Le discernement est également ce qui amène Jane à renoncer à St John : « *to have yielded now would have been an error of judgment* » (356).

Si Jane Eyre résiste à la tentation alors que Christian a besoin que l'intervention divine le remette dans le droit chemin, c'est parce qu'en plus de son

---

1. Christian montre cependant à certains moments qu'il sait résister aux tentations, comme on le note dans le passage de « *Vanity Fair* ». Lors de l'ascension du mont Hardu, Christian est d'ailleurs celui qui reconnaît le bon chemin parmi les trois qui lui font face alors que Formalist et Hypocrisy périssent pour avoir opté pour la facilité.

discernement, elle a recours à sa volonté, volonté humaine qui, selon Charlotte Brontë, n'est pas corrompue. La romancière reprend l'idée de Bunyan selon laquelle le bon chemin est long et pénible, mais ses héroïnes ont recours à des moyens essentiellement humains pour avancer. L'itinéraire personnel se caractérise par sa difficulté, comme l'indique Charlotte Brontë dans une de ses lettres : « *Two paths lie before you—you conscientiously wish to choose the right one—even though it be the most steep, straight, and rugged* » (10 juillet 1846, à Ellen Nussey ; Smith I, 482). Charlotte Brontë conçoit la vie comme une lutte (septembre 1849, à Ellen Nussey ; Smith II, 263) qui s'accompagne de souffrance. « *Strive* » et « *endure* » sont des termes qu'emploie souvent la romancière ; ils apparaissent notamment dans une lettre datée du 30 juin 1839 (« *I have never yet quitted a place without gaining a friend—Adversity is a good school—the Poor are born to labour and the Dependent to endure* ») (à Ellen Nussey ; Smith I, 193-194), ainsi que dans sa correspondance dix ans plus tard au sujet d'un voyage à Londres qu'elle redoute :

> I know what the effect and what the pain will be—how wretched I shall often feel—how thin and haggard I shall get—but he who shuns suffering will never win victory. If I mean to improve—I must strive and endure […]. *(12 avril 1850), à Ellen Nussey; Smith II, 384.*

Ce sont ces mêmes mots que prononce Jane Eyre lors de sa dernière discussion avec Rochester : « *we were born to strive and endure* » (270).

L'héroïne doit choisir la « bonne voie », expression que Charlotte Brontë utilise aussi dans ses lettres :

> The right path is that which necessitates the greatest sacrifice of self-interest—which implies the greatest good to others—and this path steadily followed will lead I believe in time to prosperity and to happiness though it may seem at the outset to tend quite in a contrary direction. *(10 juillet 1846, à Ellen Nussey; Smith I, 482-483)*

Cet extrait rappelle l'importance des moyens humains dans l'itinéraire personnel, et évoque aussi la confiance de la romancière dans l'issue trouvée, grâce au fait de suivre le droit chemin. C'est d'abord le discernement et la volonté humaine qui sont à l'origine de la progression de l'héroïne, comme l'illustre sa décision de quitter Rochester, puisqu'on note que « *I care for myself* » précède « *I will keep the law given by God* » (270). La volonté humaine accepte la volonté divine dans la foi et s'en remet à la Providence.

Jane Eyre se rapproche donc bien du roman de quête tel que l'avait conçu John Bunyan dans la mesure où le roman utilise la même structure, et se sert de l'image du voyage pour décrire le parcours de l'existence humaine. Mais il y a bel et bien réappropriation du schéma bunyanesque puisque l'objet et surtout le moteur de la quête sont différents : Christian est à la recherche de la Cité Céleste tandis que Jane vise un bonheur sur terre en accord avec son intégrité morale ; les sources d'avancement de Christian sont d'origine divine tandis que Jane Eyre a essentiellement recours à des moyens humains tels que le discernement ou la volonté. Il n'en demeure pas moins que la Providence joue un rôle important dans ce roman de quête remanié, comme nous allons maintenant le montrer.

Une (con)quête providentielle du bonheur

Avant de nous attarder sur le rôle de la Providence dans la quête de Jane Eyre, il convient de mettre en lumière le lien qui unit l'héroïne au divin. Pour ce faire, nous pouvons commencer par analyser la scène de la prière de Jane Eyre à Whitcross :

> Worn out with this torture of thought, I rose to my knees. Night was come, and her planets were risen: a safe, still night; too serene for the companionship of fear. We know that God is everywhere; but certainly we feel His presence most when His works are on the grandest scale spread before us: and it is in the unclouded night-sky, where His worlds wheel their silent course, that we read clearest His infinitude, His omnipotence, His omnipresence. I had risen to my knees to pray for Mr Rochester. Looking up, I, with tear-dimmed eyes, saw the mighty Milky Way. Remembering what it was—what countless systems there swept space like a soft trace of light—I felt the might and strength of God. Sure was I of His efficiency to save what He had made: convinced I grew that neither earth should perish, nor one of the souls it treasured. I turned my prayer to thanksgiving: the Source of Life was also the Saviour of Spirits. Mr Rochester was safe: he was God's, and by God would he be guarded. I again nestled to the breast of the hill; and ere long, in sleep, forgot sorrow. *(276)*

Dans cette scène, l'héroïne est à genoux, le regard rivé sur le ciel. Cependant la répétition du verbe « *rise* » révèle la force de Jane Eyre qui se trouve pourtant totalement isolée dans ce passage. De plus, l'extrait débute par l'occurrence du verbe « *know* » ce qui indique que l'expérience vient seulement vérifier une connaissance déjà acquise : « *we know that God is everywhere* ». L'emploi de « *we* » renforce dans un premier temps l'aspect général du propos : « *we know* », « *we read* ». Les termes relèvent d'abord de la théologie dite naturelle[1], puisque ce sont les moyens humains (intelli-

---

1. On peut reprendre ici la définition de la théologie naturelle que donne Pierre-Jean Ruff : « Par théologie naturelle, on entend une aptitude que l'homme aurait à s'approcher de Dieu et à le

gence, intuition, sentiment) qui permettent de découvrir Dieu (« *we know* », « *we feel* », « *we read* »), avant de s'orienter vers une théologie du salut : « *to save* ». C'est la nature qui témoigne de la Toute-Puissance divine ; on est alors proche du romantisme de Coleridge ou de Wordsworth. C'est cette expérience de la Toute-Puissance et de l'Omniprésence de Dieu qui prouve à Jane Eyre que Rochester est sain et sauf, l'antéposition mettant en valeur les adjectifs « *convinced* » et « *sure* » tandis que le « *we* » s'est transformé en « *I* » : « *I saw* », « *I felt* », « *I grew* ». Le changement qui s'opère alors véritablement est celui du contenu de la prière qui passe de la demande au remerciement : Jane Eyre est réconfortée à l'idée que Rochester soit en sécurité grâce à Dieu. Si Jane Eyre remercie le Tout-Puissant de prendre soin de l'être aimé, elle remercie également Dieu de l'avoir guidée dans son choix d'avoir quitté Thornfield, dans la mesure où elle pense avoir bénéficié de l'aide divine dans l'épreuve (« *God must have led me on* », 277) :

> Yes; I feel now that I was right when I adhered to principle and law, and scorned and crushed the insane promptings of a frenzied moment. God directed me to a correct choice: I thank His providence for the guidance. *(306-307)*

La transcendance est affirmée, et s'oppose à l'idée de « composition anti-chrétienne » qu'a émise Elizabeth Rigby ou à la réaffirmation d'un tel jugement[1] par M. A. Blom qui déclare :

> Jane is incapacitated for Christian faith by her reliance on her vital, autonomous imagination which forces her to conceive of death not as a prelude to an eternity of rewards and punishments, but as a doorway to nothingness—to a fathomless abyss in which the sentient self is extinguished. *(Blom 353)*

De tels propos ne prennent en compte ni le texte de *Jane Eyre* ni le contexte du roman[2] qui n'associait pas la mort au néant. La foi chrétienne n'est certes pas définie aussi précisément que dans les romans d'Anne Brontë, mais elle fait partie de l'univers de l'héroïne[3] tout comme la Providence d'ailleurs

---

connaître, sans aucune aide extérieure, donc sans Révélation, sans rien qui, du dehors, n'ouvre ses yeux à une lumière ou à une vérité qu'il ne détiendrait pas déjà en lui-même. » (Pierre-Jean Ruff, « Protestantisme libéral et théologie naturelle », *Évangile et Liberté*, 174, février 2004, http://www.evangile-et-liberte.net/elements/numeros/174/article2.html).
1. M. A. Blom part en effet du principe que les critiques n'ont pas réussi à remettre en question le présupposé d'Elizabeth Rigby : « *Although several recent and important critical studies argue that Jane Eyre's motives and acts demonstrate and confirm the worth of traditional Christian morality, reexamination suggests that Elizabeth Rigby's 1848 appraisal of Charlotte Brontë's novel as "pre-eminently an anti-Christian composition" is remarkably accurate* » (Blom 351).
2. Pour en savoir plus sur le contexte religieux des Brontë, on pourra se référer à l'ouvrage de Marianne Thormählen, *The Brontës and Religion*, Cambridge : Cambridge University Press, 1999.
3. Il est d'ailleurs intéressant de noter combien Charlotte Brontë fut amusée et étonnée de voir Jane Eyre comparée à Becky Sharp : « *I have received the Scotsman, and was greatly amused to see*

puisque, comme l'écrit Claire Bazin, « les interventions providentielles scandent le récit au rythme des déplacements dans l'espace et le temps » (Bazin 35).

Dans l'extrait de *Jane Eyre* cité précédemment (306-307), le terme « *providence* » ne prend pas de majuscule et correspond alors à un acte de la Providence, à un signe. Mis à part deux occurrences, il est cependant toujours employé avec une majuscule et désigne le principe de Providence. La Providence, comme le rappelle le *Dictionnaire critique de théologie*, renvoie à « la manière dont Dieu gouverne le monde selon des fins » (Lacoste 954). Contrairement au destin qui fixerait de façon irrévocable le cours des événements et résulterait de causes distinctes de la volonté humaine, la Providence ne prédétermine pas en principe les actions humaines et laisse l'homme libre et autonome dans le gouvernement de sa propre vie, tout en se manifestant à lui. Ce thème a attiré l'attention de critiques tels que Barbara Hardy, dans son étude de *Jane Eyre*, ou Thomas Vargish, dans son ouvrage sur l'esthétique providentielle. Barbara Hardy souligne l'importance de la Providence dans le roman de Charlotte Brontë (« *The framework of the novel is consistently Providential, but within the frame there are omissions and simplifications* », 70), mais exprime l'idée qu'en réalité la Providence viendrait s'ajouter à une foi non assumée. Au contraire, dans *Jane Eyre*, le principe de « Providence » est fondamental car il permet la coïncidence entre volonté humaine et volonté divine, en confortant la quête de l'héroïne et en validant ses choix de même que son discours pédagogique auprès de Rochester.

Dans le roman, la Providence se traduit par des signes, le plus évident étant l'appel surnaturel que lance Rochester à Jane Eyre. Il intervient au moment même où l'héroïne s'interroge sur la réponse à donner à la demande en mariage de St John. Bien que Jane sente que cette union peut menacer son intégrité physique et morale, elle est sur le point d'accepter St John comme mari. Elle s'en remet d'abord au Ciel : « *Show me—show me the path! I entreated of Heaven* » (357). La Providence conforte sa première intention de résister à St John, de refuser sa proposition (« *to have yielded now would have been an error of judgment* », 356) et de rejoindre l'être aimé. La volonté humaine centrale se voit donc approuvée par une volonté divine qui, tout en apparaissant comme essentielle, reste cependant secondaire. L'appel surnaturel a lieu après la conversion de Rochester et la Providence sous-tend donc le processus pédagogique enclenché par Jane Eyre. Celle-ci

---

Jane Eyre likened to Rebecca Sharp—the resemblance would hardly have occurred to me » (31 décembre 1847, à W.S. Williams ; Smith I, 587). Cette surprise s'explique en partie par le fait que pour l'héroïne de *Vanity Fair*, il n'existe pas de transcendance.

demandait à Rochester de respecter son intégrité et de développer son propre itinéraire de pèlerin.

Les signes, mêlés de romantisme, qu'émet la Providence ne sont pas toujours pris en compte par l'héroïne. Ainsi l'union entre Rochester et Jane Eyre apparaît compromise dès la demande en mariage sans que la jeune femme soit capable d'interpréter correctement les mises en garde auxquelles elle assiste. Cette demande est en effet immédiatement suivie d'un orage violent qui fend en deux le grand marronnier d'Inde. D'autre part, la lune, qui joue un rôle significatif dans le roman, se couvre de rouge la nuit précédant le mariage :

> As I looked up at them, the moon appeared momentarily in that part of the sky which filled their fissure; her disk was blood-red and half overcast; she seemed to throw on me one bewildered, dreary glance, and buried herself again instantly in the deep drift of cloud. *(236)*

La lune, qui est pourtant l'alliée de Jane, comme le révèle la scène où elle prend une forme humaine pour lui conseiller de fuir la tentation que représente Rochester, semble annoncer le désastre ; elle se retire après avoir transmis son message : « *the moon shut herself wholly within her chamber, and drew close her curtain of dense cloud* » (236). Jane Eyre se concentre uniquement sur l'événement de la nuit précédente, à savoir la visite de Bertha qui a déchiré son voile de mariée : « *The event of last night again recurred to me. I interpreted it as a warning of disaster* » (237). Dans la scène où la lune prend une forme humaine, Jane Eyre attend pourtant l'apparition de l'astre avec appréhension et lui confère un rôle hautement symbolique :

> the gleam was such as the moon imparts to vapours she is about to sever. I watched her come—watched with the strangest anticipation; as though some words of doom were to be written on her disk. *(272)*

Jane Eyre souligne un écho du divin au sein de la nature qui apparaît plutôt bienveillante à l'égard de l'héroïne, comme le révèle la scène où Jane Eyre, ayant fui Thornfield Hall, dort dans la bruyère : « *Nature seemed to me benign and good; I thought she loved me, outcast as I was* » (276). La nature est le témoin de la Toute-Puissance divine, comme nous l'avons vu précédemment, et qu'ils soient perçus ou non, les signes de la Providence protègent en tout cas l'héroïne. Rochester est le premier à la remercier du fait que seul le voile de la mariée ait été abîmé : « *I thank Providence, who watched over you, that she then spent her fury on your wedding apparel* » (264). Par la suite, lorsque Jane Eyre, affamée, cherche désespérément un refuge, la Providence qu'elle sollicite (« *Oh, Providence! sustain me a little longer! Aid—direct me!* », 281) lui répond par cette lumière qui surgit au loin et qui n'est autre que la maison de St John. Jane Eyre, en danger de mort, est sauvée une fois de plus dans son parcours semé d'embûches et la dernière intervention providentielle lui permet d'entendre l'appel de Rochester, après avoir lancé un ultime appel à l'aide : « *Show me, show me the path!* » (357). La Providence éclaire véritablement le chemin emprunté par Jane Eyre, aussi ferme que celle-ci soit dans ses choix.

Malgré la lettre de St John Rivers du dernier chapitre qui semble émettre certains doutes quant à l'harmonie trouvée par Jane Eyre entre sa (con)quête de la félicité et la volonté divine, la vision du bonheur qui ressort du second roman de Charlotte Brontë repose manifestement sur l'accord entre la volonté de l'héroïne et la Providence. Au fil des romans, cette Providence sera de moins en moins lisible : elle se révèle difficilement discernable dans *Shirley* pour devenir double dans *Villette* ; on a en effet l'impression que dans son dernier roman, Charlotte Brontë transpose ses angoisses de la double prédestination calviniste. Si par la suite, elle conçoit la Providence différemment, elle opte également pour un changement de genre pour ses deux derniers romans : la quête du bonheur terrestre garde toute son importance, mais *Shirley*, roman social, et *Villette*, roman beaucoup plus réaliste que *Jane Eyre*, tendent à montrer que cette conquête est de plus en plus difficile aux yeux de Charlotte Brontë.

Bibliographie

Sources primaires

BRONTË, Charlotte, *The Professor* [1853], ed., Margaret Smith et Herbert Rosengarten, The World's Classics, Oxford: Oxford University Press, 1992.

BUNYAN, John, *The Pilgrim's Progress* [1678], ed., N. H. Keeble, Oxford: Oxford University Press, 1998 ; *Le voyage du pèlerin vers l'autre monde : sous la forme d'un songe*, tr. R. Métivet-Guillaume, Lausanne : l'Âge d'homme, 1992.

CALVIN, Jean, *Confession de La Rochelle* [1571], Aix-en-Provence : Éditions Kerygma, Fondation d'Entraide Chrétienne Réformée, 1988.

SMITH, Margaret, ed., *The Letters of Charlotte Brontë: with a Selection of Letters by Family and Friends*, Oxford: Clarendon Press, *Volume I*, 1829-1847 (1995), *Volume II*, 1848-1851 (2000), *Volume III*, 1852-1855 (2004).

Sources secondaires

ALEXANDER, Christine and Margaret SMITH, *The Oxford Companion to the Brontës*, Oxford: Oxford University Press, 2003.

ALTON, Anne Hiebert, "Books in the novels of Charlotte Brontë", BST, 21: 7, 1996.

BARKER, Juliet, *The Brontës* [1994], Londres: Phoenix Press, 2001.

BAZIN, Claire, *Jane Eyre, le pèlerin moderne*, Nantes : Éditions du Temps, 2005.

BEATY, Jerome, "*Jane Eyre* and Genre", *Genre*, 10, hiver 1977, 617-654.

BERTRANDIAS, Bernadette, *Charlotte Brontë, Jane Eyre, La parole orpheline*, Paris : Ellipses, 2004.

BLOM, M. A., "*Jane Eyre*: Mind as Law Unto Itself", *Criticism, A Quarterly for Literature and the Arts*, volume 15, numéro 4, automne 1973, 350-364.

DALE, Peter Allan, "Charlotte Brontë's "Tale Half-told": the Disruption of Narrative Structure in *Jane Eyre*", *Modern Language Quarterly*, juin 1986.

EDWARDS, Philip, "The Journey in *The Pilgrim's Progress*" in Vincent Neway (ed.), *The Pilgrim's Progress Critical and Historical Views*, Liverpool: Liverpool University Press, 1980.

FISH, Stanley Eugene, "Progress in *The Pilgrim's Progress*", *English Literary Renaissance*, 1: 3, automne 1971.

GILBERT, Sandra M., "Plain Jane's Progress", *Signs: Journal of Women in Culture and Society*, 2: 4, été 1977.

LOE, Thomas, "Rejection and Progress in *Jane Eyre*", BST, 19: 8, 1989.

KNOTT, John R., "Bunyan's Gospel Day: A Reading of *The Pilgrim's Progress*" in Roger Sharrock (ed.), *Bunyan: "The Pilgrim's Progress": A Casebook*, Londres: The Macmillan Press Ltd., 1976.

HARDY, Barbara, *The Appropriate Form: An Essay on the Novel*, Londres: Athlone Press, 1964.

LACOSTE, Jean-Yves (dir.), *Dictionnaire critique de théologie* [1998], Paris : Presses Universitaires de France, 2002.

MARTIN, Robert B., *Charlotte Bronte's Novels: The Accents of Persuasion*, New-York: Norton, 1966.

MILLGATE, Jane, "Jane Eyre's Progress", *English Studies*, 50: 1-6, 1969, 21-29.

MORTIER, Daniel, « Le Wilhem Meister de Goethe ou l'origine d'un genre romanesque problématique », *in* Claude de Grève (dir.), *Dix-huitième siècle européen. En hommage à Jacques Lacant*, Paris : Aux Amateurs de Livres, 1990.

SHARROCK, Roger, "Introduction" *in* John Bunyan, *The Pilgrim's Progress*, Roger Sharrock (ed.), Baltimore: Penguin Books, 1965.

— "Spiritual Autobiography *in The Pilgrim's Progress*", *The Review of English Studies, A Quarterly Journal of English Literature and the English Language*, 24: 94, avril 1948, 102-120.

SOUSA CORREA, Delia da, "*Jane Eyre* and Genre", *in* Delia da Sousa Correa (dir.), *The Nineteenth-Century Novel: Realisms*, New-York: Routledge, 2000.

Roles and Representations of Nature in *Jane Eyre*

Xavier Lachazette

When a friend of hers, the famous essayist George Henry Lewes, advised her to write more like Jane Austen and less melodramatically than she had done in *Jane Eyre*, Charlotte Brontë wrote back, finding fault with Austen's style and indirectly defending her own. A revealing passage from this letter, which she wrote to Lewes on January 12th, 1848, goes as follows:

> Why do you like Miss Austen so very much? I am puzzled on that point. What induced you to say that you would rather have written *Pride and Prejudice* or *Tom Jones*, than any of the Waverley novels?
> I had not seen *Pride and Prejudice* till I had read that sentence of yours, and then I got the book. And what did I find? An accurate daguerreotyped portrait of a commonplace face; a carefully fenced, highly cultivated garden, with neat borders and delicate flowers; but no glance of a bright vivid physiognomy, no open country, no fresh air, no blue hill, no bonny beck. I should hardly like to live with her ladies and gentlemen, in their elegant but confined houses. These observations will probably irritate you, but I shall run the risk. *(Smith 10)*

For Brontë, Austen's novel is characterized by unjustifiable self-imposed limits (she mentions fences, borders, and the lack of open country), and by a narration whose "careful" and "neat" effects prove the writer's excessively painstaking approach. In her eyes, Austen thus deprives her novel of "bright" themes and of arresting characterization by not allowing her protagonists to interact with broad, open-air environments.

To be sure, no such absence marks *Jane Eyre*, a novel which famously opens with a melancholy description of leafless shrubbery, cold winter, and driving rain before taking the heroine on a long journey towards personal growth through mostly hostile and isolated environments. As Virginia Woolf puts it in a short essay on the Brontë sisters' *Jane Eyre* and *Wuthering Heights*:

> They both feel the need of some more powerful symbol of the vast and slumbering passions in human nature than words or actions can convey […], and so their storms, their moors, their lovely spaces of summer weather are not ornaments applied to decorate a dull page or display the

> writer's powers of observation—they carry on the emotion
> and light up the meaning of the book. *(Woolf 158)*

But another kind of danger still threatened Brontë after her failure to get *The Professor* published: that of imposing too much realism on her next narrative for the sake of truthfulness, and of excessively trying to prevent the characters, situations, and scenes from the "infernal world" of Angria, with its "burning clime" and glowing sunsets (see "Farewell to Angria", Norton 424-425), to take control over her imagination. Brontë managed to avoid this second danger, though. As one critic argued, *Jane Eyre* is even a total success because in it "she was able to accept and keep in due subordination material from her fantasy world" (Tillotson 286).

It therefore seems interesting to inquire into the kinds of representations of nature one finds here, and into the roles attributed to it by Brontë in a novel whose writing was bounded on both sides by undesired extremes. Nevertheless, since previous critics have already made extensive remarks on a number of these aspects—as David Lodge and Robert B. Heilman did when they focused respectively on the four elements, especially fire, or on the conflict between "reason-judgment-common sense" (the sun) and "feeling-imagination-intuition" (the moon)[1]—, I propose to address three different points.

First, I will stress how one key theme in the novel, Jane's dissatisfaction with forms of imprisonment or constraint, is supported by various references to natural elements and settings, and that the heroine's evolution is perceptible in her changing interaction with nature. This will allow me to show that a privileged link between the heroine and the physical world is established by the numerous natural metaphors and analogies used in the narrative. As we will then see, such a sincere and emotional closeness with nature involves potentially fatal risks but brings the eponymous character the kind of physical comfort and emotional support she requires.

The dialectic of imprisonment and liberation

Nature is given an ambivalent role right from the opening chapter of the novel. In a striking incipit, the I-narrator asserts the joy felt by herself as a child when November rain prevented her from taking a walk outside. The leafless shrubbery at Gateshead had already been visited in the morning, and Jane "never liked long walks" (5) anyway, especially in such foul "winter" weather. Nevertheless it is reading about much colder places like Norway, Siberia or the Arctic Zone which Jane chooses to do the first chance she gets,

---
1. See Heilman, p. 283-8.

those regions being more modern equivalents of the "farthest Thule" (or *ultima Thule*) of the Ancients, to which the quotation from James Thomson's *Seasons* alludes (6), that is to say the northernmost inhabitable place which previous civilizations conceived and dreamed of. Cosily and safely surrounded by the heavy moreen curtain of the drawing-room window-seat, the young girl lets her imagination wander thanks to the miniature vignettes and accompanying texts in prose or verse in Thomas Bewick's *History of British Birds*—more precisely the second volume, on water birds.

In other words, Jane's elated feelings are in paradoxical unison both with the elements raging outside and the natural descriptions in her book, and hers is not so much a dislike of the idea of nature or cold as it is a dissatisfaction with any coercive force that would compel her to get outdoor exercise or to stay in when she feels like an eager wanderer waiting to explore the world around her. Besides, her intermediary position on the window-seat, "not separating" (5) her from nature but transforming her into an observer rather than a participant, prepares the reader for the themes of her in-between status and her unfitness for society as it is, and also for the tensions in which the novel abounds—such as the conflict between society's expectations of women and the heroine's instinctive need for self-fulfilment.

As Miss Oliver insightfully remarks, Jane is "a *lusus naturae* [...] as a village schoolmistress" (314). Just like those *jests* or *sports of nature* which fascinated naturalists up to the 17th century because they defied classification—for example, the so-called Scythian lamb, or Vegetable lamb of Tartary, whose belly supposedly grew a stem or pole that fixed firmly in the ground, constraining the part-plant part-animal creature to feed only on the grass in its immediate vicinity—, Jane is one of a kind. She evades categorization and her status as "a heterogeneous thing, opposed to [the Reeds] in temperament, in capacity, in propensities" (12) is illustrated by her fascination with a china plate that is brightly painted with flowers and a bird of paradise, while John Reed's cruelty to animals and savagery to plants were underlined a few pages before.

Evading categories is not easily achieved, though, and the different stages and locales through which the heroine *progresses* all along the novel (in the way John Bunyan imagined) are marked by metaphors of natural imprisonment. Not only is the weather mostly appalling in the first eight wintry chapters, but the places themselves bear the attributes of jails. The garden at Lowood may be an oasis apart from an institution deceptively described by Mr Brocklehurst as "that nursery of chosen plants" (29), but it is only the kind of natural spot one finds in a Victorian walled garden or a "convent-like garden" (41), with no flowers yet growing in the beds assigned to the girls but complete with high, spike-guarded walls which "exclude every glimpse of prospect" (40). Likewise, we notice that great grey hills bar the horizon around Lowood, and that Jane's description abruptly passes over the natural beauties around her and analyzes them in terms of barriers beyond which some measure of happiness must lie:

> I went to my window, opened it, and looked out. There were the two wings of the building; there was the garden; there were the skirts of Lowood; there was the hilly horizon. My eye passed all other objects to rest on those most remote, the blue peaks; it was those I longed to surmount; all within their boundary of rock and heath seemed prison-ground, exile limits. I traced the white road winding round the base of one mountain, and vanishing in a gorge between two: how I longed to follow it further![1] *(72)*

This consequently erases all the romance or picturesqueness the scene may hold in actuality ("the skirts", "the hilly horizon", "the blue peaks", "white road") and the passage is marked by romanticism in the restricted sense that nature helps the heroine voice inner longings of liberation and the idea that individual needs matter more than societal constraints. Indeed, as the narrator informs us, it is precisely this view from the window at Lowood which encouraged her to better articulate her need for freedom—or for "at least a new servitude!" (72).

Interestingly, it is also a bird's-eye view of Thornfield from the "leads" (90-91), in which the reader has no choice but to see a pendant to the Lowood scene just mentioned, together with a previous glimpse of the hall from the ground up (84), which reveal the ambivalent appeal of Rochester's grounds and dwelling to Jane at first. On the one hand, the lawn, park, wood or rookery which the heroine descries from the roof all fill her with "delight". The presence of a grove, the lawn "closely girdling the grey base of the mansion", and the field "dotted with its ancient timber" all make us picture a peaceful, elegant setting along the lines of what "Capability" Brown, the celebrated landscape gardener, advocated[2]. But negative traits also crop up in this first gaze at the

---

1. This passage calls to mind a few lines from "The Teacher's Monologue", one of the poems Brontë published in 1846 alongside poems by both her sisters. At the end of a tiring day, the eponymous teacher declares: "Now, as I watch that distant hill, / So faint, so blue, so far removed, / Sweet dreams of home my heart may fill, / That home where I am known and loved: / It lies beyond; yon azure brow / Parts me from all Earth holds for me [...]." (See *The Professor...*, p. 305)
2. Except for the pavements occasionally mentioned in the narrative, in the front of the mansion and before the orchard entrance. (It is by crashing onto one of these pavements that Bertha meets her death.) Brown, on the contrary, liked to have lawns reaching right up to the foot of a dwelling, to make it look as though it had simply been built in the middle of a green scenery. For details on Brontë's plausible creation of Thornfield from a house she stayed at with her friend Ellen Nussey ("Rydings"), and another place she may also have visited with Ellen, complete with a madwoman's chamber and the property of a family by the name of Eyre ("North Lees Hall Farm"), see Leavis, p. 19.

Thornfield grounds because though pleasing, "[n]o feature in the scene was extraordinary", and the overgrown path in the "dun and sere" wood shows signs of neglect. Such traits confirm the uneasy feeling conveyed by the unexpectedly secluded aspect of the place:

> Farther off were hills: not so lofty as those round Lowood, nor so craggy, nor so like barriers of separation from the living world; but yet quiet and lonely hills enough, and seeming to embrace Thornfield with a seclusion I had not expected to find existent so near the stirring locality of Millcote. *(84)*

A certain measure of disappointment thus marks Jane's first steps at Thornfield because her hopes were initially that Mrs Fairfax's address near Millcote indicated a locality not far removed from that busy and "large manufacturing town on the banks of the A—" (75), and her joy at being hired in that particular (unnamed) shire stemmed from its lying seventy miles *closer* to the very centre of human and commercial activity, London. Whereas Jane enthusiastically describes Millcote as populous, stirring, and industrial just after getting Mrs Fairfax's letter, absolutely nothing of the sort transpires from the couple of lines devoted to the night-time discovery of the town. The reader would thus wonder whether Jane might not have struck a losing bargain in settling in a "sequestered" (93) region that she also finds less picturesque and less romantic (80), if the lower height of the hills surrounding Thornfield, mentioned in the previous quotation, did not have a metaphorical ring about it, and did not compensate for her losses by leaving her a lesser impression of imprisonment.

Conversely, in an analysis of the layout of the Thornfield grounds, it is interesting to notice that, as was already the case at Lowood, it is the central situation of Rochester's dwelling that is underlined. Surrounded by hills on all sides, from which it is therefore equally distant, the hall stands at the centre of Jane's world (91), not with the positive connotation usually associated with the idea of centrality, but with the renewed perception that what lies beyond the hills, or beyond Hay, or beyond any visible feature in the faraway landscape for that matter, is closer to whatever truth or revelation Jane is excluded from, and restlessly pining for[1]. This is the same problematic centrality as that which she meets with on stepping out of the coach at Whitcross, among a North-Midland moorland that stretches on all sides:

> There are great moors behind and on each hand of me; there are waves of mountains far beyond that deep valley

---

1. Not surprisingly Rochester's party of genteel guests momentarily toy with the idea of visiting a camp of gipsies—those symbols of freedom and vagrancy—"on a common beyond Hay" (161).

> at my feet. The population here must be thin, and I see no passengers on these roads: they stretch out east, west, north, and south—white, broad, lonely; they are all cut in the moor, and the heather grows deep and wild to their very verge. *(275)*

Centrality and distance, the hallmarks of Jane's experience in loneliness and soul-searching, can easily be contrasted with the effect derived from one of the best-known descriptions of a country seat in literature, namely Jane Austen's "Pemberley" in *Pride and Prejudice*. Indeed, the staggering beauty of Pemberley is first seen from a wooded eminence across a river that flows in an intermediary valley, before the heroine, Elizabeth Bennet, records the views of that same eminence from various windows of the Derbyshire mansion into which she then gets admittance, in an exchange of vantage points which one does not find in *Jane Eyre*. Ideas of symmetry, relativity, and reciprocity are necessarily evoked in the reader's mind by this other novel whose main themes include the meeting of opposites and the reaching of an enlightened compromise. By contrast, no such harmonious middle ground is reached in *Jane Eyre*, which chronicles the difficult triumph of a stoic, deserving heroine over adversity, together with the bringing low and maiming (some would say castration) of a formerly impetuous and coercive Rochester forced to finally bury himself in the shade and decay of Ferndean.

In this sense the circular images associated with Jane at Thornfield and elsewhere—like the numerous appearances of the moon, the crows' nests she sees in the rookery, the horse chestnut "circled at the base by a seat" (211), the hollows she seeks when lost in the moors, her village school "in the healthy heart of England" (306), etc.—can be construed as representations of what Gaston Bachelard, in a chapter on the phenomenology of circles, calls "the shape of the being that concentrates on itself[1]". Because it is a (pseudo-)autobiography and a *Bildungsroman*, Brontë's novel focuses on the personal experience and the learning processes of an "I" who sees the world from its own central and often entrenched perspective, and who, finding it hard to see beyond the "J.E."—the heroine's set of initials, quoted five times in the advertising episode of Chapter X, in a novel in which French is not infrequently spoken—, is hardly ever able to give an account of the

---

1. My translation. Though Bachelard's essay was translated into English (as *The Poetics of Space*), the whole passage might as well be quoted in French for the sake of its beauty and relevance to the present discussion: *"Il* [the poet] *sait que ce qui s'isole s'arrondit, prend la figure de l'être qui se concentre sur soi. Dans les* Poèmes français *de Rilke, tel vit et s'impose le noyer. Là encore autour de l'arbre seul, milieu d'un monde, la coupole du ciel va s'arrondir suivant la règle de la poésie cosmique"* (214).

feelings or motivations of the few other characters around her, other than through a much ulterior reconstructed narrative.

The Marsh End stage of Jane's journey is marked by the same dichotomy between freedom and imprisonment, but the appearance of St John in the third volume allows the reader to see that Jane has evolved. Already, at the end of chapter XV (129-30), the I-narrator apprised us of the fact that the night after Rochester told Jane about his belief in "natural sympathies", her younger self had been able to see a shore, in fact a sort of Promised Land[1], *beyond* the billowy waters of the sea on which her dream had taken her. Though reaching that shore was thwarted by contrary gusts of wind, it seemed then that Jane was gradually being granted the boundless visual power and the extra amount of experience that she claimed for herself. Taking this further, the Moor House episode is helpful in that it pits two restless beings against each other and shows us what course Jane's evolution is taking. Indeed, though the place is as "sequestered" as the previous locales in the novel, and only inhabited by hardy species of plants which can adapt to a hostile environment, Jane learns to love it for the sake of her cousins' regard for it. She even gives an amorous description of its features, which culminates in the powerful statement: "I saw the fascination of the locality. I felt the consecration of its loneliness" (298). Conversely, St John's relationship with nature reminds us of Jane herself at the start of the novel because the appeal of missionary life away from home prevents him from putting any store by the rugged beauty or silence of the moors. He thus feels "buried in morass, pent up in mountain" (303) because his God-given powers are turned to no earthly use. Nature to him is less a source of pleasure than a repository of intellectual images and parables whose beauty comes from Biblical tradition, while Jane becomes familiar with her adopted home by drawing sketches of the Vale of Morton and the moors around it.

Thus opposed to St John, Jane's growing closeness to nature is revealed, and the descriptions of landscapes become complex narrative pauses in which the reader is supposed to find clues as to the heroine's new state of mind or perception. In the case of St John's outdoor proposal to Jane, for instance, two levels of meaning can be found: a poetic strain in which an accumulation of choice adjectives and adverbs is systematically used to convey the beauty of the smallest detail in the glen, and a gloomier, more Gothic trend in which the *topos* of imprisonment recurs in the shape

---

1. A note on p. 1691 of the 2008 Pléiade edition of *Jane Eyre* remarks that "Beulah" is also Hebrew for "bride". In the Bible (Isaiah, 62:4), God requires the Jews to become *wedded* to the land given to them after their return from exile in Egypt—so that the land which Jane catches a glimpse of in her dream can be seen as a metaphorical representation of matrimony.

of towering hills or of "frowning" mountains. One sentence in particular makes perfectly clear this peculiar binary opposition:

> As we advanced and left the track, we trod a soft turf, mossy fine and emerald green, minutely enamelled with a tiny white flower and spangled with a star-like yellow blossom: the hills, meantime, shut us quite in; for the glen, towards its head, wound to their very core. *(341)*

Any element in the landscape thus turns into a possible objective correlative, to use the phrase coined by T.S. Eliot, that is to say into an external equivalent for Jane's personal sensations or intimate conviction, as if nature suddenly took an interest in human affairs, and sent signs or warnings to any gazer she found deserving. Endowed with the power to see through the strollers' psychology and actuated by a desire to prevent pain, Nature thus acts as a protective presence with motherly feelings for those about to err or become entangled in inextricable situations.

Emotional v. intellectual closeness with nature

Obviously, this belief in Nature's sympathy or compassion for humanity can be construed as the mirror image of the closeness which mankind tends to feel for it. It is because a nature lover like Brontë is passionate about the physical world (her poems are replete with floral metaphors) that natural elements like the moon, the rain, winds, lightnings, etc. often take centre stage in her writings—not for the sole reason then that she is following in the footsteps of a strong gothico-romantic tradition in English literature, but because ardent lovers cannot be satisfied with tepid feelings in return.

In an introduction to the 1850 publication of a few more poems of her now dead sister, Charlotte described Emily's passion for the Yorkshire moors, which closely resemble the North-Midland moorland in *Jane Eyre*. In it she stressed the role played by the imagination and the necessary projection of one's feelings onto a landscape which at heart, she argues, is stern and unromantic. Speaking of the light in the gazer's eye and the freshness in his or her heart, she asserts:

> Unless that light and freshness are innate and self-sustained, the drear prospect of a Yorkshire moor will be found as barren of poetic as of agricultural interest: where the love of wild nature is strong, the locality will perhaps be clung to with the more passionate constancy, because from the hill-lover's self comes half its charm. *(The Professor, To Which are Added the Poems of Charlotte, Emily, and Anne Brontë, 388)*

Clearly, establishing such a close correspondence with, and transferring so much of oneself into, the natural world entails a special kind of relationship, one in which direct communion and communication with fauna, flora, and the elements become possible. In such a heightened state of mind, any observed natural phenomenon is seen as a potential extension of the self or expression of the soul, and direct analogies between the two realms seem justified.

Such analogies between self and nature are rife in *Jane Eyre*. For example, the black frost in the shrubbery at Gateshead "congeals" not only the remnants of the past autumn but also the child's volition, so that she can only stand motionless and murmur to herself: "What shall I do?—what shall I do?" (32). Later at Lowood, when looking through a window after Miss Scatcherd has flogged Helen Burns, it is a markedly contrasting impression of ebullience, a "gleeful tumult", that the outside wind and chaos evoke in Jane: in perfect Romantic fashion the child wishes "the wind to howl more wildly, the gloom to deepen to darkness, and the confusion to rise to clamour" (46) to create perfect harmony between them.

Still later Jane tellingly proclaims: "The night is serene, sir; and so am I" when Rochester asks how she feels (244), while in the last two paragraphs of the second volume, it is through images of a natural cataclysm (a flood) that the heroine conveys the horror which settles upon her mind when the truth about Rochester's marriage is revealed. Interestingly, in this last example, natural metaphors are the sole form of emotional solace or relief from pain that Jane gets during that "bitter hour [which] cannot be described". Rochester is so full of his revelation and of the pain that Bertha, he argues, has inflicted on him all these years that Jane's reaction to the news is utterly taken out of the picture. Likewise, her take on the whole incident is that it was paradoxically undramatic since "no explosion of passion, no loud altercation, no dispute, no defiance or challenge, no tears, no sobs" took place (252). A mere voiceless dependent again, she needs to find a non-verbal channel for the expression of her deep sense of loss, and it is to compensatory images of a torrent flooding the dried-up bed of a river that she instinctively turns, nature ambivalently bringing her both a measure of Lethe-like oblivion through self-expression and a feeling of destruction[1].

As those examples show and previous studies have already argued, it would be in vain to try and find in the narrator's use of natural metaphors a fixed system of symbols. For example, after examining various conflicting

---

1. It must also be noticed that the water metaphors in this passage foreshadow, and in a way justify, the events in the third volume. Instances of premonition being recurrent in the novel, that Jane should be in danger of metaphorically drowning in a river foretells the risk she later runs of being "killed", as she says, by a Rivers.

images of the moon in *Jane Eyre*, Heilman comes to the conclusion that it is an "underlying, never wholly articulated meaning which the moon has for Charlotte as artist" (Heilman 297). Likewise, in his essay on "Fire and Eyre", Lodge underlines the rough similarity between the Elizabethans' hierarchical ordering of the four elements from least to most noble (earth, water, air, and fire) and Brontë's personal associations in *Jane Eyre*, only to drop the suggestion, stating that what the writer was after was "not order, but a reflection of the turbulent, fluctuating inner life of her heroine" (Lodge 121)—a statement one can but agree with, except to say that it would be over-romanticizing the novel to assert that it conveys only *turbulent* images of the self through nature. Writing, as Jane often does, the varying moods of her inner self onto the blank slate of the outside world, one must expect those biased representations to be sometimes at odds with each other: their value lies not in their logic or in the absolute truth they embody, but in the closeness between the emotions felt and the correlative used to convey them.

One can even suppose that Brontë consciously creates more or less complex networks of natural images and metaphors to make the reader sense, and inquire into, the presence of this apparent supplement of meaning.

Two cases in point are her use of the metaphor of birds and lambs. That Rochester should liken his governess to "a curious sort of bird [glancing] through the close-set bars of a cage", or to "a vivid, restless, resolute captive" who dreams of soaring to the skies (118-9), comes as no surprise, given the recurrent imprisonment theme analyzed previously. The interesting point here is that Rochester never varies in his perception of Jane. Indeed, in his eyes, she remains to the end a restless bird pining for liberty, a caged "eager bird" with large open eyes, a frail linnet who speaks and acts with a strange determination, a morning skylark which may choose to go away when the day advances (265, 266, 374). On the contrary Jane's perception of herself is apt to oscillate between acceptance and rejection of Rochester's bird metaphor, in a movement which underscores her fundamental hesitation between chafing instinctively at imposed forms of servitude and confessing her deep-set need to be of use, as when she proudly portrays herself as a helpful sparrow to Rochester's royal eagle (374).

Jane's ardent rejection of this metaphor comes during the orchard scene when Rochester's lie about sending her to Ireland cuts her to the quick:

> "Jane, be still; don't struggle so, like a wild, frantic bird that is rending its own plumage in its desperation."
> "I am no bird; and no net ensnares me: I am a free human being with an independent will; which I now exert to leave you."

> Another effort set me at liberty, and I stood erect before him. *(216)*

But the truth of the image strikes her at other moments, the I-narrator using similes which confirm and even expand the original metaphor. Describing her heart as "a bird with both wings broken" or herself as a messenger-pigeon (276, 360), depending on whether or not she is capable of flying home, she denies the previous outburst of her younger self. Picturing herself as a stray bird that feeds on Rochester's crumbs (209), in this case the little bits of happiness which his sole presence communicates to her, she adds an emotional dimension to her financial dependence on her master. Finally the proverbial association of birds with love is used in the passage where Jane hurriedly flees from Thornfield, regretting that she may not be *more* like those animals, so that the accumulation of signifieds linked to this one signifier (birds) is a form of indirect showing which helps the heroine define herself:

> Birds began singing in brake and copse: birds were faithful to their mates; birds were emblems of love. What was I? In the midst of my pain of heart, and frantic effort of principle, I abhorred myself. I had no solace from self-approbation: none even from self-respect. I had injured—wounded—left my master. I was hateful in my own eyes. *(274)*

As for the lamb metaphor, whose occurrences are far less numerous, one can say that it establishes the same kind of relationship between Rochester and Jane but takes it to more violent extremes. Indeed, during the month of courtship before the planned wedding, the I-narrator describes how she managed to keep Rochester at a safe distance. Her system, she asserts, included no "lamb-like submission and turtle-dove sensibility" (234) because she knew that she needed to put a limit to Rochester's imperious desires, habit of command, and tendency to idolize her, if a balanced relationship was to be created between them. Rochester's use of the lamb metaphor indicates that his thoughts take no such direction, though, and systematically equal *lamb* with *sacrifice*. His assertions that he would never leave his "pet lamb" near a wolf's den (Bertha's room) and that his having hurt her feelings makes him feel worse than if he had "by some mistake slaughtered it at the shambles" mean to be consoling (184, 254), but they also reveal the problem Jane needs to solve in order to reach with Rochester the kindred spirit relationship she yearns for.

Likewise, it is not coincidentally that Jane nearly falls into the (unconscious) selfish snare set by Rivers in the cause of the Holy Lamb because, throughout the novel, natural metaphors can be wielded like social, political or religious weapons whose effect is the subjugation of the young, female, initially poor and unrelated, character in the narrative. Counting as a mere nobody in the system into which she was born, it is only by sacrificing herself through the roles of the docile pupil, the more or less subjugated wife, and the missionary participating in the "last mighty victories of the Lamb", as the last page in the novel puts it, that her fictional contemporaries can envisage her.

A linguistic closeness with nature or a marked way with natural metaphors can therefore be quite effective in the political power struggle (in the broadest possible sense) in which most of the characters are engaged. Such is the case, for instance, in the concisely reported botanical conversation in which Miss Ingram puts down the more subdued, but less artificial, Mrs Dent by "[running] over its vocabulary with an air" (147) while the Colonel's wife cannot articulate her liking for *wild* flowers beyond a mere statement of the fact.

Along the same lines, it is by constantly resorting to such metaphors that Rochester manages to keep concealed the truth about his past life or his current marriage to Bertha. Indeed, on the face of it, sentences like "limpid, salubrious: no gush of bilge water had turned it [his memory] to fetid puddle" (116) aim at toning down male realities which might otherwise shock chaste female ears, and at showing through strong personal images Rochester's detestation of the sinner he implies he *used* to be. But the anomaly or semantic inconsistency usually created by metaphors (in that they are apt to establish connections between usually unrelated words) surprises the listener, and focuses his attention primarily on the logic behind them. In other words, especially in cases of metaphorical accumulations, such a rhetorical device can cause confusion and act as a smokescreen. A good illustration of this is provided by the following quote, excerpted from the first meeting of the protagonists in the orchard:

> "The glamour of inexperience is over your eyes," he answered; "and you see it through a charmed medium: you cannot discern that the gilding is slime and the silk draperies cobwebs; that the marble is sordid slate, and the polished woods mere refuse chips and scaly bark. Now here" (he pointed to the leafy enclosure we had entered) "all is real, sweet, and pure." *(183-184)*

because the numerous metaphors used here harp on the same vague idea and saturate the listener while deceptively making him think that he "gets the picture" or catches a glimpse of some imminent personal revelation.

Nature's signs and symbols

It thus appears that an emotional proximity with nature is by far preferred over an intellectual one, which makes the characters concerned lean toward artificiality and deception.

Once such a relationship is established, the sensitive self finds that his perceptive and imaginative powers expand. That is certainly the case with Jane, if we consider how she moves from a vision of nature as obstacle in the first volume to one of complicity and companionship in the other two. This shift is also made manifest by the instances of pathetic fallacy with which the text becomes interspersed each time Jane ascribes human feelings to animals or inanimate phenomena—for example, when she is displeased with birds for chirping on when her beloved master is on the brink of some revelation; when she boldly asserts that "Nature must be gladsome when I was so happy"; or when she somewhat weirdly wonders what crows must be thinking of her as they watch her survey the Thornfield grounds again after many months of absence (186-7, 219, 361).

If Nature thinks and feels as humans do, if it even watches and appraises their every action, the idea that it might also take an interest in their affairs, and talk to them, imposes itself. This, at least, is the conviction of the I-narrator who, looking back on events which took place upwards of ten years before, romantically declares her life-long faith in presentiments and in signs which, "for aught we know, may be but the sympathies of Nature with man" (187)[1].

The particular light shed by this statement makes Jane's constant passion for drawing and painting move beyond a mere artistic interest in the representation of natural scenes, and shows signs of an instinctive obsession. Whether she is fascinated by morbid miniature vignettes, draws powerful fantasy scenes in her scanty spare time, or traces in fireside embers the outline of a German castle whose picture somehow imprinted itself on her mind's eye (101), Nature's constant stimuli on her senses leave her no choice. She must inquire into the world around her and, in either conventional or highly imaginative ways, put pencil and water colours to paper in an attempt to grasp its mystery, power, and source of beauty.

This is revealed by the ekphrastic tendency evinced by the narrative, that is to say by the recurrent need the protagonists feel to try and define through the medium of one art (e.g., poetry, prose description, painting) the

---

1. The first stanza in Baudelaire's celebrated poem "Correspondances" comes to mind : "*La Nature est un temple où de vivants piliers / Laissent parfois sortir de confuses paroles ; / L'homme y passe à travers des forêts de symboles / Qui l'observent avec des regards familiers* " (published in 1857).

essence, form or spirit of another (e.g., landscape gardening, architecture)[1]. For example, Jane's description of the Bewick vignettes and of the three drawings out of her portfolio, which Rochester sets aside as highly striking and imaginative, comes into this category, though the best example of ekphrasis is to be found in the narrator's brief recounting of her "services" to her husband in the two years which elapse before he regains his eyesight:

> Literally, I was (what he often called me) the apple of his eye. He saw nature—he saw books through me; and never did I weary of gazing for his behalf, and of putting into words the effect of field, tree, town, river, cloud, sunbeam—of the landscape before us; of the weather round us—and impressing by sound on his ear what light could no longer stamp on his eye. Never did I weary of reading to him: never did I weary of conducting him where he wished to go: of doing for him what he wished to be done. *(384)*

This tendency is noteworthy because what ekphrasis does here is unite sundry viewpoints on, or sensorial perceptions of, nature as if a variety of approaches allowed for a more knowledgeable and intimate glimpse into its much lusted-after secrets. Even as a child, Jane links up parts of Bewick's introductory text with not necessarily connected vignettes, so that these in turn take on added meaning—a meaning which, for all we know, may be far from the artist's original intention. Inaccurate though this process might be it brings a degree of satisfaction to the child, who could not have been content to leave such "ever profoundly interesting" stories alone (6-7), in the same way as Rochester requires clarification of the three strange fantasy scenes which, he supposes, reveal Jane's unhappiness and frustration[2].

Nature does not reveal her secrets easily, though, and by the novel's end Jane's quest for hidden meaning has not proceeded much further than an ineradicable belief in its existence. Like Melville's Ahab in pursuit of the whale or Poe's Pym at the foot of the white veil, the episode of Jane's wanderings through the moors (275-277) even makes it clear that the longing for fusion with nature is attended with temptations of which one may as well beware—like loss of identity, suicide, or the desire to become "bee or lizard" and vanish peacefully into the wilderness or the landscape.

Yet, in *Jane Eyre*, this never-realized dream of fusion serves a purpose in that it gives the heroine a stability and strength she has not known before.

---

1. See Lawrence J. Starzyk's article on the pictorial in *Jane Eyre*.
2. Jane's watercolours fall into the ekphrastic category because she strongly visualizes her subjects and scenes "with the spiritual eye" before she tries to give them shape. Being "but a pale portrait of the thing [she] had conceived" (107), each of her works thus becomes a feeble attempt at imitating a virtual work of art.

First of all, the desolate moors around Whitcross grant her a slice of the experience she has always craved for, and shows her where her place in the universe lies, somewhere between "the mighty Milky Way" and the tiny beings into whose contact she now comes. An orphan, she is also shown the cosmic parents to whom she can turn in her hour of need, in the shape of "the universal mother, Nature", who offers Jane the "breast of her hill" to nestle to, and of her Maker, "the Source of Life" who must also protect Rochester. And finally the whole novel bears testimony to the fact that, at key moments in her daughter's life, nature sends her a series of signs for her to interpret as best she can, among which the moon, the wind, lightning, fire, and dreams play prominent parts.

This interpretation of nature's signs supposes that the observer is endowed with a subtle Romantic sensitivity, born in part of the potentially morbid desire for fusion just mentioned, because it is no easy task breaking through her code. Indeed, the vehicles for nature's messages may be few, but the tiniest variation in them must be perceived and analyzed with quasi-scientific rigour. For instance, whether ascending or fixed, waning or waxing, pale or luminous, white or blood red, glorious or veiled behind clouds, the moon imparts messages of comfort or sends urgent warnings; while the wind, "wild and high" one day, does not herald the danger another wind does when it blows "'with a sullen, moaning sound' far more eerie" (240)[1]. To boot, feelings can act as a counterforce which blurs nature's message, the blindness customarily associated with love being apt to render the most faithful observer suddenly impervious to any number of signs, as during the cataclysmic night after Rochester's proposal:

> But joy soon effaced every other feeling; and loud as the wind blew, near and deep as the thunder crashed, fierce and frequent as the lightning gleamed, cataract-like as the rain fell during a storm of two hours' duration, I experienced no fear, and little awe. Mr Rochester came thrice to my door in the course of it, to ask if I was safe and tranquil: and that was comfort, that was strength for anything. *(218-219)*

True, such examples of natural manifestations may put off some readers by seeming overly contrived or romantic in a novel which constantly hesitates between giving imagination and the senses their due and, on the other hand, depicting a realist and rational world with none of the characteristics of Charlotte and Patrick's Angria. It must be underlined, though, that what the narrator presents as a series of signs sent by the elements or the celestial

---

1. This quotation is slightly adapted from Walter Scott's *The Lay of the Last Minstrel*: "At the sullen, moaning sound, / The ban-dogs bay and howl." (I, XIII, 1-2).

bodies, the reader is free to interpret rationally as an equivalent or objective correlative of the heroine's susceptibility. Also, Brontë sometimes drops subtler and more complex natural symbols in the narrative, which must delight even the most reasonable reader—like the horse chestnut with a ring-like circular seat at the base, severed in two halves by lightning but still holding fast at the roots; or the unusual presence in Rochester's orchard of a moth which reminds the owner of a West Indian insect, as if his past must always intrude on him, even in an Eden-like setting (212).

It thus appears that nature plays a key role in *Jane Eyre* by underscoring its main themes, helping with characterization, and making possible the advent of the kind of poetry without which Brontë could not apparently have done at the time.

As we have seen, the protagonist's unconventionality, her instinctive dislike of obstacles, her thirst for freedom and experience, her quest for spiritual growth and a kindred spirit with whom to share her life are often conveyed through natural elements and through her evolving interaction with the different environments in which she is placed.

The human/nature analogies and the natural metaphors in which the narrative abounds have also shown us that, in truly Romantic fashion, a privileged emotional link is established not only between nature and Jane, whether or not she is willing and aware of the fact, but also between Jane and the like-minded Rochester, who is occasionally just as "physically influenced by the atmosphere and scene" (262) as the heroine is. On the contrary, the superficiality and foibles of characters with only an intellectual closeness with nature are brought to the fore.

As for the terms in which this closeness with the physical world is established, we have seen that, in exchange for her instinctive obsession with the idea of becoming one with a nature that is full of secrets, the protagonist often derives a feeling of harmony from the signs and symbols which she receives from the universe. As for the readers, they may choose to interpret the most striking of these natural phenomena in a rational way while enjoying the symbolic complexity and poetic unity which they lend to the narrative.

Some critics have argued that the last chapter shatters this unity because Jane disappointingly "works out her destiny in a temperate—though not idyllic—zone", or literally buries herself in "a relatively mild and ordinary marriage [which] is made after the spirit of the masculine universe is controlled or extinguished[1]." Others, on the contrary, see in Ferndean a place of regeneration, a happily secluded natural order of the protagonists' own

---

1. See Lodge, p. 143 and 117 respectively. The second sentence is quoted by Lodge from an essay by Richard Chase ("The Brontës, or Myth Domesticated").

making, devoid of artificiality *because* it is deprived of flowers and garden-beds¹. Striking and paradoxical though it may be in a novel marked by a long march from night to dawn, such an ending might still aim to show that, in the same way as Emily's *Wuthering Heights* transforms Catherine and Heathcliff into larger-than-life elemental characters, Charlotte's cataclysms, metaphorical bestiary, watchful moons, supernatural occurrences and final refuge in the wood place her protagonists under the auspices of the whole cosmos, and give the merely human love story between Rochester and Jane an unusual sunset-meets-moonrise quality. (212)

Works Cited

BACHELARD, Gaston, *La Poétique de l'espace*, Paris : Quadrige/PUF, 1981.

BRONTË, Charlotte, *Jane Eyre*, précédé de *Œuvres de jeunesse 1826-1847*, Paris : Gallimard (La Pléiade), 2008.

BRONTË, Charlotte, *The Professor, To Which are Added the Poems of Charlotte, Emily, and Anne Brontë*, London: Henry Frowde, n.d. [1912?]

GILBERT, Sandra M., "A Dialogue of Self and Soul: Plain Jane's Progress", *in The Madwoman in the Attic: The Woman Writer and the Nineteenth-Century Literary Imagination*, New Haven: Yale University Press, 2000, p. 336-71.

HEILMAN, Robert B., "Charlotte Brontë, Reason, and the Moon", *in Nineteenth Century Fiction*, 14, 1960, p. 283-302.

LEAVIS, Q. D., "Introduction", *in Jane Eyre*, London: Penguin Classics, 1985, p. 7-29.

LODGE, David, "Fire and Eyre: Charlotte Brontë's War of Earthly Elements", *in Language of Fiction: Essays in Criticism and Verbal Analysis of the English Novel*, London: Routledge and Kegan Paul, 1996, p. 114-43.

SMITH, Margaret, ed. *The Letters of Charlotte Brontë: with a Selection of Letters by Family and Friends*, Oxford: Clarendon Press, Volume II, 1848-1851 (2000).

STARZYK, Lawrence J., "'The gallery of memory': The Pictorial *in Jane Eyre*", *in Papers on Language and Literature*, 33, 3, Summer 1997, p. 288-309.

TILLOTSON, Kathleen, "*Jane Eyre*", *in Novels of the Eighteen-Forties*, Oxford: Clarendon Press, 1965, p. 257-313.

WOOLF, Virginia, "*Jane Eyre* and *Wuthering Heights*", *in The Common Reader*, London: Pelican, 1938, p. 154-60.

---

1. This is Sandra M. Gilbert's viewpoint (p. 370).

Jane Eyre : la picturalité et son inscription dans le texte

Charlotte Borie

Même si ce pan de son œuvre est moins connu, et sans doute de moindre génie, Charlotte Brontë fut aussi dessinatrice et peintre. *The Art of the Brontës*, de Jane Sellars et Christine Alexander, recense tous les dessins et peintures connus des quatre enfants Brontë, et le chapitre consacré à Charlotte, très fourni, regorge d'images, créations ou copies, par celle qui n'allait laisser de véritable empreinte dans le monde des arts qu'en tant que romancière. Pendant longtemps, Charlotte ne sut pas vraiment à laquelle des *sister arts* elle consacrerait sa carrière, mais sa mauvaise vue, entre autres choses, ne lui laissa guère d'autre choix que celui d'écrire, activité à laquelle elle éprouvait déjà tant de difficultés, étant donné le degré avancé de sa myopie. Pourtant, toute sa vie, Charlotte Brontë ressentit le besoin de mener conjointement les deux activités artistiques pour lesquelles elle avait un talent. C'est dans sa correspondance, dont le premier objectif n'était pas poétique, que l'interpénétration des deux arts est la plus frappante. Dans une lettre célèbre adressée à Ellen Nussey en date du 6 mars 1843 (dont le manuscrit est reproduit dans Smith), Charlotte dit au revoir à son amie alors qu'elle s'apprête à traverser la Manche pour retourner en Belgique pour la deuxième fois. Au bas de la lettre, Brontë a dessiné son amie, accompagnée d'un soupirant sur une rive de la Manche, et elle-même, aussi laide qu'elle se pensait, de l'autre côté, saluant Ellen de la main. Son autoportrait est accompagné d'une bulle, octroyant au personnage des paroles d'adieu. Quant à la représentation d'Ellen Nussey, elle est accompagnée d'une légende, comme celle du soupirant. La page est signée deux fois, comme une lettre, après l'écriture, et comme une œuvre d'art, après le dessin. L'intrusion du dessin dans l'écrit, puis de l'écrit dans le dessin, montre combien peu Charlotte cloisonne la pratique des deux arts, et à quel point elle ressent l'impérieuse nécessité de les employer tous les deux dans sa manière de s'exprimer. Sur un mode métaphorique aussi l'imbrication des deux arts se fait jour. Dans une lettre écrite à ses éditeurs datant du 6 novembre 1852, Charlotte s'exprime sur la composition de son dernier roman, *Villette*, et voici les termes qu'elle emploie pour décrire son art romanesque :

> I doubt whether the regular novel-reader will consider
> "the agony piled sufficiently high"—(as the Americans
> say) or the colour dashed on the Canvass with the proper
> amount of daring. Still—I fear they must be satisfied with

> what is offered: my palette affords no brighter tint—were
> I to attempt to deepen the reds or burnish the yellows, I
> should but botch. *(Lettre à W.S. Williams; Smith 80)*

Le style est comparé au geste de la main du peintre, le potentiel de l'imagination ou de l'analyse à une palette, les éléments de composition à des couleurs. Pour Charlotte Brontë, la composition d'un roman relève des techniques picturales. Mais le pictural aussi a besoin du discours, sous forme de légende, de commentaires, ou tout simplement de source d'inspiration, car finalement, parmi les nombreux dessins de Brontë, l'immense majorité est constituée d'imitations ou de dessins inféodés aux textes juvéniles. Pictural et scriptural sont destinés à se mêler dans la pratique artistique de Charlotte Brontë, et l'on retrouve comme une évidence cette interpénétration des deux mondes à l'œuvre dans *Jane Eyre*. Dans ce roman, le dessin et la peinture occupent une place thématique de choix. Et dans le même temps, comme dans la correspondance de Charlotte, le pictural ne figure pas seulement en propre dans l'œuvre mais informe l'écriture pour la colorer de ses tonalités graphiques, pour toucher les sens pendant que le discours s'adresse à l'intelligence. Le pictural ne doit pour autant pas être confiné au simple rôle de béquille qui viendrait soutenir une écriture défaillante, mais considéré comme un mode d'inscription à part entière qui fonctionne comme un véritable allié et qui est régi par ses propres spécificités, un supplément d'âme avec lequel l'écriture sait jouer, et dont elle peut aussi se départir pour exploiter à plein sa propre puissance.

La formation de l'esprit pictural

Tout le monde peut en convenir, *Jane Eyre* a une portée ekphrastique certaine. Les dessins et les peintures jalonnent le texte. Les descriptions d'images dessinées ou peintes (qu'elles soient réelles ou fictives) permettent, au-delà d'apporter une touche picturale au texte, de positionner Jane par rapport à la peinture, de lui donner un rôle dans le processus qui entoure la mise en scène des images décrites. Les scènes d'*ekphrasis* tout à la fois construisent et révèlent la tournure d'esprit de Jane, sa sensibilité visuelle, et plus encore picturale.

Jane spectatrice

Le texte est placé sous le signe de l'image dès les premières pages à travers l'évocation des gravures d'oiseaux dans le livre d'histoire naturelle de Bewick que Jane parcourt, cachée derrière le rideau de la fenêtre, à Gateshead. Cette *ekphrasis* fondatrice, crée un effet de galerie dans laquelle Jane enfant se promène.

> I cannot tell what sentiment haunted the quite solitary churchyard, with its inscribed headstone; its gate, its two trees, its low horizon, girdled by a broken wall, and its newly-risen crescent, attesting the hour of eventide.
> The two ships becalmed on a torpid sea I believed to be marine phantoms.
> The fiend pinning down the thief's pack behind him I passed over quickly: it was an object of terror.
> So was the black, horned thing seated aloof on a rock, surveying a distant crowd surrounding a gallows. *(6)*

La petite Jane est immergée dans un univers pictural, duquel l'écrit n'est pas totalement exclu même s'il n'est pas privilégié. Elle avoue : « *the letterpress thereof I cared little for, generally speaking; and yet there were certain introductory pages that, child as I was, I could not pass quite as a blank* » (6). Le pictural emporte la préférence de Jane, mais l'écrit n'est pas absent de ses préoccupations, et le poétique et le pictural se complètent pour générer un univers qui pallie l'alentour réel inhospitalier de Gateshead. Cette alliance des deux types de représentation se confirme aussitôt :

> Each picture told a story; mysterious often to my undeveloped understanding and imperfect feelings, yet ever profoundly interesting: as interesting as the tales Bessie sometimes narrated on winter evenings, when she chanced to be in good humour; and when, having brought her ironing-table to the nursery hearth, she allowed us to sit about it, and while she got up Mrs Reed's lace frills, and crimped her night-cap borders, fed our eager attention with passages of love and adventure taken from old fairy tales and other ballads; or (as at a later period I discovered) from the pages of "Pamela", and "Henry, Earl of Moreland." *(6-7)*

Dès ces premières évocations picturales, Jane met en équivalence image et discours, en expliquant que chacune des vignettes dans le livre occasionne en elle une émotion, un intérêt, semblables à ceux provoqués par les contes d'une des domestiques de la maison. Déjà, dans l'esprit de la petite Jane, le visuel et la narration sont associés, et de la même manière que chaque image raconte une histoire, on peut supposer que chaque histoire fait naître des images dans son esprit, et l'amène à concevoir le contenu du récit comme un objet visuel.

Plus tard, alors qu'elle est entrée depuis quelque temps à Lowood School, Jane entretient une brève amitié avec une des filles de l'école. Sa grande amie Helen Burns est malade, comme la plupart des enfants de l'institution, et alors que l'on se meurt entre les murs de l'école, les enfants en relative bonne santé sont livrées à elles-mêmes, passant le plus clair de leur temps dehors à profiter de l'embellie climatique qui contraste avec la morne atmosphère qui règne à l'intérieur. Un épisode de cette époque réunit donc Jane et cette camarade, et malgré son caractère anecdotique (en comparaison avec le drame qui se joue de l'autre côté du mur d'enceinte), il confirme la tournure d'esprit de la jeune Jane dans son rapport au discours :

> one Mary Ann Wilson; shrewd, observant personage, whose society I took pleasure in, partly because she was witty and original, and partly because she had a manner which set me at my ease. Some years older than I, she knew more of the world, and could tell me many things I liked to hear: with her my curiosity found gratification: to my faults also she gave ample indulgence, never imposing curb or rein on anything I said. She had a turn for narrative, I for analysis; she liked to inform, I to question; so we got on swimmingly together, deriving much entertainment, if not much improvement, from our mutual intercourse. *(66)*

Ce passage ne traite pas directement du pictural, mais il fait de Jane une spectatrice du discours de sa camarade, son oreille fonctionnant comme une rétine sur laquelle s'imprime les récits de Mary Ann, laissant derrière eux, par le jeu de la persistance, une impression de plaisir qui conforte Jane dans son attitude d'absorption. Ces échanges entre les deux petites filles ne tendent pas, du propre aveu de Jane, à la faire grandir dans son rapport au monde et à la connaissance, mais la maintiennent dans une approche immédiate, spontanée, et non construite, apprise. Jane n'a pas les qualités d'une narratrice, elle n'a pas encore accès à la linéarité et au symbolisme du discours, mais elle sait percevoir le réel, et même l'interroger. Jane, avec les années de recul qui la séparent de Lowood, écrit qu'elle avait, enfant, une certaine faculté d'analyse. Cette faculté est indissociable de celle de la synthèse, même si elles peuvent paraître antithétiques. Il semble clairement établi que Jane est sensible à l'image, c'est-à-dire à un ordre de coexistences, un ordre synthétique, qui s'oppose, au moins de prime abord, à l'ordre des successions, ordre analytique, qu'est le langage. Si elle souligne ici sa capacité d'analyse, et l'associe à sa réceptivité, c'est sans doute que Jane a déjà, dès son enfance, le regard du peintre, la capacité de voir l'image comme une composition, quelque chose qui relève à la fois de la coexistence, et de la succession, coexistence de formes et de couleurs sur la toile, succession des gestes du peintre résultant d'un enchaînement d'étapes mentales. Il n'est donc pas étonnant que Jane ne soit pas longtemps confinée au rôle de spectatrice, mais qu'elle accède, assez naturellement, au statut de créatrice. L'adaptation cinématographique de *Jane Eyre* par Zeffirelli saisit cette spécificité du personnage plus tôt encore que le roman ne la révèle, puisque l'on y voit Jane dessinant, le regard et la main sûrs, dès son enfance à Lowood.

Dans le roman, la pratique picturale de Jane ne se découvre que peu à peu, laissant d'abord entrevoir son activité comme un griffonnage enfantin, puis révélant aux yeux du lecteur l'étendue de son talent.

Jane dessinatrice

Après l'apparition fondatrice de l'image dans *Jane Eyre*, avec les vignettes dans *The History of British Birds* de Bewick, chaque phase de la vie de Jane est marquée par le dessin. A Lowood d'abord, Jane explique comment elle revoit mentalement les dessins qu'elle a effectués de jour, se raccrochant à l'idéal qu'ils représentent pour ne pas sombrer dans le désarroi de sa situation d'enfant affamée et maltraitée. Les scènes bucoliques de bétail dans la campagne, de papillons butinant les roses encore closes, d'oiseaux picorant les fruits sur les arbres, les maisons, les arbres, les nids abritant des œufs semblables à des perles (63)… Tout tend à recréer un univers charmant et chaleureux en forme d'antidote à celui de Lowood, un peu comme les oiseaux de Bewick ouvraient les portes d'un monde étrange et fascinant à la petite Jane à Gateshead. Néanmoins, une différence remarquable sépare les deux univers. Le premier était adopté par l'enfant qui découvrait sa sensibilité à l'image. Le deuxième est créé par l'écolière qui a désormais tiré les enseignements de ses premières incursions picturales, et qui sait le pouvoir de la vision. À partir de ce moment, Jane est en capacité de recréer le monde, réel ou intérieur, par son pouvoir pictural, medium privilégié pour travailler l'espace — la question du territoire et de l'appartenance étant un point névralgique de l'œuvre.

C'est à Thornfield que pour la première fois, Jane trouve un spectateur pour ses œuvres. Lors d'une de leurs premières rencontres, Rochester interroge Jane sur ses accomplissements. Sur l'annonce que Jane avait fait publier dans le journal local, elle avait déclaré avoir un bagage en français, en musique et en dessin, en plus des autres domaines habituels de l'instruction. Rochester vérifie donc d'abord ses talents de musicienne, et les juge bien pauvres. Il passe ensuite au dessin, et demande à voir le portfolio de Jane, car Adèle l'a intrigué en lui montrant des esquisses de la main de sa gouvernante. Il la soupçonne de ne pas être la seule auteure de ces dessins et exige de voir la totalité des œuvres de Jane afin, éventuellement, d'y déceler la griffe d'un maître. Jane lui apporte ses dessins et ses peintures, et Rochester la questionne alors sur la genèse de ces images :

> He deliberately scrutinised each sketch and painting. Three he laid aside; the others, when he had examined them, he swept from him. […]
> "[…] I perceive these pictures were done by one hand: was that hand yours?"

> "Yes."
> "And when did you find time to do them? They have taken much time, and some thought."
> "I did them in the last two vacations I spent at Lowood, when I had no other occupation."
> "Where did you get your copies?"
> "Out of my head."
> "That head I see now on your shoulders?"
> "Yes, sir."
> "Has it other furniture of the same kind within?"
> "I should think it may have: I should hope—better."
> *(106)*

La grande question parmi toutes celles que pose Rochester, c'est celle du modèle. Où Jane a-t-elle trouvé les images qu'elle a ensuite peintes à l'aquarelle ? Cette question centrale scinde la pratique picturale en deux, avec d'une part la technique et d'autre part la conception. Pendant son enfance à Lowood, Jane crée des dessins sans recopier des images préexistantes, mais ce sont des icônes qu'elle reproduit (maison, nid, arbre). En grandissant, elle parvient à composer des peintures en conjuguant sa capacité à imiter la nature et la puissance de son imagination. C'est donc l'esprit de Jane qui fournit les modèles de ses peintures et uniquement sa main qui les produit. Ce premier échange est suivi d'une longue *ekphrasis* menée par Jane. Elle décrit dans le détail les trois peintures qui ont retenu l'attention de Rochester. À travers cette reconstruction, le lecteur peut juger de l'étrangeté du travail de Jane, tant sur le plan thématique que sur celui de l'exécution. Les proportions semblent curieuses, et les situations semblent marquées au sceau de l'onirisme tant leur incongruité est grande. Rochester est stupéfait par tant d'étrangeté. Il qualifie les peintures de « *peculiar* », et les pensées qui les ont générées de « *elfish* ». Cette perception de l'œuvre de Jane est totalement cohérente avec la manière dont Rochester la considère. Il la croit sortie d'un conte, parente avec les sorcières ou les fées. Cette étrangeté de l'artiste et de son œuvre se retrouve tout naturellement dans sa technique. Selon Rochester, il semble évident que Jane n'a pas acquis une connaissance académique de la peinture, mais qu'elle la pratique avec inspiration, se rendant ainsi capable de représenter l'irreprésentable, qu'il s'agisse du souffle du vent ou de l'éclat irréel des yeux du personnage dans le deuxième tableau intitulé « *the Evening Star* ». Une autre question que Rochester pose à Jane est digne du plus grand intérêt : « *Were you happy when you painted these pictures?* » En posant cette question à Jane, Rochester cherche à tendre une passerelle entre la création et la psyché, comme si les dessins de Jane étaient (utile anachronisme) des photographies de son humeur. Ils auraient ainsi le pourvoir de capturer, de fixer, un état d'esprit potentiellement fugace (Rochester sait combien peu de moments de bonheur permet la vie à l'institution de Lowood). Le bonheur évoqué par Rochester est aussi à entendre sur le mode de la satisfaction. Jane a-t-elle ressenti un contentement après avoir peint ces tableaux ? Jane répond que le résultat est loin de rendre la pensée qui l'a précédé, et que ces peintures ne sont que de pâles représentations. Rochester acquiesce, qualifiant les tableaux de « shadow of your thought » (107-108).

À deux autres époques de la vie de Jane, le lecteur la voit affairée à dessiner ou à peindre. À Gateshead, où elle revenue pour accompagner sa tante vers la mort, Jane, qui ne souhaite pas prendre part aux querelles qui opposent Eliza et Georgiana Reed, s'isole près d'une fenêtre et dessine des vignettes :

> Provided with a case of pencils, and some sheets of paper, I used to take a seat apart from them, near the window, and busy myself in sketching fancy vignettes, representing any scene that happened momentarily to shape itself in the ever-shifting kaleidoscope of imagination: a glimpse of sea between two rocks; the rising moon, and a ship crossing its disk; a group of reeds and water-flags, and a naiad's head crowned with lotus-flowers, rising out of them; an elf sitting in a hedge-sparrow's nest, under a wreath of hawthorn-bloom. *(198-199)*

Parmi les sujets de Jane, on retrouve à la fois les images maritimes héritées de Bewick, la représentation bucolique de la nature, et le monde féerique dont elle semble être issue. C'est l'assemblage de ces différents mondes de référence qui fait la singularité de l'imagination de Jane, véritable kaléidoscope qui tient la gageure d'associer les images statiques et le dynamisme de son mécanisme. Le dessin extrait du mouvement de l'imagination une image et la fixe sur le papier, et la succession des vignettes reproduit la multiplicité des facettes de la pensée de Jane et leur enchaînement perpétuel. Les vignettes de cette époque, vu le caractère automatique de leur exécution (comme on parle d'écriture automatique), forment également une porte d'accès à l'inconscient de Jane. Son amour pour Rochester resurgit lors de son absence de Thornfield : alors qu'un jour Jane commence, suivant le même protocole de dessin automatique, à dessiner un visage, le portrait qui se compose sous ses yeux est celui de Rochester.

> One morning I fell to sketching a face: what sort of a face it was to be, I did not care or know. I took a soft black pencil, gave it a broad point, and worked away. Soon I had traced on the paper a broad and prominent forehead, and a square lower outline of visage: that contour gave me pleasure; my fingers proceeded actively to fill it with

> features. Strongly-marked horizontal eyebrows must be traced under that brow; then followed, naturally, a well-defined nose, with a straight ridge and full nostrils; then a flexible-looking mouth, by no means narrow; then a firm chin with a decided cleft down the middle of it: of course, some black whiskers were wanted, and some jetty hair, tufted on the temples, and waved above the forehead. Now for the eyes: I had left them to the last, because they required the most careful working. I drew them large; I shaped them well: the eyelashes I traced long and sombre; the irids lustrous and large. "Good! but not quite the thing," I thought, as I surveyed the effect: "They want more force and spirit;" and I wrought the shades blacker, that the lights might flash more brilliantly—a happy touch or two secured success. There I had a friend's face under my gaze; and what did it signify that those young ladies turned their backs on me? I looked at it; I smiled at the speaking likeness: I was absorbed and content.
> "Is that a portrait of some one you know?" asked Eliza, who had approached me unnoticed. I responded that it was merely a fancy head, and hurried it beneath the other sheets. Of course, I lied: it was, in fact, a very faithful representation of Mr Rochester. *(199)*

Ce passage est à la fois descriptif de l'image et du geste mental et manuel qui la compose. La succession de deux-points et de points-virgules atteste à la fois les ruptures de rythme entre les différentes postures de la main de la dessinatrice — correspondant aux différentes zones du visage que la jeune-femme traite — et l'enchaînement logique qui lie ces différentes étapes. Jane procède par touches, délimitant d'abord les contours, les remplissant ensuite, liant, pour finir, l'ensemble des éléments dont la disparité empêche une impression d'ensemble satisfaisante en travaillant les ombres. L'importance de cette finition est sans doute, par ailleurs, à l'origine, dans l'adaptation de Zeffirelli, d'une scène d'extérieur où Jane donne un cours de dessin à sa jeune élève. Adèle, apercevant Rochester, demande à sa gouvernante de le dessiner. Jane s'exécute avec le même naturel dont l'héroïne du roman fait preuve, esquissant en quelques traits un profil de son maître d'une ressemblance frappante. Rochester, conscient qu'on est en train de le croquer, s'approche de Jane et Adèle, voit le dessin, et en est bouleversé. Après quelques secondes d'un trouble mystérieux dont il est coutumier, Rochester demande à Jane de le suivre car il souhaite lui parler. En s'éloignant, Jane laisse des instructions à Adèle. La petite fille doit continuer à dessiner seule en se souvenant du credo de Jane : « *the shadows are as important as the lights* ». Cette phrase, lancée comme une énigme à l'esprit simple et enfantin de la petite Adèle, n'échappe évidemment pas à Rochester qui entrevoit dans la foi de la gouvernante en cette règle apparemment picturale la possibilité de lui confier sa part d'ombre sans que celle-ci ne noie dans les ténèbres la part de pureté lumineuse de son âme originelle.

Evidemment, la part d'ombre de Rochester refait surface de façon catastrophique et conduit Jane à l'exil. A Marsh End et Morton School aussi Jane dessine — des portraits de ses élèves, des paysages locaux (314). Son talent est reconnu par sa nouvelle famille, les Rivers, ainsi que par Miss Oliver, la fille du bienfaiteur local. Celle-ci, après avoir découvert avec enthousiasme les dessins de Jane, lui demande de faire son portrait. Jane accepte, en se réjouissant de l'opportunité qui lui est donnée d'imiter une si belle nature : « *I felt a thrill of artist-delight at the idea of copying from so perfect and radiant a model* » (314). Pour la première fois, Jane s'autoproclame artiste, et s'inscrit dans la grande tradition picturale de l'imitation de la nature. Le père et le soupirant de Miss Oliver s'attachent surtout à décrire la ressemblance du portrait au modèle, et la grande faculté de Jane à capturer l'éclat du regard de la jeune femme.

Saisissement, cristallisation, compréhension

Chaque dessin, chaque peinture de Jane permet une fixation, conférant ainsi à la picturalité un rôle majeur dans le rythme, le symbolisme et le développement du personnage dans l'œuvre. La pause (parfois *via* la pose) que le dessin ménage arrête la course de la narration pour créer une parenthèse, un créneau durant lequel l'esprit peut analyser à loisir la situation, et au cours duquel la même analyse, comme par un jeu de navette, se matérialise, se synthétise dans le dessin. L'objet qui résulte de ces pauses, le dessin lui-même, fait alors repère, signe intelligible d'une situation à un moment donné, signe qui demeure et qui témoigne, socle de nouvelles étapes, de nouveaux temps dans la narration. Les dessins de Jane vus et commentés par Rochester sont le saisissement de l'état d'esprit de Jane, de ses pensées, à une époque révolue, celle de Lowood. Ces dessins témoignent à la fois de l'esprit encore hanté de la jeune femme, mais aussi de sa relative immaturité sur le plan artistique puisque de son propre aveu, ces dessins ne sont qu'une faible représentation des images qu'elle avait en tête. Au moment où Jane montre ces aquarelles à Rochester, elle pressent peut-être déjà le pouvoir de saisissement du pictural. Peu après ces premiers entretiens avec son employeur, Jane prend conscience du sentiment amoureux qui naît en elle. Mais elle comprend aussi qu'elle n'est pas la seule à convoiter les regards de Rochester. Elle entend parler d'une certaine Blanche Ingram, prétendante toute désignée du maître de

Thornfield, l'un des hommes les plus riches de la région. Pour se guérir de la vanité qui lui a fait penser qu'elle pourrait inspirer à Rochester des sentiments semblables à ceux dont il est l'objet dans son cœur, Jane décide de se confronter à Blanche Ingram. Cette confrontation étant impossible dans la réalité (Blanche n'est pas encore arrivée à Thornfield et, quand bien même elle serait physiquement présente, Jane ne pourrait pas se placer à côté d'elle devant un miroir pour comparer leur apparence respective), Jane décide de la mettre en scène dans un diptyque au sein duquel chacune des deux femmes aura son portrait. C'est la sentence que prononce le tribunal de la Raison à l'encontre de Jane :

> "Listen, then, Jane Eyre, to your sentence: to-morrow, place the glass before you, and draw in chalk your own picture, faithfully; without softening one defect: omit no harsh line, smooth away no displeasing irregularity; write under it, "Portrait of a Governess, disconnected, poor, and plain.""
> "Afterwards, take a piece of smooth ivory—you have one prepared in your drawing-box: take your palette, mix your freshest, finest, clearest tints; choose your most delicate camel-hair pencils; delineate carefully the loveliest face you can imagine; paint it in your softest shades and sweetest hues, according to the description given by Mrs Fairfax […]: call it "Blanche, an accomplished lady of rank.""
> "Whenever, in future, you should chance to fancy Mr Rochester thinks well of you, take out these two pictures and compare them […]" "I'll do it," I resolved: […] I kept my word. […] I derived benefit from the task: it had kept my head and hands employed, and had given force and fixedness to the new impressions I wished to stamp indelibly on my heart. *(137)*

Cette fois encore, le thème et la technique sont en harmonie. Le portrait de Jane, une pauvre gouvernante de peu d'attraits, est exécuté à la craie. La pureté des couleurs de celui de Blanche, joyau de la noblesse, est assurée par les matériaux, pinceaux et pigments, de la plus haute qualité. Comme autour des premières images de la vie de Jane, les légendes doublent les dessins, et les ancrent plus encore dans la fixité de la formule. Ce diptyque opère un double saisissement pour Jane, à la fois sur le mode de la compréhension de sa situation sociale, et sur le mode de la pétrification des sentiments. Jane fige, à travers les traits de ses deux dessins, sa capacité à s'émouvoir et à idéaliser ce qu'elle perçoit.

Le film de Zeffirelli ne reproduit pas cet épisode en particulier, mais exploite de façon récurrente le pouvoir de saisissement de la peinture. C'est essentiellement à travers des portraits que le pictural saisit et fige le réel, en lui ajoutant parfois une dimension d'intelligibilité supplémentaire. L'apport symbolique des portraits est plus développé que dans le roman, condensant notamment en un autre diptyque la relation délétère de Rochester avec son père. Lorsque Mrs Fairfax fait visiter les appartements de Rochester à Jane, cette dernière voit au-dessus de la cheminée l'austère et gigantesque portrait en pied du père de son employeur. Le tableau semble écraser la jeune femme qui est obligée de lever la tête pour l'examiner. Puis Jane continue d'avancer dans la pièce, et trouve sur un guéridon le portrait d'un enfant. C'est celui d'Edward Rochester, son maître. Les deux portraits coexistent dans cette pièce cossue, cristallisant à jamais le drame de la vie de Rochester : avoir obéi, comme un bon fils, à la dictature de son père, épousant la femme qu'on avait choisie pour lui et qui fit son malheur. Un autre exemple du pouvoir fixateur du portrait nous ramène à l'épisode de la leçon de dessin en extérieur à Thornfield. Jane vient d'exécuter en quelques traits une esquisse très réussie du visage de son maître et, en la voyant, Rochester ne peut que se sentir saisi, doublement : surpris par le talent de Jane, et possédé corps et âme par cette jeune femme qui l'a si bien compris que ces quelques traits le représentent mieux qu'une peinture d'un grand portraitiste ne le ferait. « *You have me utterly* », avoue Rochester.

Les pouvoirs de l'image sont donc multiples dans *Jane Eyre*. D'abord objets d'observation, les dessins qui entourent Jane lui révèlent sa propre sensibilité au visuel, au graphique, et à la condensation que la toile, la page ou la vignette, toutes trois ordres de coexistence, permettent plus que le langage ou l'expérience elle-même. Le contact de Jane au monde des images forme son esprit, et bientôt sa manière de s'exprimer trouve un canal privilégié dans la pratique picturale. Les dessins et aquarelles qui remplissent alors son portfolio jalonnent la chronotopie de son existence, créant des pauses dans le déroulement de l'histoire, et ouvrant une dimension parallèle au récit, un potentiel intelligible supplémentaire qui double et améliore la diégèse. Il y a dans l'art pictural une performance qui se transmet au discours. La picturalité octroie un peu de sa nature à l'écrit qui en voit sa puissance d'évocation multipliée. Dépassant de beaucoup le statut thématique dans *Jane Eyre*, le pictural influence aussi l'expression, l'écriture, sur un plan technique.

Le pictural détourné au profit de l'écriture

Le pictural et le discursif, non contents de s'entremêler dans le texte, fusionnent parfois pour créer un langage à part entière, une écriture graphique. D'un discours autour de la peinture, le texte passe de temps en temps à un discours pictural, c'est-à-dire un mode d'écriture informé par les caractéristiques de l'image.

Sketching, observing, describing

Dans son enfance, on se souvient que Jane n'avait pas vocation au discours, mais plutôt à l'observation et à l'écoute. Arrivée à Thornfield, et après avoir exposé sa voix en passant une annonce — ébauche discursive de son profil —, Jane semble s'intéresser davantage à l'interaction, à la discussion. On peut lire avec quel plaisir elle se sent accueillie par Mrs Fairfax à son arrivée au manoir, et combien elle apprécie que cette dame, dont elle croit d'abord qu'elle est la maîtresse des lieux, s'adresse à elle comme si elles étaient sur un pied d'égalité et souhaite occuper son temps de loisir à converser avec elle. Au lendemain de son arrivée, Mrs Fairfax fait visiter Thornfield à sa nouvelle compagne, jusqu'à atteindre les appartements de Mr Rochester. C'est alors que Jane s'enquiert de son nouveau maître : Rochester est-il despotique ou est-il généralement apprécié ? N'y a-t-il rien de singulier chez lui ? À chaque question qu'elle pose à Mrs Fairfax, la réponse semble tomber à côté :

> There are people who seem to have no notion of sketching a character, or observing and describing salient points, either in persons or things: the good lady evidently belonged to this class; my queries puzzled, but did not draw her out. Mr Rochester was Mr Rochester in her eyes; a gentleman, a landed proprietor—nothing more: she inquired and searched no further, and evidently wondered at my wish to gain a more definite notion of his identity. *(89)*

Jane déplore chez Mrs Fairfax l'absence d'une caractéristique qu'elle semble s'octroyer en creux et qui consiste à savoir décrire quelqu'un avec la vivacité et l'efficacité du portraitiste, voire du caricaturiste. Elle regrette que la vieille dame ne fasse que voir au lieu de regarder, et ne soit capable de rendre compte que de ce qui est communément admis et pas d'une vision des choses qui lui soit propre et qui incarne plus Rochester que ses terres et son histoire familiale. Jane dénonce l'approche et le discours somme toute tautologiques de Mrs Fairfax — « *Mr Rochester was Mr Rochester* » — et avoue, de façon un peu détournée, qu'elle ne peut se contenter d'abstraction et qu'elle a besoin de la profondeur et de la perspective d'un portrait, au plus proche du pictural, pour satisfaire ses interrogations.

Le graphisme de l'écriture

Si Mrs Fairfax est dénuée de ce talent graphique, Jane en est dotée. Comme on pouvait l'imaginer en la sachant capable de peindre les fruits de son imagination avec prégnance et singularité, sa façon de raconter est marquée au sceau du pictural, gagnant ainsi une vivacité, une pertinence — qualités qui manquent justement au discours de Mrs Fairfax. L'influence picturale se révèle dans des techniques ou des impressions attachées à certaines scènes clés du roman, leur conférant ainsi une qualité de représentation accrue, et plaçant par ailleurs Jane dans une forme de discours autoréflexif, un mode d'écriture qui s'interroge sur ses ressorts. Jane s'inscrit alors dans son texte comme une « éditrice », décidant de la mise en page du récit de sa propre vie, de la meilleure façon de la présenter, ou de le représenter, pour donner rythme et vigueur à son récit. Deux épisodes sont, à ce titre, assez remarquables. Le premier est l'ouverture du chapitre 11. Jane a obtenu une réponse à son annonce, elle a fait le voyage jusqu'à Millcote, et attend, à l'auberge de la ville, que quelqu'un de Thornfield vienne la chercher :

> A new chapter in a novel is something like a new scene in a play: and when I draw up the curtain this time, reader, you must fancy you see a room in the "George Inn" at Millcote, with such large figured papering on the walls as inn rooms have; such a carpet, such furniture, such ornaments on the mantelpiece, such prints; including a portrait of George the Third, and another of the Prince of Wales, and a representation of the death of Wolfe. All this is visible to you by the light of an oil lamp hanging from the ceiling, and by that of an excellent fire, near which I sit in my cloak and bonnet; my muff and umbrella lie on the table, and I am warming away the numbness and chill contracted by sixteen hours' exposure to the rawness of an October day [...] *(79)*

Le nombre d'informations contenu dans ce paragraphe est incroyable. Cette ouverture de chapitre, menée sur le mode de l'hypotypose, transfère au bloc du paragraphe les qualités de ce que l'on pourrait voir sur une toile : concision, concentration, coexistence d'éléments ressortant de modes de connaissance divers — perceptions visuelle et kinesthésique, savoir partagé sur l'univers des auberges de passage et sur la civilisation anglaise, empathie avec ce personnage solitaire et engourdi par le froid. En quelques touches, à nouveau rendues par la parataxe asyndétique, Jane plante un décor et s'inscrit en son centre. La comparaison de cet épisode à une nouvelle scène dans une pièce de théâtre et l'allusion au rideau qui se lève évoquent les tableaux vivants qui précèdent parfois le début de l'action sur scène. Figeant la situation comme pour laisser au spectateur le temps d'en analyser la composition et de s'imprégner ensuite de l'atmosphère générale, ces tableaux vivants fonctionnent comme des peintures (ou encore, pour rester dans le registre théâtral, comme des pantomimes), concentrant dans une économie d'espace (ou de temps) les lignes de force de la scène, ses enjeux, évoquant à demi-mot ce qui l'a précédé, annonçant ce qui va la suivre. L'utilisation du présent renforce cette sensation de pause dans la narration, et d'immédiateté face au spectacle qui s'offre aux yeux du lecteur devenu spectateur. Ce dernier, pris à parti au travers de la fameuse adresse « *reader* », dont Jane est devenue coutumière, est placé devant ce tableau. Jane, ici clairement dédoublée en Jane narrée et Jane narrant, le fait s'arrêter à un point dans la galerie du récit, s'attarder devant le spectacle d'un tournant diégétique, se reposer un instant durant son inquiétant voyage avant d'entamer la période de Thornfield. Au sein du tableau de Jane attendant son destin à Millcote Inn, les portraits de George III et du Prince de Galles, et une reproduction du tableau de Benjamin West *The Death of General Wolfe*, mettent le pictural en abyme et dédoublent sa portée dans cette ouverture (comme dans l'œuvre), à la fois peinture d'un personnage et peinture d'une scène. Cette ouverture en forme de tableau superpose donc les deux dimensions du parcours initiatique de Jane, voyage géographique et voyage ontologique.

Un autre épisode dont les ressorts sont très proches, quoique moins affichés, de ceux de l'ouverture du chapitre 11 est celui du trajet vers l'église au matin du mariage de Jane et Rochester.

> I know not whether the day was fair or foul; in descending the drive, I gazed neither on sky nor earth; my heart was with my eyes; and both seemed migrated into Mr Rochester's frame [...] At the churchyard wicket he stopped: he discovered I was quite out of breath.
> "Am I cruel in my love?" he said. "Delay an instant: lean on me, Jane."
> And now I can recall the picture of the grey old house of God rising calm before me, of a rook wheeling round the steeple, of a ruddy morning sky beyond. I remember something, too, of the green grave-mounds; and I have not forgotten, either, two figures of strangers, straying among the low hillocks, and reading the mementoes graven on the few mossy head-stones. *(245)*

Dans la course qui entraîne les deux amoureux vers l'autel, la description de l'arrivée devant l'église fonctionne comme un arrêt sur image : Jane, à bout de souffle, obéit à la bienveillante injonction de Rochester, arrête ses pas et ouvre son regard à ce qui l'entoure. La description passe au présent, comme pour l'attente à Millcote, fonctionne par touches entre les virgules, replaçant les plages de couleur et les points qui forment les objets du décor sous les yeux du lecteur pour lui donner à voir l'impression de cette arrivée.

Le sentiment de cristallisation qui se dégage de ces quelques phrases concorde avec la prégnance du souvenir. Cet instant s'est fixé à la mémoire de Jane, et se rejoue, à travers ses « points saillants » (pour réemployer le vocabulaire pictural de Jane) dans cette évocation que la puissance anaphorique du souvenir martèle (« *I can recall* », « *I remember* », « *I have not forgotten* »). Cette scène n'est pas moins cruciale que celle de Millcote, et l'effet de ralenti puis de pause dans le récit mis en place par la picturalité soutient la solennité, le *moment* (au double sens anglais d'instant et d'importance).

Une narration picturale

À travers l'étude de ces deux passages, on décèle des caractéristiques de l'écriture qui sont directement liées aux méthodes picturales dont certaines sont récurrentes tout au long de l'œuvre : les passages au présent, les pauses entre deux phases du récit — comme on fait une halte dans un cheminement, les effets de tableau, d'arrêt sur image ou de ralenti. En fait, au-delà de l'écriture, c'est toute la narration qui porte la marque du pictural. Le roman dans son entier est structuré par ces effets picturaux. Christine Alexander et Jane Sellars remarquent, parmi plusieurs autres caractéristiques, que l'écriture romanesque est une succession de tableaux chez Charlotte Brontë, décelant « *her tendency to structure a novel as if it were a portfolio of paintings* » (Alexander and Sellars 56).

La narration du film de Zeffirelli rend compte de la picturalité sensible dans celle du roman. Le dispositif majeur de cette picturalité réside dans les effets de cadre qui jalonnent le film, et qui correspondent au positionnement dans les charnières de l'histoire. La superposition entre voyage géographique et développement intérieur, fixée lors des effets de tableaux dans le roman, se retrouve à travers des plans resserrés sur le visage de Jane, encadré par la portière de la voiture qu'elle prend pour voyager d'un point à un autre. Ce motif du visage encadré par la portière du moyen de transport est d'abord utilisé à l'arrivée de Jane à Thornfield. Le plan dure quelques secondes, avant que la portière de la voiture ne s'ouvre et ouvre dans le même temps le cadre qui fixait l'image de Jane. La même pause, mais inversée par la symétrie, a lieu lorsque Jane quitte Thornfield pour Gateshead, lorsqu'elle est appelée au chevet de sa tante. Jane s'installe dans la voiture, la caméra se centre sur son visage, et la porte de la voiture est refermée sur son occupante, enfermant par là même le visage de la jeune femme dans le cadre de la portière. La troisième et ultime occurrence du trope du cadre de la portière se trouve vers la fin du film, lorsque Jane retourne à Thornfield. Autre effet de cadre, celui permis par les arrêts de Jane devant des miroirs. Dans ces pauses picturales, la dimension du voyage géographique est perdue, et ces épisodes correspondent plutôt à des étapes du développement du personnage. Jane s'arrête devant un miroir lorsqu'elle fuit sa déception en réalisant qu'il est communément admis que Rochester doit tôt ou tard épouser Blanche Ingram. Elle s'arrête, se regarde, et s'adresse un « *You're a fool* » qui est censé correspondre à la sentence que le tribunal prononce à l'encontre de Jane « *That a greater fool than Jane Eyre had never breathed the breath of life* » (136), et à la punition qui s'ensuit, les portraits comparés de Jane et de Blanche Ingram. Cet arrêt devant le miroir crée une pause, une pétrification dans la narration, exploitant à nouveau frais le problème du cadre et du portrait mis en scène dans le roman à travers la personnification de la raison en tribunal (quoi de plus encadrant ?) et la sentence de ce tribunal (la confrontation à la représentation de soi et à celle d'autrui). Dans les deux cas, c'est Jane qui est au cœur du dispositif, à la fois source et cible — objet et reflet dans le film. La même pause spéculaire, point de basculement entre deux phases du récit, se retrouve un peu plus tard, lorsque Jane s'apprête à épouser Rochester et qu'elle se regarde dans sa robe de mariée et sous son voile.

Zeffirelli a vraiment le goût de la répétition et de la symétrie. C'est aussi par une ouverture et une fermeture en forme de diptyque qu'il inscrit son film dans la picturalité. La première image du film est une gravure, une représentation figée de Gateshead. Le spectateur voit cette gravure pendant qu'il entend la voix off de Jane adulte retracer en quelques phrases les fondements de son enfance. Par un effet de fondu, la gravure devient le premier plan filmé, et le film commence. En symétrie, à la fin du film, le dernier plan, un cadrage très large de scène d'extérieur où Jane et Rochester marchent côte à côte, devient une gravure par un fondu, et le film se termine. La première gravure n'est pas sans rappeler l'effet de tableau de Millcote ou du matin du mariage, une composition fixe qui crée une attente chez le spectateur tout en lui laissant le temps de contempler l'image et peut-être aussi de se faire sa propre vision des choses à venir, en fonction des indications données par la voix off. L'aspect patiné de la gravure place évidemment ce début sous le signe du passé, du souvenir : à partir de cette image issue de la galerie de la mémoire de Jane, la vie de l'héroïne se rejoue, reprend vie. À la fin, la cristallisation de la scène finale dans la gravure met un point d'orgue à ce récit, et fait de la totalité de l'histoire un nouveau souvenir, y compris dans l'esprit du spectateur. Le film s'est ouvert et s'est refermé à la manière d'un portfolio, comme celui que Charlotte Brontë a composé en écrivant *Jane Eyre*.

La picturalité traverse le roman en le jalonnant thématiquement et en inspirant l'écriture et la technique narrative. Mais on le voit, il n'existe pas entre l'image et le texte un rapport de subordination. À l'évidence, le pictural semble monopoliser tous les moments clés de l'œuvre, agençant son rythme, jouant avec les attentes et les sens du lecteur. Pour autant, il est possible de déchiffrer le roman comme un glissement progressif du pictural au scriptural.

De la préférence picturale à la préférence scripturale

Jamais Jane n'abandonne le dessin et la peinture, mais à la fin du roman, certains éléments permettent de penser que le discours, et notamment le discours écrit, remporte la victoire de ce qui n'est pas un conflit entre le pictural et le discursif dans le roman. On trouve des indices d'un réajustement à partir du moment où Jane n'est plus une enfant, et qu'elle accède peu à peu au monde symbolique du langage.

La théâtralité, moment de la balance

Nous avons remarqué que dans les moments clés de l'œuvre, le pictural crée une pause dans le récit. Dans cette perspective, l'ouverture du chapitre 11 forme un parfait exemple. Mais sans contredire la picturalité de cet épisode, il peut être intéressant de noter qu'une autre dimension double celle que nous avons étudiée : la théâtralité. La première phrase du chapitre ne laisse planer aucun doute : « *A new chapter in a novel is something like a new scene in a play* » (79). Ainsi, l'épisode a beau fonctionner comme un tableau, le fait qu'il soit placé sous le signe de la théâtralité rend plus complexe son statut au cœur de la problématique du pictural et du discursif. Le théâtre est double, par essence. Spectacle scénique, parlant aux sens autant qu'à l'intellect, il ne s'affranchit pas pour autant de l'écrit. La pièce n'est pas seulement un jeu d'incarnation, c'est aussi un livre. Cette double nature du théâtral place un épisode tel que l'ouverture du chapitre 11 sous le double signe du visuel et du scriptural. Vu l'importance de la théâtralité dans d'autres épisodes du roman, et notamment la soirée mondaine à Thornfield, ou encore le jeu des charades, il est possible de reconsidérer l'importance du pictural en le traitant du point de vue du scénique, reconnaissant plus encore que dans l'hypotypose, le poids de l'écrit dans ses occurrences.

Vers de nouvelles métaphores

Le langage de Jane, trouvant de préférence dans le domaine pictural la source de ses métaphores, montre donc un intérêt sous-jacent pour l'écrit. Cet intérêt se déclare plus ouvertement à mesure que le texte progresse. Deux images métaphoriques impliquent l'écrit, voire le romanesque, et semblent signer l'accession de Jane au monde de l'écriture. Alors que Rochester fait la cour à Jane, il proclame qu'il veut la parer de bijoux et de robes de grand prix. Jane, voyant dans ce désir de déverser sur elle des torrents d'or et de soie le comportement capricieux d'un sultan se délectant de voir son esclave embellie par ses richesses, menace alors son fiancé : « *I'll wear nothing but my old Lowood frocks to the end of the chapter* » (229). Cette dernière expression, qui peut se lire comme un idiomatisme, est d'une nouveauté inattendue pour le lecteur pour qui, jusqu'à ce point, toute chose était spatiale, visuelle. Ici, Jane s'inscrit dans un temps, et pour ce faire, emploie une métaphore scripturale, donnant à voir l'histoire d'amour entre elle et Rochester non pas comme un tableau, ou même une pièce de théâtre, mais comme un roman.

À la veille du mariage, Jane, pour qui la fin des fiançailles est hantée par des angoisses terribles et des pressentiments inquiétants, souhaite raconter à Rochester le moment terrifiant dont elle a fait l'expérience la nuit même. Après avoir fait des rêves de mauvais augure, elle reçoit la visite de celle qu'elle ne connaît pas encore sous le nom de Bertha Rochester. Cette dernière déchire le voile de la future mariée et le piétine, laissant derrière elle ce signe comme preuve de son passage. Pour respecter la chronologie des événements, et rendre compte de la terreur croissante de cette nuit, Jane commence par raconter ses rêves. Lorsqu'elle a terminé, Rochester tente d'amoindrir l'angoisse de sa promise en tournant la solennité du récit en dérision : «*'Now, Jane, that is all.' 'All the preface, sir; the tale is yet to come [...]'*» (241). Là où, quelque temps plus tôt, on aurait pu s'attendre à une métaphore picturale pour dramatiser les événements narrés, c'est ici une façon de parler en relation avec le récit, l'art de raconter, que Jane emploie. Il n'est plus question de poser par à-plats un décor, et de garder pour la fin l'événement que constitue la peinture du personnage, comme dans le tableau de Millcote. Ici, la composition de la tension dramatique relève de la linéarité du discours, et même de la succession logique des différentes parties d'un livre.

Dernière figure de l'enchâssement, l'autobiographie

Rien de très étonnant dans le fait que Jane narrée se révèle de plus en plus encline à l'écrit. Sa pratique artistique glisse du pictural au scriptural à mesure qu'elle se rapproche du moment où, atteignant la fin de sa course, elle se pose pour écrire son autobiographie. Ce récit a beau ne pas être « *a regular autobiography* » (70), il n'en reste pas moins l'inscription dans un livre d'une vie, celle de la femme qui écrit. Jane, écrivant, nous le rappelle de temps à autres, notamment avec l'ouverture du chapitre 10 :

> Hitherto I have recorded in detail the events of my insignificant existence: to the first ten years of my life, I have given almost as many chapters. But this is not to be a regular autobiography: I am only bound to invoke

> memory where I know her reponses will possess some
> degree of interest; therefore I now pass a space of eight
> years almost in silence: a few lines only are necessary to
> keep up the links of connection. *(70)*

Jane est gestionnaire du contenu de son histoire, éditant à mesure qu'elle l'écrit le récit de son existence, décidant de ce qui mérite d'être retenu dans la narration, et ce qui n'est pas digne d'intérêt, comptant le nombre de chapitres consacré aux diverses phases. Ces moments de réflexion sur le livre en train de se créer forment des débrayages dans la narration, comme pour désensorceler le lecteur et le rappeler à la réalité de son activité de lecture, c'est-à-dire à la fictionnalité de l'histoire. Alors même que les passages picturaux (qu'ils relèvent de l'*ekphrasis* ou de l'hypotypose) représentent un discours sur l'art qui se fond dans les préoccupations thématiques de l'œuvre, et déguisent peu ou prou leur dimension métatextuelle, les débrayages qui ramènent le lecteur au temps de la narration génèrent une véritable coupure, et ramassent en quelques phrases l'intégralité du récit entre les deux couvertures du livre. Même l'ouverture du chapitre 11, dont la picturalité n'est plus à démontrer, est enchâssée par l'écrit, d'abord par l'allusion au théâtre, et avant cela, par celle au roman : « *A new chapter in a novel is something like a new scene in a play* » (79). Ces allusions à l'écriture en train de se former préparent le lecteur à la dernière utilisation du présent dans le roman, changement de temps qui ne relève pas cette fois de la réactivation graphique du passé, mais bien de la superposition entre temps narré et temps de la narration : « *My tale draws to its close: one word respecting my experience of married life, and one brief glance at the fortunes of those whose names have most frequently recurred in this narrative, and I have done* » (383). Jane Eyre occupe désormais pleinement sa place d'écrivain. L'image de la jeune femme peignant s'éloigne au profit de celle de la femme mariée écrivant. C'est finalement l'écrit qui renferme l'ensemble du récit et l'intégralité de Jane. Il n'écrase pas le pictural : le récit se termine par un *mot* sur la vie conjugale, et un *regard* sur la vie des autres. Les *sister arts* se donnent la main jusqu'au bout, mais c'est l'écrit qui ferme la porte du récit, la couverture du livre recouvre celle du portfolio. C'est là la nature même du projet autobiographique : évoquer, avec plus ou moins de fidélité quant au contenu et aux formes de représentation, l'expérience lorsque celle-ci est arrivée à un terme (qui ne coïncide pas nécessairement avec la fin de la vie) à travers l'écrit.

Arrivée à l'âge de la maturité, Jane, devenue autobiographe, retrace son parcours géographique et intérieur, avouant les choix éditoriaux qu'elle fait et qui l'éloignent de la lettre de son existence, mais imprégnant son œuvre d'un réseau pictural — thématique, métaphorique, structurel — qui tend à rendre au plus près l'esprit de l'expérience de l'enfant et de la jeune femme qu'elle a été. Dans l'économie de cette autobiographie fictive, le pictural semble mettre en œuvre le temps de l'expérience jusqu'à ce que temps narré et temps de la narration se synchronisent et que le temps de l'écriture gagne une certaine prévalence. Cependant, temps de l'écriture et temps de l'expérience ne sont pas aussi mutuellement exclusifs qu'on pourrait le penser : la tonalité visuelle ne quitte jamais vraiment l'écriture (la vie de Jane ne se termine pas au moment où elle met le point final à son autobiographie) et semble trouver son point d'orgue à la fin du texte dans la mise en abyme des regards des Rochester père et fils, recouvrant pour l'un, découvrant pour l'autre, le spectacle du monde sensible.

Bibliographie

ALEXANDER, Christine and Jane SELLARS, *The Art of the Brontës*, Cambridge: Cambridge University Press, 1995.

SMITH, Margaret, *The Letters of Charlotte Brontë: With a Selection of Letters by Family and Friends. Volume Three, 1851-1855*, Oxford: Clarendon Press, 2004.

Charlotte Brontë's Mirthless Laughter: Comedy in *Jane Eyre*

Laure Blanchemain

Although the reader of *Jane Eyre* might remember the humorous touch in Jane and Rochester's conversations, he cannot be said to be struck by the comic side of the novel, though comedy is present, as Robin Jones rightly underlines. Neither, it seems, are the critics.

David Cecil did notice the presence of humour, but gibed at Charlotte's Brontë's attempts at comedy, branding them as a failure. His criticism is scathing:

> Painstakingly she tunes her throbbing accents to a facetious tone, conscientiously she contorts her austere countenance to a humorous grimace. Lady Ingram and Mr Sweeting remain as obstinately, as embarrassingly, unamusing as the patter of a conjuror. But though her lack of humour prevents her amusing us when she means to, it often amuses us very much when she does not. *(Cecil 170)*

Her humour is described as patently unnatural and the critic only concedes the presence of unearned irony and unwillingly comic exaggeration ("Her crudeness, her lack of restraint, and the extreme seriousness with which she envisages life, combine to deprive her of any sense of ironic proportion" [Cecil 170]). But David Cecil widely underestimated the author when he implied that she did not know what she was at.

Robin Jones recently began a re-evaluation in that field. She focused on Bertha's laugh and proved that the purpose of the novel was to show how women (and Jane) are taught not to laugh except in appropriate circumstances. There is no doubt that women were indeed extremely restrained in that respect and the ambivalent response of women writers to such limitations is of high interest but Robin Jones limited her study to laughter and smiles, that is to say the act itself, on the level of the characters only.

Robert Heilman interestingly drew a link with the Gothic when he defined the new Gothic in *Jane Eyre* as the presence of the Gothic undermined by comic elements. He thus pinpointed a crucial point which needs further development: the incongruous presence of comedy in sad or frightening moments, which is to be linked with the presence of tragic or frightening overtones in the use of humour. The reason may lie in the mirthless quality of Charlotte Brontë's humour, which cannot but evoke Bertha's mirthless laughter (91). As is often the case in works written by women, comedy in

Jane Eyre is always ambiguous because while it elicits smiles in the reader, it also reveals hidden links, opening up the reader to other, subterraneous meanings and patterns. The reader is then left to wonder, as Mrs Fairfax says about Rochester, "whether [the narrator] is in jest or earnest" (89).

Childish perceptions and hidden patterns

Though the narrator mildly pokes fun at the perceptions and language of children, the latter pervade in fact the whole text. The exaggeration in the children's perspective is a source of merriment, as when Jane compares John Reed to a murderer, a slave-driver and to the Roman Emperors (7), or when the length of the journey to Lowood acquires almost a supernatural dimension (35) and when she thinks Mr Brocklehurst and Miss Temple's conversation must necessarily revolve around her while they are addressing very material issues (52). But the adults are also prone to that kind of excess in their view of children. In Gateshead the servants' talk reveals an absurd reversal of roles as they seem frightened by Jane and even go as far as "g[iving] [her] credit for being a sort of infantine Guy Fawkes" (21).

The childish propensity to exaggeration also arises in the inability to make the difference between fiction and reality. The narrator gently mocks the division established by Jane between the characters of *Gulliver's Travels*, "a narrative of facts" according to the child, and the characters of fairytales, who are more difficult to come across (17). The reader's expectation of her discovery of the inexistence of elves is amusingly baffled and the "truth" achieved ironically undermined as Jane only believes them gone far away. This attitude however also paves the way for the fairytale mode adopted by Jane and Rochester, which echoes the narrator's much discussed allusions to fairytales like Bluebeard, Cinderella, Little Red Riding Hood, Ugly Duckling or Scheherazade's Arabian Tales.

The two characters see each other as marvellous figures, with Rochester's dog as the Gytrash and Jane as a fairy bewitching his horse and their first encounter is later turned by Rochester into a fairy tale (104, 228). Jane's mischievous answer to Rochester's allusion to the men in green is a clear echo of her response to fairy tales as a child: "The men in green all forsook England a hundred years ago" (104). The characters' playful seriousness in dealing with the marvellous strongly evokes the children's view. Rochester presents his future marriage to Jane as a fairy tale, punning on the word "honeymoon", developing at length the image of his literally taking Jane to the moon and gathering manna/honey on the moon for her (227). This play on the literal meaning of expressions is a recurrent device.

The children's inability to understand the figurative level is used as a comic ploy by the author in her literal acting out of certain expressions and in her constant use of very concrete, physical images evoking Jane and Adèle's concrete turn of mind. When Mr Brocklehurst asks Jane what she should do to avoid going to hell, she answers: "I must keep in good health and not die" (27). This wholly unexpected reply is particularly savoury because of the childlike pragmatism it betrays. In the same way, when Adèle recounts her journey to England, she focuses on physical characteristics and on objects (the chimney of the boat, the sofa, the hotel and the park, defined in terms of their physical aspect, not of their function [86]).

That very down-to-earth bias of Adèle and Jane, which makes the reader smile, resurfaces however in a more serious tone in the narrator's choice of corporeal images. After the visit of Mr Brocklehurst at Gateshead, Jane's mental suffering is depicted as if it were physical: "the whole tenor of their conversation, was recent, *raw*, and *stinging* in my mind" (29-30, my italics). Some similes and images are developed to the point of becoming literal. The figurative meaning of the word "taste" in the expression "Something of vengeance I had tasted for the first time" fades away, giving way to a much more vividly sensual development: "as aromatic wine it seemed, on swallowing, warm and racy: its after-flavour, metallic and corroding, gave me a sensation as if I had been poisoned" (31). In the same way the words "new-born agony" conjure up the concrete image of a baby that Jane strangles and cannot "persuade [herself] to own and rear" (208). Thus Charlotte Brontë reminds the reader of the original meaning of conventional similes and metaphors. The so often used image of life as a stream, a current, is brought back to life with a very detailed description of a tumultuous torrent (121).

The author goes even further in her literal approach, making the characters act out certain images. Jane cools Rochester's burning desire when she "deluges" his burning bed (127), "an almost fatally symbolic plight" (Gilbert and Gubar 353). Jane's comparison of Rochester with a "choice dish" also becomes literal when Bertha begins to sink her teeth into his cheek (250). Rochester's description of Bertha as a "fierce ragout" (251) could then explain why he does not retaliate: contrary to him, she is not a savoury dish. As those examples demonstrate, Brontë's humorous presentation of childhood uncovers a strong fascination which looms large in the novel, to the extent that childlike perceptions and attitudes frame the narrator's style and the author's choices.

The children's viewpoint is highly revealing and the author also resorts to the traditional use of naivety as a tool in satire. When Jane exclaims "they all call Mrs Reed my benefactress; if so, a benefactress is a disagreeable thing" (27), the childish definition of words is refreshing and funny but at the same time, reminding the reader of their true meaning, it also alerts him to possible deviations. This humorous touch at a moment of anguish offers some comic relief while satirically challenging Mr Brocklehurst's words.

Charlotte Brontë's "dry jokes"

The presence of comedy in the description of hardships is unexpected. The difficulties attending Jane's arrival at Lowood are wittily pointed out when the narrator writes: "My first quarter at Lowood seemed an age; and not the golden age either" (50). The pun, which seems at first sight to lighten the hardships alluded to, is in fact rather grim. Both characters and narrator are prone to such humorous or ironical remarks at frightening or melancholy moments. When Mrs Reed is about to die, there is a slight pun with Jane's drawing of a group of reeds (198) and the narrator makes fun of Georgiana's superficiality and Elizabeth's needlessly busy behaviour (200).

Rochester also adds some amusing comments in painful situations. When he narrates the discovery of Céline Varens's betrayal, the climactic moment, the arrival of Céline with her lover, is somewhat played down by the humorous exaggeration of his remark that he was "stifl[ing] with the fumes of conservatory flowers" (120). He also makes a comic allusion to Jane's rescuing him from the fire, referring to it as "that night you half drowned me" (154). When Bertha's existence is revealed, Rochester humorously presents Bertha's madness and alcoholism as a dutiful reproduction of her parents' behaviour (249) and resorts to irony to describe the extent of his misery: "I had a charming partner—pure, wise, modest: you can fancy I was a happy man.—I went through rich scenes! Oh! my experience has been heavenly, if you only knew it!" (249). The narrator partakes of this ironical mode, calling Rochester's aggressive "Go to the devil!" a "recommendation" (250). The use of irony in those two examples is of particular interest since it relies on ambiguity, on a play on opposites, which is at stake in Brontë's treatment of comedy.

Michael Mason refers to the narrator's touches of humour as "dry jokes" and according to him, the purpose of learned comic allusions like the pun on the golden age and the girls' falling asleep like Eutychus in the Acts of the Apostles is to create some complicity with the reader, to "strengthen the feeling of liking for the heroine which is so important an element in the reader's whole response to the novel" (Mason xiii). There is no denying that those "jokes", whether they are learned or not, do contribute to the reader's connivance with the narrator, but limiting them to a way of ensuring the reader's interest in the heroine's pains and difficulties implies blotting out the confusion between comedy and tragedy that is at the heart of the novel.

Tellingly, it is when the spectre of death hovers above Lowood, with the typhus outbreak, that Jane enjoys herself the most (63-65). While bleak moments are interspersed with humorous elements, comic interludes have harsh consequences or cannot be entirely perceived as funny. Charlotte Brontë favours black humour invoking images of death, as when Rochester says that Jane "half drowned [him]", and in some instances, the lurking presence of death subverts the comic effect. At the end of Jane's wanderings near Whitcross, the scene of quiet domestic happiness in Marsh End and the ignorance of the servant, Hannah, who cannot understand how the Germans understand each other, are much less entertaining because they jar in the context of the desperate situation of Jane, who witnesses all this from the outside, on the brink of death (284). The possible tragic outcomes undermine the comedy. Similarly, there is some amusing irony of situation when Mr Brocklehurst comes to Lowood and Jane, only because she is desperately trying to remain unnoticed, draws the attention on her with the fall of her slate (55). The moments of anguish that follow this amusing misstep lend it much sadder overtones.

When Jane says to Rochester "You play a farce, which I merely laugh at" (216), there is no side-splitting laughter, and not even a smile. The laugh here merely implies a satirical outlook. In the same way Brontë's comic devices do not provoke roars of laughter because they only veil a strong satire.

Comic relief and hidden satire

The burlesque vein at work in the novel with the inappropriate use of an elevated scientific vocabulary to refer to trivial activities and situations is certainly meant to entertain the reader. Mr Rochester's swear-words are called a "formula" (96) and he defines his guess concerning Jane's age as arithmetic (105). Most of the instances, however, concern women's activities. Adèle's opening of her "boîte" to discover Rochester's gifts is defined as an "anatomical process", an "operation" implying the "disembowelling" of the box and the study of "the condition of the entrails" (110). When Mrs Fairfax dresses up to meet the guests, she is said to come "in rustling state" (141), the trivial rustle of the dress standing in comic contrast with the ceremonious or scientific word "state".

Dressing is not the only feminine interest that is described in scientific terms. A domestic activity like cooking becomes a kind of alchemy (the fish and soup are "in the last stage of projection" and the cook "h[angs] over her crucibles", 142). The cook's trepidation is also delineated from a scientific standpoint as she is on the verge of "spontaneous combustion" (142). Jane the character also adopts this perspective, presenting cooking as "culinary rites" and the cleaning and tidying up of rooms as an activity demanding "mathematical precision" (332).

The contrast between the elevated and scientific language used and the domestic chores narrated is undoubtedly comic. This style can remind the reader of Adèle's incongruous seriousness when about to take part in the joyous festivities of the house ("she looked as grave as any judge", 144-145). But just as this amusing discrepancy mocks the excessive interest of the French in dress and public appearance, the misapplied vocabulary satirises, on a first level, the importance women lend to trivial activities. The text seems to ironically convey women's point of view, the scientific words becoming an expression of the way women consider those activities. What appears then at first as comic relief proves to further develop the satire. Yet the true butt is hidden. The use of burlesque in the description of domestic or frivolous activities may not so much deride female concerns as the limited world in which society would circumscribe women.

The same remark applies to the mock heroic trend that crops up occasionally. When the old "rigorous Sybil" (Rochester in disguise) asks to see the ladies, the behaviour of the latter, who react as if they were embarking on a dangerous enterprise, is certainly preposterous. Miss Ingram "r[ises] solemnly" and "swe[eps] past […] in stately silence" while her mother begs her to "pause", "reflect", as if she was about to put her life in jeopardy (165). The narrator emphasises the absurdity of Blanche's behaviour, adding that she uses a tone "which might have befitted the leader of a forlorn hope, mounting a breach in the van of his men" (165). The exaggeration, the sharp contrast between the heroic venture evoked and the commonplace encounter with a gypsy clearly satirises her behaviour. The women are all the more ludicrous as when true danger comes, they helplessly lean on men's arms, looking like "ships in full sail" (176).

Yet at the same time, the choice of a comparison with a hero, a man, is by no means fortuitous. Women's scope for action being much more limited, this might be one of the very few occasions on which a woman can behave in a heroic way. Such domestic events are in fact women's version of action. This view appears in the expression "the eventful Thursday" (334), referring to the day Diana and Mary are to come back and discover a cleaned and reorganised Moor House, and in Jane's warlike attitude towards Rochester before the wedding. The "Soft scene, daring demonstration" of Rochester's love are depicted as a "peril" against which Jane must find a "weapon of defence" (233) but this humorous mock heroic standpoint also exposes the danger surrounding Jane, namely the danger of becoming a kept mistress, the most treacherous peril of all for women because of the fall from the image of the angel in the house to that of the prostitute (a term which could include women living with men without being married).

The condition of women and the image imposed on them are also what is really at stake in the amusing episode of the girls falling asleep during the Sunday sermon:

> The Sunday evening was spent in repeating, by heart, the Church Catechism, and the fifth, sixth, and seventh chapters of St Matthew; and in listening to a long sermon, read by Miss Miller, whose irrepressible yawns attested her weariness. A frequent interlude of these performances was the enactment of the part of Eutychus by some half dozen of little girls; who, overpowered with sleep, would fall down, if not out of the third loft, yet off the fourth form, and be taken up half dead. The remedy was, to thrust them forward into the centre of the schoolroom, and oblige them to stand there till the sermon was finished. Sometimes their feet failed them, and they sank together in a heap; they were then propped up with the monitors' high stools. *(51)*

The narrator pokes fun at the girls' and the teacher's lack of endurance with the burlesque application of an elevated reference, Eutychus, and the incongruous presence of the vocabulary of medicine: weariness is described as an illness whose symptoms are yawns (the word "attested" implies that they are proofs of the presence of the "disease") and for which a "remedy" needs to be found. There is also a comic reversal of the roles of the audience, the girls, and the performer, Miss Miller, who is reading the sermon. The spectators become themselves a show, they are said to be performing a play. The scene is even close to slapstick comedy when they are thrust and propped up again and again.

This amusing interlude in the middle of the description of the girls' hardships seems to offer some unexpected comic relief. Yet it hides more savage laughter. Charlotte Brontë provides yet another concrete enactment of a conventional expression, the girls being almost literally tired to death ("half dead") but above all, the scene vividly summons the image of girls (and women) as puppets, lifeless things propped up by the rules imposed on them. Behind the entertaining surface lies then a strong satirical vein with the symbolical representation of what education can do to women. The image also evokes the "shaping hand" of men (344), who, like St John Rivers, would mould women according to their desires, turning them into lifeless statues in a reversed Pygmalion process.

The same satirical outlook pervades the text to the point of undermining its comic dimension when Mr Brocklehurst wants to have a look at the eldest girls' hair:

> Leaning a little back on my bench, I could see the looks and grimaces with which they commented on this manœuvre: it was a pity Mr Brocklehurst could not see them too; he would perhaps have felt that, whatever he might do with the outside of the cup and platter, the inside was further beyond his interference than he imagined. *(54)*

Their resistance and their comments behind his back are pleasurable, yet the episode quickly takes a much less amusing turn when the girls are submitted to Mr Brocklehurst's judgment and when he decides to have their hair cut. This decision is presented as a "sentence" passed on them, as if they were criminals, and as "the knell of doom", which emphasises women's lack of control over their own fate and again conjures up images of impending death. The girls are described as "living medals" at that point, which stresses the dehumanising effect of school. A strong satire of the education of women and of men's derogatory view of them resurfaces here and the entertaining part of the scene consists in debunking Mr Brocklehurst's authority. The narrator's (and the author's) laughter is then, like Bertha's, highly disruptive.

Debunking male authority

The first masculine butt of Brontë's comic satire is John Reed. Robin Jones asserts that though "there is no laughter at Gateshead", "we see the potential in Jane for a capacity for humor" (Jones 202). This potential arises when she muses on his ugliness at the very moment when he is going to hit her (8): the incongruous appearance of this thought in such a context makes the reader smile. Robin Jones lays emphasis on Jane's discovery of the danger of laughing openly (Jones 202) but though the character does indeed begin to understand the consequences of failing to keep such thoughts private, the narrator frees herself from that restraint and makes the reader share her derogatory stance. The portrait of John turns him into ridicule with the humorous accumulation of flaws (7) and the absurdity of his mother's view of him is disparaged with irony ("an opinion so harsh", "the more refined idea" [7]). The timing is essential, the belittling description occurring just after John Reed's assertion of his social superiority and power over Jane the character, just as the child's irreverent thought comes to her mind just before his assertion of his physical superiority. The touches of humour thus debunk the relative authority of John as Jane's superior.

This process of contrastive juxtaposition is even more successfully used to gibe at Mr Brocklehurst. As often pointed out by the critics, the arrival of his wife and daughters, wearing expensive articles of dress with a profusion of elaborately curled hair, completely disrupts the speech he has just made on women's need for sobriety in their appearance, thus undermining his authority (54-55). From the beginning, his flaws are hinted at. Jane first sees him as a black pillar (26), a comic perspective obviously linked to her small size. But this comparison has further-reaching implications, indicating either his lack of humaneness (he "has no heart at all" [Thormählen 184]) or his function as a pillar of society (Gilbert and Gubar 344, Bazin 18). He is indeed, a phallic column (Bazin 18), a symbolical representation of male power. Through him, it is then male authority that the narrator and the author are questioning.

His lectures sound ludicrous also because of their exaggerated emphasis. When he divulges Jane's alleged sin in front of the whole school, the disclosure that she is a liar comes after many allusions to the extent of her perversity, increasing the suspense and raising so much the spectators' expectations that the conclusion of this first tirade does not quite seem up to the mark (56). This excessive dramatisation is flouted by the narrator, who ironically calls his final allusion to turbid waters ("I beg of you not to allow the waters to stagnate round her") a "sublime conclusion" (57). The image he has chosen is even further turned into ridicule by an ironical echo: the beck near the school is later said to be "turbid" (64). Waters do stagnate round Jane, and there is nothing Mr Brocklehurst can do about it.

Charlotte Brontë leads the reader to share her irreverent humour and does not even spare the two male protagonists, Rochester and St John. Gilbert and Gubar have already analysed the first encounter between Jane and Rochester as a parody of romance: "what are we to think of the fact that the prince's first action is to fall on the ice, together with his horse, and exclaim prosaically 'What the deuce is to do now?'" (Gilbert and Gubar 351-52). The disruptive effect of the hero's swearing, which is hinted at here, is actually a recurrent device. Rochester's swear-words and "humph" punctuate the text, cropping up like a leitmotiv at the most intense moments, subverting the romance. Rochester's abruptness, his too honest and direct answers and his lack of manners are funny because they are unexpected in a gentleman. The contrast is alluded to by the humorous oxymoron "preciously grim" (111). This gruffness is even more incongruous in the crucial stages of courtship: the encounter of course, but also the conversations between the two lovers ("humph" [97, 103, 114], "humbug" [115]) and the moments when the lovers face dangers (he is "fulminating strange anathemas" when Jane rescues him, 127). As during the first encounter, in the last instance, the roles are reversed with Rochester as the damsel in distress and Jane as the knight coming to his rescue.

Even in the midst of a moving scene, the narrator does not hesitate to present the outward signs betraying Rochester's emotions as ridiculous: he is said to exclaim "with a twang of voice and a distortion of features equally fantastic and ludicrous" when Jane is about to leave for Gateshead and mentions her plans to obtain a position away from Thornfield (191). This comic touch undermines his emotional appeal, the bathos Jane envisages as a "gulf" (233). She also makes fun of St John's kisses, calling them "experiment kisses" (339). The humour seems to come as a defensive reflex since those kisses symbolise in fact St John's power over Jane as the comparison with "a seal affixed to my fetters" suggests (339). Turning them into ridicule is a way of fending off the servitude he represents.

In both cases, what the narrator wishes to debunk is their phallic strength. Like Mr Brocklehurst, St John Rivers is delineated as a pillar, a column (345) and the narrator alludes to his hardness, associating it with despotism (346). Jane compares St John and Rochester only to better mock their stiffness, telling Rochester: "[St John] was as stiff about urging his point as ever you could be" (377). The expression conflates various meanings, evoking the inexorable will of both and the lack of warmth of the marble-like St John but also the more bawdy image of their sexual strength as they are laying siege to Jane's virginity ("I was almost as *hard* beset by him now as I had been once before, in a different way, by another" [356, my italics]). The butt of ridicule is the very virility of those two masculine figures.

Jane Eyre is not bereft of amusing puns then, though most often at the expense of men. Not only does Charlotte Brontë laugh, an attitude condemned in her time when it did not follow the strict rules of conduct, but she irreverently laughs at men and at the patriarchal society they support and represent—as Robin Jones points out, they are supposed to be the instigators, not the repositories of the aggression laughter amounts to (Jones 202). This could explain why men and their representatives do not find her comedy really amusing. Women might take more pleasure in her "dry jokes".

Bibliography

BAZIN, Claire, *Jane Eyre, le pelerin moderne*, Nantes : Éditions du Temps, 2005.

CECIL, David, *Early Victorian Novelists* (1934), *in* Miriam Allott, ed., *Charlotte Brontë*: Jane Eyre *and* Villette: *A Casebook*, London; Basingstoke: Macmillan, 1973, p. 167-174.

GILBERT, Sandra M., and Susan GUBAR, *The Madwoman in the Attic: The Woman Writer and the Nineteenth-Century Literary Imagination* (1979), New Haven: Yale University Press, 2000.

HEILMAN, Robert, "Charlotte Brontë's 'new Gothic' *in Jane Eyre and Villette*" (1958), *in* Miriam Allott, ed., *Charlotte Brontë*: Jane Eyre *and* Villette: *A Casebook*, London; Basingstoke: Macmillan, 1973, p. 195-204.

JONES, Robin, "The Goblin Ha-Ha: Hidden Smiles and Open Laughter *in Jane Eyre*", *in* Regina Barreca, ed., *New Perspectives on Women and Comedy*, Philadelphia: Gordon and Breach, 1992, p. 201-212.

MASON, Michael, Introduction, *in Jane Eyre*, by Charlotte Brontë, London: Penguin, 1996, p. VII-XXI.

THORMAHLEN, Marianne, *The Brontës and Religion*, Cambridge: CUP, 1999.

Jane Eyre: Taking Men in and Writing out Patriarchy

Gilbert Pham-Thanh

Anatomy of (fe)male

Jane Eyre, Charlotte Brontë's most popular novel, reads like an autobiography through which the reader realizes that the representation of women and femininity in nineteenth-century fiction was always a site of tension which echoed controversies relative to the nature, place and role of women. However, it is rather masculinity that will constitute the main centre of interest in this paper. This paradoxical focus finds its basic legitimacy with the common idea that in a world based on polarities, each element of a binary structure can be analyzed through its counterpart. The approach relies on the assumption that leading male figures in *Jane Eyre* each stand—at least to some extent—for a specific type of man, and their study traces a panorama of masculinity. From what has just been posited, it follows that an exploration of Edward Rochester's characterization will yield as much information—though obliquely—on the construction of Jane-Eyre-as-a-woman as a direct inquiry into her idiosyncrasies and gendered characteristics. Hopefully, the interpretive line will intersect with those of women's identity and autobiography, so as to offer an additional perspective to the experience of reading a canonical novel.

Topography of phallocentrism

The very reference to the institution of the canon may serve as a good indicator of women's disempowerment within patriarchy and its set of prescriptive norms, which males twist to benefit, however. This is a man's world the reader is presented with, even if the biography of a young girl should prioritize the depiction, exploration and mapping of the female world. In consequence, it is no coincidence if Bertha Mason, Rochester's demented wife, is institutionalized at home, at Thornfield Hall, a parallel being drawn between State modes of restraint and domestic constraint. The laws of the fathers are almighty, and women are made to surrender to them. These "masters" are taught to claim their rights from an early age, as John Reed soon demonstrates. In the androcentric world of Gateshead, he always comes first. Moreover, his mother manages the estate like a mere accountant, but *he* can freely dilapidate the family's possessions, which are truly his, and his alone. He is enabled to enjoy this privilege fully as he is endowed with a strong element of characterization that makes him aware of being the legitimate heir: "all the house belongs to me, or will do in a few years" (8). His words spell out the truth for his mother and settle the conflicts to his advantage when he and Jane fight over Bewick's *History of British Birds*, a book she was reading. In this scene, onomastics works in a twisted way, since Eyre errs and cannot read the book, whereas Reed may not read but *he* is the heir. The same phallogocentric discourse nearly has Jane surrender to cousin St John Rivers, who persistently insists that she should follow him to India and embrace the fate of a missionary's wife, according to God's plan (cf. chapters 34 and 35). Since God himself is repeatedly equated to a father figure by St John—"my king, my lawgiver, my captain" (342)—it becomes apparent that religious power and socio-political power are complicit in keeping Jane in her existential shackles. In addition, language proves indeed a logocentric instrument of phallocentric domination, thus the phallogocentric construction mentioned previously. The arbitrariness of this system clearly shows in Mr Brocklehurst, an alter ego for St John only on a lower key, who cuts a theatrical figure by appearing dressed in black, as a "straight, narrow, sable-clad shape standing erect on the rug" (26), performatively staging authority rather than exerting it in an enlightened way. In the Lowood educational institution for the needy, this "black column" (26) manages long lines of young, silent, hungry girls in their drab uniforms, and contributes to promoting the subtext of male supremacy and female despondent dependence. Since power is better felt in abuse, he lectures them endlessly on the value of starving oneself, quoting from Matthew: "if ye suffer hunger or thirst for my sake, happy are ye" (53). He also cruelly has Julia Severn cut her long red curly hair, all the while piling miseries upon the young girls he rules and lords it over, with an inevitable reference to the Lord for legitimacy: "I have a master to serve whose kingdom is not of this world: my mission is to mortify in these girls the lusts of the flesh" (54).

Because Lowood Institution is under Mr Brocklehurst's supervision and authority, it stands out as a hyperbolic reflection of male-dominated society, be it on a minor scale. Females are tamed into obedience, and physical pain is topped by psychological torture, as exemplified when Jane is placed on a stool, a "pedestal of infamy" (57) for all to see, and then is undeservedly called a liar. Still, the repression of vital urges is so drastic that the weakest pupils literally and literarily die, among them Helen Burns, in a scene of desperate acceptance (cf. chapter 9). This purple patch leaves a lasting mark on the reader's mind, but most of all creates a site of intensification for male abuse of the female body. Discipline and punishment constitute the two regimens of presentability for women in a misogynistic universe where they are branded for and broken into acceptability. For Brontë, masculine power seems uncomfortably linked with sadism. In all the cases quoted, women are purposely made to suffer, though not always directly. John is in the habit of beating up Jane, leaving her in constant fear: "every nerve I had feared him, and every morsel of flesh on my bones shrank when he came near" (8). As for St John, he excels at inflicting psychological pain, harping on the young woman's duty towards himself and God till her reason is almost numbed into acceptance (cf. chapter 35). Even Rochester will have an occasional thrill at upsetting poor, plain Jane, by setting her up, so to speak, devising extraordinary scenarios in order to start an emotional turmoil in her that would satisfy his curiosity and compensate for his lack of self-confidence. He spreads false information concerning his marriage with "the Honourable Blanche" (135) Ingram to make Jane jealous (cf chapter 19), forces on his employee embarrassing evenings among arrogant guests (150-151), dresses up as a grotesque gypsy to manipulate her (cf chapter 19), and on each occasion, Jane is made to humour him unwittingly, while he remains in a position of command.

Of course, in such a diegetic configuration, fatherly figures proliferate freely. These would-be substitutes for the missing father in Jane's family structure re-enact the basic pattern by linking her fate to their good-will. This motif is repeated in her dependence on Rivers and Rochester for material support, in the guise of charity and a home or a well-paid occupation and accommodation, but the text makes it clear that it all comes at a cost, be it unrequited love or extra-marital sex. Fortunately, Jane's uncle, John Eyre, makes no claim whatsoever, bequeathing twenty thousand pounds to her after his death, so that this one male character does have an unreservedly positive impact on Jane. However, it is noteworthy that this notoriously childless man would hardly qualify as a model in patriarchy anyway, and even proves a traitor to his sex by protecting her from the traditional logic of subsistence for women. And yet, by making this female orphan an independent woman, he casts away all sorts of moral dilemmas which alone could have destabilized the masculine order of things. On the other hand, this agent brings in yet another shift in paradigms and is thus instrumental in reconfiguring the realist narrative into a family romance. The tale is then under the sway of the pleasure principle which organises this fictitiously autobiographical project.

Typology of masculinity

The autobiography does report the experience of a series of actual traumas, and Jane Eyre's past does exemplify men's oppression and its inherent violence, which is not always merely symbolic. Still, such a massive statement need be qualified, as individuated male characterization forms a complex grid, which might interestingly be superimposed upon the Freudian topological representation of the human psyche. This tentative interpretation is based on the study of a selection of three characters, a particularly relevant panel since John Reed, St John Rivers and Edward Rochester arguably embody the landmarks in Jane's experience of masculinity.

John Reed unambiguously stands for men's indiscriminate violence in their craving for self-assertion and self-indulgence. He is first presented both as a spoilt child and a domestic tyrant but ultimately turns into a dissolute profligate who "gambles dreadfully, and always loses" (198). He finally shames all his family, who find no support in him when money becomes scarce. In his case, irresponsibility is matched by ignorance, since he is never associated with culture or knowledge, and in consequence he is made an incarnation of blind urges. That is why for him, books are only objects whose ownership must be secured and protected against any trespasser, so that they remain available at all times—the world is reduced to a commodity. The sole posture he envisages in it is that of the spendthrift who indulges his senses to the full and acknowledges no moral boundaries in his quest for sensations. The description points to a possible identification of this sensual, self-centred, pleasure-seeking youth with the Freudian *Id*. This typical rake would then be the embodiment and fictionalization of a fundamental psychological drive. Such an interpretation is consistent with the diegetic structure, since John Reed's generalized failure reveals he is incapable of abiding by the dictates of the reality principle.

This reading finds support in the introduction of St John Rivers in the text. The partial homonymy creates a parallel reconfigured through the adjunction of a threatening "Saint", which promotes this male character's status not only above females but also beyond common earthlings, poles apart from his un-saintly counterpart. St John is the somewhat disincarnated personification of perfection, symbolically reflected in his "Greek [...] harmonious" (294) physique, his education and dedication to the welfare of the parish as well as in his utter command of himself. His determination to serve God as a missionary works to aggrandize his character, and makes him a strong moral reference for Jane. And yet by so doing, he only performs his manly duty as a guide to the straight and narrow path of virtue for misguided women. Moreover, their frequent talks develop into confrontations which usually leave the young woman speechless, for his well-informed rhetoric shows no fault and his overwhelming presence stifles any desire or capacity to differ. Still, his portraiture as a self-righteous, "cold, hard, ambitious man" (319) who gloatingly takes pride in the monument he is building of himself indicates that this idealized creature does not suit sublunary life and is not fit for worldly happiness. His overbearing demands for sacrifice and obedience to a superior goal are reminiscent of the *Superego*, with its fixation on rules, laws and norms which prevent a spontaneous response to given situations but always require adjustment and renunciation. The pleasure principle is defeated, as even marriage with Jane is envisaged as a convenient way to fulfil a godly mission. This statement rings particularly true since St John turns down the beautiful Rosamund Oliver, in spite of his reportedly genuine attachment for her. The state of affairs is phrased in a short incisive antypophora: "Rosamond a missionary's wife? No!" (318). It is his awareness that Jane is better fitted for the task at hand that explains his preference for her, even though he acknowledges his cousin's unattractiveness: "Ill or well, she would always be plain. The grace and harmony of beauty are quite wanting in those features" (289). This unsympathetic picture of the woman he later wants for a wife underpins the central part that duty plays in his characterization.

At this point, Rochester must be tested as a figure of the Freudian *Ego*, one that would be tormented by contradictory drives which would remain incompatible but might lead to solutions of compromise. He stands as a figure of authority for Jane, both as her employer and as a mature man with a position in society, and he unsurprisingly seems determined to have his way at any cost: "will you hear reason? […] because, if you won't, I'll try violence" (258). However, his discourse is ambiguous and not without self-irony: "I am not a villain: […] I am a trite commonplace sinner, hackneyed in all the poor petty dissipations with which the rich and worthless try to put on life" (116). The same distance shown in the obliquity of his courting strategy reveals his willingness to mediate his passion, to take the complexity of the situation into account. Contrary to John Reed, he does not actually resort to physical strength to subjugate Jane, and unlike St John Rivers, he negotiates his desire with her and does not dictate his terms. Neither a formidable character nor a beastly one, he is constructed as a sort of anti-hero with a past, in the romantic style. He is granted enough integrity and openness to satisfy the young woman's taste for equality and independence. In addition, he reconciles fleshly desire with a true moral sense, which is admittedly a blunted one for most of the novel, as his awful lawful spouse drives him to questionable decisions. Because he is the only male who inter-acts with reality, he evolves as a round character and gains precedence in the diegesis, much in the same way the *Ego* plays the part of the referee and is finally the only one in charge. He thus amply qualifies as a lover who in return vouches for the qualities in the person he has set his heart and soul upon.

So the analysis makes it very clear that these three characters form the milestones of a topological typology of masculinity. Yet, their systemic complementariness points to an alternative interpretation of their presence in the autobiography as projections of narrating Jane's own psyche. Through objectified others, she would try to come to terms with her past and the different choices it offered, to make sense of it, in the same way that Charlotte Brontë might have been fictionalizing part of her life dilemmas in the novel to get a firmer grip on her own personality, building a sense of identity in displacement and fiction. It follows that this systematic construction of masculine figures may serve the purpose of (re-)ordering her memories and (re-)organizing them into a narrative of edification, self-awareness and possibly self-justification. It is based on her capacity to build her own world, where over-determined elements become significant in relation to one another. In brief, an all-encompassing discourse originating in a dominant, Jane, foregrounds its paradigm to construct literarily pre-conceived meaning. In such a perspective, autobiography is seen to drift very close to auto-fiction.

Topology of resistance to phallogocentrism

If the fictitious aspect of Jane Eyre's autobiography is to be taken seriously, then it becomes possible to construe Brontë's deployment of an apparently hegemonic phallocentric universe as a base for an exercise in female empowerment. This would account for the heroine's claim, "I felt an inward power; a sense of influence, which supported me. The crisis was perilous; but not without its charm" (258), in which adversity is just another exhilarating experience in self-sufficiency. She remains the protagonist and gives the novel her name, and even if she is recurrently victimized by the representatives of male domination, she nonetheless screens every perception through the filter of her consciousness, which is then essential in the literary project and gives her pride of place. What is more, with her resilience and sharpness, she stands out as a positive figure, a survivor in a man's world, or a victor who has successfully passed the test by dodging the traps set up for her in society and the plot alike. The androcentric discourse in the narrative would be but a pretext to formulate a gynocentric alternative that would resonate at every level of the text. The strategy tilts the balance of institutions, and if Rochester can legitimately and repeatedly be called "master" by Jane, she nearly wins herself the title of "mistress" of his heart (256). Furthermore, her occupation as a governess—as the word suggests—is not without symbolic authority, not to mention Rochester's admission that he is overpowered by her: "you master me" (222). This paradoxical reversal echoes in the dramatic way men die or are maimed at the hand of an almighty narrator who supposedly reports facts, but in truth builds her own representation of reality into a world of her own. John Reed does not survive his life of debauchery, and a final description unrelentingly stages his narrative punishment: "John is sunk and degraded—his look is frightful—I feel ashamed for him when I see him" (198). St John is hardly more fortunate as he is dispatched into the middle of nowhere, far from the centre of the plot at any rate, and he colourfully writes about his weakness and impending death, which the narrator has obviously anticipated in her certainty that this is the last she ever reads from his hand (385). This is exactly what she secures by putting an end to her tale. As for Rochester, or what is left of him, he undergoes so many symbolic castrations that it is difficult to keep count. He is in constant need of Jane's assistance, as the inaugural scene of their encounter demonstrates. After he has fallen from his horse, he is just a cripple who would creep home or die on the spot, in the middle of the night on a deserted road, if Jane did not enable him to stand up. Here again, the narrative describes in detail the picture of his physical inferiority: "He laid a heavy hand on my shoulder, and leaning on me with some stress, limped to his horse" (98). This configuration repeats itself at the end, with a blind, one-armed Rochester who relies on the heroine for support. The plot unravels a structuring series of incidents, some involving Bertha Mason or her brother Richard, to assert Jane's capacity to stand in whenever her master does not prove up to the task. The insistence on these characters' failure and helplessness reads as a narratorial sanction contrived to counterbalance the effect of men's institutional dominion and reinstate women as the strong, powerful sex.

As a matter of fact, the real change of paradigm occurs as from the beginning, when narrating Jane takes control over her literary destiny. She composes an alternative image of reality and selects anecdotes that are relevant to her purpose, like the detention in the red-room at the Reeds' (cf. chapter 2). She likewise highlights events such as Helen's death, and overlooks years at Lowood, eventually turning the tale into a success story that flouts any realist code based on an understanding of society and its patriarchal tenets. Plain Jane not only claims her right to exist, but she represents herself being acknowledged in a male-dominated universe where many of her features were deemed handicaps. In fact, she pulls the narrative strings to suit a personal agenda that anticipates the feminist struggle, particularly in her ejaculation: "I married him" (382), which seems like a self-celebratory utterance, whatever the stress pattern. In addition, she might be one of the very few nineteenth-century female characters who, without any personal beauty, qualified as a heroine and made their way into diegetic matrimony. She is courted by her "betters"—coveted by a young learned Adonis and a rich powerful man—and is made an heiress by a providential uncle she has never met, not to mention the fact that she achieves heroic stature by saving Rochester's life from Bertha's first arson (127) and rescuing the Riverses from financial need, thus allowing her female cousins to marry (329). Rejecting the order of logic that rules the world as it is, she bends the laws of physics and acoustics when she contrives the psychic scene which connects her to Rochester, miles away (357). Even if she appears to be self-critical when she confesses: "to imagine such a lot befalling me is a fairy-tale" (220), she still shows no sign of regret and is only too glad to proceed with her imaginative tale. The romance now obeys new rules and meets the requirements for a happy ending and a felicitous outcome for Jane, all the while remaining within the frame of conventional narratives. To this end, men's oppressive and repressive attitudes have successfully been reconfigured within a frame devised to empower a heroine with whom women may easily identify.

Post-Mortem Male Figures and Pre-Natal Feminist Figures

For all these reasons, although *Jane Eyre* may not present a utopian picture of nineteenth-century society, it constitutes a laudable effort to lend a voice to the gendered subaltern and contributes to the elaboration of an alternative culture that does not prioritize men systematically but promotes plain Janes. Feminists will remember the lesson Brontë gave, even if they will at times regret that poor Bertha was never given a say in the matter, a possible shortcoming that Jean Rhys will redress in *Wide Sargasso Sea*, over a century later. In spite of this, what remains of Charlotte Brontë's message concerning the representation and construction of genders in the experimental field of fiction is the foregrounding of an atypical female heroine and the relative demotion of males, in a forceful gesture of appropriation of the autobiographic genre harnessed for an emancipatory project—the advent of a new woman facilitated by a narrator who strategically takes men in and subsequently writes out patriarchy.

Bibliography

ADAM, James Eli, *Dandies and Desert Saints–Styles of Victorian Manhood*. Ithaca: Cornell University Press, 1995.
ADAMS, Rachel and David SAVRAN, eds., *Masculinity Studies Reader*, Malden: Blackwell, 2002.
RHYS, Jean, *Wide Sargasso Sea* (1966), New York and London: Norton, 1999.
ROSEN, David, *Changing Fictions of Masculinity*, Chicago: University of Illinois Press, 1993.

Clothes, their Origin and Influence: Jane Eyre et la philosophie des vêtements

Laurent Bury

En décembre 1847, Charlotte Brontë eut le plaisir de découvrir dans *Fraser's Magazine* l'une des critiques les plus élogieuses concernant son roman. Ce compte rendu était dû à George Henry Lewes, qui deviendrait quelques années plus tard le compagnon d'une autre grande romancière victorienne, George Eliot. *Fraser's Magazine* comptait depuis 1832 parmi les lectures régulières des Brontë, et l'on constate l'influence de ce mensuel dans leurs écrits de jeunesse. De novembre 1833 à août 1834, un texte étrange intitulé *Sartor Resartus* y fut publié en feuilleton. Il s'agissait de la première œuvre majeure de celui qui allait devenir l'un des principaux penseurs anglais de la première moitié du XIXe siècle : Thomas Carlyle (1795-1881). On peut supposer que la famille Brontë avait lu ce curieux mélange de philosophie et de satire. Charlotte avait alors 17 ans et ne se laissa probablement pas désarçonner par la prose alambiquée de celui dont elle devait dénoncer les germanismes (Smith 74) mais dont elle admirait la vigueur (Smith 202).

Dans *Sartor Resartus*, « Le Tailleur retaillé » en latin, Carlyle invente un certain Diogenes Teufelsdröckh (patronyme facétieux signifiant « crotte du diable »), auteur d'un ouvrage intitulé *Die Kleider, ihr Werden und Wirken*, c'est-à-dire *Les Vêtements, leur origine et leur influence* (Carlyle 4). Cette philosophie vestimentaire est un prétexte bouffon qui lui permet en fait d'exposer ses conceptions complexes sur l'éveil spirituel de l'être humain. De son côté, sur un registre beaucoup moins burlesque, Charlotte Brontë retrace dans *Jane Eyre* le parcours d'une âme qui se double également d'une certaine théorie « sartoriale ».

"my bonnet, &c." (194)

On comprend que la narratrice se lasse vite d'énumérer les vêtements mis ou ôtés, et qu'elle recoure à l'expédient du "et caetera" : en effet, Charlotte Brontë ne manque jamais de signaler les très nombreuses occasions où son héroïne s'habille et se déshabille. On ne compte plus les « *I dressed* » ou « *I was dressed* » (sans oublier diverses variations sur « *I undressed* »). Dans un chapitre aussi crucial que celui de la tentative d'incendie perpétrée par Bertha Mason, les références aux vêtements se multiplient en l'espace de quelques pages : « *I had removed her bonnet and coat* » (124), « *I hurried on my frock and a shawl* » (126), « *some dry garments, if any dry there be—yes, here is my dressing-gown* » (127), « *You have a shawl on. [...] you may take my cloak yonder; wrap it about you: and sit down on the arm-chair: there—I will put it on* », « *it was cold, in spite of the cloak* », « *I heard his unshod feet* » (128). Même prolifération au chapitre 20, lorsque Mason est agressé par Bertha : « *I had put on some clothes* », « *I began and dressed myself* » (176), « *I dressed, then, to be ready for emergencies. When dressed [...]* », « *dressed as I was* », « *Are you up?[...] And dressed?* » (177).

Même dans l'évocation des autres personnages, le regard de la narratrice semble s'arrêter d'abord sur l'enveloppe extérieure : le vêtement est décrit, sans parfois que rien ne soit ajouté à propos du visage, des cheveux, des yeux, ou du caractère. A Lowood, l'une des enseignantes est « *a little dark personage, smartly dressed* » (38). La postière est « *an old dame, who wore horn spectacles on her nose, and black mittens on her hands* » (74). Aux heures les plus graves, Jane Eyre trouve toujours le temps de mémoriser la tenue de ceux qui l'entourent : « *I remember her appearance at the moment, [...] she wore a morning robe of sky-blue crape; a gauzy azure scarf was twisted in her hair* » (189-190). Seuls les deux principaux personnages masculins échappent à peu près à cet examen vestimentaire. De Rochester, nous apprenons uniquement lors de sa première rencontre avec Jane que « *His figure was enveloped in a riding cloak, fur collared and steel clasped* » (96). Quant à St John Rivers, il nous est décrit comme « *half-strangled with his white neckcloth, and stilted up on his thick-soled high-lows* » (376), mais c'est là ce qu'imagine la jalousie de Rochester, sans que le lecteur soit davantage informé à son sujet.

Par quel étrange souci d'exactitude la narratrice éprouve-t-elle le besoin d'inclure des notations vestimentaires totalement banales, du genre : « *she helped me on with my pelisse and bonnet, and wrapping herself in a shawl, she and I left the nursery* » (34) ou « *I had brushed my black stuff travelling-dress, prepared my bonnet, gloves, and muff* » (76) ? Simple « *effet de réel* » tel que Roland Barthes en identifiait dans *Un cœur simple* de Flaubert, ou « *unnecessary detail* » dénoncé avant lui par George Orwell chez Dickens (Genette 32) ? Il semble bien que cette obsession pour ce genre de détail corresponde à une stratégie plus large : *Jane Eyre* met en place un code symbolique, une philosophie des vêtements. Le roman instaure, par exemple, la correspondance entre humeur et habit : « *I took a plain but clean and light summer dress from my drawer and put it on: it seemed no attire had ever so well become me, because none had I ever worn in so blissful a mood* » (219). Tout comme la beauté est dans l'œil de celui qui regarde (149), l'élégance serait dans l'esprit de celui qui se vêt.

Au dernier chapitre du roman, ce sera grâce aux vêtements de Jane que Rochester prend conscience de son retour à la vue :

> "Jane, have you a glittering ornament round your neck?"
> I had a gold watch-chain: I answered "Yes."
> "And have you a pale blue dress on?"
> I had. *(384)*

Le film de Franco Zeffirelli rend tout à fait perceptible la métamorphose de l'héroïne qui, dans la dernière partie, après le blanc immaculé du mariage avorté, abandonne bientôt les tenues noires et étriquées de la gouvernante au profit de robes amples et claires.

Cette approche est aussi celle d'une manifestation qui s'est déroulée au cours de l'été 2007 dans la maison-musée des Brontë :

> Fans of Jane Eyre were given an insight into the fictional character's wardrobe from schoolgirl to governess at the Brontë Parsonage Museum in Haworth. […] Costume historian Gillian Stapleton wore Jane's "best dress" of silver grey silk with a replica corset, shoes and hairstyle for the presentation. She said: "We wanted to explore just how close the sartorial links between Jane Eyre and her creator really were." *(BBC News, news.bbc.co.uk/2/hi/uk_news/england/west_yorkshire/6937815.stm, 9 juin 2008)*

On voit là illustré l'un des poncifs des *success stories* : la trajectoire du personnage principal le conduit du bas de la hiérarchie sociale jusqu'à son sommet, ou du moins jusqu'à un échelon plus élevé, élévation qui se matérialise dans le passage des haillons aux plus somptueux atours.

Rags to riches

Même si elle ne porte pas les « *ragged clothes* » qui sont à ses yeux le premier des éléments caractéristiques de la pauvreté, même si elle se sent différente de ces pauvres qu'on rencontre « *washing their own clothes at the cottage doors* » (20), Jane commence son parcours dans la position de Cendrillon exclue du bal, condamnée aux vêtements ternes tandis que les deux méchantes sœurs (cousines, en l'occurrence) revêtent leurs plus beaux habits et la laissent se morfondre loin du salon auquel elle n'a pas accès : « *witnessing the daily apparelling of Eliza and Georgiana, and seeing them descend to the drawing—room, dressed out in thin muslin frocks and scarlet sashes* » (23). Jane-Cendrillon, souvent chaussée de « pantoufles » — « *My slippers were thin* » (177) — non de vair, mais de velours (182), manque perdre sa sandale pendant la fête à Thornfield, et son prince charmant la surprend alors qu'elle la relace (154).

Loin d'arborer des robes d'apparat, Jane est à Gateshead prisonnière de vêtements qui sont autant d'entraves — « *knots and strings* » —, seule sa chemise de nuit offrant une protection à plus faible qu'elle, la poupée qu'elle tient bien au chaud (23). Parmi les marques de la dépendance de Jane envers sa tante, John Reed lui reproche d'être vêtue aux frais de ceux qui l'ont recueillie : « *you ought to beg, and not [...] wear clothes at our mamma's expense* » (8). Première déchéance après l'épisode de la *red-room*, Jane est réduite à l'état de servante et revêt donc les habits utilitaires propres à ses nouvelles fonctions. Lors de la première visite de Brocklehurst, elle est présentée sous-vêtue, « *denuded [...] of [her] pinafore* », à celui qui lui apparaît comme sur-vêtu : « *the straight, narrow, sable-clad shape* » (25, 26) et, plus tard, « *buttoned up in a surtout* » (52). La réalité de son statut de pauvresse éclatera lorsqu'elle endossera l'uniforme des pensionnaires de Lowood : « *with their [...] long pinafores, and those little holland pockets outside their frocks—they are almost like poor people's children!* » (28).

L'évocation des élèves lors de l'arrivée à Lowood passe par la mention quasi obligée leur tenue « *of quaint fashion* » (36). Le même adjectif, ici nettement péjoratif, revient quelques pages plus loin lors d'une description plus détaillée de l'uniforme :

> a quaint assemblage they appeared, all [...] in brown dresses, made high and surrounded by a narrow tucker about the throat, with little pockets of holland (shaped something like a Highlander's purse) tied in front of their frocks, and destined to serve the purpose of a work-bag: all too wearing woollen stockings and country-made shoes, fastened with brass buckles. Above twenty of those clad in this costume were full-grown girls, or rather young women; it suited them ill, and gave an air of oddity even to the prettiest. *(39)*

Sans atteindre les extrêmes de la célèbre description de la casquette de Charles Bovary, Charlotte Brontë accumule ici les notations de détail pour mieux refléter le traitement infligé aux enfants. Les élèves paraissent emprisonnées (« *high* », « *surrounded* », « *narrow* », « *tied* ») dans ces vêtements qui se veulent fonctionnels mais qui sont avant tout répressifs et ne tiennent nullement compte de l'évolution de leur morphologie. Comme pour la Mock-Turtle de Lewis Carroll, « *uglification* » semble bien être l'une des matières inculquées à Lowood. L'uniforme des pensionnaires est non seulement dépourvu de toute valeur ornementale, mais il est aussi dénué de toute qualité protectrice, ainsi que le confirme plus loin la négativité des termes employés : « *Our clothing was insufficient [...]; we had no boots [...]; our ungloved hands* » (50 ; c'est moi qui souligne). Ni décoratif ni utilitaire, l'habit devient instrument de torture, comme l'était déjà la jarretière de Miss Abbot dans la *red-room* (9). À moins qu'il ne se transforme en signifiant stigmatisant : d'abord « *the untidy badge* » (57), puis l'écriteau « *Slattern* » porté en serre-tête (62). Tout aussi éloquent sera plus loin le deuil imposé au cocher Leaven lors du décès de John Reed : le « *I hope no one is dead* » prononcé par Jane Eyre n'est qu'une formule de politesse hypocrite, qu'on peut traduire par « *I know someone is dead* » puisque le crêpe noir signifie très explicitement la mort (188).

L'origine de ces uniformes reste cependant mystérieuse, car Helen Burns fournit à Jane deux informations apparemment contradictoires : « *Mr Brocklehurst buys all our food and all our clothes* » (42) et « *we make our own clothes, our frocks, and pelisses, and everything* » (43). À la charité affichée de l'homme qui nourrit ceux qui ont faim et vêt ceux qui sont nus, s'associe sans doute la discipline de fer du directeur qui impose aux enfants pauvres de fabriquer eux-mêmes leurs habits. L'art de confectionner les vêtements apparaît en effet comme l'une des compétences essentielles à maîtriser dans le cadre de la scolarité : « *mark, stitch, knit, &c.* » (46). Et l'on remarquera le long discours que tient le directeur de l'institution sur les fournitures nécessaires pour repriser (fil et aiguilles) et sur les divers sous-vêtements des fillettes (52) : là aussi, la plus grande parcimonie — « *very false economy* » selon Rochester (155) — s'impose pour éviter de renouveler ce qui peut être réparé. Les règles de l'établissement limitent aussi le nombre de vêtements propres autorisés chaque semaine. Ces contraintes s'ajoutent au régime alimentaire spartiate pour atteindre le but essentiel de l'institution : mortifier la chair, ainsi que l'explique Brocklehurst. Le corps étant abject, il convient de ne prendre aucun soin de son apparence : « *my mission is [...] to teach them to clothe themselves with shamefacedness and sobriety, not with braided hair and costly apparel* » (54). À Lowood, la parure sera métaphorique ou ne sera pas.

Ce bon principe ne s'applique évidemment qu'aux élèves, Mrs Brocklehurst et ses filles présentent à l'œil toutes les caractéristiques condamnables d'esclaves de la mode vêtues d'habits élégants, taillés dans les étoffes les plus coûteuses, où règne la profusion, la grâce et l'illusion. La dame et les demoiselles se confondent bientôt avec leur parure, perdant au passage toute trace d'humanité : « *a spread of shot orange and purple silk pelisses, and a cloud of silvery plumage extended and waved below me* » (56). Même accumulation d'accessoires lors de l'arrivée de Blanche Ingram à Thornfield : « *Fluttering veils and waving plumes filled the vehicles* » (141). Autre exemple de réification vestimentaire, la bien nommée Mrs Harden, « *made up of equal parts of whalebone and iron* » (61), baleines du corset et métal de la crinoline ou, plus vraisemblablement dans le second cas, simple métaphore. C'est la métonymie, en revanche, qui gouverne la description de Céline Varens : « *though muffled in a cloak—an unnecessary encumbrance, by-the-bye, on so warm a June evening—I knew her instantly by her little foot, seen peeping from the skirt of her dress* » (121). Le vêtement, dépouillé de toute fonction utilitaire, n'a plus pour but que de servir d'écrin à la partie du corps à laquelle se réduit l'individu fragmenté

Figurant parmi les causes de l'épidémie de typhus, les uniformes de Lowood seront ensuite réformés, au même titre que l'alimentation des élèves (71). C'est dès lors tout l'esprit de mortification propre à Brocklehurst qui disparaît et que Jane Eyre s'empresse d'oublier.

« Never mind fine clothes and jewels » (380)

Après avoir subi les préceptes hostiles à toute ornementation du corps, la jeune fille devient experte en l'art de se mettre en valeur, dans les limites imposées par la nature et par la société :

> I rose; I dressed myself with care: obliged to be plain—for I had no article of attire that was not made with extreme simplicity—I was still by nature solicitous to be neat. It was not my habit to be disregardful of appearance, or careless of the impression I made: [...] when I had brushed my hair very smooth, and put on my black frock—which, Quaker-like as it was, at least had the merit of fitting to a nicety—and adjusted my clean white tucker, I thought I should do respectably enough to appear before Mrs Fairfax [...] *(83-84)*

Le manque de beauté physique et de moyens financiers impose le recours à divers stratagèmes pour offrir malgré tout une apparence plaisante à l'œil : l'austérité puritaine des lignes et des formes n'exclut pas l'ajustement seyant, ni la propreté, gage de bonne moralité et de respectabilité.

Jane devient une grande déchiffreuse des signes extérieurs de la hiérarchie sociale, telle qu'elle se traduit à travers les nuances subtiles du code vestimentaire : ce savoir lui permet d'identifier « *a woman attired like a well-dressed servant* » (76) et de tirer des conclusions sur des tiers : « *judging from the plainness of the servant and the carriage, Mrs Fairfax is not a very dashing person* » (80). Du moins l'héroïne se croit-elle compétente en la matière. Même si les prophéties « sartoriales » de son imagination se trouvent confirmées par la réalité — « *Mrs Fairfax! I saw her in a black gown and widow's cap* » (75) ; « *the neatest imaginable little elderly lady, in widow's cap, black silk gown, and snowy muslin apron: exactly like what I had fancied Mrs Fairfax* » (81) — elle se trompe manifestement lorsqu'elle prend d'abord la gardienne du château pour la propriétaire. Par ailleurs, la tenue vestimentaire de Grace Poole devrait suffire à montrer qu'elle n'est pas la folle dangereuse pour laquelle on voudrait la faire passer : « *her brown stuff gown, her check apron, white handkerchief, and cap* » (130) font d'elle une servante des plus ordinaires et n'en laissent pas deviner davantage que sa physionomie tout aussi quelconque. Même le qualificatif ajouté plus loin (« *prim cap* », 139), s'il traduit un jugement de valeur, ne suffit pas à la rendre inquiétante. À moins qu'il ne faille, comme Teufelsdröckh, se méfier des tabliers : « *How much has been concealed, how much has been defended in Aprons!* » (Carlyle 32)…

Rochester, pour sa part, ne maîtrise pas du tout cet art de juger les inconnus sur leur apparence vestimentaire : « *He stopped, ran his eye over my dress, which, as usual, was quite simple: a black merino cloak, a black beaver bonnet: neither of them half fine enough for a lady's maid. He seemed puzzled to decide what I was* » (97). Ni assez richement vêtue, ni assez mal habillée, Jane Eyre fait figure d'individu inclassable, dont la tenue ne renseigne pas assez le spectateur.

L'arrivée de Rochester à Thornfield Hall introduit de nouveaux rites sociaux, comme celui de se changer pour passer à table. « *[I] replaced my black stuff dress by one of black silk: the best and the only additional one I had, except one of light grey, which, in my Lowood notions of the toilette, I thought too fine to be worn, except on first-rate occasions* » (102). Aussi irrémédiablement condamnée au noir que tout gentleman victorien — « *all costumed in black* », 148 —, Jane Eyre ne peut guère procéder à des variations vestimentaires qu'à travers le tissu utilisé. Ce qu'elle appelle « *my usual Quaker trim* » présente l'avantage d'être immuable ; ainsi vêtue, elle ne peut jamais être prise au dépourvu ou en flagrant délit de non-conformité à l'image impeccable qu'elle entend donner d'elle-même : « *all being too close and plain, braided locks included, to admit of disarrangement* » (110). La robe grise, associée au mariage de Miss Temple, « *and never worn since* » (145), reste taboue. Tenue de porter le noir, couleur de son ordre comme si elle était religieuse — « *a little nonnette* », dira Rochester (112) –, l'héroïne rencontre bientôt plus austère qu'elle encore. Devenue adulte, Eliza Reed affiche tous les signes d'une conversion radicale au « papisme » et prendra le voile dans un couvent lillois (206), l'intransigeance de sa foi n'ayant d'égales que la raideur empesée et la sévérité rigoureuse de sa tenue vestimentaire : « *the extreme plainness of a straight-skirted, black stuff dress, a starched linen collar, hair combed away from the temples, and the nun-like ornament of a string of ebony beads and a crucifix* » (194). La couleur du deuil se prête pourtant à toutes les variations, des plus frivoles aux plus esthétisantes, comme en témoigne la robe de Georgiana, « *as stylish as the other's looked puritanical* » (194), et comme le confirment les sœurs Rivers : « *both wore deep mourning of crape and bombazeen, which sombre garb singularly set off very fair necks and faces* » (283).

À l'opposé de ce noir obligé se situe la blancheur à l'entretien coûteux et donc caractéristique des plus fortunées : « *many were dressed in white, and all had a sweeping amplitude of array that seemed to magnify their persons as a mist magnifies the moon* » (145). Dans la haute société, le vêtement participe d'un processus général de tromperie, un travail sur les apparences qui modifie la véritable silhouette : alors que Jane Eyre porte des robes ajustées, les nobles invitées de Thornfield arborent des toilettes qui leur permettent d'occuper l'espace. Cette amplification relève de la simple illusion d'optique, comme le dénonce la comparaison à la brume devant la lune. La description des visiteuses culmine évidemment avec le trio Ingram, en commençant par la mère : « *A crimson velvet robe, and a shawl turban of some gold-wrought Indian fabric, invested her (I suppose she thought) with a truly imperial dignity* » (146). La richesse des matériaux affirme l'opulence de Lady Ingram, les couleurs connotent l'autorité (le velours cramoisi est traditionnellement associé à la monarchie) ; à défaut d'être impériale — l'incise entre parenthèses indique clairement que la dignité visée n'est pas atteinte —, cette tenue reflète du moins l'impérialisme britannique grâce à la provenance coloniale du tissu du turban. Exceptionnellement, pour ses deux filles, la description se concentre sur le visage et la personnalité, et le vêtement est vite expédié, peut-être à cause de sa simplicité affichée : « *The sisters were both attired in spotless white* » (147). C'est une pureté immaculée (« *pure white* » selon Mrs Fairfax, 135) que revendique l'aînée des sœurs Ingram, comme pour se conformer au programme que dicte son prénom, même si elle opte parfois pour la pourpre cardinalice lorsqu'elle est en habit de cheval (141). La blancheur ne signifie cependant pas que l'irréprochabilité morale, elle renvoie aussi à la froideur stérile : « *spreading out her snowy robes in queenly amplitude* » (153), Miss Ingram rejoignant les méchantes reines de contes de fées.

« You think too much of your 'toilette', Adèle » (145)

Par-delà cette réprimande adressée par la gouvernante à son élève, on peut lire une dénonciation en règle de tous les personnages pour qui les vêtements occupent une place jugée démesurée. Dans beaucoup de romans victoriens, « *Detailed sartorial knowledge is left to milliners and servants [...] In fact, there is no quicker way to vulgarize a character than to align her taste with the professional eye of the milliner* » (Bayuk Rosenman 50). Les aristocrates méprisantes invitées à Thornfield cherchent à éviter tout contact avec les pauvres hardes de la gouvernante, comme s'il existait un risque de contagion. Blanche Ingram est « *a great lady, who scorned to touch me with the hem of her robes as she passed* » (158). D'autres, en détaillant la tenue de Jane Eyre, se condamnent elles-mêmes aux yeux du lecteur en portant sur de simples vêtements un regard de professionnelle de l'habillement. Ce dédain qui est censé refléter leur supériorité sociale les rabaisse en fait à la classe des boutiquières. L'œil scrutateur de Georgiana Reed pratique à distance une sorte de fouille au corps sur la personne de sa cousine : « *sundry side-glances that measured me from head to foot—now traversing the folds of my drab merino pelisse, and now lingering on the plain trimming of my cottage bonnet* » (195).

La petite Adèle, déjà irrémédiablement marquée par ses origines françaises, se voit encore un peu plus chargée lorsque le lecteur découvre sa fascination pour la parure. L'enfant estime que regarder les dames s'habiller est une excellente forme d'instruction (142). Lorsque Rochester lui annonce son intention d'emmener Jane Eyre sur la lune, elle s'inquiète aussitôt de ce que deviendront ses habits (227). Elle est enchantée de recevoir « *a little pink frock* » qui fera d'elle un double parfait de sa théâtreuse de mère, une créature frivole et superficielle qui réserve ses extases à la découverte d'une nouvelle robe. « *A dress of rose-coloured satin, very short, and as full in the skirt as it could be gathered, replaced the brown frock she had previously worn; a wreath of rosebuds circled her forehead; her feet were dressed in silk stockings and small white satin sandals* » (119). Cette tenue de bal ou de soirée, ersatz de tutu ou véritable costume de scène, pare l'enfant des oripeaux de la maturité anticipée, en substituant à l'austère robe brune (« *frock* » peut aussi désigner la bure d'un moine) un ensemble d'accessoires bariolés qui dévoilent ou soulignent les formes. La grande réception donnée à Thornfield est pour elle l'occasion d'exhiber « *all her "toilettes", as she called frocks* » ; il lui faut pour cela donner l'illusion de l'éternelle nouveauté, nier le passage du temps : « *to furbish up any that were 'passées', and to air and arrange the new* » (139). Cette pétrification qui semble arrêter les minutes est aussi celle dont la fillette est atteinte dès qu'elle revêt ses plus beaux atours : « *the importance of the process quickly steadied her [...] under the influence of a most solemnizing impression* » (144, 145).

Si l'intérêt pour le vêtement est un penchant condamnable, pourquoi alors la narratrice elle-même s'attarde-t-elle si souvent sur la tenue des personnages ? *Jane Eyre* échappe pourtant au danger suprême, qui consisterait à s'intéresser aux habits pour eux-mêmes et non en tant que signes à déchiffrer. Le roman de Charlotte Brontë est publié en 1847, et c'est en 1848 qu'est fondé le Pre-Raphaelite Brotherhood, dont les membres consacreront des heures à peindre minutieusement le détail des costumes sur leurs toiles. Dante Gabriel Rossetti, l'un des fondateurs du groupe, en viendra lui-même à remettre en question cette pratique :

> I am beginning to doubt more and more, I confess, whether that excessive elaboration is rightly bestowed on the materials of a modern subject—things so familiar to the

> eye that they can really be rendered thoroughly (I fancy) with much less labour; and things moreover which are often far from beautiful in themselves—for instance, the flowing waistcoat of a potboy on which Brown has lately been spending some weeks of his life. *(Harding 64)*.

Dans *Principles of Success in Literature* (1865), George Henry Lewes dénonce la tendance de certains romanciers victoriens à décrire trop précisément les gilets de leurs héros : « *Of late years there has been a reaction against conventionalism which called itself Idealism, in favour of detailism which calls itself Realism* » (Lewes 83). En octobre 1856, la compagne de Lewes, Marian Evans, publie dans la *Westminster Review* un article intitulé « Silly Novels by Lady Novelists », qui tourne en dérision ces romans aux héroïnes impossibles, impeccablement vêtues en toutes circonstances.

Il serait facile d'ironiser sur l'unique récompense obtenue par le film au programme, le David di Donatello 1996 : seuls ont été jugés dignes d'un prix les costumes conçus par Jenny Beavan, collaboratrice régulière de James Ivory, « oscarisée » en 1987 pour *A Room with a View*. Adepte de la reconstitution historique minutieuse au cinéma comme dans ses (trop ?) fastueuses mises en scène d'opéra, Zeffirelli cède une fois de plus aux sirènes du « film à costumes » : « *the pejorative term "costume drama"—also known as "bonnet drama" and "Big Frock" drama, to clarify exactly whose clothing is being sniffed at* » (Baruk Rosenman 57). Selon l'expression consacrée, il ne manque pas un bouton de guêtre ou plutôt, puisque c'est la féminité qui est visée, pas une baleine de corset. « *The ease with which all clothing and furniture becomes fully commodified in modern adaptations suggests the fragility, even the deludedness, of the novels' original distinctions, but also a greater wariness and sensitivity about issues of consumption and culture* » (Baruk Rosenman 58). Cette approche paraît en effet réductrice car, loin de se limiter à une fonction réaliste, le vêtement acquiert dans le roman de Charlotte Brontë un rôle allégorique, notamment à travers la mascarade.

"I have a veil—it is down" (208)

La thématique du déguisement est omniprésente lors de la grande réception donnée à Thornfield. Dans le grand monde, tout se réduit à une comédie, que le jeu théâtral soit ou non explicitement reconnu comme tel. Les « charades » auxquelles se livrent les invités de Rochester étaient un des grands passe-temps de la haute société et un ressort romanesque employé par des auteurs aussi divers que Thackeray, dans *Vanity Fair*, ou George Eliot, dans *Daniel Deronda*. Le jeu des charades, en permettant l'inversion carnavalesque des codes (les femmes endossent des vêtements d'hommes, les riches se travestissent en pauvres), favorise le dévoilement paradoxal de vérités sous-jacentes et l'affleurement de motivations plus ou moins inavouées. Ici, les passions des différents personnages s'expriment derrière l'exotisme géographique (orientaliste) et temporel — on retrouve dans des armoires divers témoignages d'époques révolues : « *brocaded and hooped petticoats, satin sacques, black modes, lace lappets, &c.* » (155), tous ces oripeaux du passé sur lesquels se penchent les chapitres historiques du livre de Teufelsdröckh (« *Hussar cloaks, Vandyke tippets, ruffs, fardingales, are brought vividly before us* », Carlyle 28).

Nouveau déguisement, non explicitement annoncé comme tel, mais qui vise également à mettre au jour des vérités que l'on cherche à dissimuler : Rochester se fait passer pour une diseuse de bonne aventure, grimé en vieille gitane (167). Ainsi masqué, il peut commettre une sorte de viol psychologique en explorant les secrets de Jane. Quand la comédie est terminée, Rochester ne parvient pas à se dépouiller seul de son costume et il fait appel à la jeune fille pour se tirer d'embarras : « *the string is in a knot—help me* » (172). Dès que le docteur Carter a pansé les plaies laissées par la morsure de Bertha (« *dressed Mason's wounds* », 264), c'est à une comédie que se prête Jane lorsqu'elle apporte les habits dont Rochester a besoin pour dissimuler la blessure de Mason : « *take out a clean shirt and neck-handkerchief* », « *fetch a cloak* », « *bearing an immense mantle lined and edged with fur* » (181-182). Jane joue les habilleuses pour ce simulacre par lequel Rochester entend tromper son monde.

Rochester quittant son déguisement cite le roi Lear qui arrache ses habits dans la tempête : « *Off, ye lendings* ». En l'occurrence, les vêtements ne sont effectivement pas les siens, mais la référence shakespearienne autorise une autre interprétation. Rochester voudrait dire adieu au jeu des conventions sociales qui s'incarne dans le vêtement. Cette aspiration à un dénudement libérateur rejoint *Sartor Resartus:* « *In all speculations [thinkers] have tacitly figured man as a* Clothed Animal; *whereas he is by nature a* Naked Animal; *and only in certain circumstances, by purpose and device, masks himself in Clothes* » (Carlyle 2).

Cependant, une fois sa demande en mariage acceptée, l'un des premiers soucis de Rochester sera de rhabiller sa future épouse, de la couvrir de vêtements ostentatoires, mascarade que l'héroïne s'empresse cependant de dénoncer. Les voiles de satin et de dentelle seraient pour elle autant de déguisements qui non seulement masquent, mais dénaturent son identité : « *I shall not be your Jane Eyre any longer, but an ape in a harlequin's jacket—a jay in borrowed plumes. I would as soon see you, Mr Rochester, tricked out in stage-trappings, as myself clad in a court-lady's robe* » (221). Jane deviendrait un animal déguisé en humain déguisé (l'habit d'arlequin) ; la noblesse d'emprunt serait pour la modeste gouvernante aussi artificielle qu'un costume de théâtre pour son futur époux. Autre métaphore, qui assimile Jane sinon à un vêtement, du moins à un morceau de tissu : « *You might as well put a border of gold lace round that plain pocket-handkerchief you have there* » (222)

L'héroïne trouve le procédé humiliant car infantilisant, voire réifiant : « *I never can bear being dressed like a doll by Mr Rochester* » (229), la comparaison à Danaë qui suit cette phrase renforçant encore l'assimilation de Jane à un simple objet sexuel possédé par le mâle souverain. L'image orientaliste aggrave encore la tendance : « *his smile was such as a sultan might [...] bestow on a slave his gold and gems had enriched* » (229). L'épouse n'est qu'une favorite du harem, choisie ou délaissée selon le bon plaisir de son seigneur et maître. La visite à l'entrepôt de soieries prend ainsi l'aspect d'une mission imposée : « *I was ordered to choose half a dozen dresses* » (228). Paradoxalement, le futur époux de Jane Eyre semble vouloir l'emprisonner par les vêtements et bijoux qu'il compte lui offrir : une chaîne de diamants, un diadème qui encerclera son front, les bracelets se refermeront sur ses poignets, les bagues seront une charge pour ses doigts (220). La visite chez le bijoutier suscite « *annoyance and degradation* » (229).

« *How would a white or pink cloud answer for a gown, do you think? And one could cut a pretty enough scarf out of a rainbow* » (227). Rochester ne fait guère plus qu'étaler son érudition classique : dans la mythologie grecque, l'arc en ciel est en effet l'écharpe d'Iris. Pour le lecteur français, le nuage en guise de robe pourrait renvoyer à la robe couleur du temps de la *Peau d'Ane* de Perrault. C'est aussi à l'univers des contes de fées que renvoient les robes somptueuses que Rochester prétend offrir à l'héroïne : « *he might as well buy me a gold gown and a silver bonnet at once* » (229). Jane Eyre tient pourtant à se limiter au noir et au gris, seuls les matériaux (soie et satin) exprimant la richesse de celle qui les porte, ou plutôt de l'acheteur « propriétaire ». Le refus du déguisement lui inspire une véritable révolte : « *You may make a dressing-gown for yourself out of the pearl-gray silk, and an infinite series of waistcoats out of the black satin* » (229). L'habit féminin peut apparemment changer de sexe en changeant de fonction (la robe de jour devient robe de chambre) ou, au prix d'un démembrement complet, se démultiplier en une quantité innombrable d'habits masculins, habillant exclusivement le buste viril après avoir couvert tout le corps de la femme. Rochester n'a pourtant pas besoin de gilets de satin noir pour lui, mais d'un « *strait-waistcoat* » (257) pour enfermer son épouse folle dont les manifestations intempestives se multiplient jusqu'à la catastrophe finale.

« this cumbrous frame of flesh » (49)

Le vêtement est aussi une composante essentielle des apparitions les plus inquiétantes : l'habit fait le spectre, et *Jane Eyre* est plein de surnaturelles femmes en blanc et autres « *men in green* » (104). Dans la *red-room*, alors que l'épouvante de la fillette est parfaitement ambiguë, la vision restant dans une indétermination caractéristique du genre fantastique, les domestiques la réduisent à la visite beaucoup plus traditionnelle d'un fantôme en suaire : « *Something passed her, all dressed in white, and vanished* » (16). L'un des trois dessins fantastiques produits par Jane dans sa dernière année à Lowood est celui d'une géante aux traits masqués : « *Two thin hands, joined under the forehead, and supporting it, drew up before the lower features a sable veil [...] wreathed turban folds of black drapery* » (107).

Le voile apparaît en effet comme le vêtement le plus apte à se charger de mille significations métaphoriques. Il dissimule la vraie nature des individus (« *The veil fell from his hardness and despotism* », 346), mais aussi, comme on va le voir, il rend imperceptible la séparation entre le monde des morts et celui des vivants, ainsi que l'illustre la parabole de l'amant soulevant le voile de sa maîtresse qu'il croit endormie et qu'il découvre décédée (361).

Les habits imposés à Jane, et notamment son voile nuptial, créent un sentiment d'*estrangement*, d'aliénation. Elle découvre grâce à sa robe de mariée l'expérience de l'altérité : « *I saw a robed and veiled figure, so unlike my usual self that it seemed almost the image of a stranger* » (244). L'identité est comme anéantie par le simple changement de tenue. Il ne s'agit pas simplement d'une métamorphose en inconnue, en tierce personne (« *her* »), mais en spectre :

> garments said to be hers had already displaced my black stuff Lowood frock and straw bonnet: for not to me appertained that suit of wedding raiment, the pearl-coloured robe, the vapoury veil, pendent from the usurped portmanteau. I shut the closet, to conceal the strange, wraith-like apparel it contained; which, at this evening hour—nine o'clock—gave out certainly a most ghostly shimmer through the shadow of my apartment. *(235)*

Ces vêtements envahissants et arrogants relèvent de l'imposture malgré leur présence affirmée : encore en quête d'un corps, ils appartiennent à un être immatériel, non pas à un revenant mais au fantôme anticipé de celle qui ne doit exister que dans un avenir proche.

Lorsque Jane voit enfin de ses yeux Bertha Mason, « *the clothed hyena* » (250), celle-ci se présente sous un aspect d'autant plus énigmatique que son vêtement est indéfinissable. « *I know not what dress she had on: it was white and straight; but whether gown, sheet, or shroud, I cannot tell* » (242). L'indécidable ambiguïté de l'habit traduit concrètement la porosité des frontières entre le monde des vivants, celui des morts et celui des spectres. La créature du troisième étage s'empare du voile de la future mariée, rappel de ses noces avec Rochester (264) et symbole de l'événement par lequel elle doit être supplantée auprès de lui. Après avoir profané le tissu sacré en en drapant son crâne de goule, elle divise en deux cet emblème de l'union à venir, tout comme le marronnier d'Inde se fend le jour où Jane accepte d'épouser son employeur. Bertha invalide le mariage projeté en privant symboliquement Rochester du privilège de déchirer le « voile de l'hymen » (« *The ripping serves as yet another warning against the physical and psychic dangers of sex* », Maynard 108), puis elle foule au pied l'habit pour signifier son opposition à ces secondes noces. À l'issue de cette « *transaction* » — c'est ainsi que la narratrice qualifie cette profanation rituelle (242) –, le vêtement déchiré constitue pour sa part une véritable pièce à conviction qui permet la fusion de l'univers du rêve avec la réalité, la monstrueuse vision nocturne basculant ainsi dans le champ de la vérité attestée. Rochester refuse de valider cette interprétation : il préfère maintenir l'hypothèse du mi-rêve mi-réalité, et trouve lieu de se réjouir puisque l'incident connaît une fin (provisoirement) heureuse : Bertha ne s'en est prise qu'au voile au lieu de s'attaquer à celle qui doit le porter.

Ce déplacement de la colère, qui prend pour objet non pas l'individu qui la cause, mais les habits que celui-ci porte, s'apparente au phénomène que Ruskin appelait *pathetic fallacy*:

> The state of mind which attributes to [inanimate objects] these characters of a living creature is one in which the reason is unhinged by grief. All violent feelings have the same effect. They produce in us a falseness in all our impressions of external things, which I would generally characterize as the "Pathetic Fallacy" *(Modern Painters, vol. III, part 4).*

Sous la plume des écrivains, où il ne résulte plus d'un dérèglement de la raison, ce transfert des émotions sur des objets devient un procédé littéraire des plus courants.

Même s'il n'est le plus souvent qu'une enveloppe matérielle sans lien avec les mouvements de l'âme (« *with streaming garments, but with a relieved heart* », 74), le vêtement est aussi un prolongement du corps qui peut se changer en organe de perception et se substituer aux sens : « *I know my shoes [...] were soon wet with dew. But I looked neither to rising sun, nor smiling sky, nor wakening nature* » (273-274). Il peut traduire les sentiments, par exemple la colère de Mrs Reed : « *her cap flying wide, her gown rustling stormily* » (14).

Le manque de respect de John Reed envers sa mère s'exprime à travers la dégradation des habits maternels : « *[he] not infrequently tore and spoiled her silk attire* » (12). Le vêtement peut aussi se charger de connotations morales : « *besides the delicacy and richness of the fabric, I found nothing save Fairfax Rochester's pride* » (240).

Dans son exil volontaire, après l'annulation de son mariage, il ne reste à l'héroïne pour tout bien de fortune que ses habits. Son petit foulard de soie et ses gants sont des accessoires superflus qui marquent son appartenance à une catégorie sociale supérieure, en tout cas bien au-dessus de la misère à laquelle elle s'est elle-même condamnée : « *an ordinary beggar is frequently an object of suspicion; a well-dressed beggar inevitably so* » (280). Même si elle est légitime et non usurpée, cette richesse vestimentaire incongrue s'avère dérisoire et inutilisable. Comme en témoignent « *the half-worn gloves; the creased handkerchief* » (278), ces articles défraîchis, reflets de l'épuisement qui gagne peu à peu l'héroïne, s'avèrent aussi difficilement monnayables que le savoir livresque dont dispose Jane mais qui ne lui permet plus de gagner sa vie. Et ce n'est pas non plus en confectionnant de quoi habiller les autres que l'héroïne pourra se nourrir, ni en travaillant à la fabrique d'aiguilles.

Pour Jane Eyre, la marginalité tient à la contradiction entre la qualité de ses vêtements et leur saleté, résultat d'un long trajet à pied par tous les temps : « *the clothes she took off, though splashed and wet, were little worn and fine* » (289), s'étonnent les Rivers qui l'ont recueillie. Selon le proverbe anglais que rappelle Miss Scatcherd dans le film de Zeffirelli, *cleanliness is next to godliness* et la propreté retrouvée permettra à l'héroïne de surmonter la souillure morale dont elle se sent atteinte depuis qu'elle a risqué la bigamie :

> My black silk frock hung against the wall. The traces of the bog were removed from it; the creases left by the wet smoothed out: it was quite decent. My very shoes and stockings were purified and rendered presentable. [...] My clothes hung loose on me, for I was much wasted; but I covered deficiencies with a shawl, and once more, clean and respectable-looking—no speck of the dirt, no trace of the disorder I so hated, and which seemed so to degrade me, left—I crept down a stone staircase [...] *(289-290)*.

Lavée de son passé récent, Jane Eyre peut dès lors envisager une nouvelle existence, même si elle doit encore masquer ce que ses vêtements d'autrefois ont d'inadéquat par rapport au corps nouveau qu'elle s'est façonnée (ils paraissent « suspendus » à son corps comme ils l'étaient au mur). Il lui appartient désormais de rester impeccable, au sens propre comme au figuré (pour épépiner les groseilles à maquereau, il lui est conseillé de porter un tablier par-dessus sa robe, « *lest [...] I should mucky it* », 290).

Alors qu'avant d'être aimée de Rochester, son âme condamnée à l'indifférence lui semblait comme engoncée dans un habit mal taillé, comme prisonnière de chaînes bien lourdes à porter (« *to slip again over my faculties the viewless fetters of a uniform and too still existence* », 99), Jane Eyre croit pouvoir entamer à Morton une nouvelle vie grâce à sa nouvelle garde-robe, fruit de la charité publique (305). Mais un autre homme prétend bientôt lui imposer d'autres contraintes, plus mortifères encore (« *My iron shroud* », 344). Au contact de St John Rivers, elle découvre que, même chez les plus pieux, la personnalité sociale que chacun présente au regard des autres n'est parfois qu'un déguisement. De même que l'hypocrite n'est qu'un sépulcre blanchi (voir la Préface de la deuxième édition, 2), le chrétien jouit abusivement du rachat des péchés de l'humanité, qui masque ses défauts personnels en le revêtant de probité candide : « *I am simply, in my original state—stripped of that blood-bleached robe with which Christianity covers human deformity—a cold, hard, ambitious man* » (319). Étrange vêtement, dont la blancheur trompeuse est assurée par le sang du Christ...

L'arrière-plan moral de cette idée du masque de chair est très tôt annoncé par Rochester. Déjà épris de Jane, Rochester espère trouver auprès d'elle des plaisirs purs et frais mais l'héroïne, qui n'envisage pas encore d'épouser son employeur et qui refuse de devenir pour lui une maîtresse de plus, ne conçoit le plaisir que comme une tentation à fuir systématiquement. Rochester la détrompe : il s'agit d'une inspiration céleste et non d'une tentation démoniaque. « *It is no devil, I assure you; or it if be, it has put on the robes of an angel of light* » (117) : l'ambiguïté de cette phrase laisse entendre que Rochester n'est pas trop regardant et qu'il accueillerait volontiers Jane même s'il s'agissait d'une diablesse déguisée en ange. L'héroïne persiste, incitant Rochester à la méfiance, et celui-ci s'entête, il affirme vouloir accueillir la visiteuse surnaturelle, qu'elle soit ou non ce qu'elle paraît être : « *I have received the pilgrim—a disguised deity, as I verily believe* » (117). Echappant au modèle chrétien, Jane prend alors l'aspect d'une déesse de la mythologie grecque, qui emprunte l'apparence d'une simple mortelle pour visiter les humains ; ses facultés surnaturelles seront confirmées lorsqu'elle entendra, comme par télépathie, l'appel de Rochester au chapitre 35.

Dans une lettre du 2 juin 1848, Charlotte Brontë explique à W.S. Williams qu'elle ne souhaite pas utiliser la presse comme vecteur de ses opinions. Elle laisse ce soin à d'autres plumes : « *Currer Bell is not Carlyle, and must not imitate him* » (Smith 70). C'est notamment devant l'extrémisme carlylien qu'elle semble reculer. Pour Teufelsdröckh, tout est vêtement : « *Whatsoever sensibly exists, whatsoever represents Spirit to Spirit, is properly a Clothing, a suit of Raiment, put on for a season, and to be laid off. Thus in this one pregnant subject of Clothes, rightly understood, is included all that men have thought, dreamed, done, and been : the whole External Universe and what it holds is but Clothing ; and the essence of all Science lies in the Philosophy of Clothes* » (Carlyle 55). Même si une certaine philosophie des vêtements imprègne Jane Eyre, même si le rôle attribué aux habits reflète les différentes composantes du roman (réalisme, symbolisme, etc.), l'objectif de Charlotte Brontë est évidemment tout autre. Pourtant, lingerie féminine et plaisir du texte semblent faire bon ménage, puisque les meilleurs souvenirs de Jane à Gateshead Hall sont ceux qu'elle associe aux récits de Bessie Lee, future Mrs Leaven : « *when, having brought her ironing-table to the nursery-heath, she allowed us to sit about it, and while she got up Mrs Reed's lace frills, and crimped her night-cap borders, fed our eager attention with passages of love and adventure taken from old fairy tales and older ballads* » (7). Dans *Jane Eyre*, que son auteur n'hésite pas à présenter comme une vaste entreprise de dénudement des hypocrites (Préface de la deuxième édition), les habits masquent les corps mais dévoilent les âmes, ils parlent avec éloquence, eux-mêmes complices de la narration.

Bibliographie

BAYUK ROSENMAN, Ellen Bayuk, "More Stories about Clothing and Furniture", *in Functions of Victorian Culture at the Present Time*, ed., Christine L. Krueger, Athens: Ohio University Press, 2002, 47-62.
CARLYLE, Thomas, *Sartor Resartus*, Everyman Classic, London: Dent, 1984.
GENETTE, Gérard, *Nouveau Discours du récit*, Paris : Seuil, 1983.
HARDING, Ellen, ed., *Re-framing the Pre-Raphaelites, Historical and theoretical essays*, Aldershot: Scolar Press, 1996.
LEWES, George Henry, *Principles of Success in Literature*, Boston: Allyn and Bacon, 1891.
MAYNARD, John, *Charlotte Brontë and Sexuality*, Cambridge: Cambridge University Press, 1984.
SMITH, Margaret, ed., *The Letters of Charlotte Brontë, with a selection of letters by family and friends*, Vol. 2, 1848-1851, Oxford: Clarendon Press, 2000.
THOMAS, Julia, *Pictorial Victorians, The Inscription of Values in Word and Image*, Athens: Ohio University Press, 2004.

"I am not a liar": Interpellation and Counter-interpellation in *Jane Eyre*

Catherine Lanone

Although *Jane Eyre* met with widespread recognition when it was published (Queen Victoria herself could hardly put it down) and has become part of the academic canon as a set text as well as the focus of countless feminist studies, it was in 1847 very much a novel written from the margins of society. The Brontës were, at the time, unknown spinsters whiling their lives away in Haworth, hardly the center of Victorian society. Charlotte Brontë's deliberately unfeminine pen name, Currer Bell, aimed to ward off gender prejudices, while the book itself focused on a deliberately atypical heroine, a poor, plain governess, depicting her own journey from childhood to adulthood. The novel thus fits in with the Victorian fascination for the genre of the *Bildungsroman*, the novel of formation of personality, a genre best exemplified by Dickens's masterpieces *David Copperfield* or *Great Expectations* (two books which were published after *Jane Eyre*)—but it adds a significant twist, focusing on an unglamorous female protagonist and her journey towards identity and a decent social position. The novel's early scenes may have been inspired by Charlotte Brontë's miserable memories of Carus Wilson and Cowan Bridge, the school which caused the death of two of her sisters, but they also function as defining moments, significant rites of passage where Jane as a child seeks to articulate her liminal position as a female outsider (*i.e.* a poor relation), struggling against degrading interpellation in order to achieve a kind of counter-interpellation, as we shall see. We shall study first the mechanisms of oppression and alienation. Then we shall pay attention to modalities of resistance, through the use of irony, or figures of speech like the hyperbaton, signalling the shift from oppression to self-identification and resistance, or in other words, from interpellation to counter-interpellation.

The stages of oppression

Initial alienation

As is the case for most *Bildungsromane*, Jane is an orphan, forced to make her way in the world by relying on her own self. Brontë's novel thus explores the unfamiliar territories of female experience, no longer the safe world of the gentry as in Jane Austen's novels, but the insecure uncertain experience of a woman forced to earn a living.

The shift away from Jane Austen's world is signalled by the opening sentence of the novel. A first chapter is supposed to display crucial information, laying down the basic foundations of the plot as quickly and as neatly as possible; the opening paragraph is meant to answer a series of questions, who, where, when, why, how. In Jane Austen's *Emma*, for instance, the opening lines seem straightforward enough:

> Emma Woodhouse, handsome, clever and rich, with a comfortable home and a happy disposition, seemed to unite some of the best blessings of existence; and had lived nearly twenty-one years in the world with very little to distress or vex her. *(Austen 1)*

The opening paragraph of *Jane Eyre* strays from such conventions: the first-person speaker refrains from disclosing her own name, though a "Mrs Reed" is mentioned (similarly, the second paragraph introduces Bessie and a cluster of names, "Eliza, John, and Georgiana Reed", but no Jane Eyre, as if to signal implicitly the drastic divide which separates the speaker from the aforementioned characters). Jane is neither rich nor handsome, and, unlike Emma, there is much to "distress or vex her"; indeed, the cold winter winds and somber clouds become objective correlatives for a child who remains always, figuratively speaking, under a cloud, that is to say, who is constantly in disgrace and disfavour, under suspicion—whatever she does, however hard she may strive to please, she is "termed naughty and tiresome, sullen and sneaking, from morning to noon, and from noon to night" (12), as she muses later on in the "red-room" (10). Besides, instead of building a steady referential frame, the novel favours the affect of a bleak atmosphere. We are left to infer what kind of a house this is (Gateshead is not yet given a name); the somewhat enigmatic opening sentence thrusts the reader *in medias res*: "There was no possibility of taking a walk that day" (5). Such a sentence relies on the mere impact of negation; we are about to learn that the season is winter, but "that day" is specified no further, so that the deictic is actually cataphoric: "that" day stands out, not so much because there was no walk, but because of what subsequently happens in the chapter.

Such a deliberate refusal to build a traditional, realistic frame of reference allows Charlotte Brontë to create instead what Jean-Jacques Lecercle calls "a structure of feeling" (Lecercle 216). As has often been noted, the opening scene functions according to a binary system which recurs throughout the novel, the symbolic opposition between warmth and cold. Here, the Narrated I is clearly excluded from warmth, expelled on the cold margins of the family scene—no wonder that Mrs Reed should later be given an "eye of ice" which "[dwells] freezingly" on Jane (30). The narrator quickly sketches a living *tableau*, in a brief hypotyposis which stresses the conventional postures of the reclining mother and the clustered children, all beaming by the fireplace, a sentimental scene apparently connoting all the domestic values that were to be celebrated during the Victorian era. But the hearth is no haven for the cold, isolated child, dismissed from the family circle by word and deed.

Mrs Reed's speech, which is quoted at length, reveals the hypocritical play on normativity, as verbs like "regretted" or "must" imply that she is abiding by ethical constraints upon which she has no control: "She regretted to be under the necessity of keeping me at a distance […] she really must exclude me from privileges intended only for contented, happy little children" (5). Not only is language cold here, it is extremely formal, not at all the kind of endearing language usually addressed to children (see stiff expressions like "regretted to be under the necessity" instead of "sorry to have to", or "endeavouring in good earnest" rather than "try hard"). Jane is thus doubly distanced, in spatial and in linguistic terms, from the hearth. The text shows the way in which the woman wields her power to attempt to crush the little girl, by adding insult to injury. The girl is not simply excluded, she is blamed for exclusion. Words are made to wound. This is a case of what Judith Butler, following Althusser, calls interpellation. For Butler, linguistic injury interpellates and constitutes a subject. One is called by a derogatory, demeaning name, and one's identity, as it were, is suddenly crystallized, or paralyzed, fixed by that name. The insult (Jane is a naughty child) "hails" the child into the subservient position of the inferior subaltern hovering on the margins of the true family nucleus. Butler points out that the mode of address is equally important; linguistic injury does not simply depend on words, but on the way in which they are uttered. Here, the dismissing of the little girl who is not allowed to join the group and is deliberately silenced —"until you can speak pleasantly, remain silent" (5)—is enhanced by the clichéd posture of the mother gathering her children by the fireside. There is a process of alienation at work, attempting to disguise exclusion as a petrifying necessity, blaming Jane for not being a contented, happy child, as if it were in her power to transform herself into Eliza or Georgiana.

In John Reed's coarser version of interpellation and alienation, duplicating the mother's speech but stripping it of its hypocritical circumlocutions, Jane is more clearly abused, called names such as "Madame Mope", "bad animal" (7), or "Rat! rat!" (9), all expanding upon the fury and contempt unleashed by the mother's definition of Jane, a "dependent" (8). Linguistic wounding is this time materialized by an actual blow, as the boy throws a book, which makes Jane fall and bleed.

The crimson crypt

The episode of the "red-room", which follows Jane's brief struggle, marks a further step in the process of alienation. No longer a proper *bed*room, since it is never used, the room has become a hyphenated *red-*room through significant paronomasia. The hyphen becomes a graphic symptom of connection and disconnection, pointing to the real meaning of the room. On the one hand, the room functions as a prison where the child is locked and punished. The room transposes Gothic motifs—like an ancient Gothic castle, it is cold (no fire is ever lit there) and huge, "one of the largest and the stateliest chambers in the mansion", with its "massive" mahogany bed (10); the room is steeped in red (with its curtains of "deep red damask", its "red carpet" and "crimson cloth") while the snowy white bed creates a striking contrast; the colour scheme desperately brings to mind spilled blood and a ghastly bloodless corpse, all the more so as the room is presented as a tomb, moulded by the memory of Mr Reed's coffin. As in a Gothic novel, the text builds up a progression from terror to "horror" (13), when Jane takes the quivering gleam of light for a visitation from the beyond, leading to the climactic swoon which ends many a Gothic scene: "unconsciousness closed the scene" (14).

The shift from the Gothic to the domestic reveals the evil stepmother's death-wish, locking up the child as if to get rid of her once and for all. Indeed, in a scene which parallels Cathy's vision of herself as a ghost at the Grange in *Wuthering Heights*, Jane catches a spectral glimpse of herself in the mirror: unable to identify her own reflection in the cold, dark, "visionary hollow", she sees a hybrid being, "half fairy half imp", "the strange little figure there gazing at me, with a white face and arms specking the gloom, and glittering eyes of fear moving where all else was still" (11). Jane's face is consumed by fear, her body becomes almost unsubstantial, immaterial. Instead of offering a Lacanian mirror stage, the glass signals dangerous fragmentation or alienation, as the child literally perceives herself as Other.

This fading corresponds to the psychic wound inflicted by Mrs Reed: Jane is indeed beside herself with fear, "or rather *out* of [herself], as the French would say" (9), coming dangerously close to the edge of psychic dissolution.

The traumatic experience of the red-room must also be connected, not simply with punishment, but with secrecy. A "rebel slave" (9), Jane has been robbed of her true identity, like all slaves. The sense of alienation reveals the hollow space within the child, the foreign entity which she harbours unawares, giving rise to an inexplicable feeling, the somatic signs of what Abraham and Torok call a psychic phantom, or transgenerational secret. What Jane dimly senses is what is indeed encrypted within that tomb of a room, Mr Reed's last words and the secret of Jane's uncle in Madeira, a secret which the text hints at without fully disclosing it:

> Mrs Reed herself, at far intervals, visited it to review the contents of a secret drawer in the wardrobe, where were stored divers parchments, her jewel-casket, and a miniature of her deceased husband; and in those last words lies the secret of the red-room—the spell which kept it so lonely in spite of its grandeur. *(11)*

The spell-binding secret is not fully disclosed yet.

The "straight, narrow, sable-clad shape" (26)

According to Jean-Jacques Lecercle, "interpellation is an on-going process" (Lecercle 166). Interpellation is caught in a wider social process: "the hailing speech act is always-already caught up in a serial arrangement, which means that the hailer is not the originator of the act, but only a mouthpiece" (Lecercle 166). Mrs Reed's rejection of Jane is thus part of a wider social process which ascribes to the child the position of a social nonentity as an orphan. The coercive process of spatial enclosure and verbal injury which culminates in the red-room is both interrupted and continued by the arrival of Brocklehurst—interrupted, because Lowood will allow growth and personal interaction; and continued, because Lowood is yet another kind of potentially lethal prison, under the supervision of Mr Brocklehurst, a narrow-minded agent of social order and sexual domination. Jane's encounter with Brocklehurst is a clear case of interpellation. The child's hesitation on the threshold of the room shows her awareness of having been *summoned*, for better or for worse. The threshold which is about to be crossed is a significant limit, signalling a new stage in Jane's progress. The repetition of the verb "feared" stresses the child's dilemma, while the colons and semi-colons create significant pauses in the sentence, conveying fear and paralysis, mimicking mental hesitation as little Jane is torn between the desire to escape and the awareness that she is compelled to enter that room: "I feared to return to the nursery, and feared to go forward to the parlour; ten minutes I stood in agitated hesitation: the vehement ringing of the breakfast-room bell decided me; I *must* enter" (26). The italics stress the sense of obligation, but also the sudden decisiveness of the child making up her mind to face whatever lies out there, on the other side of that door.

Like the policeman in Althusser's paradigmatic scenario of interpellation (by saying "hey you" a policeman turns each person into a guilty subject), Brocklehurst embodies patriarchal law. The child's viewpoint dehumanizes him, perceiving him as a stiff, vertical, petrified shape which is not merely phallic, as almost all commentators point out, but as rigid as a blind, unfair social system. Jane is dwarfed by the formidable figure. The use of pronouns ("*He*, for it was a man" 26) turns Brocklehurst into a monstrous apparition, a cog in a system rather than a human being. Everything about him is stern, dark and monumental:

> […] I looked up at—a black pillar! such, at least, appeared to me, at first sight, the straight, narrow, sable-clad shape standing erect on the rug: the grim face at the top was like a carved mask, placed above the shaft by way of capital. *(26)*

The contrast between the dark pillar and the small child is enhanced by details entailing pathos, such as the way in which Jane needs both hands to turn the handle, or the way in which Brocklehurst notices that she is small for her age. Once more, the dialogue aims to assign guilt, and breed in Jane a sense of unworthiness and inferiority. Using a Christian rhetoric, harping on psalms and pamphlets, Brocklehurst becomes an echoing chamber magnifying Mrs Reed's accusations: "'Deceit is, indeed, a sad fault in a child'" (28).

The process of interpellation is made more graphic at Lowood. The aim is to stamp the child, to print on it a performative label, constructing body and soul as infamous. In two archetypal scenes, the child is shamed, written on, "[appropriated] by the pragmatic structure" (Lecercle 167). After a long speech purporting to isolate and alienate Jane (she must be shunned for she "is a little castaway: not a member of the true flock, but evidently an interloper and an alien", 56) Brocklehurst concludes dramatically: "—this girl is—a liar!" (56). The dash signals the process of interpellation. Exposed on a stool turned into "a pedestal of infamy" (57), Jane is crushed by shame and reduced to tears after her ordeal. Similarly, Helen Burns is branded by Miss Scatcherd, binding the word "Slattern" across Helen's "large, mild, intelligent, and benign-looking forehead" (62). Charlotte Brontë's interest in phrenology makes this accumulation of adjectives even more significant, stressing the gap between Helen's innate qualities and the label shaming her.

Ironic distance

Such devices of interpellation aim to breed within the subject damaging and self-defeating assumptions. The kind of religion upheld by Brocklehurst becomes the language of coercion and social domination, supposedly breeding content and passivity in orphans. The discourse is clearly patriarchal; infuriated by a girl's red curls, Brocklehurst has all the girls cropped, yet his own daughters may flaunt feathers and his wife "a false front of French curls" (55). The poor girls' bodies are deliberately unsexed, while the master delights in parading his own bourgeois family before the enslaved orphans.

But while interpellation threatens the integrity of body and soul, the victims may develop strategies of liminal negotiations challenging cultural, social and even gender differences. Interpellation may be displaced, or countered.

The process of reaction is constantly stressed by the Narrating I, filtering the perceptions of the past with an irony which conveys anger. In the opening scene, for instance, the narrator instantly deconstructs the happy little family scene she is creating with scathing innuendoes: Mrs Reed reclines with "her darlings about her" (5) but the text instantly qualifies this by recalling that they usually spend their time bickering. Similarly, at Lowood, the hypocritical Brocklehurst girls apply their handkerchiefs to their "optics" rather than their eyes (56) whereas Brocklehurst's pompous heavy speech sentencing Jane to isolation is sarcastically deemed "sublime" (57). The narrator's irony casts a critical light upon the situations weighing upon little Jane. But Jane as a child also finds ways of voicing her rebellion.

Voicing resentment: the role of hyperbatons

The shift from interpellation to gradual counter-interpellation may be traced stylistically. Hyperbatons play a significant role in conveying resilience and self-definition, as opposed to the process of oppression. This figure of speech uses deviation from natural word order to create a specific effect. In the case of Jane Eyre, such a deviation reflects the way in which little Jane strays from the norm which society imposes upon her, the system of constraints which constructs her as a plain social nonentity, and nothing else. On the opening page of the novel, a striking hyperbaton is used first to graphically reproduce the system of isolation (like the pronoun "me" with its comma, Jane is cut off from the family) and a dawning sense of identity stemming from this very process of rejection: "Me, she had dispensed from joining the group" (5).

When Brocklehurst comes to Gateshead, Jane fights back, relying on fairy-tale patterns to channel her fear; the series of exclamations cast Brocklehurst as the big bad Wolf and Jane as a diminutive Little Red Riding Hood: "What a great nose! And what a mouth! And what large prominent teeth!" (26). She sensibly discards the great fears of Hell Brocklehurst tries to breed in her, dispelling coercion with her delightfully "objectionable" answer: "I must keep in good health and not die" (27). The voice of ideology, which was figured as a voice almost impossible to refuse, a sovereign power, is suddenly radically undermined by the child's refusal to play the part of the scared victim. A much more significant victory is won when Jane fights back and uses Mrs Reed's own insult. The demeaning term "liar" delineates the space which Jane is going to occupy at Lowood, it becomes a performative ritual meant to prolong the process of isolation, cutting Jane off from teachers and potential friends. But, as Lecercle points out, "there are such things as insurrectionary speech acts": "Speech acts do not merely reflect dominant relations of power: they can be turned around, and sent back against their temporary authors" (Lecercle 167). A series of short clauses mimics Jane's motion towards and away from the door; the central semi-colon marks the sudden breach of behaviour, as she breaks the bounds of passivity and turns around, walking slowly back to confront her aunt: "I got up, I went to the door, I came back again; I walked to the window, across the room, then close up to her" (30). Jane is ready to hurl the insult back at the oppressor. The hyperbaton signals the shift from interpellation to counter-interpellation, as the sentence loops back on itself, seeking the way forward: "*Speak* I must; I had been trodden on severely, and *must* turn: but how?" (30). The use of italics, of the significant verb "turn", the powerful repetition of the modal "must" shows how the subject is already displaced from the place ascribed by interpellation. The chain of authority is broken, as the silenced self is about to "speak" indeed, smashing guilt and passivity: "I am not deceitful", Jane claims suddenly, "*You* are deceitful!" (30). Symptomatically, the sense of liberation is expressed by a powerful series of hyperboles ("strangest", "I ever felt"), binary rhythms ("expand/"exult", ""freedom"/"triumph") mimicking elation and unleashed energy, while the sentence is prefaced by the word "Ere", recalling through homophony Jane's own name, Eyre, as if to strengthen the sense of a newly-gained identity: "Ere I had finished this reply my soul began to expand, to exult, with the strangest sense of freedom, of triumph, I ever felt" (30). As a frightened Mrs Reed murmurs "*sotto voce*" in a kind of theatrical aside, turned into a mere puppet or actress rather than a full agent, Jane is left "alone—winner of the field" (31); isolation is no longer imposed upon her, it has been conquered, solitude has become a sign of empowerment.

Lowood acts as an ambiguous space where Jane is faced with further oppression and unhealthy living conditions, but where she is also allowed to build her stern, resilient self. Claire Bazin underlines this significant shift which takes place from the start even when Jane is placed on the stool, which for Bazin is transfigured by the expression "pedestal of infamy": "*L'expression honnie se transforme en victoire bénie. L'humiliation s'estompe devant la dignité recouvrée, grâce, en partie, à la position debout, impossible dans la chambre rouge*" (Bazin 21). Warmed by Helen Burns's kind, passing glance, lifting her head up, taking "a firm stand on the stool" (57), Jane stands the test. The formative aspect of Lowood is emphasized by one of the nicest shots in Zeffirelli's movie, where little Jane, bending before Helen's tomb, rises up as the serene, adult Charlotte Gainsbourg. In the book, Jane's shift to adulthood as she takes her destiny into her own hands, is signalled by the third, discrete hyperbaton. Seeking a way out of Lowood, the adult Jane lapses once more into fairy-tale language: the suggestion that she should advertise for a job has been dropped on her pillow by some kind fairy. The anteposition of "scheme" in the following sentence stresses the moment of empowerment, as Jane takes one of the most significant decisions of her life, freeing herself from the servitude and solitude of Lowood (once again, the use of a central colon in the middle of the sentence marks a turning point in Jane's life): "This scheme I went over twice, thrice; it was then digested in my mind: I had it in a clear practical form; I felt satisfied, and fell asleep" (73).

The three hyperbatons thus stress Jane's progress, as she shifts from being a dependent to resilience and hard-won independence (though her independence as a governess is of course relative, it is clearly a step forward in her life's pilgrimage).

Jane's creativity

Helen Burns is the passive angel whom Jane cannot resemble. Margaret Atwood in her book entitled *Survival* has defined four "basic victim positions" (Atwood 36). Helen Burns corresponds to Position Two, which means, in the words of Atwood, "To acknowledge the fact that you are a victim, but to explain this as an act of Fate, the Will of God, the dictates of Biology (in the case of women, for instance)" (Atwood 37). Helen Burns does not deny the fact that she is a victim, but she does not rebel either, considering that her own shortcomings entail punishment, and submitting to the will of God. Jane, on the other hand, refuses to abide by the law of inferiority. She thus moves from Position Three ("To acknowledge the fact that you are a victim but to refuse to accept the assumption that the role is inevitable", Atwood 37) to Position Four ("To be a creative non-victim", Atwood 38).

Jane's imaginative powers are foregrounded from the start; excluded from the family scene, she shifts from the malignant Reeds to reading; seclusion is turned into a refuge, rather than a punishment; "shrined in double retirement" (5), Jane turns the space delineated by the crimson curtains into an inner theater, a discovery space. The evocation of the blank death-realms of the Arctic creates a sublime version of the bleak winter day outside. Bewick's *History of British Birds* provides a series of visions which deeply shape Jane's soul as an artist. Indeed, the landscapes which Jane describes foreshadow the eerie visions Rochester will find so fascinating in her own drawings:

> The words in these introductory pages connected themselves with the succeeding vignettes, and gave significance to the rock standing up alone in a sea of billow and spray; to the broken boat stranded on a desolate coast; to the cold and ghastly moon glancing through bars of cloud at a wreck just sinking. *(6)*

As Jane grows up, reading and drawing become ways of defining her own identity. Two months after her arrival at Lowood, she sketches her first cottage (63). Psychologists study the way children draw houses in order to assess their mental balance. Jane's cottage has clumsy walls (with characteristic self-derision she claims that they rival the leaning tower of Pisa) but it is significantly associated with Jane's first French lessons and her ability to say "the verb *Etre*" (63). Both drawing and verbs are emblems of a more stable identity, of new powers of expression and self-definition which are beginning to emerge; as she goes to sleep, Jane dreams of being able to draw "freely pencilled houses and trees", "Cuyp-like groups of cattle", butterflies and roses and birds' nests, picturesque scenes connoting a safe haven, and recaptured intimacy; later, when Bessie comes to visit her for the first and last time, Jane is able to display her ladylike accomplishments, duly playing the piano or displaying a pretty "landscape in water colours" (78). Such pretty landscapes Rochester will quickly sweep aside, to single out the more original visionary scenes imagined by Jane, the cormorant and the sunken corpse, the evening Star and the iceberg, allegories of dismay and formlessness, troubled emblems of Romantic creativity.

Thus the novel portrays the ways in which Jane grows, from an oppressed orphan to a creative non-victim, able to draw striking visions and to write the story of her own life. Susan Gilbert and Sandra Gubar have shown that Victorian critics like Matthew Arnold or Elizabeth Rigby were shocked by Jane's undisciplined spirit, her rebellion: "In other words, what horrified the Victorians was Jane's anger" (Gilbert and Gubar 338). We have attempted to show that, unlike passive Helen Burns or unlike her dark fierce double, the madwoman in the attic, Jane Eyre manages to channel and voice her resentment in order to devise strategies of resilience and counter-interpellation. Jane's pilgrimage leads her to grow both as a woman and as an artist, as she leaves Lowood to become a governess, neither a servant nor a member of the gentry, then is forced to struggle against temptation, leading her towards the somewhat ambivalent, dialogic ending of the novel, as Bernadette Bertrandias reminds us: "*Jane Victrix n'en demeure pas moins, à jamais, Jane l'exclue: mais dans cet irréductible paradoxe réside toute la force de sa parole*" (Bertrandias 112).

Bibliography

ATWOOD, Margaret, *Survival* [1972], Toronto: McClelland & Stewart, 1996.
AUSTEN, Jane, *Emma*, ed., Stephen M. Parrish, Norton Critical Edition, New York: Norton, 1972.
ABRAHAM, Nicolas, et Maria TOROK, *L'Écorce et le noyau*, Paris : Flammarion, 1992.
BAZIN, Claire, *Jane Eyre, le pèlerin moderne*, Nantes : Éditions du Temps, 2005.
BERTRANDIAS, Bernadette, *Charlotte Brontë: Jane Eyre, la parole orpheline*, Paris : Ellipses, 2004.
GILBERT, Sandra, and Susan GUBAR, *The Madwoman in the Attic*, New Haven, London: Yale UP, 1979.
LECERCLE, Jean-Jacques, *Interpretation as Pragmatics*, London: Macmillan, 1999.

Secrets, Lies, Concealment and the Quest for Truth in *Jane Eyre*

Jacqueline Fromonot

Charlotte Brontë's 1847 preface to *Jane Eyre* is ample proof of the novelist's admiration for William Makepeace Thackeray, the satirical essayist and novelist to whom she dedicates the second edition of her novel. She particularly praises his capacity to speak truthfully, regardless of courtesy or decorum:

> There is a man in our own days whose words are not framed to tickle delicate ears: who, to my thinking, comes before the great ones of society, much as the son of Imlah came before the throned Kings of Judah and Israel; and who speaks truth as deep, with a power as prophet-like and as vital—a mien as dauntless and as daring. *(2)*

Now Thackeray was a prominent literary figure at the time; he was famous—and notorious—for his social satires and his portrayal of the real rather than the ideal. His tendency "to look into the depths of a loathsome truth", as a critic of that period put it (Ray 257), did not often "tickle delicate ears"; indeed, they rather set teeth gnawing, just as Brontë's novel did, to a certain extent. Although her work became very popular immediately after publication, there was also widespread censure of the text, owing to its supposed coarseness in the portrayal of emotions and its critical representation of religious sentiment through an attack on Evangelicalism. The respect and admiration expressed by Brontë in her homage must have been mutual, for Thackeray in his turn eulogized her as he wrote the editorial introduction to her last text, *Emma*, published in the *Cornhill Magazine* five years after her death. This contribution gave him an opportunity to emphasize the very qualities she liked about him, among which "the indignation at wrong" and "the burning love of truth" (Wheeler 62). The two artists saw each other—and probably themselves too—as outspoken moralists, which significantly points to their ethical concerns and aesthetic preoccupations as writers.

In *Jane Eyre*, the eponymous heroine unsurprisingly shares the author's desire to favour truth over appearances and humbug. Throughout her diegetic life Jane is tirelessly made to denounce all kinds of lies, whether individual or social, thus putting forward an ethic of her own, based on sincerity and authenticity, in other words the capacity and willingness to tell the truth. One might even go as far as saying that the omnipresent themes of deceit and disguise are explored only to offer the heroine the possibility to expose the surrounding world of make-believe. In fact, Jane's role is to "restore to rectitude the warped system of things" (1847 preface, 2), within the fictional space created by the text and maybe outside it too. This, however, does not lead Brontë to write a latter-day pamphlet, for the status of the truth is affected by the constant tension between the two distinct codes of romance and realism in this fictional autobiography.

A World of Secrets and Lies

Lying is such a central element in *Jane Eyre* that it shapes its plot and becomes one of its main driving forces. As an impediment, it has a complicating function within the structure of the narrative. Very early in the plot, although it is revealed rather late in the narrative, Mrs Reed has Jane's uncle believe that his niece is dead, thus depriving her for a time of a genuine family link and her inheritance (204). The aunt's breach of faith reads as another form of deception, though to a lesser degree, when she refuses to fulfil her promise to take good care of Jane. As a result, Mrs Reed—decidedly the treacherous villain of the tale—causes Jane to be bullied and humiliated. In the opening chapters, this triggers a chain of events leading to the red-room crisis and Jane's subsequent departure from Gateshead. Therefore, these falsehoods prove to be dynamic elements in Jane's destiny; they contribute to turn the penniless orphan into a strong, independent and resilient woman, in other words to allow her to achieve maturity as a character and credibility as an authoress, in this *Bildungsroman*, or apprenticeship novel. Given the onomastic symbolism of "Gateshead", the Reeds' property, Jane was never meant to stay there; the "gate" is a threshold for the journey she is forced to undertake, and lying actually stands out as just another diegetic strategy which prompts the appropriate response. It is a powerful means of eliciting answers as well, and it unexpectedly helps the characters deal with complex inter-subjective relationships. For instance, Rochester, a manipulative character, propagates false rumours like his impending marriage with Blanche Ingram to see if it arouses Jane's jealousy; then, he has Miss Ingram believe he is not as rich as she thinks to confirm his suspicion about her mercenary motives (217). He even poses as a fortune-teller to tell Blanche how little he thinks of her (165) and to trick Jane into a confession. Through his transvestite impersonation of a gypsy, he fosters freedom of expression, in a world where truth is difficult to obtain and truthfulness hard to put into practice. This, however, should not obscure the fact that the whole process reads as a metafictional *mise en abyme* of the way tales themselves are productive of truth.

However, lying is not only used as a tool for heuristic purposes; it appears as a central theme whose many facets and figures are detailed, particularly in the Thornfield episode. Rochester's life has become a web of lies: a sort of Bluebeard (91) with a past he keeps secret, he is surrounded by mystery, and Jane is "purposely excluded" (140) from what is referred to as the "third story" (90) of the mansion. Now the expression "third story" is a polysemic one, whose meanings have to be deciphered according to contexts. Firstly, it obviously refers to the top floor of the building, where Rochester's wife Bertha is kept under lock and key. A psychoanalytical approach may also link it to the Freudian *Id* and its threatening urges, which have to be confined to a separate sphere. In addition, the very wording "third story" implies the existence of three narratives altogether—those of Bertha, Jane and Rochester. In a literary attempt to reach unity so that Jane's and Rochester's become a single destiny, the third pole, one too many, has to be denied or even eliminated. Rochester's lies about his wife have to grow ever more elaborate as her presence becomes harder to conceal. Mere lying by omission, that is passively withholding the truth about Bertha's existence, develops into intentionally false declarations, like the misinformation about the anomalies in his home. In order to cover up the attempt made on Mason's life, Rochester has to launch into the following tale to set his guests' minds at rest:

> A servant has had the nightmare; that is all. She's an excitable, nervous person: she construed her dream into an apparition, or something of that sort, no doubt; and has taken a fit with fright. Now, then, I must see you all back into your rooms; for, till the house is settled she cannot be looked after. *(176)*

This elaborate speech draws its power to convince from its coherence and likelihood. It borrows elements from diegetic reality, mentioning a psychologically unstable person, while no identity is disclosed. The efficient rhetoric is based on the speaker's trusting that no-one will care or dare to enquire who this "servant", a mere subaltern, could be. Furthermore, the forged explanation is well-devised, with a strict logic about it, a string of causes and consequences all leading to the request that the party should leave—for lies are indeed constructions. Finally, Rochester intentionally commits deceptive acts, behaving in such a way as to lay false trails and making arrangements behind people's backs, so to speak, when he attends to his brother-in-law, significantly carrying him out through the "side-passage door" at the back of the house and using the "back-stairs" (183). One should bear in mind that in the traditional stately home, space is organized according to strict laws to maintain the distinction between the various areas according to function. For example, the back stairs are reserved for the servants. Therefore, when Rochester uses the staircase that is not intended for him, he can easily hide from the public gaze. However, he cannot afford to be "upfront", both literally and figuratively, and has to take advantage of the architectural design to preserve his double life.

The exploration of secrecy and its resulting deception through the Thornfield episode is completed by a more general reflection on lying, through the analysis of some 19th-century mores, namely the restraint society expects from individuals. Women in particular are required to conceal their bodies and repress their feelings: they are taught to be what the patriarchal society has decided for them, chaste, demure and subdued. That is why Bertha, with her insatiable sexual desire, can no longer make a presentable wife, and is therefore kept away from the public sphere. Innate dispositions in girls have to be disciplined, as the Puritan reverend Brocklehurst puts it: "We are not to conform to nature" (54). Consequently the Lowood boarders are made to wear austere outfits which cover as much flesh as possible, "brown dresses, made high and surrounded by a brown tucker about the throat" (39), in utter denial of the flesh (54). A strict hairstyle hides away curls or wisps of hair, as signs of deviant naturalness, for hair recalls the animal and it is what brings a human being close to wild, impulsive, irrational—natural—forces. Significantly enough, Bertha is dishevelled; she is said to have "shaggy locks" over her face (250), and her "mane" (250) likens her to an animal. In response, Lowood cages the beast, according to principles best defined by Rochester, who tells Jane: "The Lowood constraint still clings to you somewhat; controlling your features, muffling your voice, and restricting your limbs" (118). The three verbs evoke the repression of one's true nature under socially acceptable images. All spontaneity is gone, and the portrait is reminiscent of English governesses as described by the French historian Hyppolite Taine:

> Ce n'est pas un rôle agréable que celui des gouvernantes en Angleterre; voyez là-dessus les romans de Charlotte Brontë. La plupart de celles que j'ai vues s'étaient fait un visage de bois ; rien de plus étonnant quand ce visage est jeune. Le ton, la démarche, tout est artificiel et de commande, composé et maintenu de façon à ne jamais donner prise. *(Taine 120)*

Hard wood has replaced the flesh and its drives, whose presence is not to be tolerated in women in charge of children's education in the best circles. For Taine, governesses themselves initiate this process of lignification, maybe as a result of defensive deception, according to which the individual agrees to conform, at least outwardly. This may indeed be the only way to survive from the Lowood treatment at any rate, with its essentially repressive and punitive education. Brocklehurst himself seems to set an example by mastering his own body to the point of being a "black pillar", in the eyes of a dismayed little girl:

> I looked up at—a black pillar! Such, at least, appeared to me, at first sight, the straight, narrow, sable-clad shape standing erect on the rug: the grim face at the top was like a carved mask, placed above the shaft by way of capital. *(26)*

Here, the image of the "black pillar" is not just a comparison (no link word such as "like" is used), but a metaphor, a running one even, for the idea is taken up again by "shaft", pointing to the shape of the column and of the tall, upright body, and "capital", meaning both the top of a pillar and the head. The reference to stone evokes a process of petrifaction, this time, for Brocklehurst has stifled his humanity and humaneness, shamefully forgetting the teachings of Christ. Besides, the "mask" he seems to be wearing inevitably conjures up the idea of artifice and questions the authenticity of such a display of virtue. Brocklehurst can easily be suspected of being a Pharisee, a believer whose faith is not genuine. The confirmation comes with the revelation that he is but a hypocrite whose class double standards lead him to think that humility needs to be taught to the poor, while the rich can enjoy all kinds of privileges. In this respect, his emphasis on modesty in dress does not concern his own family, for instance (55). Therefore his homilies are mere "cant", a variety of lying whose Latin etymology *cantare* relates it to a song. His lectures are merely superficial talk about moral principles, which he uses to pretend he is better than he claims. One might think that this indictment of extreme Evangelical zeal through the treatment of Brocklehurst may be counterbalanced by that of the other key religious figure of the novel, St John Rivers, the statutory embodiment of charitable, humanistic Christian values. Yet, the narrator describes him with the very same image of a "column" (345), made harder still through a conspicuous network of mineral elements, "marble" and "stone" (350). In this case there is no room for doubt as to the authenticity of his faith; nevertheless Rivers is so cold and ruthlessly moral that he would not hesitate to bend Jane to his will, turning her into a mere "useful tool" (354) for the sake of his high-minded religious ideals. Consequently, just as the heroine turns down Rochester's offer to pass off as his wife, she refuses to marry Rivers for want of true passion between them. Indeed, both cases are unacceptable for her, as they require the sacrifice of feelings and moral sense so as to save mere social appearances. In other words, Jane is caught up in a diegetic destiny which leads her to refuse compromises with her inner sense of truth, and her quest is aimed at finding it.

The Quest for Truth and Truthfulness

In Brontë's set-up, it is essential to develop the right focus to visualize reality, so Jane is endowed with acute sight that enables her to get to the truth. She is eager to see through things and people, who might then feel ill at ease: "your eyes […] are directed piercingly to my face", Rochester says (112). Jane's innate skill is reinforced by acquired knowledge, as is shown by the way she reconstructs Rochester's inner psyche: "his full nostrils, denoting, I thought, choler; his grim mouth, chin and jaw—yes, all three were very grim and no mistake" (102). Her analysis is reminiscent of 19th-century sciences, like physiognomy and phrenology, which were used at the time as reliable means of deciphering personalities, an ambition echoed by the final words "no mistake". What is most striking in Jane, whose driving principle is the unveiling of truth, is that as a child, she constantly had to face accusations of being false. Her aunt points to her "tendency to deceit" (28), a verdict that becomes hyperbolic with Brocklehurst, who repeatedly accuses her of being a "liar" (28, 56). The apparent paradox can be explained away by the writer's careful characterization of the heroine. Jane's natural taste for truth is implicitly enhanced by the recurring charges of propensity to lie, which she and the reader know to be unfounded. This assumption is in keeping with the autobiographic code, which tends to establish causal links between the early years and adult life. Jane's craving for authenticity has predictable consequences on her character, and they reinforce its coherence. The heroine significantly despises luxury and artifice in dress, for example, and insists on wearing "nothing but [her] old Lowood frocks" (229) once she is engaged to marry. She rejects the trappings of conventional femininity, which are so essential to the construction of Blanche Ingram and Céline Varens. Even as a narrator addressing the reader directly, she makes no compromise about her ideal of truthfulness at the risk of shocking idealistic readers; hence her propitiatory remark when it comes to noting Grace Poole's drinking problem, uttered apologetically like an aside, in brackets, but present still: "(Oh, romantic reader, forgive me for telling the plain truth:)" (93). Jane's crusade is not restricted to persons; it also aims at higher levels of meaning, as when she counters traditional beliefs in the matter of children's education—admittedly a sensitive subject. She means to stand her ground, as is exemplified in a metatextual commentary, "I am not writing to flatter parental egotism, to echo cant, or prop up humbug; I am merely telling the truth" (92), which recall the content and tone of the 1847 preface to the novel, previously quoted.

More generally, the heroine refuses to live by common standards of sociability and she thinks little of courteous exchange. When Rochester asks her if she finds him handsome, she apparently blunders, by her own admission: "the answer somehow slipped from my tongue before I was aware: —'No, sir.'" (112). This discourteous retort just comes out uncensored by any sense of propriety, and its bluntness is emphasized by the monosyllabic and monolithical negative form "No". As she is embarrassed at what is likened to a *lapsus linguae*, or "slip of the tongue", Jane hastily puts together a new version:

> "Sir, I was too plain: I beg your pardon. I ought to have replied that it was not easy to give an impromptu answer to a question about appearances; that tastes differ; that beauty is of little consequence, or something of that sort." *(112)*

The terseness of the previous answer is replaced by a linguistic proliferation, with the extensive use of circumlocution and approximation; and yet the conventional speech sounds hardly more satisfactory, for Jane gives vent to her scorn for its artificiality as she utters it. She uses a dismissive closure, "or something of that sort," to distance herself ironically from the ready-made formulae often resorted to when a straight answer is impossible to give. She also points to the possibility of adding an endless string of nice-sounding euphemisms, because just like a lie, a softened version of reality admits of multiple formulations, released as it is from the necessity of representing the truth, supposedly unique. An independent, uncompromising woman, Jane does not feel bound to conform; she refuses affectation and intends to mean what she says and say what she means. In this perspective, a dramatic and unexpected reversal proves her right. As it turns out, Rochester does appreciate Jane's sincerity, as he confesses later on, while he despises the hypocrisy of Céline Varens, who referred to his "beauté mâle" in his presence, but to his physical "deformities" when she flirted with a new lover (123). In other words, Jane's remarkable departure from deceptive conventions had a felicitous outcome in true romance.

Facts are revealed not only through the resources of language, assertions, conversations and admissions, but also in appropriate courses of action, which organize a process of gradual revelation within an aptly-staged plot. Every mystery is finally cleared out, and in Thornfield Hall, for instance, reaching for the heart of the secret is literally shown as passing a series of material obstacles: "the tapestry was now looped up in one part, and there was a door apparent, which had then been concealed" (178). Space is being reconfigured, since ordinary, familiar places originally perceived as closed-in units are now passage-ways to unknown recesses. After the wedding misfires, Rochester takes the whole party to see his actual wife, in a long ascent towards the truth: "We mounted the first staircase, passed up the gallery, proceeded to the third storey" (249-250). This implies that more layers of tapestries have to be removed (250), without a word, as it might disturb the enlightening initiation aimed at uncovering the *corpus delicti*. And indeed the attic of Thornfield Hall, which is called a "shrine of memory" (90), not only contains materialized testimonies of the past, like discarded objects and old furniture, but also fleshly skeletons in the closet, for Bertha's haunting presence finally resurfaces at this time of anamnesis. To the modern reader, the process recalls psychoanalysis: the patient searches the past and gradually retrieves long-gone memories. Confronted with the truth, Jane can symbolically "discern that the gilding is slime and the silk draperies cobwebs" (184). In other words, she realizes at last that the "splendid mansion" (183) is built on illusion and treachery, gaining knowledge and experience from her journey through appearances. This gradual unveiling process is a metaphor for the development of the whole plot; yet, the very mechanisms at work in the revelation of these truths are not without complexity and deserve undivided attention.

The Poetic Manipulation of Truth

In this perspective, it is the nature of the text itself that should be examined. Like any standard autobiography, *Jane Eyre* is based on narration in retrospect, with a first-person, limited point of view. It is a double-voiced narrative too, which means that the referent of the pronoun "I" oscillates between two different Janes, the mature woman writing her story long after the events have occurred, that is the narrator, and the younger self she used to be, submerged in the narrated situations, the focalizer, most of the time. In accordance with the genre, these two voices differ in tone, and efforts are made to retrieve the perception of the past as faithfully as possible. For example, when little Jane meets Brocklehurst, she exclaims: "What a great nose! and what a mouth! and what large prominent teeth!" (26). The underlying reference to the big bad wolf of *Red Riding Hood* is meant to render a child's construction of meaning from folklore and its fairy-tales, one of the main forms of culture available to her at the time. However, the dissociation of the two viewpoints might be hard to perceive for the reader, because the voice of maturity will inevitably merge with that of childhood, and this will result in unstable focalization. Indeed, the ironical comment on the appearance of the Brocklehurst family, "They ought to have come a little sooner to have heard [the reverent's] lecture on dress" (54), does not really sound like a young girl's utterance. Furthermore, the numerous references to the enigmas of Thornfield Hall are made in bad faith, so to speak, because the narrator has solved them since then. Under the pretence of reporting events, she slips into her former self's restricted understanding to keep the unfolding of the diegesis going. In addition, the retrospective nature of the tale inevitably leads her to select and organize moments that suit her purpose, according to the metatextual principle that "This is not to be a regular autobiography" (70), thus revealing the fictitious part of any autobiography, also known as autofiction. Hence the basically unreliable nature of Jane's story and the reader's legitimate questioning of the very truthfulness of the diegesis. In a comment on a conversation with Miss Temple, the heroine herself confesses to the charge: "Thus restrained and simplified, [my account] sounded more credible" (60). The implicit message is that sometimes the actual truth departs so much from the standards of verisimilitude that the most convincing way to reveal it is to tamper with it, in anticipation of the narratee's reception.

The manipulation relies on the close bond created between the narrator and the reader, who is often addressed directly through apostrophes so that a relation of plain, honest communication is established. Nonetheless, the narrative strategy demands that some facts should be held back, a necessity which is made explicit: "Stay till [Rochester] comes, reader; and, when I disclose my secret to him, you shall share the confidence" (235). The candidly outspoken manoeuvre titillatingly delays the release of information. This controlling process applies to the whole novel, which classically rests on the conflict between two opposite forces. The first one is a dynamic and relentless movement towards disclosing the outcome; the other tends to postpone the revelations by stalling action or setting up all sorts of obstacles, so as to build expectation. This is achieved with the help of "dilatory morphemes" (Barthes 82), like incomplete answers, misrepresentations, withheld information, ambiguities and red-herrings, some of which can be spotted in Brontë's text. For instance, Bertha's laugh is at first wrongly attributed to Grace Poole (91), a misleading clue given by the narrator herself. Then, Rochester leaves his sentences unfinished when he alludes to his past, as in "how long have I abhorred the very thought of it; […]. How I do still abhor—" (121). Of course this is a somewhat likely reaction from a psychological viewpoint, because the character finds it difficult to articulate painful experiences, not to mention the fact that he has to keep a secret. More importantly from a narrative point of view, however, it is necessary to preserve suspense and thus intensify the enjoyment of the reading experience, setting an erotic logic in motion, in which the object of desire is given *and* partially refused at the same time, in a teasing way. Therefore it becomes apparent that narrative truthfulness does not import so much; it is the reader's pleasure that counts—especially at a time when very few sources of excitement are even condoned…

This may also account for the poetic truth in the novel, which draws from an extensive use of romantic imagination. Although the story reaches a high degree of authenticity, it is hard not to call it a romance, on account of the part idealization plays in it, regarding in particular the providential nature of the world depicted. It cannot be denied that *Jane Eyre* unfolds through a combination of good luck and implausible, heavy-handed coincidences. There is a blatant case of poetic justice, for instance, when the reader learns that the good, deserving Riverses are actually part of Jane's family and are rewarded for this very reason, since thanks to her, they get their very share of the Eyre inheritance they had been denied (328-29). Besides, the text teems with obvious symbols and omens, like the storm splitting the chestnut tree in two the night after Rochester proposes (219). Finally, there comes the help of the supernatural to reunite the two lovers, when Jane hears Rochester's calls (357). These elements do not belong to realism, which advocates the depiction of things as they are, not as they should be. However, their presence makes sense in terms of narrative framework. The narrator has adapted the laws of rationality to capture a kind of poetic truth with a logic of its own that defies the world as it is.

As Mrs Gaskell notes in her *Life of Charlotte Brontë*, the writing of *Jane Eyre* is said to have started with a challenge. Brontë reportedly warned her sisters, who favoured beautiful, romantic heroines, "I will prove to you that you are wrong; I will show you a heroine as plain and as small as myself, who shall be as interesting as any of yours" (Gaskell 317). This project was clearly a departure from romance in favour of the budding genre of realism. However, the authoress proves unable to free herself totally from the romantic code and may have lost her bet, but in this respect one may say that it is thanks to the very mixture of the two literary traditions that Jane Eyre is a true literary master-piece.

Bibliography

BARTHES, Roland, *S/Z*, Collection Points Littérature, Paris : Seuil, 1970.
GASKELL, Emily, *The Life of Charlotte Brontë* (1857), London: Smith Elder, 1900.
TAINE, Hyppolite, *Notes sur l'Angleterre* (1871), Paris : Hachette, 1876.
RAY, Gordon N., "*Vanity Fair*: One Version of the Novelist's Responsibility." *The Victorian Novel: Modern Essays in Criticism*, edited by Ian Watt, New York and Oxford: Oxford UP, 1976.
WHEELER, Michael, *English Fiction of the Victorian Period (1830-1890)* (1985), Longman Literature in English Series, Second Edition, London and New York: Longman, 1994.

Legacies of the Past: The Buried Stories of Thornfield Hall

Laurence Talairach-Vielmas

> No reflection was to be allowed now: not one glance was to be cast back; not even one forward. Not one thought was to be given either to the past or the future. The first was a page so heavenly sweet—so deadly sad—that to read one line of it would dissolve my courage and break down my energy. That last was an awful blank […]. *(273)*

When Jane Eyre turns her back on Thornfield Hall and turns the page of her failed romance with her master to start a new chapter afresh, the fictionalization of the heroine's life typifies the novel's obsessional play with the stories that define, frame or haunt women's lives. As Susan Gubar and Sandra Gilbert have long underlined, Brontë's novel exemplifies nineteenth-century female writing haunted by and entrapped in male texts, fated to reproduce "male expectations and designs" (Gilbert and Gubar 12). The governess's love story has been erased by the master's narrative, blotted out into an "awful blank" which denies the female character any attempt to write her own story. In the same way as the novel's secret is locked up in/on Thornfield Hall's third story, Charlotte Brontë's narrative is hinged upon the scripts that traumatize women, the stories that threaten to entrap the heroine as they have incarcerated the women before her. Seen from this perspective, Brontë's adaptation of prototypical Gothic tales with the heroine entering a mysterious house and "find[ing] herself in love with a mysterious man who appears to be some kind of criminal [whom] she [suspects] of having killed his first wife […] or of being out to kill someone else, most likely herself", to quote Tania Modleski's phrasing of the genre, appears less as a commercial lure than as a means of highlighting the narratives that fuel women's lives throughout the eponymous heroine's journey into femininity (Modleski 59). *Jane Eyre* functions as a series of embedded horror texts, of frightening textual layers which conflate Brontë's Gothicism with textuality, highlighting, in David Punter's terms, how the Gothic functions as a "paradigm of […] all textuality" (Punter 1).

Brontë's debt to eighteenth-century Gothic and her adaptation of stock devices is indeed most to be seen in the novel's play on textual motifs, starting with the red-room where a secret drawer in the wardrobe conceals parchments together with the haunting portrait of Jane's deceased uncle.

Dusty texts, paintings of the dead, buried manuscripts host the secrets of the past, typifying, as we will see, the shameful material that the household seeks to repress and that society hushes. Uncle Reed's parchments thus set the tone of a narrative paced by textual layers, buried fictions and inherited scenarios recounting woman's fate in patriarchal society. Obviously, as we may guess, Brontë's revision of Gothic motifs and plot patterns is no adaptation of the Male Gothic tradition, to follow Anne Williams's definition of the gender-oriented formula; that is, *Jane Eyre* is no tragic plot aimed at eradicating the woman whose transgressive sexuality endangers the patriarchal order. As a result, we will not here follow Juliann E. Fleenor's construction of the mad arsonist Bertha Mason as a visual reproduction of female rage and passionate nature whose body needs to be domesticated by being put away and locked up in an attic. On the contrary, this paper intends more to focus on the dark aspects of the imprisoned female body, hence engages with Brontë's narrative from the female Gothic perspective.

Fleenor's definition of "female Gothic", which encapsulates and redefines Ellen Moers's initial coining of the term, claims that Gothic narratives are grounded on the patriarchal paradigm that "the woman is motherless, defective, and defined by a male God" (Fleenor 11). In this way, the self-divided heroine is a "reflection of patriarchal values", and her quest frequently leads her to investigate "whether she is anything but reflection" (Fleenor 12). Such feminist views posit that, even if the threats jeopardizing the life of the heroine are often dispelled by the end of the novel, the plots foreground female victimization in order to dramatize woman's self-abnegating role within patriarchy. Similarly, in a more recent study of the genre, Anne Williams traces the "Gothic myth" in the patriarchal family, with Lacan's "Law of the Father" as the leading principle of the cultural order. Williams interestingly uses the tale of *Bluebeard* as a staple of Gothic structure, typically hosting the villain's crimes in secret chambers and seeking to castigate its curious heroine. By trying to affirm male power, the tale exposes significant structures of cultural power, limiting woman's freedom and staging man's superior position (Williams 43).

As feminist criticism has frequently noted, Brontë's novel does revise Radcliffean Gothic where the female protagonist is lost in an unknown dwelling and faced with images of women—whether as rebellious and murderous *femmes fatales* or as passive and self-abnegated Griseldas—meant to map out her future as a wife. The series of female versions functions as so many hints at woman's fate in patriarchal society, with the Gothic villains embodying patriarchal power, ruling over the derelict castles and concealing their worst secrets. Similarly, in *Jane Eyre*, the plot conflates a prototypical Gothic spatial imagery with the heroine's dread that her marriage might be but a repetition of the past, that what is locked up in the attic might stand for her own situation as a married and dependent woman. The ghost from the past haunts the present and only scares women on the brink of marriage, leading the female text to a climax of hysteria when the heroine unveils the main textual secret: the truly married woman *is* the mad woman. However, Brontë's encoding of the perilous story of woman's entrapment and alienation in a male-dominated society through a stereotyped mode of writing is not merely a series of images borrowed from an earlier popular genre: it can also be analysed as a lesson in reading through texts. Indeed, by leading the reader to decipher the literary layers that compose her own novel, Brontë may well hint at the fact that the recycling of genres might be turned into a metatextual mirror: entrapping women's stories into a genre to mimic the formula-ridden lives of domestic women. Revamping in this way the prototypical motif of the manuscript, Brontë changes images of buried writing into a precast scenario emmured in the Gothic mansion, thence using the cliché in its literal sense: the stock device of the manuscript does not so much contain the secrets of the past as it hosts a preset text and predicted story, a fatal trope which literally binds woman to a narrative and warns the eponymous heroine of her fate. Poisoned, murderous and criminal, the narrative's buried texts are threatening remains, hollowed out into dead metaphors conveying the spectre of patriarchy and prophesying woman's live burial in patriarchy's textually haunted castle. The Gothic imagery is therefore brought into play not solely, as Fleenor argues, to suggest the female body, sexuality and physiology through locked/unlocked rooms and dark recesses (Fleenor 13), but rather to reinscribe the mysterious manuscripts as the narratives that pen women's lives and that they have absorbed and physically experience, as shall be seen. Reading through the codes and precast texts that have been scattered throughout Thornfield Hall may thus highlight Brontë's educational project, in her description of a heroine faced with female stories and attempting to write her own story, her "autobiography".

As Gubar and Gilbert's analysis of *Jane Eyre* emphasizes, the novel is teeming with male enigmas, with Rochester's Sphinx-like sentences, speaking in riddles, lying or disguising as a woman. Whether he masquerades as a gipsy and mesmerizes the listeners with enchanting words, plays with double-entendres and manipulates words in charades, or invents stories to set his guests as rest, Rochester's mystery and mastery lie in words, stories or fictions that all encode the secret of male potency: textual lies and textual charades are what Jane must learn to decode, reading Rochester as a weaver of fictions seeking to delude women (Gilbert and Gubar 356). Obviously, the most pregnant narrative that Jane must read is the tale of

Bluebeard, which functions as a leitmotif in Brontë's novel, encapsulating Rochester's "secret of male sexual guilt" and illustrating Jane's and her master's relationship in gender terms, that is, from a patriarchal standpoint (Gilbert and Gubar 354). Right from the beginning of the heroine's arrival in the haunted dwelling, her discovery of the house and of the mysterious passage leading to the third story, "narrow, low, and dim [...] like a corridor in some Bluebeard's castle" (91), instantly activates the patriarchal narrative. The third story is instantly bound to her discontent regarding her situation as a woman, destined to "making puddings and knitting stockings, to playing on the piano and embroidering bags" (93), a frustration which she vents by walking along the corridor of the third story, backwards and forwards. Her own indirection, mimicking the "boredom of repetition in women's ordinary lives" (Delamotte 202)—and reflected in all the other female characters inhabiting the third story, from Grace Poole, walking in and out of the kitchen, to Bertha Mason, crouching and swaying to and fro in her prison—is paralleled with the character's storying out female fantasies of "incident, life, fire, feeling" (93), romantic stories that allow her to escape the constraints of domesticity. Ironically enough, these very fantasized romances of her own making exist as living tropes beneath the tapestry in an inner chamber of the third story. By walking along the story, Jane has manifestly been contaminated by the text. Voicing their anger through an uncanny laughter or monosyllables, Bertha Mason and Grace Poole twist Jane's female stories into mysterious scripts of muteness where incident, fire and feeling punctuate horror narratives. The tale of *Bluebeard*, walled up and embedded in Thornfield's third story, recounting a Gothic nightmare of isolation and imprisonment and equating women's lives with horror, haunts the women who walk along the place. Thus spatialized, *Bluebeard* quickens the young heroine who is thirsty for action and passion, enrages the married Creole heiress and reduces to silence the servant whose uncanny monosyllables encode the potency of her master's power. The female bodies, wandering to and fro along the chapters of the macabre tale, experience the same story over and over again, entrapped as they are in/on a story they cannot master.

Thus, if Jane is no prototypical Gothic heroine locked up in a bedchamber, she nonetheless experiences narratives of female enclosure, narratives which Thornfield Hall's master pens and orchestrates. Female entrapment is therefore both literal and figurative, turning space into stories the better to secure female obedience to the male law. Right from the beginning of the novel, texts and books function as metonymical reflections of the houses Jane inhabits. At Gateshead, John Reed presents both his books and his house as his possessions ("they *are* mine; all the house belongs to me", 8), reminding Jane of her inferior position by claiming back the book she is reading. The novel increasingly draws links between space and texts. When Jane vanishes into one of the recesses of the drawing-room to read one of her cousin's books, she mounts on the "window-seat" and draws "the red moreen curtain" so as to be "shrined in double retirement" (5), that is, in fact, so as to be concealed behind the folds of the drapery and behind the fictional material. The spatial recess, like a box within a room, echoes the intertextual depth, the story within the story which the narrative exposes. Furthermore, Jane reads about "the haunts of seafowl" and "forlorn regions of dreary space" and "death-white realms" (6) to forget about her own exclusion from the picture of domestic harmony her cousins and aunt shape before her. Suddenly, space creates plots, multiplies plots, and Jane recalls Bessie's fairy tale stories while looking at the pictures in the book. Yet, the intertextual fairy tale soon turns into a textual nightmare when John Reed discovers her hideaway and shatters the protective spatial frame. To assert his ownership and masculinity, John hurls the volume at the female protagonist; Jane falls on the floor and wounds her head. Hence the book rewrites the story, changes its plot to hit and make the female body bleed. Jane's imaginary marvellous realm, her fictional fold, has been turned into a nightmarish tale where blood stains the main narrative, spreading the tinges of the moreen curtain all over the text, with John Reed as the "murderer" (8) and tyrannous male. The metaphor of the "shrine" displays its macabre undertones and thereby shrouds the woman's body.

As an additional punishment for her disobedience to the male law, Jane's bleeding body is then locked up in the red-room, as if her wound were reflected on the walls of the haunted chamber. Brontë's female Gothic is here foregrounded in a scene which overtly conflates the setting with a discourse on interior space: the heroine's quest for her self flashes on the surface of the glass where Jane reads her own alienated self in the depth of the mirror, rewriting her body as fairy and imp stories. However, her tale instantly turns into a Gothic narrative with vindictive ghosts eager to claim vengeance looming behind the looking-glass. The depth of the mirror, the "visionary hollow" (11) reveal vaults and graves entrapping the female mind and body: the imaginary story contaminates Jane's body and locks her up in her own psychic space. She faints, horrified and mesmerized by the tale she has read in the glass. Hence, whilst space always opens up fictional creativity, not only do the romance or fairy intertexts always turn into Gothic intertexts, but the female body seems always to function as a surface that absorbs and experiences layers of narrative, as an alternative space to write and read female stories, or tales about female bodies. Caught in a vicious metafictional narrative, woman thus physically experiences the violence of words.

This idea of textual bondage awaits the heroine further as soon as she arrives at Thornfield Hall. Mrs Fairfax's presentation of the premises as an isolated place where one needs to read to fight seclusion instantly associates reading with imprisonment. More significantly still, Leah feels reading is too "confining" (82). As a revision of Radcliffean Gothic castles, Thornfield Hall sets into pace a female body bound to texts which function as prisons and deadly metaphors, as when Jane comes back to Thornfield at the end of the novel, discovering a heap of ruins and rendering the discovery through a necrophiliac comparison with a female corpse:

> A lover finds his mistress asleep on a mossy bank; he wishes to catch a glimpse of her fair face without waking her. He steals softly over the grass, careful to make no sound; he pauses—fancying she has stirred: he withdraws; not for worlds would he be seen. All is still: he again advances: he bends above her; a light veil rests on her features: he lifts it, bends lower; now his eyes anticipate the vision of beauty—warm, and blooming, and lovely, in rest. How hurried was their first glance! But how they fix! How he starts! How suddenly and vehemently clasps in both arms the form he dared not, a moment since, touch with his finger! How he calls aloud a name, and drops his burden, and gazes on it wildly! He thus grasps and cries, and gazes, because he no longer fears to waken by any sound he can utter—by any movement he can make. He thought his love slept sweetly: he finds she is stone-dead.
> I looked with timourous joy towards a stately house: I saw a blackened ruin. *(361).*

Obviously, Thornfield Hall is a literary trapping. As a pivotal narrative device, the house, with its "coffin-dust" relics (90), hosts, encapsulates and embeds the clichés that define and construct woman's deadly fate in patriarchal society, "shrin[ing]" womanhood (90) in a macabre way. As a literary embodiment of Brontë's feminist discourse, therefore, Thornfield Hall illustrates the texts that define and frame women. This is why when Jane arrives on the Gothic site, she constructs the building as a repository of other stories. In fact, part of Jane's experience consists in learning how to decode the mysteries she encounters, "puzzling [her] brains over the enigmatical character of Grace Poole" (132), trying to read the relationship between Rochester and Blanche Ingram or, of course, deciphering the frightening laughter of the third story. As a matter of fact, the building as a whole encapsulates three stories Jane must read to grasp the truth about her own femininity.

Indeed, if the surface story of Thornfield Hall is that of the potential romance between its enigmatic owner and the governess, it is bound to be brought to a stop so long as the other two stories have not been solved. The fairy-tale references that pepper the narrative are far too numerous to be mentioned and have frequently been analysed by feminist criticism. Let us note, however, that the first encounter between the lovers engages with the heroine's romantic construction of the scene, using once again Bessie's fairy tales to depict the apparition. Interestingly enough, Rochester partakes in Jane's fantasy, comparing the meeting to a fairy tale ("I thought unaccountably of fairy tales", 104). Rochester's contribution to the creation of their romance in fairy-tale terms is very significant: in fact, his frequent association of Jane with fairy creatures aims less at constructing her as a feminine ideal, celestial, otherworldly and morally superior, than at confining her in a plot where he plays the main part. As a matter of fact, he has literally written their romance: when Jane meets him on her way back from Gateshead, with "a book and a pencil in his hand" (208), he is penning their story in fairy-tale terms, as he later tells Adèle when on their way to Millcote to buy Jane's wedding dress and ring. However, constructing Jane as a fairy coming from Elf-land (228), he also rewrites his future bride in economic terms, as a social inferior, as a slave, as a coquette, as a creature likely to be devoured by an ogre or later as self-sacrificing woman dying for her husband. Ironically, their story drifts from the fairy tale to an Oriental narrative, then moves towards the tale of a kept mistress and concludes on a horror story and a macabre song. All through the shift in Rochester's narrative, female types merge, offering Jane multiple visions of her awaiting doom, from becoming Rochester's mistress (like Céline Varens, the vain kept woman), to being a double of Blanche Ingram, Rochester's expected bride, playing the part of the Israelitish princess enslaved to her master, or to becoming his wife, another Bertha, a monstrous goblin and a living-dead prisoner. In this way, if Jane refuses to become dependent and literally share the ogre's dinner as a savoury dish, she is yet intertwined in a series of fateful stories which she cannot master. Unable to hear about her own fate—as when the gipsy recounts Rochester's fortune instead of her own—and caught within other women's narratives, Jane must unearth Rochester's past stories to rewrite her own.

In fact, it stands to reason that the closure of the first story mostly depends on the third story, since the leading secret inhabits the third story, being as it were literally embedded in the motifs of the "shadow[y]" wallpaper—the tapestry covering the entrance of the inner chamber where Bertha is confined (179). But Jane keeps misreading the story concealed beneath the paper, the living manuscript, as she misreads all the other secrets of the mansion, turning Grace Poole into a former lover holding Rochester in her power or painting Blanche's bewitching looks and devising her marriage to a master entranced by her beauty. Moreover, when she finds herself locked up in the third story "fastened into one of its mystic cells" to look after Mason, "dip[ping] [her] hand again and again in the basin of blood and water, and wip[ing] away the trickling gore" (179), Jane again misreads the story as a tale of female power. Overlooking in this way Mason's submissiveness to her master's orders or the fact that the "beast" she believes is locked up seems "spell-bound" (179) after Rochester's visit, Jane again misinterprets Rochester's potency as the keeper of the keys and weaves a tale of male victimization and female rage. And yet, she is locked up in the third story, striving, like Bluebeard's wife, to wash the blood off the stained key, to blot out the traces of the secret she has just discovered and hush Rochester's dark mysteries, the live burial of his wife, as he tells Mason: "you may think of her as dead and buried" (181).

What the narrative of the third story tells us, in fact, and which many a feminist critic has already underlined, is how Brontë may have intertwined a legal discourse with the Gothic motifs of the labyrinthine castle and its secret chambers, where a rich and independent wife has been locked away by her husband. Bertha's literal bondage is symbolically a textual bondage: the female character functions as a living trope of patriarchy's criminal double-standard, a legal narrative of male domination and female subordination where the wife is "sequestered" (179) that is, secluded, deprived of her self and of her fortune. Consequently, the Gothic thematics provide, in Punter's terms, an "image language" for the female body whose live burial emblematizes woman's voicelessness and lack of legal identity (Punter 14). If Punter associates premature burials with "case[s] that will not be heard", Bertha's shrine in the attic is a legal text made uncanny, spectral, haunting—her live burial denouncing patriarchy as "the signature of the crypt" (Punter 103). In this way, Bertha becomes a "crime [...] incarnate" (179), an embedded legal text concealed in a secret room, another room within a room, a fleshly representation of a legal system that shaped women as *femmes couvertes*, that is, whose legal existence was literally covered and suspended by the husband. This is why, Eugenia C. Delamotte argues, the law of coverture found a symbolic representation in Gothic narratives, hiding women, subjecting them to "barbaric law" and burying them alive the better to express "the writers' sense of subjection to the legal power that they nonetheless experience as illegitimate" (Delamotte 157). Hence, in Brontë's narrative, the law of coverture becomes a performative text, the very means, as Punter underlines, "by which the law retains its tenacious hold on the body" (Punter 7). Brontë's female Gothic is therefore hinged upon a complex interplay between space and text, placing the female body as a significant axis to uncover the power relationships at stake in the novel. Whilst space releases deadly metaphors, words seem made of flesh, wounding, binding, sequestering the female inhabitants/characters of the third story. The key to deciphering the mystery of the third story depends thus on reading "sexual 'difference' as the 'key' to the secrets of the patriarchal power structure", as Anne Williams posits (Williams 43).

However, if the symbolical significance of Bertha's story seems to be magnified throughout the text, and possibly over-interpreted by feminist criticism, what may be more meaningful to read is the second story, the female narrative which is barely hidden, which sounds domestic and is yet horrific, and which stands right in between the fairy-tale story and the nightmarish Gothic tale. Indeed, the very first mystery which triggers off Jane's curiosity once she starts working at Thornfield Hall as a governess is, in fact, the story of her own pupil Adèle Varens. As a matter of fact, the secret concerning the illegitimate daughter of a fallen woman is the first female story of the past Rochester hides from Jane, even if the mystery is quickly solved. If the story is hinged upon some fateful repetition, the fallen woman's sin tainting her daughter's life, nothing seems yet to point out any potential link between the Bluebeard tyrant, who has imprisoned and buried his wife alive on the third story and whose heart is a "charnel" (117), and the innocent Rochester who has agreed to be the guardian of a child who is certainly not his own and who claims he is "not a villain" (116). However, my point here is to show that deeper connections can be perceived between the two ostensibly antagonistic male protagonists, and that therefore Rochester is as much Bluebeard in the Gothic nightmarish third story as in the domestic second story of a fallen woman's daughter.

Indeed, first of all, the redoubling of female models is Rochester's doing. When he comes back to Thornfield Hall, the presents he has brought to his ward have a view to changing Adèle into a ghost-like miniature model of her own mother ("a miniature of Céline Varens", 119). Beneath the offerings the text spreads clues concerning Rochester's murdering potential, his capacity to change little girls into dead figures of the past, to renew his macabre cabinet of curios. Besides, the box he has brought Adèle, which contains porcelain and ivory works of art, as well as clothes, objectifies the little coquette and fashions her as a commodity woman, but also emphasizes Rochester's criminal propensity: the little chest hosts a deadly manuscript. In fact, Rochester's generosity aims at dissecting the little girl's vanity, so as to show, to quote his own words, how coquetry "runs in her blood, blends with her brains, and seasons the marrow of her bones" (119). Rochester-the-ogre ("Do you suppose I eat like an ogre, or a ghoul, that you dread being the companion of my repast?", 230), whose first wife is to him a "fierce ragout" (251) and whose sexuality is often seen in terms of "hunger and thirst" (269), has manifestly a taste for female flesh ("he seemed to devour me", 271). Rochester's description of Adèle's opening of her present strengthens the parallel with the murderous male, since the box—a metonymical image of the commodity woman—changes the male protagonist into an anatomist, eager to dismember the female body:

> "Yes—there is your "boîte" at last: take it into a corner, you genuine daughter of Paris, and amuse yourself with disembowelling it [...] And [...] don't bother me with any details of the anatomical process, or any notice of the condition of the entrails: let your operation be conducted in silence— tiens-toi tranquille, enfant ; comprends-tu ?" *(110)*

The figure of the anatomist, as Elizabeth Bronfen's discussion highlights, brings into play how the female corpse, as "a perfect, immaculate aesthetic form", not only suggests erotic pleasure through its inaccessibility but above all encapsulates male power (Bronfen 5). The anatomist, who cuts open female bodies to produce authoritative texts, who verifies texts by thrusting his knife into the female flesh, is a particularly significant example of male desire for the dead female body (Bronfen 6), cloaking unequal gender relationships beneath a scientific discourse and rewriting the fetish in power terms. Beautified because dead, exposed yet contained by the male scientist's knife, Adèle is a revised image of the actress who has evaded Rochester's power and denied the patriarchal scripts: the doll-like stereotype is turned into a ghostly figure doomed to die (as her own mother Céline did), trained in the handling of the tropes of her own death by playing with ivory bits and pieces, as so many body parts dismembered. In this way, female bodies, whether symbolically disembowelled by the master or metaphorically buried in Thornfield Hall, are all "companionless [...] prisoner[s] in [their] dungeon[s]" (140) whom the master seldom visits, bringing them poisoned gifts merely meant to reflect and reinforce their impotent position as morbidly fetishized objects. The boundaries between Bertha and Adèle collapse, as both are isolated, not to be shown to visitors, and are constructed as living embodiments of capitalism (as heiress or commodity). Hence, Jane witnesses the disruption of liminal structures so typical to female Gothic narratives, gradually realizing that the self and the other are one and the same, that all women are alike and that woman's fate in patriarchal society is a mere repetition of stories always telling the same story (the "fateful third story", 177), whether the heroine is a beautiful and rich—thus independent—Creole turned into a devilish wild beast or a poor sexually degraded actress changed into a doll lying on the table of the male anatomist.

As already suggested, Rochester interweaves the female models, fuses the stories, holding the key to interpret male power. The fallen, monstrous, Oriental female models that partake of Rochester's sexual past are all living-dead female characters haunting the three stories of Thornfield Hall, and always appearing as potential wives for the omnipotent master. The ghost-like Adèle, as a visionary reproduction of Rochester's mistress, who sings and dances to mimic her mother; the beautiful Blanche Ingram who plays the part of a bride happily well provided for to mime the famous prison Bridewell in the charade scene, ironically donning the costumes from the wardrobes of the third story, and who merely repeats "sounding phrases from books" (158); and of course Jane, just before her wedding, when she sees her own nuptial garments and compares them to the ghostly belongings of the future bride:

> Mrs Rochester! She did not exist: she would not be born till to-morrow, some time after eight o'clock A.M.; and I would wait to be assured she had come into the world alive before I assigned to her all that property. It was enough that in yonder closet, opposite my dressing-table, garments said to be hers had already displaced my black stuff Lowood frock and straw bonnet: for not to me appertained that suit of wedding raiment, the pearl-coloured robe, the vapoury veil, pendent from the usurped portmanteau. I shut the closet, to conceal the strange, wraith-like apparel it contained; which, at this evening hour—nine o'clock—gave out certainly a most ghostly shimmer through the shadow of my apartment. *(234-235)*

The vision of selfless, alienated and ghostly women, brides, or mistresses locked up in the attic, in a prison, in a box or in a closet changes the main plot into a series of murderous subplots. Therefore, as the narrative suggests, Jane's initial reference to *Bluebeard*'s tale, or rather *Bluebeard*'s tales ("some Bluebeard") seems to be the ideal narrative short-cut to rework Gothic images and insert them within a clichéd plot. As we have seen, the *Bluebeard* textual layer directs the narrative less towards the secret of sex and male sexual guilt than towards a reading of the story of woman's fate within the institution of marriage. The murdered wives hanging on the ceiling, dripping blood, hint at the fate of the newly wedded bride, mirroring her own position and pointing out her future: the horror story of femininity in a male-dominated society. Through her rewriting of Gothic motifs of death, dread, and boundlessness, of frightful timeless figures, Charlotte Brontë creates a world of ghostlike women, a collection of potential corpses all hanging in the attic of Thornfield Hall and awaiting their doom. The child's tale becomes an adult's horror story—a Gothic tale rooted in the world of reality: as a horrible fairy tale foregrounding the husband as a serial killer, *Bluebeard* stands out as the most pregnant Gothic narrative to magnify a macabre process of repetition leading women to experience the same fate over and over again.

The closure of the fairy-tale story, Jane's romance with her master, thus depends on the changes Jane makes in the scenario to rewrite "the end of the chapter" (229). It is only through deciphering the fictional material of her own existence that she can add new scenes to a crystallized plot and change the male "despot[…]" (234) into a new version of Prince Charming. Jane will indeed not "pluck out [her] right eye" or "cut off [her] right hand" (254) as the voices of the female characters from *Cinderella* seem to intimate to her. On the contrary, she will have the male protagonist suffer physical mutilation before marrying him. In this new story, the woman holds a "penknife" (112) to carve the hero of her dreams, and she magically gains her own independence whilst the man suffers in silence and obedience. Far from the novels of Ann Radcliffe, with their female characters left to starve and die locked up in a turret or passively awaiting their saviors, mad with anxiety, Brontë's fiction proposes an alternative way of phrasing her perception of the horrors of domesticity within the world of Victorian England. Her heroine's exploration of the scripts which define women, her search for independence and her attempt at freeing herself from textual bondage seems then to secure her marital happiness, thereby matching the positive aspects Anne Williams reads in female Gothic quests. However, disturbingly enough, Jane is never given a chance to actually *read* the third story, the latter being read to her on her wedding day, forcing her passively to consume a Gothic tale instead of consuming her marriage. Worse still, though Bertha's setting fire to the story purges Thornfield Hall from the patriarchal scripts of enclosure and allows Jane to rewrite her romance in more equal terms, in an uncanny way, Adèle's story never burns, nor crumbles into dust, leaving one fatal manuscript to continue haunting the heroine's story. Put away in a school, pale, thin and unhappy, Adèle is trained into female education, and "corrected [from] her French defects" (383) so to be moulded and shaped as a docile creature. Dysphoric notes do jar at the end of the tale, therefore, with all the female characters happily married, whilst little Adèle, thoroughly secluded, is patiently educated and learns how to abide by the laws of patriarchy.

Bibliography

BRONFEN, Elizabeth, *Over her Dead Body: Death, Femininity and the Aesthetic*, Manchester: Manchester University Press, 1992.

DELAMOTTE, Eugenia C., *Perils of the Night: A Feminist Study of Nineteenth-Century Gothic*, Oxford: Oxford University Press, 1990.

FLEENOR, Juliann E., ed., *The Female Gothic*, London: Eden Press, 1983.

GILBERT, Sandra and Susan GUBAR, *The Madwoman in the Attic: the Woman Writer and the Nineteenth-Century Literary Imagination* [1978], New Haven: Yale University Press, 1984.

MODLESKI, Tania, *Loving With a Vengeance: Mass-produced Fantasies for Women* [1982], London: Routledge, 1990.

MOERS, Ellen, "Female Gothic", *Literary Women*, London: The Women's Press Limited, 1978.

PUNTER, David, *Gothic Pathologies: The Text, the Body and the Law*, London: Macmillan, 1998.

WILLIAMS, Anne, *Art of Darkness: A Poetics of Gothic*, Chicago: University of Chicago Press, 1995.

La construction de l'ipséité textuelle dans *Jane Eyre* à partir de certaines figures archétypales de rebelles et de tyrans

Pascale Denance

Publié en 1847, à une époque où le personnage féminin a peu d'antécédents littéraires de grande envergure encore et reste très largement à construire, *Jane Eyre* frappe par la complexité de sa composition, la diversité de ses emprunts, et la profondeur de son personnage principal. Alors que la conception du personnage féminin qui prévalait alors n'était pas très différente de celle qu'entretenait Aristote, la première moitié du XIXe siècle, grâce notamment à des auteurs comme Charlotte Brontë, a été transformée en période d'expérimentation, dans laquelle s'est constitué un véritable laboratoire de recherche à propos du genre en littérature (le terme est entendu ici au sens de *gender*). Les matériaux disponibles, c'est-à-dire, de fait, quelques héroïnes shakespeariennes, de rares personnages au cours du siècle précédent, ainsi que les *persona* de certains romans de Jane Austen, doivent donc être utilisés au mieux. Plus en amont, certaines figures anciennes représentent une source d'inspiration, mais aussi un paradigme dangereux. Parfois figés en stéréotypes, ces modèles prestigieux sont en effet susceptibles d'entraver, autant que de faciliter, l'élaboration de ces constructions discursives que sont les personnages.

Le fait d'examiner, dans le roman de Brontë, les traces intertextuelles de trois figures archétypales, Lilith, Antigone et la femme de Barbe-Bleue, permet de faire apparaître un *pattern* dans ce dernier, mais aussi d'apprécier les stratégies argumentatives spécifiques qui sont les siennes. Posant un regard sur le monde à partir d'un point de vue différent, cette œuvre se préoccupe de subjectivité littéraire en privilégiant l'exploration d'une conscience de femme. La perspective de genre et la complexité du personnage éponyme sont à l'origine d'une vision novatrice du sujet, qui annonce les concepts ricœuriens de mêmeté et d'ipséité. Selon Ricœur, qui explique dans *Soi-même comme un autre* que l'altérité fait partie du sujet à part entière par le biais de ce qu'il nomme l'ipséité, il convient en effet de « dissocier deux significations majeures de l'identité, selon que l'on entend par identique l'équivalent de l'*idem* ou de l'*ipse* latin » (Ricœur 12). Il s'agit ici de lire la construction en palimpseste de *Jane Eyre* à la lumière de ces concepts.

La figure d'Antigone

Plus que tout autre roman du XIXᵉ siècle, *Jane Eyre* est l'expression d'une révolte, un cri de souffrance et de colère, comme beaucoup de critiques l'ont souligné. Certaines scènes de l'enfance de l'héroïne sont d'une grande violence. Le premier acte de rébellion se situe au tout début du roman, quand Jane, dont l'indignation est plus forte que sa terreur, se résout à se défendre contre l'agression de son cousin, un adolescent brutal et tyrannique qui la persécute continuellement. Cette révolte rappelle celle d'Antigone, laquelle demeure la figure classique de la rébellion d'une femme contre un pouvoir patriarcal. La version proposée par la tragédie de Sophocle ne laisse en effet aucun doute sur le fait qu'il s'agit de la révolte d'une femme face au pouvoir d'un homme. Créon le précise de façon explicite, qu'il s'adresse directement à Antigone : « Moi vivant, ce n'est pas une femme qui fera la loi » (v. 524), ou à son fils : « Il ne faut jamais plier devant une femme. Je tomberai s'il le faut, mais sous les coups d'un homme. On ne dira pas qu'une femme m'a vaincu » (v. 678-680). Comme Lacan l'a indiqué, Antigone est du côté de la mort : « Antigone mène jusqu'à la limite l'accomplissement de ce que l'on peut appeler le désir pur, le pur et simple désir de mort comme tel. Ce désir, elle l'incarne » (Lacan 1986, 329). Jane Eyre, quant à elle, apprend à faire face aux nombreuses vicissitudes qui sont les siennes. Elle envisage de « se laisser mourir » lors de son enfermement dans « la chambre rouge », enfermement qui est une épreuve redoutable pour elle, car il a lieu dans la pièce où était décédé Mr Reed (12), et la tentation de mourir survient de nouveau après qu'elle s'est enfuie de Thornfield (281), mais elle n'y cède pas. Elle précise d'ailleurs que sa fuite ne s'accomplit pas dans un esprit de sacrifice, mais qu'elle est nécessaire pour préserver sa dignité. Adrienne Rich l'a noté :

> In this whole portion of the novel, in which Jane moves through the landscape utterly alone, there is a strong counterpull between female self-immolation—the temptation of passive suicide—and the will and courage which are her survival tools. *(Rich 480)*

Jane Eyre incarne la révolte d'Antigone épurée de l'obsession pour la mort. En combinant les pulsions de vie et de mort, en refusant le schéma passif de la tentation du suicide représenté par le modèle d'Antigone et en choisissant de façon répétée la vie sur la mort, le texte de Charlotte Brontë illustre de façon magistrale l'observation de Levinas : « Il y a dans la mort la tentation du néant de Lucrèce, et le désir de l'éternité de Pascal. Ce ne sont pas deux attitudes distinctes : nous voulons à la fois mourir et être » (Levinas 66).

Il y a aussi un aspect dérisoire à la rébellion d'Antigone, qui suscite l'incompréhension (tout cela pour quelques poignées de poussière ! serait-on tenté de s'exclamer—ou bien encore : « *much ado about nothing* ») car elle est vouée à l'échec, ce qu'Ismène, moins téméraire, certes, mais peut-être aussi plus sage que sa sœur perçoit bien :

> N'oublie pas que nous sommes femmes et que nous n'aurons jamais raison contre des hommes. Le roi est le roi : il nous faut bien obéir à son ordre, et peut-être à de plus cruels encore. Que nos morts sous la terre me le pardonnent, mais je n'ai pas le choix ; je m'inclinerai devant le pouvoir. C'est folie d'entreprendre plus qu'on ne peut. *(Sophocle, v. 58-67)*

Le roman de Charlotte Brontë reprend, à travers la confrontation entre Jane et Helen, le couple d'oppositions constitué par Antigone et Ismène, non sans lui avoir fait subir un certain nombre de transformations décisives. C'est Helen la soumise, subissant son sort sans se plaindre, qui meurt, alors que Jane, la révoltée, partant sans cesse en guerre contre les injustices en se heurtant au mur d'*impedimenta* érigé par son environnement, garde la vie sauve.

À l'instar de l'héroïne de la pièce de Sophocle, Jane Eyre, Antigone moderne, se pose comme un sujet. Elle attache la même importance au fait de renoncer dans la dignité à tout ce qui choque son sens de la justice. Mais il existe une différence de taille : contrairement à son modèle, elle reste en vie. Peut-être consentir à mourir reviendrait-il à accepter prématurément, et donc inutilement, la métamorphose en objet. Dans la grammaire du genre et de ses représentations, Antigone ne fonctionne-t-elle pas comme l'exception qui confirme la règle, renforçant ainsi, au lieu de l'affaiblir, le stéréotype qui confine les femmes dans une sphère restreinte ? Le dessein de la réécriture de l'archétype à laquelle se livre le roman de Charlotte Brontë est au contraire de sortir le personnage féminin de son statut d'exception, poursuivant en cela la vaste entreprise de réalignement de ce dernier qui commence au début du XIXe siècle avec Jane Austen. L'ambition n'est plus seulement de déroger à la règle qui constitue le masculin en référent générique, mais de changer cette règle — en faisant pression sur la grammaire du sujet et en inaugurant pour ce faire une référence dédoublée.

Le mythe de Lilith

Le mythe de Lilith est très présent dans *Jane Eyre*, dans lequel est transposé le triangle formé par Lilith, Adam et Eve. Lors de la tentative de mariage avortée, Rochester compare défavorablement à Jane Eyre sa première femme,

Bertha, jugée déplaisante et malfaisante. Le contraste entre les deux femmes est tel que la première rappelle Lilith, tandis que la deuxième, jeune, soumise, innocente, évoque Eve telle qu'elle est décrite avant la faute. Mais qui est Lilith ? Elle est décrite ainsi dans *Le Judaïsme au féminin* :

> Lilith, dans la littérature midrachique, fut la première femme créée par Dieu. [...] Dans l'Alfabeta de Ben Sira, du IXe ou Xe siècle, Lilith est mieux définie. Première femme donnée par Dieu à l'homme, tirée elle aussi de la terre, elle se heurte à Adam pour s'assurer de sa prééminence; leurs querelles sont constantes. Lilith, n'y tenant plus, prononce le tétragramme — YHWH, un des noms de Dieu qu'il est interdit de prononcer — et disparaît dans les airs. *(Gdalia et Goldmann 164-165)*

Lilith concentre les phantasmes de l'inconscient collectif qui se sont organisés autour du mythe de la première femme, morte ou disparue dans des conditions étranges. Représente-elle la radicalité de l'autre exemplifiée dans l'opposition binaire entre le masculin et le féminin ? Comme le fait remarquer plaisamment Lacan, considérer l'effacement de la présence de Lilith ne résout pas les contradictions apparentes dans l'épisode biblique de la création d'Adam et Eve :

> Il n'est pas vrai que Dieu les fit mâle et femelle, si c'est le dire du couple d'Adam et Eve, comme aussi bien le contredit expressément le mythe ultra-condensé que l'on trouve dans le même texte sur la création de la compagne.
> Sans doute y avait-il d'auparavant Lilith, mais elle n'arrange rien. *(Lacan 1966, 849-850)*

Le personnage de Lilith n'apparaît effectivement pas en tant que tel dans la Bible, ce qui incite à supposer que certains de ses traits apparaissent dans la représentation qui est proposée d'Eve. Figure double, cette dernière semble en effet être une synthèse résultant de la condensation de deux entités plus anciennes. Cette dualité se retrouve dans l'ambiguïté de ses évocations en littérature, où son image est tantôt celle de l'innocence, tantôt celle de la culpabilité. Certains personnages combinant ces deux aspects, un glissement s'opère parfois de la figure d'Eve vers celle de Lilith au cours du texte, comme c'est le cas dans *Jane Eyre*. C'est la figure d'Eve avant la faute qui semble stabilisée dans le personnage éponyme ; mais malgré toute l'innocence que lui prête Rochester, Jane fait néanmoins la grave erreur de tenter d'avoir accès à la connaissance, provoquant une mise en garde : « *don't turn out a downright Eve on my hands!* » (223). Et elle se révèle également capable de prononcer une remarque déterminante qui semble venir tout droit du discours revendicatif de Lilith : « *equal,—as we are!* » (216).

Helen et Bertha, qui encadrent Jane Eyre, meurent toutes deux, la laissant ainsi au centre de l'intrigue. En tant que, respectivement, « actant adjuvant » et « actant opposant », selon la terminologie de Greimas (voir Greimas 178-180), elles ont rempli leur fonction dans le roman, celle d'aider la protagoniste à s'acheminer vers la maturité et la réalisation de soi. En tant qu'éléments symboliques, elles fonctionnent comme des projections de l'héroïne et représentent ses parties reniées, peu acceptables ou peu humaines. Enfin, elles correspondent aussi à deux grands archétypes littéraires, la folle et la sainte. Le même parallélisme se retrouve dans le traitement des personnages masculins, Rochester se trouvant lui aussi encadré de deux personnages extrêmes, l'un dans la sainteté, l'autre dans l'abjection. L'onomastique venant renforcer l'effet de parallélisme dans l'opposition, ils sont d'ailleurs appelés John et St John. Eux aussi seront éliminés du récit par le biais de leur mort au niveau de la diégèse. Est ainsi instauré dans chaque cas un continuum positionnant chaque personnage principal au mitan d'une ligne bornée par deux points extrêmes, de sorte que ce personnage semble se situer dans un juste milieu. Comparée à celle de Bertha, la révolte de Jane Eyre paraît ainsi « modérée ».

Lilith est celle qui surgit du passé, « d'auparavant », comme le précise Lacan. Certaines des traces qu'elle a laissées dans la figure biblique d'Eve sont incorporées dans *Jane Eyre* à travers le couple d'oppositions constitué par Jane et Bertha, mais surtout à travers Bertha elle-même, qui, ayant été mise à l'écart, revient sans cesse troubler les vivants, et dont les attaques inattendues symbolisent ce que Lacan nomme « le retour du refoulé ».

Réécriture du conte de Barbe-Bleue

L'emprisonnement du personnage de Bertha correspond aussi à celui de la femme de Barbe-Bleue et à celui de « toutes les femmes que la Barbe bleue avait épousées et qu'il avait égorgées l'une après l'autre » (Perrault 223). *Jane Eyre* est, en un sens, une réécriture du célèbre conte. Plusieurs échos permettent de discerner cette filiation directe : la tour, l'escalier, le couloir menant à la pièce dans laquelle est enfermée une femme, le leitmotiv de la clef et du sang, et enfin, l'interdit arbitraire, qui semble cacher un terrible secret. Contrairement aux mythes d'Antigone et de Lilith, qui sont seulement évoqués, ce conte imprime dans le roman, sous la forme du château de Barbe bleue, lequel est explicitement mentionné, une trace intertextuelle manifeste :

> Mrs Fairfax stayed behind a moment to fasten the trap-door; I, by dint of groping, found the outlet from the attic, and proceeded to descend the narrow garret staircase. I lingered in the long passage to which this led, separating the front and back rooms of the third story: narrow, low, and dim, with only one little window at the far end, and looking, with its two rows of small black doors all shut, like a corridor in some Bluebeard's castle. *(91)*

La descente qu'effectue Jane Eyre est une reprise de celle de la femme de Barbe-Bleue, qui doit descendre « par un petit escalier dérobé » pour atteindre le « cabinet » interdit. L'environnement métonymique renvoie donc cette fois-ci le personnage de Jane Eyre à la femme de Barbe-Bleue, ce que notent Sandra Gilbert et Susan Gubar, dans *The Madwoman in the Attic*, ouvrage dont le titre a été inspiré par ce personnage de Bertha dans Jane Eyre :

> And just above this sinister corridor, leaning against the picturesque battlements and looking out over the world like Bluebeard's bride's sister Anne, Jane is to long again for freedom [...] *(Gilbert and Gubar 348)*

Le passage dans lequel Jane est enfermée avec un inconnu, qui, blessé, doit être soigné de toute urgence, se caractérise par l'accent mis, d'une part, sur le lien métonymique entre deux motifs empruntés au conte (les clefs et le sang qui ne cesse de s'écouler) et sur la présence opaque du secret ténébreux, d'autre part. La concentration des motifs omniprésents dans *La Barbe bleue* font de cet épisode comme un microcosme du conte. Il y a un écho direct du texte de Perrault dans la description que propose la narratrice de sa nuit de veille :

> Here then I was in the third story, fastened into one of its mystic cells; night around me; a pale and bloody spectacle under my eyes and hands; a murderess hardly separated from me by a single door [...] *(179)*

Les citations comparatives permettent de faire émerger non seulement l'intertexte, mais encore les déplacements par rapport au schéma initial. L'insistance sur la réapparition du sang qui s'écoule de la blessure (« *You will sponge the blood when it returns* », 178) constitue une reprise de celle, dans le conte, sur le sang qui refuse d'être effacé : « il y demeura toujours du sang, car la clef était Fée, [...] quand on ôtait le sang d'un côté, il revenait de l'autre ». Dans un phénomène de transsubstantiation littéraire, le sang des femmes mortes de *La Barbe bleue*, qui s'était imprimé de façon indélébile sur la clef enchantée, a été transféré sur un homme, Mason, le frère de Bertha. Dans un entrelacs complexe d'oppositions et de croisements, c'est le personnage éponyme qui est devenu « Fée », Jane étant souvent qualifiée ainsi par Rochester, qui décline tous les synonymes du terme, pour finalement jeter son dévolu sur une appellation duelle : « *fairy-born and human-bred* » (373). Au-delà du questionnement sur l'appartenance au monde féerique et à travers la réalité singulière de ce questionnement à propos de Jane, le problème posé ici est celui, plus général, de la dualité identitaire.

Lors de cette longue veille macabre, Jane ne manque pas de se poser des questions : « *What crime was this, that lived incarnate in this sequestered mansion, and could neither be expelled nor subdued by the owner?—What mystery, that broke out, now in fire and now in blood, at the deadest hours of night?* » (179). Par le biais d'expressions convenues, comme « *sequestered mansion* », qui renvoie à un univers gothique, ou bien encore de la métaphore figée du superlatif « *the deadest* », l'énonciation renforce le déplacement entre la situation de la narratrice dans la diégèse et l'univers métaphorique convoqué par ses mots, qui lui donnent une posture d'héroïne de conte. Les similitudes et les écarts sont de nouveau apparents : l'interdiction de parler dont est frappée Jane Eyre n'est pas si différente de celle, plus littérale, d'ouvrir une porte, ressort principal de l'intrigue dans *La Barbe bleue*, car métaphoriquement, l'interdit verbal correspond à la défense d'ouvrir la porte sur un autre monde. Rappelons également que Jane a été sommée d'éviter l'étage où est enfermée (dans le plus grand secret) la première femme de Rochester. Plus tard, lorsqu'elle formule à haute voix ses questionnements, sa curiosité rencontre l'effroi de Rochester. Il craint ses questions—elle pressent un lourd secret. Mais contrairement à son homologue dans le conte de Perrault, elle ne tente pas de passer outre l'interdit.

À travers l'opposition entre les personnages de Bertha et de Jane, c'est le conflit entre deux aspects de la condition féminine qui est retracé dans *Jane Eyre*. L'évocation littéraire de l'ambivalence entre l'attirance pour le prince charmant et la crainte du tyran contribue à mettre en scène la tension entre deux états conflictuels du sujet. L'étude de la réécriture de symboles récurrents, comme la clef et la tour dans laquelle la princesse est retenue captive, éléments métonymiques signifiant l'enfermement symbolique du personnage féminin, permet d'appréhender ce roman dans sa dimension de conte. Jane Eyre, par contraste, échappe à ce destin convenu. Elle devient autonome à la fin du roman, à une époque où seule l'indépendance financière pouvait apporter l'autonomie à une femme, mais grâce à l'héritage d'un oncle, ce qui ne la rend pas dépendante de son futur mari. Rochester jouerait volontiers au despote, il est comparé à plusieurs reprises à un pacha ou un sultan, mais il en est empêché par la diégèse. Les subversions de l'hypotexte se font toutes dans l'atténuation. D'une part, la prisonnière est vivante, contrairement aux femmes de la Barbe bleue, qui ont été assassinées. D'autre part, Jane Eyre a la possibilité de s'enfuir lorsque le secret est éventé et Rochester n'est pas tué à cette occasion, mais rendu aveugle.

La construction du personnage

Jane est différente selon l'aune à laquelle elle se voit mesurée : elle ressemble à Antigone quand elle est comparée à Helen, qui est un parangon de soumission, mais elle a l'innocence d'Eve par rapport à Bertha, qui a des accents de Lilith. Un personnage est une conception composite, un ensemble de mots créant un effet de sens et une apparence de spécificité. Une sélection s'opère, par exérèses répétées, par évidements, comme l'on détacherait des éléments d'un bloc à sculpter, mais aussi par l'amalgame d'une série de *je* successifs, de fragments de sujet, qui participent à la construction d'une entité élusive. A cela s'ajoutent les modalités illocutoires du personnage, c'est-à-dire les façons qu'a l'instance narratrice de s'adresser à l'instance narrataire, que le narrateur peut appeler « *reader* », comme le fait Jane Eyre. Le personnage, en tant qu'élément textuel, est construit par la lecture, dans un processus permettant de le faire apparaître et nécessitant l'adhésion du lecteur, qui doit accepter d'admettre l'existence de l'unité illusoire du personnage ainsi créé. Pour permettre la démarche que Coleridge nomme « *that willing suspension of disbelief for the moment* » (Biographia Literaria, chapitre 14), le texte doit nécessairement donner quelques éléments d'illusion d'unité ; nous devons pouvoir croire, au moins un instant, en la structure qui nous est présentée.

Après les scènes de l'enfance, une remise en question des schémas convenus du XIXe siècle apparaît de façon plus élaborée dans l'épisode Thornfield, par exemple dans un monologue intérieur fréquemment cité :

> Anybody may blame me who likes [...]. Women are supposed to be very calm generally: but women feel just as men feel; they need exercise for their faculties, and a field for their efforts as much as their brothers do; they suffer from too rigid a restraint, too absolute a stagnation, precisely as men would suffer; and it is narrow-minded in their more privileged fellow-creatures to say that they ought to confine themselves to making puddings and knitting stockings, to playing on the piano and embroidering bags. It is thoughtless to condemn them, or laugh at them, if they seek to do more or learn more than custom has pronounced necessary for their sex. *(92-93)*

Ce passage a souvent été commenté. Comparons deux lectures fort différentes, voire opposées : Virginia Woolf considère que ce passage trahit l'indignation et la colère de son auteur :

> One might say, I continued, laying the book down beside *Pride and Prejudice*, that the woman who wrote those pages had more genius in her than Jane Austen; but if

> one reads them over and marks that jerk in them, that indignation, one sees that she will never get her genius expressed whole and entire. Her books will be deformed and twisted. She will write foolishly where she should write wisely. She will write of herself where she should write of her characters. *(Woolf 66-67)*

En d'autres termes, la conscience de l'oppression et l'expression de la colère ne devraient pas apparaître en littérature, ce qui correspond à l'opinion de nombreux critiques du XIXe siècle et du début du XXe siècle. Voici maintenant l'analyse que fait Adrienne Rich du même passage de *Jane Eyre* :

> The phrase ["anybody may blame me who likes..."] introduces a passage which is Charlotte Brontë's feminist manifesto. Written one hundred and twenty-six years ago, it is still having to be written over and over today, in different language but with essentially the same sense that sentiments of this kind are still unacceptable to many, and that in uttering them one lays open to blame and to entrenched resistance [...] *(Rich 475)*

Rich pense au contraire que non seulement ce type d'expression n'est pas incongru en littérature, mais encore qu'il est important de lui accorder une place. Les deux critiques n'écrivent pas à la même date et n'ont pas le même recul. Cela semble indiquer que la lecture critique, qui prend la forme plus précisément ici de la discussion de ce qui devrait ou non entrer dans la composition d'un personnage, ne saurait être totalement exempte de biais idéologique. De fait, on assiste dans *Jane Eyre* à une transformation des dispositifs rhétoriques qui construisaient jusqu'alors l'image de la femme en littérature. L'image d'une nouvelle construction, « *The New Woman* », n'est pas encore en place pour venir suppléer au modèle victorien de « l'Ange du foyer », *the Angel in the House*. Un nouveau paradigme est en train de se former, dans un espace conceptuel controversé. Le texte prend ainsi des allures de Janus à deux visages : soumission aux mœurs d'une époque d'un côté et ruse offensive de l'autre. Mais le trait le plus frappant dans la construction du personnage de Jane Eyre demeure la multiplicité et la diversité des références qui participent à son élaboration :

> In *Jane Eyre*, Brontë attempts to depict a complete female identity, and she expresses her heroine's consciousness through an extraordinary range of narrative devices. Psychological development and the dramas of the inner life are represented in dreams, hallucinations, visions, surrealistic paintings, and masquerades; the sexual experiences of the female body are expressed spatially through elaborate and rhythmically recurring images of

> rooms and houses. Jane's growth is further structured
> through a pattern of literary, biblical, and mythological
> allusion. *(Showalter 112-113)*

La constitution d'un texte donné se fait à partir d'un texte extérieur, dont il se sépare tout en l'intégrant en partie—auquel il ressemble sans pourtant être semblable. Métaphore la plus exacte de la subjectivité, la réécriture, et plus particulièrement celle du personnage, met ainsi au jour la dialectique de la mêmeté et de l'ipséité :

> Dans la fiction littéraire, l'espace de variations ouvert aux rapports entre les deux modalités d'identité est immense. À une extrémité, le personnage est un caractère identifiable et réidentifiable comme même : c'est à peu près le statut du personnage des contes de fées et du folklore. Quant au roman classique — de *La Princesse de Clèves* ou du roman anglais du XVIIIe siècle à Dostoïevski et Tolstoï, on peut dire qu'il a exploré l'espace intermédiaire de variations où, à travers les transformations du personnage, l'identification du même décroît sans disparaître. On se rapproche du pôle inverse avec le roman dit d'apprentissage et, plus encore, le roman du courant de conscience. Le rapport entre intrigue et personnage paraît alors s'inverser : au contraire du modèle aristotélicien, l'intrigue est mise au service du personnage. C'est alors que l'identité de ce dernier, échappant au contrôle de l'intrigue et de son principe d'ordre, est mise véritablement à l'épreuve. On atteint ainsi le pôle extrême de variation, où le personnage a cessé d'être un caractère. *(Ricœur 176)*

L'ipséité du personnage à l'intérieur du texte est problématisée dans *Jane Eyre*, roman qui peut être situé assez près du pôle de l'ipséité dans le continuum déterminé par Ricœur : par son patchwork identitaire, sa vision kaléidoscopique du personnage éponyme, *Jane Eyre* nous semble très moderne, très proche par certains côtés du courant littéraire désigné sous l'appellation de *stream of consciousness*.

La réflexion sur sujet et genre dans ce roman s'inscrit dans une faille, qui n'est pas seulement littéraire, mais qui reflète également les conceptions du sujet-femme dans la première moitié du XIXe siècle en Angleterre. Le décalage entre l'ancien schéma qui n'est plus suffisant et le nouveau qui est encore à construire engendre un espace de transition, un espace paradoxal, oxymorique, fait à la fois de douleur et d'espoir : « *the Angel in the House* » n'est plus crédible, « *the New Woman* », très inspirée par les modèles américains, n'est pas encore en place. Il n'y a pas d'échappatoire possible, car les structures ne sont pas encore là. Le texte littéraire est paradoxal, en ce sens qu'il expose les vides, les absences, en même temps qu'il crée des potentialités. En montrant les aspirations très fortes d'un personnage et l'inadéquation avec le contexte socioculturel de l'époque, le roman de Brontë non seulement construit des mondes conceptuels mais encore contribue par son écriture à l'existence de ces nouvelles éventualités.

Certains seulement des archétypes qui ont présidé à la construction de Jane Eyre ont été examinés ici. Il est important de souligner leur métamorphose : la révolte d'Antigone, qui, impuissante dans sa rébellion, représente une cause perdue d'avance, a été transformée en révolte de vie. Lilith l'exclue, la rebelle dangereuse, a été intégrée dans une revendication d'égalité. La femme de Barbe-Bleue, qui finit par triompher dans son combat contre l'injustice et par se libérer du joug d'un despote, cesse d'être une figure anonyme. Jane Eyre intègre la force du mythe sans toutefois céder à la tentation du stéréotype. Ces archétypes renvoient, par associations métonymiques, à d'autres, et sont ainsi autant de synecdoques de systèmes plus larges. Transférables, évolutifs, les mondes sémiotiques et identitaires convoqués, dont les frontières s'entrecroisent dans le roman, se dilatent, se contractent ou s'estompent dans la réécriture. De leur plasticité dépendent la complexité et la polysémie de ce roman en forme de palimpseste, qui représente l'aboutissement d'une condensation d'éléments, dans un ensemble de convergences littéraires.

L'étude des adaptations dont ces archétypes sont l'objet met également au jour la difficile intégration de l'ipséité dans la construction identitaire. L'entrelacs des références tisse une identité kaléidoscopique et conflictuelle permettant d'aller au-delà du modèle cartésien sans pour autant enfermer le sujet divisé ainsi créé dans une conception aporétique. La tension entre les éléments reconnaissables de l'hypotexte et la trace des transformations de ce dernier dans le texte étudié est une mise en abyme de la dialectique entre la mêmeté et l'ipséité à l'œuvre dans *Jane Eyre*. Ce roman iconoclaste, qui célèbre le refus en tant que ressort de changement, met en lumière le lien entre l'ipséité du personnage, ses vacillements et glissements identitaires, et sa révolte. Ce n'est en effet qu'en refusant tour à tour les modèles identitaires insatisfaisants qui lui sont proposés tout au long de son parcours que Jane Eyre se trouve en mesure de surmonter la peur et la souffrance, tant physique qu'émotionnelle, de puiser dans l'énergie de la révolte les moyens de sa survie, et enfin d'accéder à l'équilibre, si fragile soit-il, qu'elle finit par atteindre à la fin du roman. Le devenir de l'être, semble suggérer le texte de Brontë, passe par le refus d'être, puis, en dernière analyse, par celui de ne pas être…

Bibliographie

ARISTOTE, *Poétique*, tr. M. Magnien, Librairie Générale Française, Livre de Poche classique, 1990.

COLERIDGE, Samuel Taylor, *Biographia Literaria* (1817), London: J.M. Dent & Sons, New York, Dutton & Co, 1947.

GILBERT, Sandra, and Susan Gubar, *The Madwoman in the Attic: The Woman Writer and the Nineteenth Century Literary Imagination*, New Haven and London: Yale University Press, 1979.

GDALIA, Janine, et Annie Goldmann, *Le Judaïsme au féminin*, Éditions Balland, 1989.

GREIMAS, A.J., *Sémantique structurale*, Paris, Librairie Larousse, 1966.

LACAN, Jacques, « Antigone dans l'entre-deux-morts », *Le Séminaire, livre VII, L'éthique de la psychanalyse*, Paris, Éditions du Seuil, 1986.

— « Position de l'inconscient », *Écrits*, Paris, Éditions du Seuil, 1966.

LEVINAS, Emmanuel, *Le Temps et l'autre* (1948), Paris, Presses Universitaires de France, 1983.

PERRAULT, Charles, *Barbe-Bleue*, (1697), *Contes*, Classiques de Poche, Paris, Librairie Générale Française, 2006.

RICŒUR, Paul, *Soi-même comme un autre*, Paris, Éditions du Seuil, 1990.

RICH, Adrienne, « Jane Eyre: The Temptations of a Motherless Woman », *in* Charlotte Brontë, *Jane Eyre*, ed., Richard Dunn, New York, London: Norton, 2001.

SHOWALTER, Elaine, *A Literature of Their Own, British Women Novelists from Brontë to Lessing*, London: Virago, 1978.

SOPHOCLE, *Antigone, Théâtre complet*, tr. R. Pignarre, Paris, Garnier-Flammarion, 1964.

WOOLF, Virginia, *A Room of One's Own* (1928), London: Panther Books, Granada Publishing, 1963.

Le théâtre intérieur ou le sens caché de *Jane Eyre* : « *the secret voice* » (133), « *the still small voice* » (172)

Max Duperray

À l'instar des narrateurs de la première personne, l'héroïne de Charlotte Brontë est beaucoup sujette à l'introspection. Au comble du mélodrame, Jane est la proie d'un débat intérieur impérieux. Dans le premier exemple de la page 133, elle se penche sur la culpabilité possible de Grace Poole après avoir sauvé le maître de son lit enflammé. La voix secrète l'arrête là où commencerait le soupçon d'histoires sentimentales non dites, de liaisons dangereuses. Plus tard cette même voix corrige ses souhaits extravagants. Rochester a menti par omission, il faut partir et la petite voix articule peur et désir, dans le combat qui oppose la tête et le cœur, interprète fidèle des dictats de la conscience morale. Mais, dans la tirade échevelée qui suit, l'autre voix s'exaspère : « *I think I rave in a kind of exquisite delirium* ». La conscience (morale) ne parvient pas à faire taire cette autre voix exquise et tout aussi secrète, révélatrice d'un subconscient que le discours véhicule. Jane parle ici de maîtrise : « *So far I have governed myself thoroughly* », mais en même temps elle demande au personnage de « Miss Eyre », en un dédoublement significatif, de se lever et de quitter la scène. Elle revient à la métaphore du spectacle : « *the play is played out* » (172). Dans ce sursaut d'autocensure s'entend l'affirmation d'un déni : le refus de dire ce qui tiendrait à la vérité de la personne, trop imposante pour qu'on la laisse faire.

Car, selon son patronyme explicite, Jane « erre ». Rochester le lui en fait la remarque judicieuse — « *Dread remorse when you are tempted to err, Miss Eyre: remorse is the poison of life* » (116) –, lui qui renvoie la pensée de l'errance (« *I have roamed half the globe* », 114) et l'y associe (« *bonny wanderer* », 117). Cette angoisse de l'erreur est en effet le poison qui condamne Jane à d'incessantes marches ou allées et venues frénétiques et le moteur puissant de projection des fantasmes sur la scène intérieure, tenus à distance par la « gouvernance » de soi, sur la scène sociale cette fois, remémorée de façon rétrospective. Redoutant le spectacle de la fête à Thornfield, elle cherche refuge dans le sanctuaire de la salle de classe (« *my sanctum of the schoolroom* », 141) où elle pourra à plaisir réfléchir à l'ambiguïté de sa position, ancillaire mais éducatrice, et à la résolution du mystère dont elle est exclue : « *there was a mystery at Thornfield; and [...] from participation in that mystery I was purposely excluded* » (140).

L'histoire qu'elle rapporte — et qu'elle a peur d'entendre quand, à la fin, l'aubergiste lui raconte les derniers jours de Thornfield — est celle d'une dramatisation, une mise en scène gothique, des phobies inconscientes que sécrètent les exclusions. Notons au passage que l'aubergiste en question, contre toute attente, ne trace pas d'elle un portrait flatteur, contrairement à tous ceux qui, selon ses dires, la vénèrent : elle aurait exercé sur Rochester une mauvaise influence.

La mise en scène des phobies est aussi importante que leur résultat, les mystères de Thornfield, après ceux d'Udolphe et avant ceux de Bly, aussi paradigmatiques que le Bildungsroman féminin. Car, comme toutes les confessions disertes à un lecteur convoqué à grand renfort d'apostrophe, la parole est d'autant plus vive qu'elle est empêchée. Elle rejaillira sur le mode de la rhétorique romantique de la fusion élémentaire — les courants, l'eau et le feu, le déluge biblique et l'irruption volcanique, l'appel à la mère... Nature (« *the universal mother, Nature* », 275).

D'entrée de jeu, l'orpheline méditative, « *Madame Mope* » (7), a remplacé la parole par la lecture ou la contemplation des images. Bewick introduit la terreur, les pages de *Pamela*, l'espoir d'une sagesse récompensée par un ordre social providentiel et le texte d'une femme qui consigne son désir dans des lettres : Pamela, son ancêtre, reconnue comme sa fille par la Providence, cette même Providence dont se réclame la narratrice en fin de course. Enfant, Jane proteste avec véhémence contre la parole empêchée ; gouvernante, elle écoute le maître qui est celui du verbe, acerbe, grandiloquent, histrionique même. La punition est celle de l'internement répété, dans la chambre des supplices, dans l'institution de charité ou dans la patience que lui enseigne la religion puritaine de la parole révélée bien comprise (Helen Burns) ou mal comprise (Brocklehurst ou St John Rivers). Dans la demeure ancestrale du maître, elle constate l'enfermement sans en saisir le pourquoi et sans comprendre le silence obligé qui l'entoure. Projetée dans le drame consécutif à la venue de Mason, elle veille le blessé, contrainte de ne pas échanger avec lui le moindre propos. Partout, comme en une lancinante reprise, la séquestration se répète jusqu'à un diapason morbide. A Moor House on lit *Marmion*. Le poète écossais y parle d'une nonne qui pour avoir brisé ses vœux subit le châtiment indicible d'être enterrée vivante — Rochester l'avait traitée plaisamment de « *little nonnette* » (112). Le discours ascétique de St John la condamne au linceul de fer (« *My iron shroud contracted round me; persuasion advanced with slow sure steps* », 344)

Voyant les énigmes — la bonne société se distrait du théâtre des charades : le sens est à deviner — elle entend la réponse : Bridewell, la célèbre prison. Bride ? la voilà face à sa problématique. Well ? le puits de sa perplexité, son propre esprit dont elle a si vite et si bien perçu le fonctionnement : « *all the servants' partiality [...] turned up in my disturbed mind like a dark deposit in a turbid well* » (11). Sous le coup du sort, elle se rebiffe en projetant de tracer à la craie, à la surface du miroir, l'autoportrait dérisoire, avilissant, comme en un négatif de défiance, en un geste d'autopunition, affirmé et dénié, à la craie, provisoire. « *Listen, then, Jane Eyre, to your sentence: to-morrow, place the glass before you, and draw in chalk your own picture, faithfully; [...] write under it, "Portait of a Governess, disconnected, poor, and plain"* » (137).

À ce miroir-support répondent les autres, la grande glace de la chambre rouge à Gateshead et le miroir oblong de Thornfield qui déforme le visage monstrueux de la femme. Dans ces espaces réflexifs, le regard instinctivement fouille des profondeurs : « *my fascinated glance involuntarily explored the depth it revealed* » (11). L'enfant qui s'y reflète est un esprit, un fantôme en miniature. Dans le cas du second, Jane narratrice rapporte les faits à l'auditeur : c'est un autre esprit, un autre fantôme qu'elle a vu s'insinuer dans l'intimité et vivre de sa vie propre. Comme Pamela dans ses pages pouvait lui offrir une version ancienne de sa propre ontologie, la folle du logis lui en procure une autre, autoréflexive, à consonance mélodramatique et tragique. C'est le personnage sauvage du Romantisme allemand, « *The Vampire Life in Death* » de la poésie romantique (« *the foul German spectre—the Vampyre* », 242), l'image déformée de la narratrice elle-même qui déclenche la catharsis : elle déchire le voile de mariée. Si Bertha appartient à l'onirisme sombre, les gouvernantes aussi qui, de l'avis des gens bien informés, sont des « incubes » (« *governesses [...] all incubi* », 150). La vision de l'autre, prédatrice, agressive, vorace — sexuellement aussi, apprendra-t-on du récit de Rochester — est un contrepoint que la virginité puritaine réprime envers et contre tout. « *Bertha is put in place of Jane's double [...] through the image of the nightmare which becomes a fluid medium through which they exchange position* » (Wolstenholme 65)

Pourtant si la folle déchire le voile de la soumission ou de la méconnaissance, elle réalise bien l'espoir secret de l'héroïne : « *I have a veil—it is down* » avoue cette dernière à une autre occasion (208). Se séparant du voile qui, métaphoriquement, la dissimule, elle proclame son identité et crie son nom à ceux qui, soudainement handicapés, ne la reconnaîtraient plus. Mrs Reed sur son lit de mort ou Rochester à Ferndean, devenu aveugle, Elle invite les autres à la lire comme Rochester le fait quand il lui demande d'approcher son visage de la flamme de l'âtre dans l'épisode de la « bohémienne ». Cette lecture est difficile et en convoque d'autres. En effet, dans l'histoire de sa vie tourmentée avec sa femme aliénée que Rochester raconte, il se souvient d'elle devant Thornfield, semblable aux sorcières de Macbeth : « *"You like Thornfield?" she said, lifting her finger; and then she wrote in the air a memento, which ran in lurid hieroglyphics all along the house-front [...]. "Like it if you can!" "Like it if you dare!"*» (122). Une apostrophe énigmatique que Jane reprend à son compte, comme si elle en était la destinataire, plutôt que Rochester lui-même. Ne lui a-t-on pas demandé, à elle, lors de son arrivée, si Thornfield lui plaît ? C'est Mrs Fairfax qui pose la question en des termes voisins : « *How do you like Thornfield?* » (85).

Dans ses dessins pourtant elle donne à voir le personnage féminin hiératique où se confondent héroïsme et morbidité. La noyée dont le bijou a été volé par le cormoran, comme une âme arrachée, et surtout le buste colossal de la femme au voile noir, avec les traits blafards du désespoir (« *the glassiness of despair* » — toujours le signifiant du miroir). Dans cette image surlignée par ce commentaire tiré du *Paradis Perdu* « une forme qui n'en a pas une », entre la dimension du triomphe et les stigmates de la mort (107).

Mais il faut revenir à ce défi que la folle lance à son mari face à sa demeure et aux histoires secrètes des familles. Qu'y aurait-il à déchiffrer dans les hiéroglyphes tracés au fronton du château et ces mots qui se répètent aux oreilles de la gouvernante ?

À un moment de son séjour à Thornfield, stimulée par la confiance du maître, Jane renaît à la vie ; ce bonheur lui fait oublier ses désirs et ses soucis. Or ce sont des désirs et des soucis de famille : « *So happy, so gratified did I become [...] that I ceased to pine after kindred* » (125). Certes le foyer manquant angoisse l'orpheline et motive sa quête, mais la parenté désirée est aussi un syndrome de réflexivité, l'indice d'un mystérieux rappel, la hantise qui conditionne l'histoire : « *family secrets* » (249) comme le dit Rochester à Thornfield, « *a home of the past: a shrine of memory* » (90).

Car tout tourne autour d'un défaut, d'un malaise, d'un mal-être aux sources des histoires, des ratés du symbolique. Amour déplacé, frustration létale, loi défaillante, sacrilège. Jane issue de parents sacrifiés, abandonnée aux mains d'une marâtre, Adèle sans mère si ce n'est la langue maternelle où le signifiant « mère » est présent, Rochester sacrifié au nom de l'intérêt du père et de la pérennité de la propriété indivise, devenu, dès lors, à proprement parler hors-la-loi, St John Rivers sacrifié au nom de sa loi, du fondamentalisme de la doctrine.

Le cri de Bertha devant Thornfield laisse entendre que la propriété de Rochester est suspecte. La biographie compliquée et/ou lacunaire (fin du chapitre XIII) de cet homme comme membre d'une fratrie où l'un ne ressemble pas à l'autre a abouti à un dessaisissement. La propriété lui est échue sans testament. Il y a un relent d'usurpation qui pollue d'entrée de jeu le personnage du déplacé. Rochester, l'exotique. Il s'habille de la défroque du potentat oriental sur la scène des charades, avant de s'affubler du déguisement de la fausse bohémienne qui devrait prédire l'avenir plutôt que ressasser le passé. Il prête à la loi du mariage une dimension grotesque : le spectacle est un mime pour un mariage pantomime qui fait entendre encore une fois le thème du mariage catastrophe : « *A ceremony followed, in dumb show, in which it was easy to recognise the pantomime of a marriage* » (156). Ce mariage catastrophe est la fin convenue des histoires (« *[they] promise to end in the same catastrophe—marriage* », 169). Jane lui signale d'ailleurs l'inadéquation du vêtement rapporté, quand il veut la vêtir en princesse, comme le remarque Margaret Smith (« *I would soon see you, Mr Rochester, tricked out in stage-trappings, as myself clad in a court-lady's robe* », 221).

Cette usurpation diffuse ramène le roman dans l'orbite d'*Hamlet* encore plus que dans celle de *Macbeth*. Rochester a une image curieuse quand il se pose en victime et reproche à Jane de le faire souffrir : « *you stick a sly penknife under my ear* » (112). Quant à Jane, l'absence qu'elle vit dès le drame de la chambre rouge se glose par l'image du vide qui vient se creuser dans la réalité : « *All looked colder and darker in that visionary hollow than in reality* » (11).

Cette absence commande le retour des morts et il s'accomplit d'une certaine manière grâce aux œuvres de la narratrice elle-même : sa mère riche héritière avait joint son destin à un pauvre vicaire désargenté. La mort en avait été le prix... le mariage d'amour sans rime ni raison. St John Rivers la mettra en garde contre toute reprise de ce schéma, contre toutes les erreurs qui feraient d'elle une mauvaise mère. Car le drame se déroule au sein d'une vaste famille. Jane, potentiellement Jane Eyre Reed (JER) pourra devenir soit Jane Eyre Rochester soit Jane Eyre Rivers en dupliquant John Eyre Rivers (JER), le JE, les initiales inaltérables comme dans « Jane Elliot » (Currer Bell comme Charlotte Brontë), sublimées ou aliénées par le R (R comme romance, que Charlotte prétend ne pas écrire, ou R comme répétition ?). Sur la scène de l'ailleurs géographique, lointain, du bout du monde (Madère ou les Antilles), les destins se sont scellés et John Eyre, l'oncle providentiel, l'autre face de St John Eyre R., a libéré Jane des entraves économiques qui la liaient à sa famille de Moor House. Comme la créature de Frankenstein à la porte des De Laceys, elle avait contemplé de l'extérieur les habitants de Moor House où elle était revenue sans le savoir, étrangère, à sa famille authentique (Charlotte revenue à Haworth), cette famille qui voudra vite lui imposer sa loi, même si la Providence efface le défaut de sa biographie et allume le feu qui ravage le lieu carcéral du même.

Tout au long de son périple, Jane arpente sans relâche, fébrilement, cette autre scène dans ce creux de la réalité, où se profile la femme au voile noir. Là, les rêves égrènent les icônes du gothique dont on a pu dire qu'elles donnaient une forme symbolique à la thématique réaliste. On a pu dire, à propos du *Tour d'Ecrou* de Henry James : « *James's story is powerfully haunted by the example of* Jane Eyre, *borrowing openly from its gothic aspect influenced more covertly by its themes of class and femalehood. And as in* Jane

Eyre, *the gothic element gives the realist themes symbolic form* » (Bell 100). Le rêve prémonitoire est sans doute une icône obligée, mais il y a d'autres rêves qui réitèrent la problématique féminine en tant que représentative d'une angoisse ontologique que l'imaginaire formule en images, semblables à celles que Jane conserve dans ses carnets à dessiner — images réflexives encore, à n'en pas douter.

Dans la biographie évasive de Rochester, la mère fait défaut. Encore que, de fil en aiguille, Mrs Fairfax puisse ressembler à un substitut maternel. Son mari avait pour cousine la mère de Rochester, une Fairfax (chapitre XI) — encore le lien familial —, mais c'est une « mère » ravalée au rang d'intendante et congédiée après le mariage manqué… pour avoir trop parlé ? (c'est l'hypothèse de Sutherland qui veut faire de Rochester un Barbe-Bleue sans foi ni loi). Jane de son côté comme préceptrice se substituerait à la mère d'Adèle. Et Rochester lui en accorde plaisamment le statut dérisoire : « *petite maman Anglaise* » (210), dans la langue d'Adèle qui est aussi celle dans laquelle Jane a appris à conjuguer le verbe « Être » — pour conjurer son mal-être ? Beaucoup de lectures à orientation psychanalytique ont bien sûr repéré le chaînon manquant et le vide laissé par la mère de Charlotte/Jane. À Moor House elle se glisserait vite dans ce rôle. Mais il ne faut pas y voir l'idéal sentimental que le récit compensatoire et gratifiant et ses visions combleraient. Bien au contraire, le rapport à la figure maternelle perdue appartient sur l'autre scène au devenir catastrophique du sujet, s'exprimant dans l'ambiguïté de la fonction maternelle. Dans le premier rêve clé où l'enfant apparaît, au début du chapitre XXI (« *a dream of an infant: […] a wailing child this night, and a laughing one the next* »), l'enfant est un annonciateur de mort comme le personnage du double dans les fictions du fantastique ; c'est une image de la répétition à l'inquiétante étrangeté : « *I did not like this iteration of one idea* » (188). Dans le second rêve, au beau milieu de son idylle, Jane est troublée par un songe identique : « *I was burdened with the charge of a little child* » (240) ; elle voit Rochester s'éloigner sur le chemin. Les perceptions d'une maternité oppressante, coupable, et oppressée, jouxtant l'apocalypse comme le cauchemar annonce l'incendie final du château, placent au centre de la représentation l'image de la femme fascinante liée au principe lunaire — la récurrence de l'astre nocturne en témoigne — avec sa connotation de démence.

Dans une lecture mythopoétique, un critique schématise le roman en le plaçant sous le signe de Dionysos affrontant Apollon, le principe de l'imaginaire débridé face au contrôle. Orphée en est le médiateur. Il y a une logique onirique qu'il faut savoir suivre dans le discours de Jane Eyre, ou *Aire* selon Adèle, l'*air*, l'aérien, ou le chtonien : *l'aire*, le domaine, le foyer où l'on revient après le pèlerinage.

La « voix secrète » n'est pas celle que Jane allègue, pour l'édification du lecteur, celle qui peut en fait ne pas l'être puisqu'elle s'articule sur une morale consensuelle. C'est plutôt celle qu'il faut lire dans la substance textuelle de ses propos, en filigrane... écouter un discours qui dépasse la diégèse reléguée au roman type de l'orpheline inquiète faisant son chemin. C'est pourquoi on ne suivra pas David Lodge quand il sous-estime l'aspect gothique au profit de la « vérité » du roman : celui de l'éducation. « *The "gothic" elements [...] constitute only a small part of Charlotte Brontë's debt to Romantic literature [...] far more important is [...] the struggle of an individual consciousness towards self-fulfilment* » (Lodge 114). Plus qu'un trajet édifiant de la connaissance de soi, le roman reprend la leçon du gothique, non pas celui auquel pense Robert Heilman dans son approche du « *New Gothic* » de *Jane Eyre* et qui serait un décor... « *mere thrillers* », une littérature du sensationnel. L'intensité psychologique a informé le gothique littéraire depuis le *Château d'Otrante* et les mystères de Mrs Radcliffe jusqu'au *Melmoth* de Maturin. Emily St Aubert, la séquestrée du château d'Udolphe, pourrait réclamer sans mal sa part d'héritage. On préférera sans doute au concept de « *new gothic* » — qui ne se confirme pas dans le roman de Charlotte Brontë, si ce n'est par la façon dont il est évacué — celui de « *post-gothic* » de Wolstensholme qui s'en tient prudemment et judicieusement à une dénotation chronologique.

Plus pertinente est en effet la question de savoir comment l'histoire archétypique de la femme assujettie et subjuguée, passant par les affres de la séparation et/ou de l'aliénation familiale selon une formule consacrée a pu perdurer dans la littérature par-delà l'histoire des sociétés et même le déclin du patriarcat. Tout à la fin du XIXe siècle, James revient à *Jane Eyre* pour sa gouvernante qui parle de « mystères d'Udolphe ». Il consigne son personnage dans un château qui abrite un secret ou dans une salle de classe où elle écrit au maître qui le lui a interdit. Les fantômes qui la visitent sont ceux d'un couple illicite de serviteurs corrompus. James expurge son récit de tout mélodrame explicite pour concentrer l'attention du lecteur sur le texte retrouvé de la gouvernante hantée. À cette époque, Freud établit une nouvelle science psychique : la psychanalyse, une méthode pour lire les confessions et les délires. Le trope gothique de la femme séquestrée se poursuivra dans de multiples récits, depuis Le Fanu et son *Uncle Silas*, Daphné Du Maurier et son *Rebecca*, Charlotte P. Gilman et la femme de la chambre au papier peint jaune, entre autres.

C'est que la voix secrète, obstinée et obsédante qui s'abîme dans ces textes est d'une plus grande longévité que les histoires de maturation de la personne dans un contexte social évolutif : le discours, spéculaire, la voix secrète, au miroir d'encre, derrière la mobilité des diégèses, spectaculaires.

Bibliographie

BELL, Millicent, « Class, Sex and the Victorian Governess: James's *The Turn of the Screw* » in *The American Novel. New Essays on Daisy Miller and The Turn of the Screw*, ed. Vivian R. Pollack, Cambridge: Cambridge University Press, 1993.

HEILMAN, Robert, « Charlotte Brontë's 'New' Gothic *in Jane Eyre* and *Villette* » *in* Ian Gregor, ed., *The Brontës: A Collection of Critical Essays*, Twentieth Century Views, New Haven: Yale UP, 1970.

HUGHES, R.E., « Jane Eyre: the Unbaptized Dionysos », *Nineteenth-Century Fiction*, vol.18, n° 4 (March 1964), 347-364.

LODGE, David, « Fire and Eyre: Charlotte Brontë's War of Earthly Elements », *The Language of Fiction*, London: Routledge and Kegan Paul, 1966, 114-143.

RAPAPORT, Herman, « *Jane Eyre and the Mot Tabou* », *MLN*, vol. 94, n° 5 *Comparative Literature* (Dec. 1979), 1093-1104.

SMITH Margaret, Introduction to *Jane Eyre*, Oxford, New York: OUP, The World's Classics, 1975, rpt 1990.

SUTHERLAND, John, *Can Jane Eyre Be Happy?: More Puzzles in Classic Fiction*, Oxford and New York: OUP, The World's Classics, 1997.

WOLSTENHOLME, Susan, « Charlotte Brontë's Post-Gothic Gothic », *Writing Women as Readers: Gothic (Re)visions*, State University of New York Press, 1993.

"The red-room" (9-14) : Explication de texte

Claire Bazin

The episode of the red-room which is the first narrative unit in the novel, be it because of its place or of its significance, can be read as a paradigm of further events, as what Lacan would call a *"moment fécond"* in Jane's psychic life. She is both subject and object of the narration—the enunciative instance is dissociated from the acting one: "emotion recollected in tranquillity" (Wordsworth, preface to *Lyrical Ballads*). At each crucial stage in her life, Jane will remember this episode, a pivot on which the schema of incarceration and flight—reiterated in the course of the narration—will revolve. The red-room is situated at the top of the house: "I was borne upstairs" (9), another proleptic similarity with the attic where Bertha is kept prisoner. John Reed might be to Jane what Rochester is to his mad wife, and the two "regions upstairs" are two enclosed spaces where madness may be controlled, even walled-in. The mad girl—"mad cat", "rat", "bad animal" (9, 8, 7)—in the red-room is the budding image of the mad woman in the attic ("clothed hyena", "grovell[ing] on all fours", 250). If Bachelard speaks of the rationality of the roof which he opposes to the irrationality of the cellar—*"cave ventrale et grenier cervical"* as Durand would put it –, it does seem that the values are reversed here. The ascent to the red-room and later on to the attic is a descent into Hell. Jane, as the victim of the injustice of her aunt whose son vicariously satisfies her tyranny by striking the intruder, is carried away to the red-room by two servants who even use some garters to tie her down in a scene which conjures up scenes of flagellations in Victorian pornography: "Whipping girls to subdue the unruly flesh and the rebellious spirit was a routine punishment for the Victorians, as well as a potent sexual fantasy" (Showalter 116).

Later on in the narration, when Bertha attacks Rochester, he eventually manages to tame her with a rope, which reinforces the animal imagery, very pregnant in Bertha's case: she is tamed like a horse—or, the night/mare—to which her bulging Fuselian eyes link her. The motif is reiterated at Lowood when Helen is whipped by Miss Scatcherd. Karen Chase rightly underlines that it is usually women who punish other women in this male-dominated society where they merely execute orders or, as in Mrs Reed's case, they are the slaves of their sons' desires. The enclosed space of the red-room cannot but conjure up the "female inner space", a womb or a tomb, where Jane will undergo the rite of passage necessary to become a woman: "*Dans tout rituel d'initiation, se présente une épreuve qui est le passage par une chambre secrète qui symbolise le lieu de la mort du vieil homme et de la naissance de l'homme nouveau"* (Chevalier et Gheerbrant 223-224).

The child Jane needs to die to give birth to the adult. Because of the homophony, we could even go as far as to interpret: "I was borne upstairs" symbolically. Like any rite of passage, the experience is however painful and traumatic, as rooms are often dangerous places. Jane first sees the room in a proliferation of symbols: reality undergoes a negative transformation. The functional imagery is the expression and the vehicle of the inexpressible, a device of semiological repression. After a brief description of the place that tries to remain objective (the narrative I is at stake) and stick to reality, Jane gradually loses her control as her perceptions slowly undergo a metamorphosis, a distortion. The vast, naked and solitary room ("never", "spare", "seldom") endows each object—and each object stands out as if gifted with life in this place of death—with the importance that Jane's tormented psyche is prepared to inscribe on it. In this episode, which could be analysed as a fit of madness, the paranoid phase, foreshadowed by the use of the strange and hostile pronoun "they", paves the way to the experience of schizophrenic dissociation, when Jane looks at herself in the mirror, an object that had formerly been forbidden to her by her cousin ("Go and stand by the door, out of the way of the mirror and the windows", 8) and doesn't recognize herself. The scene ends with her fainting, a rehearsal of her other fainting at Thornfield as well as a *"petite mort"*, the necessary stage in the process of her rebirth as a more subdued and submitted Jane.

In the first paranoid stage of what could be analysed as a fit of madness, the surrounding world gradually turns into a vast metaphor.

Right in the middle of the room, the bed is its focal point, its promontory: a coffin, or as Jane calls it, a tabernacle, it stands erect like the statue of the Commander or like Brocklehurst's marmorean figure. It is both a place of birth and death and in the present case, it is more obviously associated with the latter: it is in this very bed that Mr Reed "breathed his last", hence its venerable character, the prevailing sense of "dreary consecration" (11). The whole surrounding space is magnified, emphasized: "scarcely less prominent", the locks are doubly bolted: "no jail was ever more secure", the angles are twice as sharp. Jane is belittled (a tiny imp) in a world of giants that have turned into so many enemies; all the more so, as to the prevailing impression of hugeness, is added one of abundance and wealth: "massive pillars of mahogany". The furniture and the setting represent what Jane will never have or what the whole Reed family, going as far as to negate her very existence by ostracizing her before actually declaring she is dead (204), desperately tries to deny her. John Reed accuses her of being "a dependant", an insult that is resumed by Abbott: "They will have a great deal of money and you will have none" (10). Locking Jane in the red-room has the same function as Rochester's relegating Bertha in the attic. It metaphorizes the wish to forget some cumbersome elements that tend to threaten the established order: "I was a discord in Gateshead Hall" (12). In the red-room, Jane will almost literally die of fear: the piled-up mattresses and pillows are so many ghosts or corpses thrown upon the bed, which is reinforced by the choice of "shrouded": it is a funerary place, a euphemized sepulchre, where the always drawn curtains ("muffled windows") keep their terrifying secret or can even help to hide another…

The whole room is the mirror of Jane's growing fear, as she is reduced to a terrifying tête-à-tête with her only self. This abysmal space rouses the spectre of eternal damnation, of the fire of Hell. The dark red of the room is anxiogenic. Its initiatic and funerary significance turns the whole place into a huge coffin: *"Le rouge sombre est nocturne, femelle, secret et à la limite centripète"* (Chevalier et Gheerbrant 831).

Even before the secret of the red-room is revealed (red or Reed room?), the setting is drawn. To the prevailing, invading red becoming hypnotic in its "languid fullness of detail" (Maynard 101)—"red damask", "fawn", "red carpet", "crimson cloth"—is opposed the blinding, spectral and immaculate white, the symbol of absolute silence: "Its colour scheme of red and white appears almost thematically in Charlotte Brontë's work, a scheme of violent contrast between the cold purity of white and the hot crimsons and scarlets" (Oldfield 34). The colour white, as the outcome of diurnal life, represents a limit: it is the colour of passage, of death and rebirth. The snowy counterpane conjures up a virgin land, but it is also the colour of shrouds and ghosts and it could probably raise the late Mr Reed's ghost, like Jane's wedding veil—aren't we dealing with two rites of initiation?—will raise the apparition of Bertha who comes to kill the future bride before her actual "death" in the church next day. But at this point in her psychic itinerary, Jane has not yet reached the hallucinatory stage and Mr Reed's death is only evoked as a past event. Mr Reed is still encased in the portrait his wife carefully keeps in a jewel casket which she opens only occasionally, like a miser looking at her riches, unless it might hold a more Freudian meaning, underlined by Eva Figes who sees it as a masturbatory activity. Jane, who, for her part, rarely enters this sacred place, is slowly undergoing its spell. She remains riveted to her stool, the only safe point in the vast enclosed space which is gradually turning into an enemy, lest the slightest movement animate one of these spectral objects.

Reality becomes specularized: as in *Wuthering Heights*, the high, dark wardrobe also plays the part of a moving mirror with "broken reflections" where only threatening shadows can be reflected. In this second phase, the surrounding space is specularized: the wardrobe, the windows and the mirror itself all send back to Jane some anxiogenic images that her disturbed psyche is ready to receive: "prepared as my mind was for horror" (13). The three "mirrors" tend to deform the I (the reverse of Lacan's theory about the mirror as constitutive of the emerging I), perverting an already vacillating reality. The very object itself, like the wardrobe, has an impressive size and aspect, in osmosis with the place: "subdued, muffled, great". In its "vacant majesty", the mirror reverberates the enclosed claustral space of the room: "A mirror is also a sort of chamber, a mysterious enclosure in which images of the self are trapped like divers parchments" (Gilbert and Gubar 341).

Its central position, between the windows and the wardrobe, duplicates that of the bed "standing in the centre", sharing with it its huge, solemn character. The whole room is embedded in this abysmal mirror. It is a hollow depth, a "bottomless pit" says Rochester to describe Hell (262), where a metaphorized reality reinforces its threat in the reflection: "colder and darker" (11). "*Les miroirs sont des portes par où va et vient la mort*", Cocteau wrote. The mirror in the red-room is an optical echo to the mirror at Thornfield, "a dark, oblong glass" which is also frightening in its external aspect. Here, Jane is terrified at the idea of passing in front of the unavoidable mirror, though her fear is mixed with a sort of attraction for the mysterious depth: "My fascinated glance involuntarily explored the depth" (the very adjective is resumed at the end of the hallucinatory phase). Her quest ends on a discovery that turns out to be as traumatic as the preceding experiences: the abyss reveals an evil presence:

> the strange little figure there gazing at me, with a white face and arms specking the gloom, and glittering eyes of fear moving where all else was still, had the effect of a real spirit: I thought it like one of the tiny phantoms, half-fairy, half-imp, Bessie's evening stories represented as coming out of lone, ferny dells in moors, and appearing before the eyes of belated travellers. *(11)*

Each part of the body acquires a life of its own, moving like a puppet against darkness. The sight sends back to Jane a terrifying image of herself: "a real spirit", an oxymoron on which stumbles a more and more frightening reality, steeped in the superstitious creeds that are scattered through the Brontës' works. The "half-fairy, half-imp" which Jane sees in the mirror is the best expression of the experience of her schizophrenic dissociation, Jane fears she might never be able to enter into a normal human relationship: "am I a monster?" she will later wonder (226). It is impossible for her to recognize herself in this image of a self that is seen as a terrifying other. Furthermore, the split reflection, a faithful hybrid reproduction of a fragmented self reveals its two aspects in a sort of manichean superstitious way: "half-fairy, half-imp". The mirror underlines the growing difference, the distance from the usual self. Jane is, to quote her own words: "beside [her]self; or rather *out* of [her] self" (9). Jane's face is no longer hers but *"dérive vers un ailleurs"*. Later in the narration, when Jane meets Rochester for the first time in Hay Lane and comes to the rescue in a scene that is worthy of a fairy tale or of Coleridgean poetry, she appears to him like a witch or a spirit: "When you came on me in Hay Lane last night, I thought unaccountably of fairy tales, and had half a mind to demand whether you had bewitched my horse" (104).

Could she be the fairy "coming out of lone ferny dells"? When Jane comes back to Rochester at the end of the novel, he resorts to the same vocabulary: "changeling—fairy-born and human-bred" (373). The ghost-child with "white arms specking the gloom" will haunt Jane's nights at Thornfield before her own aborted wedding. When she leaves Rochester, Jane also becomes the "belated traveller" of Bessie's stories, "a wanderer on the face of the earth" (194), as if she were actualizing the childhood stories. In the restrictive space of the red-room, her fate is made clear: Jane is looking for an identity that the Reeds deny her and that is slowly dissolving in the broken reflections of the mirror. The scene, as a psychological seism, is closely linked to another scene at Thornfield, in another room.

The day before her wedding with Rochester, Bertha pays Jane a visit that is announced by a gleam, usually the prerogative of ghosts—the word is used both in the red-room and at Thornfield. Rochester's mad wife is locked up in the attic like some living dead, a living body wearing the mask of death, a disfigured figure which must be kept away, like Jane at Gateshead. Jane discovers Bertha's presence through the mirror, in an indirect way, revealing the *"Unheimlich"*, an image that is even more terrifying than the "half-fairy, half-imp" of the red-room. Bertha actualizes the woman in Jane's painting with her dark wild eyes and her Fuselian mane: "the eyes shone dark and wild; the hair streamed shadowy, like a beamless cloud torn by storm or by electric travail" (107). She also anticipates the last vision the reader gets of her before her jumping from the roof: "… and had long black hair: we could see it streaming against the flames" (365).

Bertha's appearance is more of an apparition: "half dream, half reality" says Rochester (243), once again underlining the closeness between the two women. As if she were galvanized by Jane's presence at Thornfield and the coming wedding which exemplifies Rochester's wish to forget her very existence by, so to speak, burying her. If we were to believe 19th-century physicians, Bertha's regular attacks on Jane and Rochester could be said to follow the menstrual cycle:

> Menstruation could drive some women temporarily berserk, destroying furniture, attacking family and strangers alike … Those unfortunate women, one doctor suggested, should, for their own good and that of society, be incarcerated for the length of their menstrual years. *(Showalter 121)*

Bertha's fits of madness, materialized in her pyromaniac tendencies, are an echo to Jane's crises at Gateshead and Lowood, and Bertha is a grown-up, uglified resurgence of a Jane who thought she was dead. As the legitimate wife, Bertha, dressed in white—like a ghost who might have borrowed the red-room sheets or Mr Reed's shroud—appropriates the usurper's veil to play again the scene of her own past wedding, to become re-married. With the veil, she is altogether Jane's double and a self-parody playing again Rochester's first wedding. Here, gothicism is subtly modified by the prevailing symbolism of the scene: Bertha tears the veil in two which foreshadows the aborted wedding, and is also another version of the old horse-chestnut at Thornfield split in the middle by the thunderstorm. In her rage, Bertha stamps upon the veil. As in the red-room, Jane sees in the mirror a terrifying obscure, exacerbated double, her "own hunger, rebellion and rage" which is miming her to warn her of her coming destruction. What is unrepresentable though paradoxically represented by Bertha dares to do what Jane does not. She would like to postpone a wedding that is a cause of worry because she feels threatened in the process, gradually losing her identity, being reified by Rochester whose toy she is aware of becoming: "an ape in a harlequin's jacket" (221). On the morning of her wedding to please Sophie, the chambermaid, Jane eventually accepts to look at herself in the mirror, and she once again sees a figure there that she does not recognize: "I saw a robed and veiled figure, so unlike my usual self that it seemed almost the image of a stranger" (244). She is but the "visionary bride [...] who had melted in air" (273), the homophony stressing the painful fact that Jane should remain Eyre. In the game of charades, when Jane so easily guesses who is hiding behind the disguise, she exclaims: "all were familiar to me as my own face in a glass" (172), an example of total contradiction. On the contrary, the novel offers Jane visions of herself which she disowns; she is often literally beside or beyond herself.

In the red-room, Jane first chooses rebellion—she sees red—which follows the phases of paranoia and schizophrenia but her rebellion is only short-lived: she is soon assailed by guilt and the terror of the Hell she has made out in the mirror, all the more so as the shadows invading the darkening room seem to become endowed with life though they are more like harbingers of destruction and death. This is an ideal setting for the appearance of a ghost, which Jane both wishes and dreads: she is now entering the last phase in her fit of madness. She will be the prey of hallucinations which renew and confirm the initial paranoid fear: the image of the benevolent father is as anxiogenic as the monstrous furniture or as Jane's own deformed reflection in the mirror; and the child doesn't even dare to breathe for fear that the slightest movement might raise the ghost from the dead. Instead of being a compensatory memory, the very idea is but another threat: "This idea, consolatory in theory, I felt would be terrible if realised" (13). Her isolation has become all the more unbearable as, paradoxically enough, the prospect of a visit from the world beyond, threatens to put an end to it:

> The thought of Reed who might appear is an incident which furnishes a paradigm of the novel's imaginative movement: the pressure of Jane's situation summons forth a character (here an imaginary spectre) who exacts new demands, poses new problems or incites new terrors.
> *(Chase 72)*

The absence of a father will find a negative compensation in the character of Brocklehurst. In this last stage preceding her fainting, fear dominates: her rebellion gradually merges in a miming of death: "cold as stone". Jane is so to speak dying of fear; and whereas death had first appeared as a possible escape:—"letting myself die"—it now becomes a terrible threat. She perceives her initial rebellion as a sacrilege that must be punished. The red-room is but the antechamber of Hell, reserved to those who are not "fit to die". The tribunal of Gateshead has passed its sentence: "All said I was wicked", which Mrs Reed will later resume on her death-bed: "she talked to me once [...] like a fiend" (197). Hence Jane's dramatic ironical question about her real self: "am I a monster?" which sends her back to the most obscure part of herself, embodied in the character of Bertha Rochester. Rochester himself stresses the link when he says: "consider the resolute, wild, free thing looking out of it, defying me, [...] the savage, beautiful creature" (271).

Jane is unable to circumscribe that self which is distorted in the mirrors, escapes or refuses to submit. It is only at the end that the self will appear, liberated, freed from its extremes—the christic figure of Helen Burns and Bertha, the femme fatale, between which she wavers throughout the novel. If the narrating I remains stable, the acting I is far less so; and this is best exemplified in the episode of the red-room: for the two to coincide, Jane needs to undergo her five rites of passage: "Charlotte Brontë exploits the doubleness in the narrating I which points us both to the moment of mature utterance and the moment of immature experience" (Chase 51); a statement that finds a significant illustration in the author's own analysis: "I can now conjecture readily that this streak of light was, in all likelihood, a gleam from a lantern, carried by some one across the lawn" (13), whereas her *hic et nunc* reaction can't be but hysterical. The fear of seeing a ghost visitor appearing is expressed in highly sexual terms: "My heart beat thick, my head grew hot; a sound filled my ears" (14), which once again stresses the difficulty of becoming an adult: Jane significantly begs to be brought back to the nursery before sinking into unconsciousness.

The world around her which had first undergone the metamorphoses of metaphorization and specularization before giving birth to hallucinations, now disappears: "unconsciousness closed the scene" (14). It has become too unbearable, too laden with concrete frightening or invisible—but nonetheless powerful—presences and it must vanish. Jane sinks into the visionary hollow, a rehearsal of her second fainting at Thornfield: "I lost consciousness: for the second time in my life—only the second time" (242). The two scenes are due to hallucinatory visions from the world beyond: Mr Reed's ghost or the "foul German spectre, the Vampyre" who, unlike ghosts, runs away at dawn: "it saw dawn approaching" (242). Jane's fainting enables her to escape an unbearable reality while also favouring the completion of the rite of passage: the rebellious slave must give birth to a tamed Jane—it is the end of the tomboy—submitting to her jailer's orders: "Fainting is the point of physical submission" says Eva Figes (121). The stay in the red-room bears some striking resemblances with Catherine Earnshaw's stay at Thrushcross Grange: both incarcerations help to turn the two wild girls into young women who are taken care of, like precious objects: "lifting me up and supporting me in a sitting posture, and that more tenderly than I had ever been raised or upheld before" (15).

Jane "must be borne upstairs". When she wakes up, the nightmare goes on: the whole place is also red and she thinks she is still a prisoner: "and seeing before me a terrible red glare, crossed with thick black bars" (14-15). The never ending nightmare however takes on a new meaning: the return to life, echoing the "preface to death" Jane has just been through, symbolized by the fire that was absent from the red-room.

Gateshead, which could easily be parodied into Gateshell, is the first logical and chronological narrative unit in Jane's existence: for her, each new episode is a confrontation with the unknown which must help her in her self-discovery. The initial situation at Gateshead is one of deprivation: Mrs Reed and her children are the negative images of what a real family should be and the mere evocation of the dead father is a source of terror. Jane's rebellion against the injustice of this world leads to her punishment: the prolonged stay in the enclosed space of the red-room, a microcosmic mirror of the external world—breeds superstitious fears that slowly turn into a fit of madness. Rebellion is followed by guilt and Jane finally faints. The red-room has a cathartic function: Jane's rage—a metaphoric parallel to the more literal fire where Bertha loses her life—dies there. For Jane to live, Bertha must die, both literally and metaphorically: "As long as Bertha is, Jane cannot be" (Twitchell 72). There is not enough room for two or for what is excessive—too Bertha-like—in Jane. The red-room used as a safeguard against Jane whose fits of anger must be punished, reveals her rebellious self which is however sometimes assailed by doubts as to its ability to belong to the chain of beings (to which Bertha no longer belongs because Rochester has no doubts at all). Jane must grow up to exorcise the demons of her childhood, her "bad propensities" (16), to enter the symbolic order, to conjugate the different versions of an unstable I: "when the Bertha in Jane falls from the ruined wall of Thornfield and is destroyed, the orphan child, too, as her dream predicts, will roll from her knee—the burden of her past will be lifted—and she will wake" (Gilbert and Gubar 362).

Bibliography

BACHELARD, Gaston, *La Terre et les Rêveries de la Volonté : essai sur l'imagination des forces*, Paris : José Corti, 1948.
CHASE, Karen, *Eros and Psyche: The Representation of Personality in Charlotte Brontë, Charles Dickens, and George Eliot*, New York and London: Methuen, 1984.
CHEVALIER, Jean et Alain GHEERBRANT, éd., *Dictionnaire des Symboles*, Paris : Laffont, 1969.
DURAND, Gilbert, *Les Structures anthropologiques de l'imaginaire*, Paris : Bordas, 1969.
FIGES, Eva, *Sex and Subterfuge, Women Writers to 1850*, London: Macmillan, 1982.
GILBERT, Sandra M. and Susan GUBAR, *The Madwoman in the Attic: The Woman Writer and the Nineteenth-Century Literary Imagination*, New Haven and London: Yale University Press, 1979.
MAYNARD, John, *Charlotte Brontë and sexuality*, London: Cambridge University Press, 1984.
OLDFIELD, Jenny, *Jane Eyre and Wuthering Heights, a Study Guide*, London: Heineman Educational Books, 1976.
SHOWALTER, Elaine, *A Literature of their Own: British Women Novelists from Brontë to Lessing*, London: Virago Press, 1978.
TWITCHELL, James, *The Living Dead: The Vampire in Romantic Literature*, Durham, NC: Duke University Press, 1981.

Jane Eyre : l'œuvre en création

Stéphanie Bernard

« *There was no possibility of taking a walk that day* » : l'œuvre s'ouvre sur la désolation d'une petite orpheline. Elle n'est pas jolie et n'attire d'autre attention que la colère de son entourage. Dans ce *Bildungsroman*, la petite fille va pourtant faire entendre sa voix et affirmer sa volonté. De spectatrice elle deviendra actrice, d'objet du discours des autres et de leurs brimades elle deviendra sujet de sa propre histoire. La fin du récit la présente comme une maîtresse femme sur qui son mari infirme peut s'appuyer. Elle est son guide, ses yeux, ses mains. Lui est abaissé dans son corps, elle est élevée : socialement par son héritage, esthétiquement par sa fonction de narratrice clairement appuyée dans les dernières pages du roman. Elle est le sujet parlant du texte, par qui nous voyons et entendons tout ce qu'il nous est permis de connaître de l'univers du roman.

Ce qui nous intéresse ici est ce parcours du personnage, à la fois digne de celui d'un héros de Dickens et cause de la subversion des codes de l'écriture romanesque du XIXe siècle. Dans *Jane Eyre*, le romantisme rencontre le réalisme ; le feu qui ravage Thornfield et mutile Rochester écorche aussi le traditionnel « *happy ending* ». Le glacis de la première personne se fissure et la dimension réflexive du texte se donne à voir. Nous tenterons de discerner en quoi ces renversements font de *Jane Eyre* un roman qui s'offre à la réécriture, au cinéma comme dans la littérature, et qui pose du même coup la question du féminin.

La romance de Jane : de l'ombre à la lumière

Roman du XIXe siècle influencé par le réalisme naissant, *Jane Eyre* s'efforce de nous faire parvenir une image unifiée et cohérente du monde. L'équilibre entre respect des codes et innovation se reflète dans le traitement des lieux. Thornfield est l'espace emblématique du récit : c'est là que vit Rochester, héros sombre et romantique à la façon de Byron. Près de là a lieu la première rencontre entre les deux protagonistes ; puis dans le jardin se déroule la demande en mariage au cours d'une scène dont Franco Zeffirelli, dans son adaptation cinématographique, a su faire ressortir le mystère et la douceur à la fois, tel un « rêve étrange et pénétrant ». Au dernier étage de la bâtisse se tapit la folie sous les traits de Bertha, dont les cris, les rires et la violence enveloppent les lieux d'une atmosphère gothique.

De ce point central — sur le plan diégétique et esthétique — jaillit le romantisme qui irradie au point que le lecteur en oublie la complexité chromatique de l'œuvre.

> Charlotte Brontë's narrative strategy [...] lets many of us get too closely involved with young Jane, too uncritically accepting of her worldview, enabling—virtually determining—the reading of *Jane Eyre* as a novel of rebellion and the legitimate assertion of the sovereignty of the self. *(Beaty 491)*

En effet, les tristes années à Gateshead puis la dure réalité de Lowood d'une part, l'austérité de la vie à Moor House d'autre part, constituent un cadre rigide qui empêche — ou devrait empêcher — les ingrédients gothiques et romantiques de contaminer l'ensemble du roman. Jane découvre par exemple à Moor House un endroit simple et tranquille :

> I could see clearly a room with a sanded floor, clean scoured; a dresser of walnut, with pewter plates ranged in rows, reflecting the redness and radiance of a glowing peat-fire. I could see a clock, a white deal table, some chairs. The candle, whose ray had been my beacon, burnt on the table; and by its light an elderly woman, somewhat rough-looking, but scrupulously clean, like all about her, was knitting a stocking.
> I noticed these objects cursorily only—in them there was nothing extraordinary. A group of more interest appeared near the hearth, sitting still amidst the rosy peace and warmth suffusing it. Two graceful women—ladies in every point—sat, one in a low rocking chair, the other on a stool [...] *(282-283)*

Comme à Thornfield, un feu de cheminée revêt la scène de charme et de douceur et rassure Jane à son arrivée. Pourtant l'ambivalence de Thornfield Hall est d'emblée suggérée par les lumières qui éblouissent l'héroïne, annonçant peut-être le brasier qui détruira les lieux :

> she ushered me into a room whose double illumination of fire and candle at first dazzled me, contrasting as it did with the darkness to which my eyes had been for two hours inured; when I could see, however, a cozy and agreeable picture presented itself to my view. [...] A more reassuring introduction for a new governess could scarcely be conceived: there was no grandeur to overwhelm, no stateliness to embarass [...] *(81)*

Malgré l'insistance de la narratrice sur l'absence de démesure dans la construction et sur l'accueil bienveillant qu'elle reçoit, le lecteur tend à retenir l'atmosphère inquiétante et les recoins obscurs du manoir.

Moor House, au contraire, est un symbole d'authenticité. Le bâtiment — « *black, low, and rather long* » (282) — est moins élevé que Thornfield — « *three stories high, of proportions not vast, though considerable: a gentleman's manor-house, not a nobleman's seat* » (84). L'atmosphère y est paisible et accueillante.

Cependant, le texte ne se fige pas dans une opposition binaire. Moor House n'est pas un havre de paix : c'est ce que laisse discrètement entendre l'adjectif « *black* ». La présence des deux jeunes femmes dans cet endroit rustique souligne également une certaine singularité : « *A strange place was this humble kitchen for such occupants!* » (283). L'extrême simplicité du décor annonce l'ascétisme de St John Rivers. Jane se retrouve dans un environnement totalement différent du précédent mais qui la met tout autant au défi. Cette fois, l'intégrité de son être est menacée par l'envers de la passion : « *Reason, and not Feeling* » (320) pour citer St John. Comme si chacun de ces lieux trouvait son âme en l'homme qui l'habite.

Après son séjour auprès de la famille Rivers, Jane est prête à poser un regard nouveau sur Rochester. La première description de Ferndean confirme cette évolution du personnage :

> […] presently I beheld a railing, then the house—scarce, by this dim light, distinguishable from the trees; so dank and green were its decaying walls. Entering a portal, fastened only by a latch, I stood amidst a space of enclosed ground, from which the wood swept away in a semicircle. There were no flowers, no garden-beds; only a broad gravel-walk girdling a grass-plat, and this set in the heavy frame of the forest. The house presented two pointed gables in its front; the windows were latticed and narrow; the front door was narrow too, one step led up to it. The whole looked, as the host of the Rochester Arms had said, "quite a desolate spot." It was still as a church on a week-day: the pattering rain on the forest leaves was the only sound audible in its vicinage. *(366-367)*

Ferndean est un autre lieu isolé, un manoir sans éclat pris dans le sombre écrin d'une épaisse forêt mais qui n'a rien de l'atmosphère gothique de l'ancienne demeure de Rochester. La description anticipe et souligne plutôt l'authenticité de la relation qui s'établit désormais entre les deux protagonistes. Chacun a fait la paix avec sa propre histoire. Rochester a reconnu sa faute, le feu l'a débarrassé de tout orgueil et a mis fin à la triste union avec Bertha. Aucun artifice, nulle dissimulation n'est possible ici.

La forêt alentour menace d'engloutir la maison qu'on distingue à peine, comme si le soleil ne parvenait plus à y briller. Cependant peu à peu une étincelle apparaît : dans la scène des retrouvailles, Rochester essaie de « voir » Jane avec ses mains (369), puis il avoue distinguer la lueur du feu (372). Plus tard il retrouvera partiellement la vue : le personnage masculin progresse symboliquement des ténèbres vers la lumière. Le traitement du décor confirme cette progression. La pénombre et la pluie qui accompagnaient Jane lors de son arrivée à Ferndean se dissipent pour laisser place, le matin suivant, à une belle éclaircie : « *"It is a bright, sunny morning, sir," I said. "The rain is over and gone, and there is a tender shining after it: you shall have a walk soon"* » (374). La scène se déroule ensuite à ciel ouvert. La forêt toute proche est évoquée, mais Jane et Rochester s'en éloignent pour se retrouver, à l'écart du monde, dans un paysage radieux :

> Most of the morning was spent in the open air. I led him out of the wet and wild wood into some cheerful fields: I described to him how brilliantly green they were; how the flowers and hedges looked refreshed; how sparkingly blue was the sky. I sought a seat for him in a hidden and lovely spot: a dry stump of a tree [...] *(374)*

Ce mouvement reflète le cheminement de l'héroïne depuis Gateshead — « *with its clouds so sombre* » (5) — jusqu'à la douce lumière de Ferndean, lieu de la maturité. Le personnage peut doucement, inostensiblement y rejoindre la narratrice pour devenir Jane Rochester : une autre femme.

Cendrillon ou femme libérée ?

Le dernier voyage de Jane est sa réponse à l'appel de Rochester : elle accourt et va véritablement le sauver. Le lecteur assiste en quelque sorte au dénouement d'un conte renversé : la jeune femme devient le prince charmant qui libère l'autre blessé et prisonnier d'une fin misérable. « *I love you better now, when I can be really useful to you, than I did in your state of proud independence, when you disdained every part but that of the giver and protector* » (379). Jane est maintenant celle qui donne et protège, celle qui conduit et ordonne. Ainsi, le mariage ne la « domestique » pas : elle est actrice de son histoire. A Moor House et Morton, elle acquiert l'indépendance sociale, d'abord par son travail, puis par son héritage. Elle n'est plus orpheline. Elle trouve sa place dans l'histoire socio-familiale et affirme : « *I told you I am independent, sir, as well as rich: I am my own mistress* » (370).

Néanmoins le déplacement vers une fin conventionnelle est indéniable. L'héritage providentiel n'est pas le fruit des efforts de l'héroïne. De plus, dans l'Angleterre victorienne, le mariage demeure la norme à laquelle Jane ne peut échapper : il est le prix de son intégration dans la société. Adrienne Rich rappelle qu'il n'y a pas d'indépendance possible pour la femme victorienne, aussi riche soit-elle (Rich 470). Tout sujet est pris dans le maillage des lois sociales. Par l'affirmation de sa liberté, Jane semble dire qu'elle ne risque plus d'être pareille à Cendrillon, dont le bonheur ne tient qu'à une union salvatrice avec un prince riche et charmant. Mais pour Sandra M. Gilbert l'illusion est fragile : « *Who is the slave, the master or the servant, the prince or Cinderella? [...] The prince is inevitably Cinderella's superior, Charlotte Brontë saw, not because his rank is higher than hers, but because it is* he *who will initiate* her *into the mysteries of the flesh* » (Gilbert 485-486).

En réalité, l'héroïne doit mener une lutte de chaque instant pour acquérir ce semblant d'indépendance. A Thornfield Hall, Rochester se laisse aller à une idéalisation de Jane qu'elle ne peut tolérer : « *You are a beauty, in my eyes; and a beauty just after the desire of my heart,—delicate and aërial. [...] I will make the world acknowledge you a beauty too* » (220-221). Les efforts répétés de la jeune femme pour ne pas succomber à cette hérésie sentimentale s'avèrent vains : consciente du danger (« *he was either deluding himself, or trying to delude me* », 221), usant habilement de l'aiguillon de l'ironie, elle cède cependant : « *My future husband was becoming to me my whole world* » (234).

L'hésitation entre le réalisme froid et sarcastique du personnage féminin et le romantisme passionné de son amant reflète d'ailleurs les hésitations de l'œuvre entre ces deux pôles : les chapitres XXIII et XXIV sont un retour vers le rêve — « *I thought over what had happened, and wondered if it were a dream* » (219) — encadré premièrement par la dureté de l'enfance de Jane, ses remarques ironiques pour contrer Rochester, les rappels incessants de l'absence de beauté chez elle, deuxièmement par la désillusion et la recherche affirmée de son indépendance après que la jeune femme s'est enfuie de Thornfield.

A Ferndean, au contraire, tandis que Rochester doute de ses sens, la réponse de Jane lève toute ambiguïté : « *"In truth?—in the flesh? My living Jane?" "You touch me, sir,—you hold me, and fast enough; I am not cold like a corpse, nor vacant like air, am I?"* » (369). À la question : « *Am I hideous, Jane?* », celle-ci répond avec franc-parler : « *Very, sir: you always were, you know* » (373). La première demande en mariage aura été la répétition de ce qui se déroule ici. A Thornfield, les paroles sont connotées et lourdes de sens : le terme « *bride* » (217) renvoie à Jane dans la bouche de Rochester, Blanche dans celle de Jane, alors qu'il s'agit en réalité de Bertha. Mais à Ferndean, le couple est comme seul au monde.

De plus, le temps n'est plus aux hallucinations ni aux voix désincarnées. Le langage fonctionne dans sa dimension d'échange. L'étrange appel entendu par Jane à Morton reçoit une justification rationnelle et prend l'aspect quasi-conventionnel d'un dialogue :

> "As I exclaimed 'Jane! Jane! Jane!' a voice—I cannot tell whence the voice came, but I know whose voice it was—replied, "I am coming: wait for me;" and a moment after went whispering on the wind the words—"Where are you?" [...]
> Reader, it was on Monday night—near midnight—that I too had received the mysterious summons: those were the very words by which I replied to it. *(381)*

Les paroles sont humanisées et les corps qui les produisent s'offrent au regard du lecteur. La relation se fait tactile, les mains se touchent :

> Then he stretched his hand out to be led. I took that dear hand, held it a moment to my lips, then let it pass round my shoulder: being so much lower of stature than he, I served both for his prop and guide. We entered the wood, and wended homeward. *(382)*

Rochester ayant fait acte de repentance (382), son savoir sur le corps et la sexualité — « *the mysteries of the flesh* » — n'est plus un obstacle et trouve même sa justification dans les Écritures. La Bible plus que le conte de fées pose son empreinte sur le texte. La réalité charnelle de la rencontre entre les protagonistes est rappelée avec d'autant plus de force qu'elle est en nette opposition avec le discours de St John Rivers et qu'elle marque l'accomplissement de la parole biblique du Livre de la Genèse :

> I hold myself supremely blest—blest beyond what language can express; because I am my husband's life as fully as he is mine. No woman was ever nearer to her mate than I am: ever more absolutely bone of his *bone and flesh of his flesh*. *(384, je souligne)*

Ferndean se fait ainsi le reflet du jardin d'Eden. La seconde demande en mariage se déroule à l'extérieur. Le couple doit traverser la forêt — la frontière de l'Eden — pour rejoindre la maison — microcosme de la société. Leur bonheur n'est véritablement possible que hors du monde, loin du jugement social. C'est seulement dans ce lieu isolé et presque invisible que le conte peut s'inverser : il n'y a que de l'autre côté du miroir — ou de la forêt — que Jane, jeune épouse victorienne, a accès à l'indépendance et à la liberté.

Dans le dernier chapitre, le récit file du passé de la diégèse vers le présent de la narration. Jane disparaît peu à peu. « *My Edward and I, then, are happy* » (385) dit la narratrice. Rochester est appelé par son prénom, ce qui renforce l'impression qu'a le lecteur d'être le voyeur non désiré — voire non autorisé — d'un bonheur simple et authentique. Le passage par la forêt est semblable au corridor qu'emprunte Antoinette dans *Wide Sargasso Sea* avant de mettre le feu à Thornfield Hall et de mourir, le lieu d'un impossible à dire qui s'écrit pourtant : « *The flame flickered and I thought it was out. But I shielded it with my hand and it burned up again to light me along the dark passage* » (Rhys 156).

Jane : l'œil et la voix du texte

Jean Rhys choisit pour son roman une narration fragmentée ; le « I » est tantôt Antoinette, tantôt Rochester. La fin du texte est énigmatique : celle qui nous parle meurt dans l'incendie qu'elle déclenche si l'on en croit, cette fois, la narratrice de Charlotte Brontë. Ce détour nous ramène à *Jane Eyre* et à l'unité de ton que produit le choix du genre autobiographique. La voix de Jane harmonise un texte à la limite des genres littéraires ; son regard — « *eye* » qui s'entend dans « I » — lie des ingrédients variés, voire contradictoires.

Jane Eyre attire le lecteur dans une intimité avec l'héroïne. Les appels au « *gentle reader* » sont nombreux : le destinataire est nommé, invité au cœur du récit et Jane lui livre ses sentiments profonds. L'auteur limite encore le détachement du lecteur en peignant une héroïne sans artifice et même plutôt commune — « *disconnected, poor, and plain* » comme l'écrit Jane au-dessous de son autoportrait (137) — dans un monde crédible. Ce que vit Jane, le lecteur pourrait aussi le vivre : « *Gentle reader, may you never feel what I then felt! May your eyes never shed such stormy, scalding, heart-wrung tears as poured from mine* » (274).

Le récit nous parvient avec une immédiateté qui rappelle le roman épistolaire. L'acte de lecture fait se rejoindre le passé et le présent, Jane personnage et Jane narratrice. Ce faisant, dans les moments d'intense émotion, la narration tente d'abolir le temps qui passe avec le recours au présent : « *And where is Mr Rochester?* » (148) se demande Jane confrontée aux invités mondains venus à Thornfield ; quand il arrive enfin, l'indifférence qu'il manifeste envers sa gouvernante ne fait que rappeler douloureusement les instants de quasi-complicité qu'ils ont connus. De même après que Jane s'est enfuie de Thornfield : « *Two days are passed. It is a summer evening* », dit-elle (275).

Cependant Jane n'est pas une figure monolithique : entre le premier épisode de Gateshead et le bonheur retrouvé à Ferndean, l'héroïne apparaît à trois âges différents —enfant, jeune fille, puis femme —, si bien qu'elle offre au lecteur une vision plurielle. Tantôt tout détachement est abandonné ; tantôt, au contraire, la narratrice condamne les excès de sa jeunesse, notamment par le recours aux commentaires d'autres personnages. « *But you are passionnate, Jane, that you must allow* » dit Mrs Reed (31) avec un calme tel que ce ne peut être que sincère. A Lowood Helen Burns, son amie, la rappelle à l'ordre : « *Hush, Jane! you think too much of the love of human beings, you are too impulsive, too vehement* » (59).

Parfois enfin la narration s'éloigne de Jane pour se focaliser sur d'autres personnages : tel est le cas avec la mort de Helen au pensionnat ou plus généralement lorsque le texte décrit la vie à Lowood afin d'ancrer le récit dans une réalité froide et crédible, ou encore quand le roman se clôt sur les paroles de St John Rivers.

C'est enfin avec un certain détachement que Jane déclare dans le dernier chapitre : « *I have now been married ten years. I know what it is to live entirely for and with what I love best on earth* » (383-384). Il ne nous est pas permis de pénétrer l'intimité du mariage avec Rochester. Le présent est gardé secret, chuchoté seulement. Narrée à demi, cette histoire spectrale empêche la clôture traditionnelle du conte de fées d'opérer. D'autre part, si le personnage s'est dévoilé dans le récit, la narratrice demeure, elle, dans l'ombre, devenant spectrale à son tour. Lorsque Jane réapparaît après tout ce temps passé à l'abri de la forêt, elle ne se devine qu'à travers ce qu'elle nous a dit de son double diégétique.

L'unité recherchée dans le style biographique est un leurre. Même si le lecteur se laisse entraîner dans une relation privilégiée avec la narratrice, il n'a jamais en face de lui une Jane unique, mais des facettes, des étapes d'un personnage multidimensionnel. Le texte se construit au rythme de la lecture et la vision du monde y est un puzzle dont les pièces s'emboîtent peu à peu pour former une image cohérente. C'est là l'illusion réaliste sur laquelle s'appuie *Jane Eyre*.

Derrière cette façade se révèle la qualité polyphonique du roman. Des voix étrangères, c'est-à-dire hors du « je » narratif — des voix hors-jeu — résonnent. Tel est l'effet de la voix que Jane entend comme venant de nulle part et sans origine rationnelle : « *I might have said, "Where is it?" for it did not seem in the room—nor in the house—nor in the garden: it did not come out of the air—nor from under the earth—nor from overhead. I had heard it—where, or whence, for ever impossible to know!* » (357). L'épisode de la Chambre Rouge attire davantage l'attention sur l'hallucination visuelle ; l'enfant n'entend pas des voix mais croit percevoir un fantôme (31).

Ces deux passages suggèrent combien le personnage progresse au fil des années. Jane apprend peu à peu à accepter l'Autre : ce qui diffère d'elle, ce qui ne se cantonne pas aux frontières de son esprit. Le personnage devient de plus en plus semblable à la narratrice qui ménage une place dans son récit à des paroles venues d'ailleurs : des paroles bibliques qui parsèment le texte (41), des poèmes (98) ou des chansons (17-18). De manière significative, les derniers mots du roman reviennent à l'austère St John Rivers (385). Le cocon que Jane tisse avec Rochester doit rester entrouvert sur le monde. La narratrice se positionne donc entre l'acceptation de l'Autre et le refus du monde à Ferndean. Les deux penchants de Jane sont en quelque sorte réconciliés au travers du silence qui se fait sur sa vie : nous ne savons rien vraiment des dix années de mariage ; la voix de Jane s'efface pour laisser s'élever la prière de Rivers et ménage ainsi un espace où peut résonner la voix du lecteur, la pensée victorienne, l'opinion du critique... Cette narration habitée d'autres voix s'offre au jeu de l'intertextualité et à l'imagination des autres. *Jane Eyre* demeure une œuvre en création.

Un texte qui se regarde

Nombreuses sont les occasions où Jane se met en scène en train de raconter son histoire plutôt que de la vivre. À la fin du roman, celle-ci rappelle la qualité fictive et quelque peu artificielle de son récit : « *My tale draws to its close: one word respecting my experience of married life, and one brief glance at the fortunes of those whose names have most frequently returned in this narrative, and I have done* » (383). À demi-mot, l'auteur nous rappelle à travers sa narratrice que *Jane Eyre* n'est pas une autobiographie mais une œuvre de fiction, créée et tissée d'illusions. Ainsi, Jane ne s'attarde pas, comme elle l'avance, sur la vie de ceux dont l'histoire a le plus parlé — rien n'est dit sur la famille Reed ni sur Miss Temple par exemple — mais de ceux qui, en fin de compte, marquent l'âge de la maturité pour elle.

L'aveu d'un *projet* d'écriture apparaît plus tôt dans le roman : « *Hitherto I have recorded in detail the events of my insignificant existence [...]. But this is not to be a regular autobiography: I am only bound to invoke memory where I know her responses will possess some degree of interest* » (70). Cette révélation évoque du même coup le temps qui s'écoule au fil du récit. Lorsque Jane écrit, elle n'est plus celle qui a vécu tous ces événements.

La narratrice cherche à maintenir la distance qui la sépare de son double diégétique afin de ne pas sombrer dans le sentimentalisme, tout comme le personnage tente de le faire avec Rochester : « *but I'll not sink into a bathos of sentiment: and with this needle of repartee I'll keep you from the edge of the gulf too; and, moreover, maintain by its pungent aid that distance between you and myself most conductive to our real mutual advantage* » (233). Cette pensée par laquelle elle s'efforce de résister aux envolées passionnées de celui qui la courtise se transpose aisément à la relation qui unit et sépare à la fois le personnage et la narratrice. Les pointes de sarcasme qu'elle adresse à Rochester trouvent leur écho dans le jugement narratif qui s'abat parfois sur la jeune héroïne.

A Lowood, la voix de la narratrice évoque discrètement la complexité du personnage de Jane ainsi que ses talents de conteuse :

> I resolved, in the depth of my heart, that I would be most moderate—most correct; and, having reflected a few minutes in order to arrange coherently what I had to say; I told her all the story of my sad childhood. Exhausted by emotion, my language was more subdued than it generally was when it developed that sad theme; and mindful of Helen's warnings against the indulgence of resentment, I infused into the narrative far less of gall and wormwood than ordinary. Thus restrained and simplified, it sounded more credible: I felt as I went on that Miss Temple fully believed me. *(60)*

Ces lignes parlent des difficultés de tout écrivain à mettre suffisamment de passion dans ses mots pour éveiller l'intérêt du lecteur tout en satisfaisant aux lois de la vraisemblance. Jane apparaît ici en tant que personnage mais aussi en tant que narratrice : l'autocritique opérée vise l'enfant trop sincère, la jeune pensionnaire de Lowood qui dose habilement les ingrédients de son histoire, et enfin la narratrice qui sait mieux encore manipuler le langage et agencer les données de son récit.

Jane se reconnaît donc en tant qu'être parlant (« parlêtre » dirait Lacan) et a clairement conscience du monde qui l'entoure. Cela la conduit à adopter une attitude réflexive vis-à-vis de sa fonction dans l'œuvre. Les micro-récits qu'elle fait de-ci, de-là de sa propre histoire (ou qu'elle entend lorsque l'aubergiste raconte l'incendie de Thornfield et la fin de Bertha au chapitre XXXVI) renvoient autant de reflets de son cheminement. Ils sont une mosaïque dont *Jane Eyre* est le cadre.

Par là, l'acte d'écriture tient l'illusion réaliste en suspens. À maintes reprises le roman attire notre attention sur sa surface graphique et linguistique, avec les trois dessins de Jane par exemple (107) et la sollicitation insistante du lecteur. Le style de *Jane Eyre* se singularise par l'utilisation répétée d'une imagerie biblique ou empruntée à la nature et les allusions à d'autres textes ou à différentes peintures. Ces références à l'art apportent une résonance interne à l'œuvre de Charlotte Brontë. L'écriture se trouve sans cesse mise en abîme, donnant au texte une épaisseur soulignée très tôt par la scène de la Chambre Rouge où la jeune héroïne voit son reflet dans un miroir : « *Returning, I had to cross before the looking-glass; my fascinated glance involuntarily explored the depth it revealed. All looked colder and darker in that visionary hollow than in reality* » (11).

Le roman fonctionne comme un autre miroir déformant dans lequel l'image n'est jamais vraiment fidèle à l'objet qu'elle reflète. L'acte d'écriture transforme la réalité, soit en l'embellissant, soit en la montrant « plus froide et plus sombre » qu'elle n'est. Quant à la parole donnée ou la phrase écrite, elle n'est jamais univoque puisqu'elle est toujours traversée par des voix étrangères : « Aucun membre de la communauté verbale ne trouve jamais des mots de la langue qui soient neutres, exempts des aspirations et des évaluations d'autrui, inhabités par la voix d'autrui. Non, il reçoit ce mot par la voix d'autrui, et ce mot en reste rempli » (Todorov 77). Tout comme Jane qui ne peut véritablement prétendre à un état de fusion avec l'homme qu'elle aime, et ce malgré l'isolement de Ferndean, le roman de Charlotte Brontë est soumis aux idées de son temps, au poids du passé et aux aspirations du futur.

Jane Eyre se perçoit donc au cœur d'influences croisées : dans l'équilibre entre la vision romantique, le mouvement réaliste qui s'attache à donner l'illusion d'un monde vrai, et la dimension réflexive de l'écrit se manifestant dans sa matérialité. Cette ouverture d'une œuvre à première vue si intimiste s'offre à des lectures diverses, et par là au jeu de la réécriture.

Renversements

L'initiative de ce jeu revient à Charlotte Brontë elle-même, qui publia ses premières œuvres sous le pseudonyme de Currer Bell. Dans une notice biographique destinée à l'édition de 1850 de *Wuthering Heights*, Charlotte justifie cette stratégie adoptée par les trois sœurs Brontë :

> Averse to personal publicity, we veiled our own names under those of Currer, Ellis and Acton Bell; the ambiguous choice being dictated by a sort of conscientious scruple at assuming Christian names positively masculine, while we did not like to declare ourselves women, because—without at that time suspecting that our mode of writing and thinking was not what is called "feminine"—we had a vague impression that authoresses are liable to be looked on with prejudice; we had noticed how critics sometimes use for their chastisement the weapon of personality, and for their reward, a flattery, which is not true praise. *(Brontë 31)*

Sa véritable identité dévoilée, elle signe pourtant cette notice du nom de Currer Bell. L'auteur semble se complaire dans ce jeu de rôle qui entretient l'ambiguïté des positions masculines et féminines et qui fait écho à la fin peu conventionnelle du roman.

Charlotte Brontë se défendit ainsi de son audace dans sa Préface : « *Conventionality is not morality. Self-righteousness is not religion. To attack the first is not to assail the last. To pluck the mask from the face of the Pharisee, is not to lift an impious hand to the Crown of Thorns* » (1). Consciente des codes qu'elle enfreint, elle manipule les conventions sociales et littéraires — dont celui d'une écriture masculine sérieuse opposée à une écriture féminine de second rang. Cette subversion des codes dans et par le roman explique sans doute l'intérêt que Jane Eyre suscite, tant chez les écrivains que chez les cinéastes.

Jean Rhys écrit *Wide Sargasso Sea* en 1966. Elle renverse la position narrative de *Jane Eyre* pour donner voix à Bertha, la femme folle, rebaptisée Antoinette. Ce nouveau nom la libère, en tant que narratrice, de son double grossier et hurlant à Thornfield Hall. Jane devient l'intruse, l'autre, la troisième personne. *Wide Sargasso Sea* est le reflet en négatif de *Jane Eyre*, tout comme Antoinette est le double inversé de Jane. Une des preuves textuelles de ce renversement est la répétition de la scène de la Chambre Rouge, cette fois vécue par Antoinette à la fin de son histoire : « *It was a large room with a red carpet and red curtains. Everything else was white. I sat down on a couch to look at it and it seemed sad and cold and empty to me, like a church without an altar. [...] Suddenly I felt very miserable in that room* » (Rhys 111).

Le travail de réécriture est particulièrement bien évoqué par Jean Rhys elle-même dans sa correspondance lorsqu'elle parle de son personnage principal :

> She must be at least plausible with a past, the reason why Mr Rochester treats her so abominably and feels justified, the reason why he thinks she is mad and why of course she becomes mad, even the reason why she tries to set everything on fire, and eventually succeeds. (Personnally, I think that one is simple. She is cold—and fire is the only warmth she knows in England.)
> I do not see how Charlotte Brontë's madwoman could possibly convey all this. [...] Another "I" must talk, two others perhaps. Then the Creole's "I" will come to life.
> [...] Lastly: her end, I want it in a way triumphant!
> (Wyndham and Melly 156-157)

La difficulté fut de déplacer la focalisation sur Bertha, qui devient alors la jeune et jolie Antoinette. Le personnage féminin se reconstruit au fil du récit. En tant que narratrice, Antoinette montre, par son intimité avec le lecteur, qu'elle n'est pas folle, ou tout au moins pas quand elle écrit.

C'est en ce sens que la fin de la narratrice de *Wide Sargasso Sea* est « triomphante » : elle parvient à s'écrire, elle qui n'a d'autre voix que des cris dans *Jane Eyre*. Jusqu'au bout, elle suit le chemin de l'écriture pour s'affranchir de l'ordre patriarcal qui l'emprisonne, jusqu'au bout elle affirme sa différence. Pour Jane aussi, l'écriture est vecteur d'indépendance. Cependant, elle s'arrête au bord du précipice : après s'être enfuie pour préserver sa liberté et échapper à l'humiliation, elle revient vers Rochester. Elle accepte un héritage puis un mariage qui l'inscrivent dans l'ordre social. Son indépendance est à ce prix. Avec *Wide Sargasso Sea*, la pensée victorienne laisse place aux incertitudes du XXe siècle qui modifient le travail d'écriture et ouvrent la voie à l'inscription de la femme dans un univers patriarcal fissuré.

Le film de Franco Zeffirelli, réécriture récente de l'œuvre, opte pour un esthétisme épuré et un sens maîtrisé du mystère par le choix des couleurs, des paysages et des musiques ainsi que par l'agencement des faits. Ainsi, la scène de la première rencontre entre Grace Poole et Jane montre que l'héroïne n'est pas totalement dupe : Jane sait que le rire n'est pas celui de Grace mais qu'il vient d'une pièce close par une porte massive sur laquelle elle pose son regard. La folie de Bertha qui revêt Thornfield d'une atmosphère gothique dans le roman apparaît de façon concrète dans le film, comme un mutisme forcé et une violence exacerbée.

En outre, les coïncidences perdent leur caractère énigmatique : l'arrivée de Jane chez la famille Rivers s'explique aisément par le lien avec la famille Reed. La voix désincarnée de Rochester qui l'appelle au secours semble poussée par le vent et s'insère assez logiquement dans le récit, au moment où la voix off de la narratrice nous dit combien les pensées du personnage sont occupées par le souvenir de sa vie à Thornfield. Enfin, l'annonce de l'héritage faite par St John Rivers n'a rien de soudain puisque les évènements s'enchaînent rapidement après la visite de Jane à Mrs Reed qui, sur son lit de mort, lui apprend l'existence d'un oncle qui souhaitait l'adopter.

Cette adaptation insiste sur le réalisme de l'œuvre et offre en même temps une vision d'ensemble qui privilégie le thème amoureux. Elle ancre le récit dans le XXIe siècle : l'importance donnée à l'enfance de Jane à Lowood, la présence récurrente d'Adèle à Thornfield, la capacité de Rochester à se montrer tel un père tendre lorsque la petite fille est attristée par l'absence de Jane, répondent à des préoccupations contemporaines. Une famille recomposée s'agrège autour de Jane à Ferndean. Dans les derniers instants du récit, alors que le livre insiste sur l'éducation que reçoit l'enfant pour devenir « *a pleasing and obliging companion* » (383), le film dit clairement que Jane est devenue une mère pour elle. La fin du film est ainsi moins problématique que celle du roman. Les derniers mots de la voix off, « *our happiness is complete* », sont absents du roman. Ils suggèrent que rien ne vient troubler l'union avec Rochester. La dernière image montre le couple dans un paysage bucolique. Nulle allusion n'est faite à d'autres personnages. La note est donc positive, le « happy ending » reprend ses droits.

La modernité de *Wide Sargasso Sea* et sa revendication d'une écriture féminine d'une part, l'esthétisme élégant et sobre du film de Franco Zeffirelli d'autre part, mettent en relief la malléabilité du roman de Charlotte Brontë et l'ouverture sémantique qui autorise une diversité de lectures. L'une des plus récentes et des plus atypiques est celle de Jasper Fforde qui, en 2001, écrit *The Eyre Affair* : le ton est léger, voire parodique. Rochester y apparaît très romantique et sombre, Bertha désespérément folle (« *She cackled maniacally* », Fforde 338). Fforde souligne la complexité narrative de *Jane*

Eyre liée au style autobiographique. Son jeu d'écriture insiste sur les codes manipulés par Charlotte Brontë et qu'il manipule à son tour. Ainsi, l'appel de Rochester est réécrit, par l'intrusion de Thursday Next, l'héroïne de Fforde, dans l'univers de *Jane Eyre* :

> There, as the words etched themselves across the paper, was a new development in the narrative. After Jane promised St John Rivers that if it was God's will that they should be married, then they would, there was a voice—a new voice, Rochester's voice, calling to her across the ether. But from where? It was a question that was being asked simultaneously by nearly eighty million people worldwide, all following the new story in front of their eyes.
> "What does it mean?" asked Victor.
> "I don't know," replied Plink. "It's pure Charlotte Brontë but it definitely wasn't there before!" [...]
> They read delightedly as Jane changed her mind about India and St John Rivers and decided to return to Thornfield.
> I made it back to Ferndean and Rochester just before Jane did. I met Rochester in the dining room and told him the news; how I had found her at the Riverses' house, gone to her window and barked: "Jane, Jane, Jane!" in a hoarse whisper the way Rochester did. *(Fforde 346-347)*

Le lecteur, représenté par Thursday, se fait ici auteur à son tour, mais le style reste celui de l'écrivain. Les personnages romanesques deviennent bien plus que des êtres de papier, étant condamnés à vivre et revivre sans cesse la même histoire. Les conventions littéraires sont irrévérencieusement subverties. Mais le respect de la grandeur de l'œuvre demeure. « *And it is this mixture of Celtic dreaming with English realism and self-control which gives value and originality to all they do* » (Ward XXIV) : c'est en ces termes qu'à l'aube du XXe siècle Mary A. Ward parlait de Charlotte Brontë. C'est ainsi également que pourrait être décrite l'atmosphère qui se dégage de *Jane Eyre*.

La narration s'efforce de tendre vers la vraisemblance tout en rappelant cependant que le récit est fiction et que la littérature n'existe que par l'acte de lecture. Le réalisme se teinte des couleurs de l'imagination romantique. Sous l'apparente conventionalité du style autobiographique se devine un travail original et singulier par lequel Charlotte Brontë parvient à esquisser le trait qui sépare la réalité factuelle de l'ordre du langage — le réel du symbolique. L'absence qui s'affirme et se comble à la fois dans l'espace entrouvert entre les mots et les choses s'écrit dans l'histoire de *Jane Eyre* qui est tout à la fois l'œuvre, le personnage, la narratrice, au point de devenir insaisissable. « *I am Jane Eyre* » affirme l'héroïne à deux reprises, mais qui est-elle vraiment ?

La question que pose la modernité sur l'absence qui fonde le langage s'entend déjà dans *Jane Eyre* : roman sur les origines, il n'occulte pas le mystère mais y prend sa source. La réponse divine n'est pas rejetée mais elle est tout de même confrontée à l'ordre social et à la force de la vision d'un sujet, féminin qui plus est. L'audace de Charlotte Brontë est d'avoir créé un chef-d'œuvre célébré depuis sa publication en 1847. Femme écrivain qui se fait passer pour un homme, auteur d'une autobiographie fictive qui s'offre à des voix étrangères et s'inspire de mouvements littéraires contraires, elle parvient à forger son style et inspirer chaque page de cette mosaïque imaginaire : *Jane Eyre*.

Bibliographie

BEATY, Jerome, "St John's Way and the Wayward Reader", *in* Charlotte Brontë, *Jane Eyre*, ed., Richard Dunn, New York, London: Norton, 2001.

BRONTË, Charlotte, "Biographical Notice of Ellis and Acton Bell", *in* Emily Brontë, *Wuthering Heights*, Harmondsworth: Penguin, 1965.

FFORDE, Jasper, *The Eyre Affair*, Harmondsworth: Penguin, 2001.

GILBERT, Sandra M., "A Dialogue of Self and Soul: Plain Jane's Progress", *in* Charlotte Brontë, *Jane Eyre*, ed., Richard Dunn, New York, London: Norton, 2001.

RHYS, Jean, *Wide Sargasso Sea* [1966], New York & London: Norton, 1999.

RICH, Adrienne, "Jane Eyre: The Temptations of a Motherless Woman", *in* Charlotte Brontë, *Jane Eyre*, ed., Richard Dunn, New York, London: Norton, 2001.

TODOROV, Tzvetan, *Mikhaïl Bakhtine, le principe dialogique* suivi de *Écrits du Cercle de Bakhtine*, Paris, Éditions du Seuil, 1981.

WARD, Mary A., "Introduction to *Jane Eyre*", *in* Clement Shorter, ed., *Life and Works of the Sisters Brontë*, vol. 1, London: Harper, 1899.

WYNDHAM, Francis, and Diana MELLY, eds., *The Letters of Jean Rhys*, New York: Viking, 1984.

Partie II –
Jane Eyre à l'écran

Jane Eyre : quel usage faisons-nous des classiques à l'écran ?

Dominique Sipière

Ça se passe tout à côté, mais c'est vraiment très différent : le *Pride and Prejudice* de 2005 a été filmé à Chatsworth par le presque débutant Joe Wright alors que le *Jane Eyre* de 1996 avait été réalisé par le vétéran Zeffirelli, à 4 miles de là, précisément à Haddon, sur la commune de Bakewell, dans le Derbyshire, au sud du Peak District (on trouve ces belles demeures sur la carte Michelin n° 403, dans le même carré, p. 24 …).

Les rapprochements entre le film du précédent programme et celui de cette année ne s'arrêtent d'ailleurs pas là : d'abord ils ont été réalisés « *on location* », en décors naturels, dans l'Angleterre des *Heritage Films* qui ont proliféré dans les années 90. Ensuite, leurs récits partagent l'itinéraire *édifiant* — il faut ici prendre ce mot au sérieux ! — d'une jeune fille jugée « inférieure » (mais il y a plusieurs façons de l'être) vers un mariage heureux et somme toute improbable. Les deux contes de fées doivent donc beaucoup à l'histoire de Cendrillon, mais on voit aussitôt que c'est dans le plaisir de la variation autour d'un même dessin que tout va se jouer. On aura aussi remarqué que les romans et leurs auteurs ont plusieurs points en commun : Jane et Charlotte sont deux célibataires, filles de pasteurs modestes, que 40 ans séparent (mais quelles années !) ; le roman de la première a été publié l'année même de la naissance de la seconde (1816) ; et, surtout, il s'agit de l'adaptation de deux *classiques* confirmés, jamais oubliés, toujours repris sur la scène, puis au cinéma et à la télévision.

Mais le jeu des ressemblances conduit vite à celui des différences, tant d'un roman à l'autre qu'entre les deux films étudiés. Par exemple, certains ont regretté que Keira Knightley soit vraiment trop jolie pour incarner Elizabeth Bennet et voici que Charlotte Gainsbourg semble délibérément enlaidie par son metteur en scène (Au point qu'on soupçonne bientôt un effet rhétorique). C'est que, dès les romans, l'idée de hiérarchie entre les deux sœurs (Jane Bennet / Elizabeth), ou l'insistance sur le fait que Jane Eyre soit jugée (et se trouve elle-même) « *plain* » ne signifie évidemment pas le même rapport à soi et aux autres (même si c'est toujours aux « vraies valeurs » et à des attraits jugés plus « authentiques » que la leçon chrétienne renvoie). Si les trente et un ans qui séparent *Pride and Prejudice* de *Jane Eyre* n'ont pas tout changé, le lecteur est quand même frappé par deux types de différences liées au changement d'époque : ainsi, la *voix* narrative n'est plus du tout la même ; l'*action* austenienne, entièrement centrée sur les pouvoirs et sur les règles de la société, est remplacée par l'enjeu de la mort (comme chez Camus[1], la question de la mort et du suicide passif est lisible dès le début du roman), des souffrances physiques et de la destitution, seulement entrevue derrière le personnage de Wickham en 1816.

Dès le début, la vie ordinaire de Jane est *perçue* physiquement dans la peur (red-room), la rage, l'inconfort (le froid, la faim) et la douleur (les coups infligés à Jane par John Reed, puis à Helen par Miss Scatcherd). L'idée même d'une Bertha — la Folle dans le grenier — ne viendrait jamais au lecteur de Jane Austen. Et d'ailleurs, le lecteur d'Austen pouvait *se passer des corps* de ses personnages, de sorte que le sang versé dès les premières pages marque une rupture profonde entre les deux univers. Enfin, et surtout, à l'absence fascinante de *descriptions* (de quelle couleur sont les yeux d'Elizabeth ?) des objets et des corps chez Austen se substitue une forêt *lisible* de visages et de paysages.

Autant dire que si la méthode de travail préconisée pour *Pride and Prejudice* l'an dernier reste un outil de départ, on se concentrera ici sur d'autres signes, d'autres thèmes et une autre problématique. Je vais quand même, dans un premier temps, reprendre ces outils et continuer à comparer les deux adaptations, en espérant rappeler de bons souvenirs à certains et en encourageant ceux qui ne connaitraient pas *Pride* à le découvrir un jour. Mais j'inviterai surtout les candidats à explorer quelques *thèmes* (des idées et des débats) et quelques *motifs*[2] (des fragments narratifs, des images...) et à analyser leur évolution du roman aux films, selon les époques et selon les *usages* que les lecteurs et les spectateurs ont fait de *Jane Eyre*.

Premières explorations

Ne partons pas sans outils et sans fil conducteur — même si un visionnement « naïf » est à la fois légitime et utile pour comprendre ce que le réalisateur a probablement recherché en s'adressant à un assez large public. Il n'est même pas impossible que certains d'entre vous soient amenés à voir le film avant d'avoir lu le livre et cette expérience — refusée aux autres — mérite réflexion. Ce ne seront plus des pertes mais des « ajouts » que vous allez mesurer en passant du film au roman... Mais aussi, curieusement, une sorte de coup de force des images qui imposent alors un visage et une atmosphère, que le roman ne *dit* pas. Dans le film, Blanche *était* blonde et rayonnante, la

---

1. Au début du *Mythe de Sisyphe*. On me pardonnera cet anachronisme, mais Jane, dans sa révolte, pense d'abord à se laisser mourir.
2. Pour le dire encore plus simplement, on travaillera sur deux versants : celui des signifiés (dits et non dits) et celui des signifiants (délibérés ou non).

voici brune et presque athlétique et on se demande alors pourquoi les deux versions ont choisi l'une ou l'autre (J'y reviens bientôt)…

Après le premier visionnement spontané — qui laisse toute leur place aux critiques et aux soupirs — il faut s'équiper un peu. Comme l'an dernier, je suggère donc de commencer par une *verbalisation* écrite du film, puis de travailler sur les grands transferts de l'adaptation en passant en revue les composantes de la construction *diégétique* (espace, temps, personnages, motifs récurrents…). Enfin, une rapide exploration des étapes habituelles de la *genèse* de tout film permettra sans doute de dégager quelques pistes supplémentaires : élaboration du script (des mots aux images) ; choix des lieux et des décors ; scénographie (organisation de l'espace et des décors) ; *casting* (selon les personnages et la persona des acteurs), puis filmage et montage…

On commencera donc par une *verbalisation* personnelle du film, c'est-à-dire qu'on ne se contentera pas de la mémoire pour y repérer des échos, des reprises et des différences. On notera le mouvement du *récit* (de grands pans vont ainsi disparaître dans le film où toute la fin du roman — un livre entier, 132 pages ! — semble débouler en huit minutes), les dialogues (le film de 1997, dont on pourra se dispenser, « modernise » la langue de Jane et de Rochester), la bande son (bruits, musique, etc.) et, bien sûr, les *images* elles mêmes c'est-à-dire les décors, les costumes, les lieux, les corps et les mouvements — ceux qu'on observe *dans* le cadre autant que ceux effectués *par* le cadre. Il me semble que cette transcription personnelle ne peut pas être proposée par quelqu'un d'autre que vous : elle relève de l'*appropriation* des textes par chacun, à la fois aussi exacte que possible mais également orientée par les préoccupations et les intérêts de chaque candidat. Elle permettra de naviguer entre les versions du récit sans, bien sûr, faire l'économie de leur visionnement.

Un rapide retour aux étapes de la *construction diégétique* va me permettre de comparer le film de Wright avec celui de Zeffirelli. Là encore, le jeu des ressemblances et des différences peut servir de boîte à idées. Ainsi, il était assez évident que l'*espace* et le mouvement s'offraient dès l'incipit de *Pride and Prejudice* comme le point fort du réalisateur, à la limite de la virtuosité gratuite, mais sans jamais tomber dans l'horripilante agitation d'un Branagh. Vue ainsi, l'économie dynamique de Zeffirelli (presque contemporaine des excès du *Frankenstein* de Branagh) mérite qu'on s'y arrête. Habitué à la fois aux décors flamboyants de l'opéra (mais aussi aux nécessités statiques du chant) et confronté à un roman qui se prêtait aux pires délires visuels, Zeffirelli choisit une relative discrétion, des couleurs froides ou pastel (les camaïeux de bruns) et un bi-chromatisme (le rouge / le bleu) somme toute assez intellectualisé. C'est donc le paradoxe de la (relative) *retenue* de

Zeffirelli que la comparaison suggère, même si au reproche de *brontëisation* d'Austen encouru par Wright ne saurait correspondre celui d'*austenisation* de Brontë par le réalisateur italien !

Le *temps* est traité avec la même linéarité que chez Joe Wright, même si le point de départ est ici très différent : le temps de Brontë est bien plus suggestif et plus fluctuant — un temps vécu et des *durées* élastiques, plus expressives, plus verbales aussi, que narratives. Cela dit, tous les films préservent très sagement l'ordre initial des événements — ce qui ne va pas de soi au cinéma.

Il y a beaucoup de *personnages* dans *Jane Eyre* et leur traitement d'un film à l'autre mérite une étude à lui seul. Notons tout de même la disparition pure et simple de Bessie chez Zeffirelli et, au contraire, son gonflement en 1944 (merveilleuse Sara Allgood, ronde et entre deux âges dans le film de Stevenson) ; le remplacement (en 1944) du pharmacien Lloyd par un certain Dr Rivers, dès le début du film, qui vise à donner une continuité plus lisible au récit. La disparition pure et simple de plusieurs personnages (En 1996 Rivers n'a plus qu'une seule sœur...) et ainsi de suite : à chaque fois on pourra s'interroger sur les raisons mécaniques, psychologiques ou symboliques de ces modifications et sur leurs « effets secondaires ». Par exemple, la blondeur de Blanche — évoquée plus haut — tient d'abord au choix d'Elle MacPherson, « *supercover girl* » très en vue en 1996[1]. Sa persona à l'extérieur du film a quelque chose d'un corrélat objectif pour le spectateur, un équivalent de l'effet produit sur Jane par une sorte de Princesse de la société de son temps : à chaque génération ses modèles d'idéal social, à chaque héroïne les figures pour l'intimider ; à chaque époque ses inquiétudes, sa Jamaïque, et la *couleur* du visage des Mason : peut-on faire moins caraïbe que Maria Schneider, livide dans le rôle de Bertha ? Mais la blondeur de Blanche rend plus visible encore la *symétrie* entre les deux « femmes fatales » dont parle Claire Bazin : l'une qu'on montre et l'autre qu'on cache, l'une diurne et l'autre nocturne.

La première question posée par l'adaptation de *Pride and Prejudice* était celle de la voix narratrice (troisième personne) et de la subtile ironie pré-jamesienne du roman de 1816. Le lecteur apprenait vite à se méfier de tout. Ici les choses ont beaucoup changé, mais les difficultés demeurent pour le cinéma : l'*intelligence surplombante* d'un narrateur pince sans rire est remplacée par l'*autobiographie fictive*, capable certes de distance envers la Jane narrée (donc passée), mais elle-même (la Jane narratrice des années 1840) sujette à ses idiosyncrasies, à un certain manque de fiabilité et, bien sûr — sur une troisième plan — à la vision du monde propre à un auteur et à son époque (1847). Une fois de plus, la voix off est parcimonieuse (d'autres films la renforcent un peu,

---

1. L'Australienne Elle Mac Pherson est une habituée des magazines internationaux. En 1986 elle était pour *Time* « The Big Elle » en couverture.

comme en 1944, mais sans grand effet d'ironie) et son usage est assez dérisoire devant l'étendue du problème. Il va falloir y revenir car, là où le cinéma paraît manquer de *profondeur* — ou plutôt de multiplicité des plans de réalité — il apporte aussi une forme d'*épaisseur*, de présence et d'émotion grâce aux voix, aux intonations et aux rythmes. Je n'arrive pas à pardonner à Zeffirelli d'avoir presque supprimé l'appel *télépathique* de Rochester au moment où Jane est sur le point de succomber à Rivers[1]. Quand les films le préservent, cet *instant vocal* (comment un grand metteur en scène d'opéra a-t-il pu manquer cela ?) qui transcende l'image est d'une superbe intensité, en particulier dans la version télévisée de 1983. La *voix* de Timothy Dalton, adressée à Jane, me saisit et me *transporte* au-delà des images un peu trop sages du téléfilm.

Je vais passer plus vite sur le troisième outil d'investigation qui suit les étapes supposées de la *fabrication* des films, en particulier parce que les informations sur le travail de Zeffirelli sont assez minces et parce qu'on n'est pas très sûr de les trouver intéressantes. On regardera quand même de près l'élaboration des *dialogues*, pas seulement ce qui est coupé et ce qui est préservé, mais aussi l'arrangement et les équilibres entre les personnages, entre ce qui est dit et ce qui est montré (diegesis / mimesis) et bien sûr les *silences* qui sont, notons le sans trop d'ironie, un des points forts du cinéma quand on le compare à l'écrit.

En revanche, la mise à plat du choix des *acteurs*, de leur physique et de leurs rôles antérieurs (persona) risque de déborder de toutes parts et on devra se concentrer sur l'essentiel, c'est-à-dire sur les modifications intentionnelles et/ou révélatrices : un ancien James Bond[2]; le héros de *The Avengers*[3] (en 1957) ; ou William Hurt, le bel Américain aux yeux clairs et à l'air accablé de 1996. Tout semble possible, même le plus invraisemblable, puisque Charlton Heston — Moïse et Ben Hur ! — fut le Rochester d'une série télévisée de 1949. Plus intéressant sans doute, dans un film par ailleurs très décrié, George C. Scott, à la mine sombre et spécialisé dans les rôles autoritaires et assez peu sympathiques (Delbert Mann, 1970). On admirera le masque de la terrifiante Miss Scatcherd de Geraldine Chaplin ou le très convaincant Brocklehurst de John Wood en 1996 (malgré son âge ?). Mais on se demandera comment ces visages, ces voix et ces attitudes (l'air *intelligent et las* de Mr Hurt) modifient la lecture des mots du roman. La *scénographie* et le *filmage* mériteront évidemment une étude : paysages, bâtisses, corridors, escaliers et miroirs sont choisis et regardés selon des éclairages, des angles et des enchainements très délibérés.

---

1. On entend à la place un discret appel « Jane » dans les arbres et le vent, mais dans une atmosphère calme et paisible sans rapport avec celle du roman.
2. Timothy Dalton, dans la version BBC de 1983.
3. Patrick MacNee était le John Steed de *Chapeaux melons et bottes de cuir*.

Interroger les textes

Il convient maintenant de nous donner quelques pistes de recherche, quelques *questions* pour interroger la relation entre le roman et ses films, car l'inventaire ci-dessus ne doit pas être lancé sans quelques arrière-pensées : sur le classicisme, sur l'injustice et la révolte, sur le destin et l'ordre du monde ; sur les fables, les contes de fées et la religion ; sur l'égalité, le sexe et les genres (*gender*) ; sur le dire et le voir, les pertes et les profits d'une époque à l'autre et sur quelques autres aiguillons de la lecture.

Jane Eyre pose frontalement la question des œuvres du passé et de leur *classicisme*. Comment un roman qui a choqué en son temps devient-il assez sage et rassurant pour qu'on en recommande l'étude dans les écoles ? D'où les trois questions : que devient « an extremist heroine in an extremist book[1] » au XXe siècle ? Au cinéma ? Chez Zeffirelli ? On voit bien qu'il s'agit ici de trois interrogations différentes, qui s'alimentent les unes les autres.

Dès l'incipit du *Jane Eyre* de 1996 on peut séparer ce que le film préserve du roman et ce qu'il en perd. Jetée d'emblée dans la chambre rouge (on la sortait d'un placard claustrophobe en 1944) Jane éprouve terreur et sentiment d'injustice, mais les mots manquent au film pour dire sa révolte et son désir de mourir. De même, on retrouve le sentiment de solitude et d'enfermement (moins qu'en 1944), mais pas l'extraordinaire phrase d'ouverture et la presque joyeuse revendication d'autonomie du deuxième paragraphe :

> There was no possibility of taking a walk that day [...] I was glad of it...

Ou encore, Mr Brocklehurst suscite bien la même protestation devant l'injustice de ses accusations de sournoiserie (« *I am not deceitful!* »), mais il ne déclenche pas l'extraordinaire obsession de vérité et d'*authenticité* qui traversera tout le roman.

On remarquera au passage que ce récit et sa rhétorique particulière appellent souvent trois niveaux d'analyse : 1) comment une scène sert-elle à susciter des émotions et une réaction chez le lecteur ou le spectateur (ici : révolte et sympathie) ? ; 2) comment la scène de fiction renvoie-t-elle au monde social réel (à Lowood : les écoles pour jeunes filles nécessiteuses) ? ; 3) quelles réponses successives le récit suggère-t-il dans la fiction et dans la réalité : révolte, acceptation, dépassement(s) par la *fiction* ; action et dépassement dans la *réalité* ? Revenons sur quelques thèmes qui s'imposent dès le début du roman.

Injustice, révolte et pouvoir. Il faut bien reconnaître que ce que nous éprouvons en sympathisant avec Jane (y a-t-il personnage plus *aimable* dans la littérature ?) relève du malentendu : c'est d'abord le conte de fées qui nous

---

1. Richard Alleva, June 1, 1996, *Commonweal*

touche, l'injustice grossière faite à la sœur plus modeste, directement héritée de Cendrillon et de ses épigones (*Pride* ne faisait en vérité qu'effleurer le versant enfantin du conte). Mais il y a beaucoup de rhétorique et d'artifice dans l'usage que nous faisons du roman et des films : dans un temps très lointain (« *once upon a time* ») des gens « comme vous et moi » ont souffert ce que souffrent *aujourd'hui* de tout autres déshérités, dans de tout autres continents… Bref, il est assez clair que nous ne lisons pas, sauf dans un effort d'historiens ou d'archéologues de la littérature, ce qui se lisait en 1847. Belle évidence, que les films sont parfois sommés d'oublier : ils accentuent alors l'effet de parallaxe et ils nous renseignent autant sur leurs intentions que sur nos évolutions, le plus souvent parce qu'ils s'efforcent de dire ce que leurs auteurs imaginent répondre à nos attentes. Et, au bout du compte, cette Jane-là est-elle toujours aussi *aimable* qu'en 1847 ?

Au début du film, le sentiment d'*injustice* est donc projeté à la face du spectateur (l'écran devient entièrement rouge) dans sa forme la plus massive et la plus révoltante : chez Zeffirelli (mais le ton n'est guère différent dans les autres adaptations), une marâtre à moitié hystérique, entourée d'une progéniture repoussante (le John Reed de 1996 est loin d'être le pire), veut se débarrasser de l'héroïne et elle la confie à un vieux rapace dont la mauvaise foi saute aux yeux ! Certes, le conte de fées utilise les outils du réalisme, mais une fois acquise la sympathie du spectateur, que dénonce-t-on ici ? Un cas de favoritisme indécent, une injustice sociale, ou un Destin individuel ? Dans *Pride and Prejudice*, ce que j'ai appelé l'*ordre des choses* pour marquer à quel point il semblait accepté par Austen restait un moteur de l'intrigue, la cause première (à savoir l'*entailment*) postulée pour que le récit ait lieu. Les choses sont plus complexes dans *Jane Eyre*, ne serait-ce que parce que la narratrice doit se dédoubler pour séparer le vrai du faux.

Intertextes. Là encore les récits-doubles ne manquent pas, autobiographies, contes ou fables édifiantes : en 1850, l'autobiographie déclarée — mais imaginaire — d'*Alton Locke* par Charles Kingsley raconte la vie (et le départ vers l'Empire) d'un héros qui traverse les drames sociaux de son temps et plaide la cause du Chartisme ; au contraire, en 1857, la vie et la mort d'*Emma Bovary* renvoient à une autobiographie déguisée de Gustave Flaubert : ici l'écriture de soi sert à crédibiliser une fiction sociale ; là une fiction apparente garde à distance le récit de soi. Le conte émouvant et vengeur de l'*Ugly Duckling* (Vilain petit canard) convient beaucoup mieux à Jane qu'à Elizabeth Bennett, car l'héroïne de Charlotte Brontë est une *héritière* (tout le monde le savait déjà puisqu'elle s'appelle Jane Heir !), dont la trajectoire était dessinée d'avance et dont le *pattern* sous jacent — nous savons depuis le début ce que Jane doit progressivement découvrir — permet le double jeu de la distance et de l'émotion. Quant à *From Rags to Riches*, la fable d'Horatio Alger déjà évoquée à propos d'Austen, elle semble résumer le message social *apparent* de 1847: tout est possible à ceux qui travaillent, « aide toi le Ciel t'aidera ».

Liberté et déterminisme. Il faudrait donc vérifier les choix que chaque version suggère entre la *révolte* et l'*acceptation* de l'ordre des choses. On notera d'abord que les contraintes et les refus de cet ordre s'expriment visuellement de deux façons antagonistes — centripète et centrifuge — tantôt par l'*enfermement* dans les règles arbitraires (Lowood), les contrats hasardeux (le premier mariage de Rochester) ou la séquestration (Chambre rouge, grenier de Bertha) ; tantôt par la *fuite*, vers le Nord pour Jane, vers Marseille (dans le roman) si elle avait écouté Rochester. On insistera ensuite sur le soustexte biblique omniprésent que les films effleurent à peine, souvent de façon caricaturale (En 1996, Brocklehurst cite un verset). Car le roman est habité par une croyance multiforme au *déterminisme*, tantôt proche du positivisme, tantôt sur des bases chrétiennes : phrénologie, correspondance entre le physique (inné) et le mental, confiance dans une typologie des caractères et des dons[1], lisibilité des visages ; mais aussi naissance, hérédité et héritages, volonté divine et nécessité de suivre les traces du Christ. Il faut alors choisir entre la conformité à la *nature* de chacun et la volonté de réformer la Nature pour atteindre, selon les mots de Brocklehurst, la Grâce !

Autrement dit, on se demandera ce que les films préservent de l'*anatomie de la morale chrétienne* si patiemment décrite par Brontë : acceptation des punitions infligées, de la mise en conformité et de la mort pour Helen Burns, dont le Destin manifeste est d'être un Ange (En 1944, Elizabeth Taylor se rapproche de l'original) ; bonne volonté et vision très adoucie chez Miss Temple ; caricature hypocrite chez son patron et lecture totalitaire et inquiétante chez St John Rivers, qui faute d'être un Ange, rêve de devenir un Saint. Seuls les films TV ont le temps et le goût (anglais ?) pour ces choses là. Si, à propos d'Helen Burns, Zeffirelli évite soigneusement de tomber dans le sulpicien, c'est peut-être pour esquiver une autre révolte — façon Michel Onfray — contre les méfaits d'une religion qui préfère la mort à la vie.

Hommes et femmes. On aura deviné mes doutes sur ce versant du récit[2] et ma sympathie pour l'autre : la formidable *revendication égalitaire* de Jane, sociale, sexuelle et ontologique, telle qu'elle s'exprime dans le roman :

> Do you think, because I am poor, obscure, plain, and
> little, I am soulless and heartless? *(216)*

Tout un programme et un rude apprentissage pour Rochester — car il faudra aussi quand même s'intéresser à *son* point de vue ! — qui lâche un

---

1. Helen admire le don de Jane qui sait dessiner.
2. Pourtant très stimulant pour l'historien des idées.

touchant (et complaisant ?) « *I was your equal at sixteen*[1]! » (p. 116). Après les inégalités de classe et de fortune (« *your place* » !) l'étude des inégalités entre hommes et femmes s'impose et on se demandera en quoi les films réalisés par des femmes (BBC 1973 et 2006 par exemple) sont différents des autres. Mais c'est aussi la place de la *sexualité* suggérée ou visible dans les films, qui varie d'époque en époque, au point que la version 2006 montre Jane et Rochester enlacés sur la pelouse, que le châtelain insiste « *We are not the platonic sort, Jane* » et que Bertha retrouve la parole pour lancer à Jane une insulte espagnole assez suggestive : « *Puta!* » Là plus qu'ailleurs, le différentiel de temps entre un roman de 1847, des lecteurs de 2008, des films d'il y a plus de cinquante ans (dans une Amérique très puritaine), ou le film prudent de 1996, invite à lire entre les lignes ou derrière les images. Ce qu'on a déjà dit des sœurs Bennett reste vrai : la découverte probable de la sexualité masculine sur des statues de *marbre*[2] laisse supposer que Jane Eyre aura beaucoup à explorer, alors même que son époux — comme beaucoup de mâles de son temps — a au contraire *beaucoup vécu*, comme on disait alors. Les mots ici en disent déjà long sur la différence entre les sexes.

Dire et voir. C'est justement cette relation entre les mots et les choses, entre le dire et le montrer, qui se trouve au cœur de la relation particulière entre le roman de Brontë et ses films. La narratrice revient plusieurs fois sur la capacité ou le talent de certains pour la description et d'autres pour l'analyse et le questionnement, ce qui insinue d'ailleurs une hiérarchie, surtout quand il s'agit de sa camarade de Lowood, Ann Wilson, manifestement inférieure à Helen Burns, mais qui « *had a turn for narration* ». Jane ajoute aussitôt « *I for analysis* » (66). *Jane Eyre* analyse, commente et, surtout, *décrit* ses personnages, les lieux et la nature qui les entourent et le roman paraissait — à première vue — un support idéal pour une adaptation cinématographique. On a compris que les choses sont bien plus compliquées et que là où le roman se fait minutieux (à la lecture on croit *voir* Rochester, un sorte de Lino Ventura athlétique et trapu d'outre Manche), les films s'empressent de tout changer.

Là encore, Brontë aime les *comparaisons* et elle offre une typologie de plusieurs statuts du dessin afin de mieux comprendre de quoi on parle avant de penser à évaluer. A Lowood, Jane sait d'abord *reproduire* les visages et la gracieuse vivacité de ses gestes devant Helen Burns, qui a pris la pose dans le soleil, est déjà celle d'une experte. Mais sa réussite tient aussi à son aptitude à voir le détail caractéristique, le mouvement juste — c'est-à-dire que voir suppose aussi une forme de rencontre entre l'image reçue et l'image

---

1. Je suis un peu de mauvaise foi : « equal » ici, veut surtout dire « comme vous ».
2. Dans le film de Joe Wright (2005).

projetée par le dessinateur. Même les films préservent les conceptions de l'art impliquées par le livre. Rochester demande d'abord si les dessins de la gouvernante sont des *copies* d'après d'autres dessins ; puis s'ils *représentent* des lieux réels. Mais Jane se plaint aussi de n'avoir pas su « re-présenter » ses *images intérieures*, faute de technique : car le dessin (ou la peinture) est encore la reproduction d'une image qui existait déjà, elle-même associée à un référent plus ou moins matérialisé : *objet* réel, *image* d'un objet déjà représenté, image d'un objet vu en *esprit* (en rêve, de façon télépathique, ou animée par une force transcendante … car la métaphore romantique de la Harpe Eolienne n'est pas très loin) ; image d'un objet suscité par des *mots*…. Seuls manquent au film de 1996 le dessin-comparaison à visée édifiante (Jane à la craie / Blanche Ingram *imaginée* sur l'ivoire, p. 137) et, surtout, le portrait « télépathique » de Rochester, guidé par l'inconscient (ou par le Destin …).

L'étude des films ouvre ainsi la vaste question d'une sorte de symétrie entre la monstration par les mots et la « parole par les images » : soit que les mots se substituent aux images (jusqu'au cas extrême de l'ekphrasis), soit que les images tentent à leur tour de parler à la place des mots, voire de les gauchir ou de les contredire. Brontë est déjà fascinée par l'articulation entre un monde organisé selon le *verbe* (et d'abord la Bible) et l'immédiateté apparente du monde des *sens*. Chez elle, sans doute plus qu'ailleurs, le monde est un texte à lire et à déchiffrer. On est alors frappé par le fait qu'avant même que le cinéma existe, la littérature a déjà été confrontée à des questions qui le traversent depuis plus d'un siècle.

Que faire des classiques ?

Il faut enfin revenir à la question initiale de la *fortune des classiques*. Si on considère l'*usage* que les films et les lecteurs-spectateurs font maintenant du récit, il faut répéter que l'essentiel de *Jane Eyre* est désormais rejeté dans un ailleurs de l'Histoire et de la fiction : les châtiments corporels ont disparu des écoles, les lecteurs potentiels du roman ne meurent plus de faim en Angleterre et ils n'y gâchent plus leur vie à cause d'un mariage arrangé avec une malheureuse devenue folle, séquestrée dans un château enfin équipé de détecteurs de fumée[1] ! Les films sont pourtant contraints d'ignorer l'*historicisation* des enjeux du roman (le noyau dur ici est l'évidence selon laquelle Rochester aurait obtenu le divorce, depuis plus d'un demi-siècle en Europe), faute de quoi le récit s'effondrerait comme la charpente de

---

1. Il faut bien sûr séparer les évolutions technologiques (nostalgie et couleur locale) des institutions et des idéologies. Mais, surtout dans un univers aussi chargé symboliquement, elles se répondent et s'articulent.

Thornfield. Autrement dit, à de rares exceptions près, notre appropriation des classiques passe par un double mouvement d'historicisation et de métaphorisation : l'injustice de telle époque trouve toujours un équivalent symbolique (lectures féministes) — parfois universel (comment lisons-nous *Lear*?) — dans l'univers présent du spectateur.

On sait donc bien ce que les films risquent (plus ou moins) de rater : la voix, l'ironie et la rage intérieure de Jane ; l'inquiétude intergénérique liée au recours au gothique ; la *physicalité* des enfermements et l'angoisse de se trouver à la croisée des chemins (Whitcross) sans aucun recours ; le continent entrevu d'un *ailleurs* dérangeant que constituent l'Empire patriarcal et l'esclavage ; la *croyance* enfin à un univers de *correspondances* où une sensibilité aiguisée associée à une intelligence vigoureuse peut déchiffrer son destin. Dans tous ces cas, les manques ou les variations imposées par les films serviront d'autant de « *foils* » dans un retour à l'esprit de 1847. Mais les deux siècles suivants ont aussi apporté leurs éclairages, leurs besoins et leurs aspirations : une doxa de méfiance à l'égard de l'image photographique dissimule encore la richesse du visible. Les belles images de la Nature, des visages et des animaux, de la lumière et des textures… tout cela est ignoré comme allant de soi, simple technique de reproduction doublement suspecte de mercantilisme et de conservatisme. Or ce n'est pas parce qu'un réalisateur n'est pas au dessus de tout soupçon que le cinéma doit subir un tel aveuglement. Peut-être pourrait-on sortir de ce malentendu en se souvenant que le directeur de la photographie, David Watkin[1], était un remarquable artiste qui a photographié plus de soixante films depuis 1955, dont *Mademoiselle* (Tony Richardson, 1966), *The Charge of the Light Brigade* (Richardson, 1968), *The Devils* (Ken Russell, 1971) et *Out of Africa* (Sidney Pollack, 1985)…

On suivra alors les pistes que suggèrent les évidences supposées de notre temps : notre regard devenu un peu fuyant sur les *enfants*, pour qui les dangers redoutés ont beaucoup changé ; ou le statut des *victimes* (naguère et aujourd'hui). On remarquera par exemple la richesse des réponses du roman, ses refus (auxquels nous adhérons évidemment) mais aussi ses *consentements* (que nous prendrions parfois aujourd'hui pour des complaisances) — car sans le Deus ex machina promis d'emblée, Jane, redevenue victime, aurait bien fini par s'allonger dans le linceul de son destin. De même, les films, dans leur hâte, nous épargnent les moments de tranquille xénophobie sur les paysans étrangers :

> for after all the British peasantry are the best taught, best mannered, most self-respecting of any in Europe: since

---

1. David Watkin, né à Margate en 1925, mort en 2008.

> those days I have seen paysannes and Bäuerinnen: and the
> best of them seemed to me ignorant, coarse, and besotted,
> compared with my Morton girls. *(331-332)*

Sans parler des trois belles continentales testées par Rochester. Après la Parisienne, infidèle et obsédée par ses toilettes, voici l'Italienne et l'Allemande :

> She had two successors: an Italian, Giacinta, and a German, Clara; both considered singularly handsome. What was their beauty to me in a few weeks? Giacinta was unprincipled and violent: I tired of her in three months. Clara was honest and quiet; but heavy, mindless, and unimpressible: not one whit to my taste[1]. *(266)*.

Merci pour elles, mais on aura mesuré les effets d'un genre et des habitudes de lecture d'une époque. Autrement dit, on se demandera en miroir ce que sont devenues les nôtres.

La plupart des adaptations n'ont pas su ou voulu trouver un équivalent de la merveilleuse page 266-267 où — dans un retour émouvant et audacieux — Rochester raconte *sa* rencontre avec Jane le premier soir[2], pour lui-même, pour Jane et pour nous : « *I saw a quiet little figure… I passed it… negligently…* » Mais :

> Once I had pressed the frail shoulder, something new—a
> fresh sap and sense—stole into my frame. […] I heard…
> I thought of you… watched for you… observed you…
> fancied your thoughts… etc.

Moment de pure grâce romanesque, aboutissement du dispositif narratif de l'*Ugly Duckling* par lequel on revit l'instant du doute avec les yeux du bonheur. Le cinéma pourtant excelle dans le jeu des échos, des retours sur le même et sur la différence. Tout reste donc à faire ? Et si, finalement, la visite était quand même intéressante ?

---

1. Dans cet exemple où c'est Rochester qui parle on peut supposer l'ironie, mais pas dans le cas de la narratrice à propos des paysans.
2. Voir plus bas l'étude de Nicole Cloarec.

Jane Eyre de Franco Zeffirelli (1996) : la glace sans le feu.
Lectures croisées de la première rencontre entre Jane et Rochester

Nicole Cloarec

Les récents travaux sur la question de l'adaptation d'œuvres littéraires au cinéma ont montré combien la notion même d'œuvre source est problématique[1] et qu'une adaptation filmique est le produit d'un nombre de facteurs aussi différents qu'un possible projet personnel du réalisateur, les attentes du public, la vision contemporaine d'une époque révolue, les conventions de narration cinématographique dominantes au moment du tournage, sans oublier les exigences commerciales des compagnies de production[2] ... C'est bien pourquoi on continue d'adapter les classiques au cinéma. Zeffirelli lui-même, interrogé sur les motifs qui l'ont poussé à adapter le roman de Charlotte Brontë[3], déclare que chaque génération a droit à « son » *Hamlet*, à « son » *Romeo et Juliette*[4] et à « sa » *Jane Eyre*. La question devient alors : que nous dit le film de notre réception de *Jane Eyre* en cette fin de XXe et début du XXIe siècle ? À quelles attentes du public le film répond-il, ou, plutôt, le film répond-il à ce que l'on pense être ce que le public acceptera comme la vision la plus « adéquate » — sachant que le dit public comprend aussi bien des fins connaisseurs de l'œuvre que des

---

1. Voir l'excellent article de Donna Marie Nudd « The Pleasure of Intertextuality: Reading *Jane Eyre* Television and Film Adaptations », in *Jane Eyre*, Charlotte Brontë, A Norton Critical Edition, Third Edition, Edited by Richard J. Dunn, 2001, p. 522-523: « But for filmmakers, the notion of the original text becomes even more complicated than just choosing which generic interpretation to emphasize. [...] For filmmakers, the original text is perhaps not Charlotte Brontë's novel but rather the most famous Jane Eyre film made before the one the filmmakers are working on. Or perhaps it is all the *Jane Eyres* (stage plays, films, books, television adaptations, cassette recordings, one-person shows, reviews, critical essays) with which the filmmakers have made themselves familiar. The original text might also be the compromised, idiosyncratic, historically situated interpretation of Brontë's novel as it emerges through the collaborative vision of a particular director, producer, and screenwriter, and their performers, musicians, set and costume designers, and editors. Or the original text might just be the novel as the filmmakers or their producers perceive the audience as having read, yesterday or thirty years ago—the *Jane Eyre* as imagined in the collective audience mind.»
2. Voir le tout aussi excellent article de Jeffrey Sconce « The Cinematic Reconstitution of *Jane Eyre*», in *Jane Eyre*, Charlotte Brontë, A Norton Critical Edition, *op.cit.*, p. 515-516.
3. Interview donnée à Charlie Rose le 04/04/1996, disponible sur Internet : http://www.charlierose.com/shows/1996/04/04/3/an-interview-with-franco-zeffirelli
4. *Romeo & Juliet* (1968) et *Hamlet* (1990) sont deux des précédentes adaptations de Franco Zeffirelli tirées du canon littéraire britannique, auxquelles on peut ajouter *The Taming of the Shrew* (1967).

spectateurs pour qui le livre n'est plus qu'un vague souvenir, si ce n'est un simple nom du canon littéraire britannique, ou encore des souvenirs d'autres adaptations filmiques ou télévisuelles[1]?

Fidélité en trompe-l'œil

On peut être surpris d'apprendre dans la version de 1934 que Rochester est l'oncle d'Adèle et qu'il entreprend très tôt de faire annuler son mariage, mais ces changements sont vite compréhensibles quand on les replace en pleine époque de la mise en place du code Hays : la morale est sauve, même si le maître de Thornfield s'est montré coupable d'impatience, en planifiant son second mariage avant l'arrivée des papiers. On peut être tout autant surpris dans le film de Zeffirelli de voir Jane revenir vivre à Thornfield sans qu'à aucun moment elle n'ait eu connaissance du sort de Bertha. Est-ce en raison de l'évolution des mœurs ? Mais la fin du film continue de consacrer l'union matrimoniale, reprenant non seulement l'adresse au spectateur en voix off « And so I married him » mais figeant le couple au centre d'un véritable tableau pastoral à la composition symétrique[2]. Serait-ce alors qu'implicitement le dilemme moral de Jane n'a plus lieu d'être dès lors que le spectateur ne le ressent plus, ayant été témoin de l'incendie ?

Le titre américain incluant le génitif de l'auteur (*Charlotte Brontë's Jane Eyre*) semblerait indiquer que le film de Zeffirelli s'inscrit pleinement dans la vogue des années 1990 d'un « retour au texte », à l'instar du film de Francis Ford Coppola *Bram Stoker's Dracula* (1992) et de celui de Kenneth Branagh *Mary Shelley's Frankenstein* (1994). De fait, le film de Zeffirelli est l'un des rares à insérer en séquence pré-générique l'épisode séminal de la chambre

---

1. Voir à ce sujet Jeffrey Sconce qui mentionne l'étude effectuée à la demande de Selznick en vue du *Jane Eyre* de Robert Stevenson (1944): « Incredibly, the single most remembered scene in Brontë's novel, according to the ARI survey, was an event that is only indirectly represented in the novel. The burning of Thornfield Hall was by far the most vividly remembered scene in the book, despite the fact that Jane, who serves as the novel's first person narrator, is not present to witness the blaze.» *op.cit.* p. 519-520.
2. À l'instar de toutes les autres adaptations, la fin du film de Zeffirelli élimine toute ambiguïté pour ne conserver que la figure du « happy end» qui n'est troublée ni par les dernières paroles de St John Rivers ni par l'exclusion d'Adèle qui revit en fin de compte le même sort que Jane enfant. Cf Nina Schwartz: « Jane's treatment of Adèle disturbingly repeats both Mrs Reed's conduct toward Jane herself and the behaviour of Mr Burns to his daughter Helen following his second marriage: in each case, a young girl is exiled from a domestic space because her presence is inconsistent with the adults' conception of family. » « No Place Like Home: The Logic of the Supplement in Jane Eyre », in *Jane Eyre*, Charlotte Brontë, Ed. By Beth Newman, Bedford Books of St Martin's Press, Boston — New York, 1996, p. 563. Dans le film de Zeffirelli, signe des temps, Jane indique en voix off qu'Adèle revient faire partie de la nouvelle famille « recomposée ».

rouge[1] (volume I, chapitre II). En dehors des mini-séries télévisées qui disposent d'une plus grande latitude temporelle, seule la version de 1997, donc postérieure, traite cette scène. Dans ce film, la scène est filmée à l'aide de lentilles déformantes qui brouillent la perspective en images convexes, traduisant le point de vue de la petite Jane victime d'hallucinations sonores comme visuelles : alors qu'un lourd rideau rouge s'agite, on entend des rires lointains et pourtant proleptiques, et dans un plan subjectif rapide, on voit même le cadavre de son oncle allongé sur le lit. Enfin, le miroir en pied dans lequel Jane s'abîme présente comme un trou béant en insérant le reflet d'un autre miroir en son centre.

Dans le film de Zeffirelli, la scène est également filmée en alternant plans rapprochés sur le visage terrifié de Jane et plans subjectifs traduisant la vision de la fillette, comme l'atteste le plan de Mrs Reed filmée dans l'encadrement de la porte en contreplongée. Jane est violement projetée contre la psyché, qui basculant, reflète une chambre rouge très sombre et fondamentalement instable. À l'image des cadres serrés, l'impression dominante est celle de claustrophobie, toute perspective étant bouchée par la porte qui se referme, les rideaux et tentures rouges qui entourent la pièce entière. Le dernier plan, avant un fondu au noir évocateur d'une syncope, montre Jane de face tapie dans l'ombre.

Les deux versions divergent radicalement dans la mesure où le film de Zeffirelli, à l'inverse de la version de 1997 qui exploite la dimension proleptique de la scène par l'entremise des rires, du miroir aliénant et de la rigidité de la figure paternelle, isole totalement la scène du reste du récit. Ainsi, le film omet la visite nocturne de Bertha l'avant-veille du mariage de Jane qui, réveillée, aperçoit le reflet de la folle voilée dans le miroir. De même, le sentiment d'aliénation de Jane face à son reflet en robe de mariée n'est pas traité dans le film dans lequel le miroir, bien que multipliant les reflets, renvoie une image « objective[2] », celle d'une jeune femme sans charme immédiat (« I am a fool »). Enfin, la référence au fantôme de l'oncle disparaît, laissant supposer que l'intensité de la détresse éprouvée par Jane est provoquée par l'arbitraire et la violence du rejet que lui manifeste sa famille d'adoption. La voix off ouvrant le récit semble corroborer l'idée que l'enjeu central du film est bien l'amour — le manque et le besoin d'aimer et d'être aimé(e) : « My parents died when I was very young. I was sent to

---

1. Voir par exemple Sandra M. Gilbert : « And that Brontë quite consciously intended the incident of the red-room to serve as a paradigm for the larger plot of her novel is clear not only from its position in the narrative but also from Jane's own recollection of the experience at crucial moments throughout the book. » « Plain Jane's Progress », in *Jane Eyre*, Charlotte Brontë, Ed. By Beth Newman, *op. cit.*, p. 477.
2. Dans le film de Zeffirelli, le miroir tient davantage le rôle tenu dans le roman par l'auto-portrait que Jane dessine pour mieux se déprécier en comparaison du portrait imaginé de Blanche.

live with my aunt Mrs Reed and her children at Gateshead Hall. For nearly ten years I endured their unkindness and cruelty. They did not love me. I could not love them. »

Comme l'atteste la réécriture de l'incipit, le film de Zeffirelli procède à autant de modifications, omissions et condensations que les autres adaptations, ce qui ne saurait surprendre. Il est cependant fascinant de voir à quel point l'incipit écrit par Charlotte Brontë a fait l'objet de réécritures, alors même que les textes sont filmés en insert, selon la figure conventionnelle du cinéma hollywoodien classique qui fait coïncider le début du film avec l'ouverture d'un livre[1]. Afin de cerner davantage les choix esthétiques opérés par l'adaptation de Zeffirelli, nous nous pencherons sur la scène emblématique de la rencontre entre Jane et Rochester.

Un conte d'hiver

De nombreux critiques ont remarqué que le chapitre XII s'ouvre sur un appel au changement[2], l'insatisfaction inquiète de Jane se manifestant par d'incessantes allées et venues le long du troisième étage[3] ou de longues marches sur les landes environnantes et une propension à laisser vaguer son imagination. Après l'accélération temporelle du sommaire itératif retraçant sa vie à Thornfield pendant les trois mois d'automne, la narratrice se concentre sur les circonstances particulières d'une promenade un soir d'hiver. Elle commence par décrire minutieusement le décor en insistant sur le lieu mais aussi sur le moment de la journée si propice aux rêveries de Jane :

> I walked slowly to enjoy and analyse the species of pleasure brooding for me in the hour and situation.[...] the charm of the hour lay in its approaching dimness, in the low-gliding and pale-beaming sun. *(94)*

---

1. La version de 1934, pourtant proche du théâtre filmé, opte pour la note atmosphérique : « The cold winter wind had brought with it somber clouds and penetrating rain. ». Dans la célèbre version de 1944, le texte, qui apparaît à l'écran alors qu'il est lu en voix off, insiste sur le contexte historique et biographique : « My name is Jane Eyre. I was born in 1820, a harsh time of change in England. Money and position seems all that mattered. Charity was a cold and disagreeable word. Religion too often wore a mask of bigotry and cruelty. There was no proper place for the poor or the unfortunate. I had no father or mother, brother or sister. As a child I lived with my aunt, a Mrs Reed of Gateshead Hall. I do not remember that she ever spoke one kind word to me. » Dans les deux cas, il s'agit bien d'apporter une caution littéraire et non de suivre un texte !
2. Il s'agit du troisième paragraphe : « Anybody may blame me who likes when I add further that now and then, when I took a walk by myself in the grounds [...]—that then I longed for a power of vision which might overpass that limit... » p. 93.
3. « I could not help it: the restlessness was in my nature; it agitated me to pain sometimes. Then my sole relief was to walk along the corridor of the third story, backwards and forwards [...] and, best of all, to open my inward ear to a tale that was never ended—a tale my imagination created, and narrated continuously » p. 93.

L'attente de Jane est ainsi traduite par l'extrême minutie apportée à la transcription des moindres frémissements de la nature au sein d'un paysage hivernal figé par le gel. La rencontre proprement dite, elle, se déroule en trois temps.

Dans le premier temps, alors que Jane, réchauffée, fait une pause pour admirer le soleil couchant et la lune naissante, c'est une intrusion sonore qui vient interrompre sa contemplation : les monosyllabes « a rude noise broke » viennent littéralement cogner la mélodie coulante des « fine ripplings and whisperings ». L'approche sonore oxymorique — « at once so far away and so clear » — et donc étrange parce que contradictoire, déclenche l'imagination de la jeune femme qui se prépare (de même que le lecteur) à une rencontre surnaturelle :

> In those days I was young, and all sorts of fancies bright and dark tenanted my mind: the memories of nursery stories were there amongst other rubbish; and when they recurred, maturing youth added to them a vigour and vividness beyond what childhood could give. *(95)*

De façon remarquable, l'identification du bruit comme martèlement des sabots d'un cheval ainsi que l'irruption du chien ne viennent que confirmer la vision irréelle de Jane :

> As this horse approached, and as I watched for it to appear through the dusk, I remembered certain of Bessie's tales, wherein figured a North-of-England spirit, called a "Gytrash", which, in the form of horse, mule, or large dog, haunted solitary ways, and sometimes came upon belated travellers, as this horse was now coming upon me. It was very near, but not yet in sight, when, in addition to the tramp, tramp, I heard a rush under the hedge, and close down by the hazel stems glided a great dog, whose black and white colour made him a distinct object against the trees. It was exactly one mask of Bessie's Gytrash—a lion-like creature with long hair and a huge head. *(95)*

Le deuxième mouvement de la rencontre est marqué par l'apparition du cavalier qui brise le charme féerique de la scène[1] de façon d'autant plus abrupte que sa première action est de chuter. Edward Rochester est un héros déjà déchu et c'est toute la perversité de Jane que d'être attirée par la part sombre du protagoniste qui mobilise chez elle un désir d'apporter aide et rédemption. Enfin, le troisième mouvement de la rencontre est dédié au dialogue, qui se déploie lui-même en deux temps, séparé par le portrait de Rochester et les sentiments que son apparence éveille en Jane. Il est frappant

---

1. "The man, the human being, broke the spell at once". p. 96

de noter que l'attirance de Jane pour Rochester est largement décrite en termes négatifs, engendrant un long passage hypothétique qui culmine en un condensé de termes quasi antithétiques (c'est moi qui souligne) :

> *Had* he been a handsome, heroic-looking young gentleman, I should *not* have dared to stand thus questioning him *against his will*, and offering my services *un*asked. I had *hardly ever* seen a handsome youth; *never* in my life spoken to one. I had a theoretical reverence and homage for beauty, elegance, gallantry, fascination; but *had* I met those qualities incarnate in masculine shape, I should have known instinctively that they *nei*ther had *nor* could have sympathy with anything in me, and should have shunned them as one would fire, lightning, or anything that is bright but *anti*pathetic. *If* even this stranger had smiled and been good-humoured to me when I addressed him; if he had put off my offer of assistance gaily and with thanks, I should have gone on my way and *not* felt any vocation to renew inquiries: but the *frown*, the *roughness* of the traveller, set me at my *ease*. (97)

D'emblée la rencontre place la relation entre Jane et Rochester sous le signe du paradoxe et du déni, que la narratrice traduit par l'accumulation des négations et des contradictions juste après la narration de la scène (c'est moi qui souligne) :

> The incident had occurred and was gone for me: it was an incident of *no* moment, *no* romance, *no* interest in a sense; *yet* it marked with change one single hour of a monotonous life [...] trivial, transitory *though* the deed was, it was *yet* an active thing, and I was weary of an existence all passive. *(98)*

La rencontre de Jane et de Rochester est donc une scène complexe, marquée par de rapides changements de rythmes, de tonalités et de registres, passant du fantastique au trivial, marquée par l'ambiguïté des sentiments et ses expressions contradictoires. Il est bien sûr illusoire de vouloir retrouver toutes ces nuances dans une adaptation filmique, qui répond à d'autres contraintes narratives et exploite un autre système sémiotique. Il ne s'agit donc en aucun cas d'établir une hiérarchie entre roman et film ou même entre différentes versions filmiques mais bien d'explorer des lectures spécifiques de la scène, emblématiques des choix esthétiques à l'œuvre dans les films.

Dans la célèbre version de 1944, la scène de la rencontre s'ouvre sur un paysage nocturne et couvert de brume ; bien que filmé en studio, le jeu d'éclairage très contrasté, résolument gothique, traduit un espace qui semble illimité et sans repère, dans lequel les sons sont amplifiés à l'instar du crescendo musical qui suit le timbre régulier d'une cloche lointaine et prend des tonalités de musique de chasse. La tension créée par la bande son se traduit alors par le cadre resserré sur le visage inquiet de Jane, quand celle-ci manque d'être renversée d'abord par un énorme molosse puis par un cheval noir qui se cabre, filmé en contre-plongée. À chaque fois, l'apparition soudaine émerge de la brume épaisse juste devant Jane, de même que le cavalier se relève de sa chute à ses pieds, comme un diable qui sort de sa boite. Edward Rochester reste jusqu'au bout une apparition, une émanation de la brume dans laquelle il disparaît à nouveau vers le fond de l'écran après être remonté en selle sans l'aide de Jane. La scène ne laisse aucune ambiguïté possible : nous sommes en plein conte gothique où chaque séquence est ponctuée par des portes qui se referment, où le secret inavouable que représente Bertha reste un hors champ inaccessible au spectateur, sa présence inquiétante étant suggérée par la bande son, des jeux d'ombre ou, lorsque Rochester la présente à Jane, une paire de mains qui surgissent du bas de l'écran.

La version de 1970 met également l'accent sur l'aspect onirique de la scène sans pour autant conserver sa dimension nocturne et gothique. Filmée en décor naturel, la scène montre Jane en haut d'un escarpement surplombant une vallée à la tombée du jour. La caméra adopte alors la vision subjective de Jane, totalement éblouie par le soleil couchant alors que sur la bande son, des martèlements de plus en plus distincts viennent couvrir la musique, évoquant des battements de cœur qui s'accélèrent avant de se transformer en bruit de galop frénétique. Suit un montage très découpé alternant des plans serrés sur les pattes du cheval et sur le visage de Jane. La soudaineté de l'apparition de Rochester et le choc de la rencontre sont ici dramatisés à l'extrême par les effets sonores et visuels subjectifs et la rapidité du montage.

La version de 1997 présente au moins deux variantes majeures. Si elle reprend le motif de la brume qui stagne au ras du sol, elle déplace le moment de la journée, puisque qu'il s'agit d'un après-midi froid et clair. Jane se promène près d'un ruisseau qui se révélera être le point de la rencontre. La silhouette d'un cavalier noyée dans la brume apparaît dans trois plans très rapides, filmée au ralenti afin d'accentuer l'impression de vitesse, et c'est la seconde originalité de cette scène car ces plans ne sont logiquement rattachés à aucun point de vue. Deux interprétations sont alors possibles : effet de suspense comme un classique montage parallèle ou vision hallucinée par Jane dont l'imagination vient d'être stimulée ? La rencontre proprement dite se traduit par le jaillissement des eaux qui éclaboussent la jeune femme. Ce choix d'une eau nullement gelée vient toutefois souligner la symbolique aquatique si prégnante dans le roman[1] et indique clairement la nature passionnée de la future relation telle qu'elle se développe dans le film.

Au-delà des différences considérables qui existent dans le traitement de la scène, les trois versions mentionnées plus haut partagent une vision de la rencontre comme un choc violent, physique (dans la collision évitée de justesse) et émotionnel. C'est ici que le film de Zeffirelli diffère considérablement et offre une lecture où dominent au contraire distance et retenue[2]. Située dans un paysage gelé de fin d'automne d'une grande beauté, la scène respecte dans les grandes lignes l'action et le dialogue sans chercher à rendre quelque aspect que ce soit de la narration subjective qui prépare à la rencontre puis l'analyse. De fait, la scène se caractérise par le refus du moment dramatique : le montage est sans effet de surprise, ne créant pas d'attente particulière, de tension ou d'appréhension subjective des événements, mais reste au contraire extérieur à ces derniers, observant en plans larges puis en plans serrés et en champ contre champ deux êtres se croisant. De la même façon, la bande son reste sobre, avec un fond musical discret puis des aboiements dénués de mystère qui annulent tout effet de surprise de la rencontre.

Surtout, la scène refuse tout soupçon d'une imagerie symbolique susceptible de former un réseau signifiant, comme celle de la présence tutélaire de la lune, mentionnée dans le roman à chaque événement décisif : ainsi, le choix d'un moment indifférencié de l'après-midi presque hivernal donne à l'image des tons passés à l'image du ciel presque incolore. De façon significative, le même choix par omission est opéré lors de l'appel télépathique de Rochester à Jane, filmé en plein jour près de la tombe d'Helen et qui se trouve comme « naturalisé » par le bruissement du vent dans les feuilles de grands arbres que deux plans viennent isoler.

En dépit du conseil de Jane à Adèle « and remember : the shadows are as important as the light » [48], le décor s'efface en épure destinée à mettre en valeur le jeu des acteurs, que vient souligner les multiples plans rapprochés sur le visage de Jane-Charlotte Gainsbourg et le traditionnel champ contre-champ des regards. Ici, plus qu'à une collision suggérée dans les autres versions, l'insistance est sur la rencontre des regards. Ce procédé sera d'ailleurs réitéré dans la plupart des séquences : la caméra commence par planter un décor à la photographie léchée, parfois proche d'un véritable tableau (récurrence des compositions symétriques) pour finir par un champ contre champ en plan serrés sur les visages des deux protagonistes principaux.

---

1. Voir par exemple Bernadette Bertrandias, *Jane Eyre : la parole orpheline*, Ellipses, coll « Marque-page », 2004, en particulier le chapitre « Physique élémentaire », p. 39.
2. Je parle ici de la mise en scène et de ses effets. Si les deux termes correspondent tout à fait au jeu de Charlotte Gainsbourg, ils ne sauraient qualifier les mimiques appuyées de William Hurt.

On peut sans doute voir dans l'importance presque exclusive accordée aux acteurs l'influence de la scène opératique[1] et l'ouverture sur un dessin de façade de maison, telle un décor de fond de scène, tendrait à corroborer cette hypothèse. De façon révélatrice, le type de dessin choisi est une grisaille, mettant en valeur les détails mais refusant les contrastes violents, comme si elle était programmatique de la photographie du film, souvent très sombre mais sans véritables ombres parce que l'espace n'est jamais l'enjeu de la scène.

Si on ne s'étonne plus de voir que les adaptations filmiques omettent systématiquement la dimension du pèlerinage religieux, il est beaucoup plus surprenant de rencontrer une version qui ne cherche pas à dramatiser visuellement la passion et l'excès qui font la force et l'originalité de l'écriture de Charlotte Brontë. C'est aussi l'originalité incontestable du film de Franco Zeffirelli que de traiter *Jane Eyre* avec une extrême retenue, au risque de réécrire le roman en un conte d'hiver, de glace sans le feu.

Filmographie

Jane Eyre (1996) réalisé par Franco Zeffirelli, produit pour Rochester Films Ltd, Flach Film et Cineritmo SRL, avec Charlotte Gainsbourg (Jane Eyre) et William Hurt (Edward Rochester).
Jane Eyre (1934) réalisé par Christy Cabanne, produit pour Monogram Picture, avec Virginia Bruce (Jane Eyre) et Colin Clive (Edward Rochester).
Jane Eyre (1944) réalisé par Robert Stevenson, produit pour Twentieth Fox Century, avec et Joan Fontaine (Jane Eyre) Orson Welles (Edward Rochester).
Jane Eyre (1970) réalisé par Delbert Mann, produit pour Guillotine Films, avec Susannah York (Jane Eyre) et George C. Scott (Edward Rochester).
Jane Eyre (1997) réalisé par Robert Young, produit pour London Weekend Television et A&E Television Networks, avec Samantha Morton (Jane Eyre) et Ciaran Hinds (Edward Rochester).

Bibliographie

BERTRANDIAS, Bernadette, *Jane Eyre : la parole orpheline*, Ellipses, coll « Marque-page », 2004.
GILBERT, Sandra M., « Plain Jane's Progress », *in Jane Eyre*, Charlotte Brontë, ed., By Beth Newman, Bedford Books of St Martin's Press, Boston—New York, 1996.
NUDD, Donna Marie, « The Pleasure of Intertextuality: Reading *Jane Eyre* Television and Film Adaptations », *in Jane Eyre*, Charlotte Brontë, A Norton Critical Edition, Third Edition, Edited by Richard J. Dunn, 2001.
SCHWARTZ, Nina, « No Place Like Home: The Logic of the Supplement in Jane Eyre », *in Jane Eyre*, Charlotte Brontë, ed., By Beth Newman, Bedford Books of St Martin's Press, Boston—New York, 1996.
SCONCE, Jeffrey, « The Cinematic Reconstitution of *Jane Eyre* », *in Jane Eyre*, Charlotte Brontë, A Norton Critical Edition, Third Edition, Edited by Richard J. Dunn, 2001.

---

1. Franco Zeffirelli est connu pour ses mises en scène d'opéras. Tout récemment (30 mars 2008), il a reçu les honneurs du New York Metropolitan Opera où il a monté douze productions.

Commodifying culture and the politically correct in the 1990s: Franco Zeffirelli's *Jane Eyre* (1847)

R. Costa de Beauregard

Among the major shots one remembers of the film which epitomizes the dramatic screening of Jane Eyre as a romantic heroine, I wish to quote a long distance shot framing the battlements of Thornfield Hall (alias Haddon Hall, "a medieval manor house ...wholly enclosed within a twelfth-century containing-wall"[1]) on the crest of a hill. The high angle on Jane as she crosses the green pasture below the woods and their castle, frames her black figure as a tiny speck in a pastoral landscape: in shots such as this one the film relies on our expectations in two very different ways: either the viewer knows nothing of the novel and enjoys what we are told is a typical Yorkshire view, or we are familiar with the novel and are expecting her encounter with the "Gytrash". The representation of the heroine in the film is thus divided between tourist information made more attractive by a careful delay of information for the former, and the difficulties of screening a text whose interest lies primarily in its narration for the latter. Bearing this in mind, I will try to examine the screening of a Yorkshire tour for a stranger, and the delay of information which preserves a degree of violence for the various crises of the heroine's struggle against predestination, only slightly addressing the latter viewer's expectations.

In the novel places are given names which symbolize periods in Jane's growth from childhood to adulthood; in the film, these places primarily allow us to reconstruct her Yorkshire[2] surroundings. For example, the

---

1. As D. Sipière kindly reminds me, the DVD does say it was shot on location, *i.e.* Haddon Hall (Bakewell, Derbyshire) and this ought to be for the interiors such as "the Long Gallery with the unusual windows and fine panelling". The façade of Haddon Hall is a beautiful Elizabethan one with a great many large windows, but there also is a tower on the older façade; the colour of the stone makes it "warmly welcoming". As for the shot of Jane and Adele on the terrace overlooking the gardens, it is clearly shot from the terrace. Cf. G. Hogg, *A Guide to English Country Houses*, London: Country Life, 1969, p. 28-9. There is a tradition today that Charlotte Brontë had visited Norton Conyers and used the place as a model for "Thornfield"; the present owners are members of the National Trust, (ref. on Google).
2. Yorkshire is shown in the film using the clichés of a Tour in what is now called Brontë Country: though no photographs of Haworth are apparently included in Zeffirelli's film, yet the outdoor shots on the moors are faithful to the "staggeringly beautiful Yorkshire landscape" (*Brontë Country*, by Liam DALE (2001), DVD, ed. Delta Music, 222 Cray Avenue, Orpington, Kent, BR5 3PZ, U.K.) while the northern light is carefully rendered (clouded skies, low-key lighting) by the photography of David Watkin in reference to Burke and Girtin's 'Sublime'. The general feeling of chilling dampness which characterizes Haworth is enhanced by the motif of the

characteristic deep-grey colour of Yorkshire stone gives the facades of its buildings a grim quality which a tourist visiting what is now known as Brontë Country cannot fail to notice, being so different from the brickwork of colourful villages in such places as southern Kent for instance. Flowers do add flashes of colour in the spring, but the film carefully restricts these to a short span of happiness during Jane's first stay at Thornfield Hall. Interestingly, the film opens on a black and white photograph of a frontal view showing an eighteenth century Georgian façade which, in Yorkshire, is characterised by the lack of windowsills, a feature which gives the large rectangular windows an expression of forbidding resilience. The Tudor castle's surrounding walls exhibit an equally dark stonework for the battlements; but the film uses a facade with a lighter yellow coloured stone, and its mullioned windows add more ornament by this piece of Renaissance stonework. The choice of a vertical top to bottom crane-shot to describe its tower down to the pointed arch and heavy wooden door offers a sharp contrast with Jane's earlier dwellings; instead of making the more ancient period look the darker of the two, the film's architectural choices enhance the pleasure of escaping from a gloomy modern era into a magic past. Thus when the camera pulls back to a low angle of Jane ascending the front steps and cuts to a final close-shot of her huge black bonnet as she rings the bell, her confrontation with an unknown place is free from any foreboding sense of an ominous future.

The frontal angle on Gateshead (dvd. ch.1&2) first as a black-and-white photograph then in its authentic grey garb) makes its façade appear like a screen within the screen and the windows suggest more the iron bars of a gaol. By the addition (for the film?) of a coat of arms bearing three marks on it which are weirdly empty and not unlike a skull[1], Gateshead façade is made to suggest the Gate of an Inferno, an impression immediately confirmed as the voices of quarrelling children are overheard and by the shutting up of little Jane in the red-room. The Palladian façade—two rows of windows, no apparent roof, and a portico for the entrance door, thus seems to be subverted from its original pleasurable Georgian elegance. While a historical tour of Yorkshire provides the foreigner with an account of social unrest and proletarian exploitation in the industrialisation of the North, the

---

graveyard in the film, and tourists are told about the Haworth tragedy which killed over 40% of the children in the lifetime of the Brontë sisters (lack of hygiene caused by the water supply from the top of the filtered through the graves in which bodies were buried without coffins before being used in the village below). The raised slabs shown in the film are the result of a decision from the Board of Health to outlaw flat gravestones thought to increase the downhill running of the poisoned water.

1. Ironically different from the Byron family coat of arms at Newstead Abbey (Nottinghamshire) dated 1631, this coat of arms fits oddly on a typically eighteenth century building; this is relevant if the character of Rochester is taken from Lord Byron himself.

interiors of Gateshead, which were presumably done for the film, suggest the enforced rigidity of eighteenth and nineteenth century British upper middle class traditions by the absolute symmetry of the decoration. The fire-place is encased in a flat white marble chimney-piece above which the eighteenth century Italian, *i.e.* Claudian, landscape faintly but distinctly recalls the decoration of well-known tourist sights such as the double-cube-room at Wilton House, or the Canaletto red-rooms in Woburn[1]. The rigidity of the setting is duplicated by Brocklehurst's upright silhouette and Mrs Reed's equally formal demeanour in a cliché scene of the British tea ritual; Georgiana entertains their guest by playing the pianoforte, while the other two children stand respectfully in attendance; sources for the XVIIIth century iconography of such family gatherings might be found in Hogarth's family portraits. However the film is not making a caricature of a class but restricting its focus upon the two unbearable snobs who have the upper hand over Jane's destiny. From the first shots of the film, the Reeds and the Brocklehursts of Jane's childhood are redolent with faint reminiscences of Dickens's own *Oliver Twist*, not however with any other subtext than a reference to what have become the clichés of Victorian ill-treatment of lower class children.

The unfair remarks which Mrs Reed (Fiona Shaw) makes about Jane all add up to a general victimization of the heroine: we are shown John bullying Jane in the stairs, and close shots of her 'benefactress' as she spills out her venom underscore the perversity of her character. The portico is used to enhance Mr Brocklehurst ceremonious entrance and by contrast rings with the echoes of little Jane's voice as she turns round before leaving and returns the accusation of deceit: here the text of the novel is inserted faithfully, introducing the theme of predestination and the heroine's constant struggle to regain control over her destiny.

The ensconced facade of the more rural and medieval looking building which was used to shoot the exteriors of Lowood (dvd ch 3 & 4) is equally shot frontally, and its gaol-like connotations are highlighted by the additional signpost in the foreground: 'Lowood Charity School'. But the changes from the novel are indeed telling: while the novel tells us that little Jane travels alone to a school which she has asked for, and that she has several weeks to establish her reputation before she is charged with being a liar and forced to stand on a stool, significant narrative elements which establish

---

1. Another place which would be imitated by the Reeds for the interior decoration of Gateshead, and rather nearer Haworth in West Yorkshire, might be Harewood House near Leeds, which was built in the eighteenth century and contains decoration and furniture by Robert Adam and Chippendale, and has a Capability Brown designed landscape garden. The typical white/red colour scheme is recalled in the white/red colours of Mr Reed's bedroom in which little Jane believes she meets his spectre.

the heroine's own part in her emancipation, the film shows her as a victim captured by Brocklehurst for his own purpose: reinforce the ban on social mobility for the lower classes. The ill-lit schoolroom has a low vaulted ceiling which frames the icons of power: Brocklehurst himself, and Miss Scatherd (Geraldine Chaplin) are carefully centred in the middle of the archway while the children are either shown in rows (inspection scene) or in the ill-lit dormitory which is also used for the recreation scene. The children are always shown indoors, but the cold is nevertheless visualised by the ice sheet on the water basin which they have to break in the morning. There is ice in the novel but it is only linked to Helen's unclean fingers in Jane's mind: Jane marvels at Helen's silence, and takes her cue from Helen's capacity to retreat within her own private self in such circumstances. But, in the film, Helen complains that the water was too cold for her to clean her hands, and the scene clearly departs from the novel in its tendency towards pathos. Arguably, the novel avoids pathos and manages to make cruelty quite convincing because it is grounded on a general treatment of all the pupils in the school, the film focuses on Helen as a scapegoat without showing us that the violence against her is also inflicted to other children. Thus it is the very significance of the scapegoat as a social ritual which is lost on the spectator; instead one infers that some unaccountable dislike causes Miss Scatcherd to torment Helen (though the novel does suggest something of the sort, but we are told for instance that the child whose hair is cut short is another one, anonymous, besides).

Such is indeed also characteristic of Jane's introductory ordeal in the film as Brocklehurst seems to be the instrument of Mrs Reed's neurosis. No rehabilitation scene is made possible, while the novel introduces an interesting piece of metatextual comment at that moment. Jane is addressing Miss Temple, the ideal Victorian lady—proleptic of Lady Colonel Dent later—and Jane's own ideal too:

> I told her all the story of my sad childhood…my language was more subdued than it generally was…mindful of Helen's warnings against the indulgence of resentment, I infused into the narrative far less of gall and wormwood than ordinary. Thus restrained and simplified, it sounded more credible: I felt as I went on that Miss Temple fully believed me[1].

By enhancing Jane's helplessness in the scenes of revolt, the film fails to bring to our attention what the novel persistently underscores, *i.e.* the increasing power Jane exercises on her own fate to escape determinism, as the example of the control she exerts over her own story shows. For example,

---

1. *Jane Eyre*, chapter 8 (p. 60 Norton edition).

the novel makes her reply: "I must keep in good health" to escape Hell, a symbol of her rebellion against predestination, and it is soon followed by her outcry of hatred for the Reeds which she calls the truth. The film keeps these two key sentences, but emphasizes her small size, her powerlessness and the cruel punishment her rebellion will call upon her, rather than showing this is an early step in a more lasting emancipation of the heroine. In similar fashion, when later, instead of an anonymous girl, it is Helen Burns who is singled out as the girl whose red curls have to be cut off, Jane is made to offer her own hair to be cut short also; though the actress (Anna Paquin) contrives to express her defiance in her look, the general effect is one of disproportionate cruelty since they were only drawing and reading. Brocklehurst is heard preaching against vanity, which aptly recalls that the Reed girls had just such hair and wore it long, but did not arouse his wrath: in the novel, however, the parallel is even more ironical because it is his own daughters who visit Lowood school in state, and exhibit just such a mass of golden curls: they therefore provide for the children, and Jane in particular, a telling instance of injustice which does not escape them. In the film the possible indictment of Brocklehurst is thus barely perceptible and not connected to Jane's observation in any manner.

As for the choice of Jane making a portrait of Helen, nowhere to be found in the novel, if I am not mistaken, this also subverts the view that Jane is emancipating from her condition at Lowood, despite the plan which was to make her into a servant. Instead we are introduced to a moment of intimacy between the two children which serves to motivate one of the key scenes in the novel when Jane gets into Helen's bed and wakes to find her dead. Helen in the novel gives Jane the secret to achieve a form of independence which is grounded on the life of the imagination, even though more religious minded than Jane will ever be. This major contribution to Jane's evolution is thus obliterated and replaced by a more acceptably common view of two children's natural friendship. The graveyard shots only express Jane's grief as she is shown kneeling near the raised gravestone and laying a bunch of white wild flowers; we are not allowed to realize Helen's double message: independence and religious faith, nor how the heroine only follows the ideal of independence but rejects its religious dimension.

Thus Lowood in the film is not the place of emancipation for Jane which eventually causes her to advertise for a governess's job in the newspaper (Miss Temple's getting married being her essential motivation, *i.e.* a model of emancipation by marriage), Miss Temple does not get married but remains a prisoner of her fate which she mildly accepts in a manner recalling Helen Burns' submissive attitude instead of the major character Miss Temple is in the novel. Miss Temple says goodbye in a setting displaying the erect gravestones and church in the background recalling Haworth to the tourist, and the typhus epidemics in the novel for the reader in the know. As to the delay of information, the shot on the graveyard frames Jane in her huge black bonnet and tall dark silhouette again without suggesting she made the decision on her own; rather the camera shoots her inside the coach and we hear Mrs Fairfax's voice over reading aloud her own letter. The information is thus delayed until we share Jane's trip and are shown a new view of the Yorkshire landscape; while the succession of hills was framed in the depth of the shot for her trip to Lowood, we now see these in the background as the carriage crosses the frame from left to right; the landscape is very much the same, yet the effect is different: in the first case we are heading towards a rather gloomy horizon embodied by the hills, while in the second case the hills are a mere backdrop to a more exciting adventure. We shift from predestination and childhood (Lowood) to free choice and adulthood (Thornfield).

By enhancing adult violence and child ill-treatment, the film underscores the repressive nature of Victorian adults towards children without the symbolic analogy with the behaviour of the Victorian higher middle class society regarding the lower classes which the novel implies; its corruption which is materialized by the fall of John Reed in the novel is not related to a criticism of a class in the film but once again only focused on individual behaviour. Again, in the novel, the meeting between Jane and the dying Mrs Reed which in the novel is an opportunity for Jane not only to practice charity and mercy, but also to make her cousins rely on her, the profligate as well as the egotistic nun, which emphasizes the "true lady" model which Jane embodies. The film only stresses Mrs Reed's unaccountable and clearly neurotic dislike for Jane, thus diminishing the self-reliance Jane has reached at this stage of the novel.

Lowood as a symbolic place has vanished in the film, despite the fact architectural setting and clever lighting schemes (David Watkin) do have a degree of symbolic significance. What the film achieves in that respect, and the following discussion of the equally symbolic Thornfield will confirm this, is a reduction to literal monovalence of a story which, in the source novel, derives much of its impetus from its symbolic significance. By reducing to literalness the narrative, the film depends only on the delay of information to sustain the viewer's interest, and therefore addresses only viewers who have no familiarity with the novel; rather than an adaptation, therefore, the film stands on its own as far as sustaining the viewer's interest goes, distilling information about Yorkshire living standards in a nondescript industrial North to the foreigner, and providing effects of surprise as when Jane stands by her friend and they both bow forward as if for decapitation.

Such interesting subversions of the novel's ideology by means of the setting and the suppression of significant episodes in the novel are also observable in the film's treatment of Thornfield (dvd ch.5-11 & 12-13).

With the Tudor architecture which is used for Thornfield, the lattice windows also look like a gaol when we get a glimpse of Bertha's fingers as a clue to some living human being's imprisonment. However, the shot is edited with other shots on an open lattice window framing Jane's expressionless face and Adele's inquisitive gaze and the object of their interest: a high angle on Blanche Ingram's (Elle Macpherson) "royal" blue coat on her white horse alighting in grand style with the help of Rochester's hand. The façade now plays the part of a balcony in a theatre, with the two female spectators gazing at the show which the high society guests are acutely aware of enacting for the benefit only of their own members. Architecture is thus given a double semiotic function as it is not only a visual metaphor of imprisonment but now also becomes the setting for a comedy of manners.

The indoors setting uses the latticed windows to yet another purpose, staging the play of warm—*i.e.* golden coloured—sunlight upon the characters' faces and figures in the bow-window scenes between Jane and Adele making sums on a blackboard. The warm sunlight provides a telling contrast with the dimly lit schoolroom at Lowood, while it establishes a clear parallel with similar warm coloured effects from the firelight in moments of family-like happiness in evenings.

However, the camerawork also uses the interior architecture to convey the gothic tale motif of the haunted house; Jane is taken by Mrs Fairfax (Joan Plowright) to visit the house: the staircase with its huge latticed windows filtering a grey light introduces gothic elements such as wood panelling, canopied wooden beds, large bookcases, and the necessity of candles as well as fire throughout most of the scenes. The new family Jane is introduced to is clearly defined by natural affinities, which is the case in the novel as well, a family in which Adele does not know Rochester is her father, Jane does not know Rochester's wife lives upstairs, Mrs Fairfax is only Rochester's distant relative, and therefore Jane's integration as an outsider is less unexpected—the intertextuality with Richardson's *Pamela* is not suggested, while it plays an important part in our reading of the novel[1]. Indeed the achievement of the novel partly relies on a splitting up of the Pamela character into two heroines, the gradually emancipating one, Jane,

---

1. In Richardson's novel, Pamela is neither a servant nor a lady; this leaves room for a governess such as Jane who eventually turns out to be a wealthy middle class heiress, thus avoiding any suggestion of class change in both novel and film. Nor is for that matter an even more fascinating sub-text, Richardson's other novel *Clarissa*, and its links with Rochester's works and epistolary style. See Gillian Beer, *Arguing With The Past—Essays in Narrative from Woolf to Sidney*, London: Routledge, 1989, p. 69.

who manages to avoid being a servant, and the imprisoned one, Bertha (Maria Schneider) who is doomed both by predestination (her madness is hereditary) and by the iron determination of her husband to lock her up (her very existence is uncertain until the marriage discovery scene, both in the novel and the film (dvd ch.13)).

The film hints at the motif of the haunted house by the sounds which Jane hears, but preserves till the end the likelihood of Jane's ignorance by erasing most of the clues which the novel provides. We do see Grace Poole (Billie Whitelaw) and her quiet demeanour is clearly incompatible with the fire accident. Her sudden appearances and disappearances along the third floor corridor are mysterious enough to make Jane's continued ignorance acceptable; besides the mystery is in keeping with the genre that the architecture of Thornfield introduces, as I suggested above, mainly the code of the fairy tale and its magic characters. Jane's ignorance is contrasted with her education as a governess and epitomizes her innocence as far as the 'facts of life' are concerned. Adele is unwittingly given a central part in the masquerade, and the film makes much of the pretty child-actress (Josephine Serre), the tale of her unreliable mother, a French dancer, and the picture of Rochester as unable to cope with women: led into marrying a lunatic, he then is betrayed by a manipulative woman who manages to make him pay for Adele's keep.

Thornfield is thus haunted by another woman, Adele's mother, whose portrait Rochester says he sees in the child's performance of a dance in front of the fireplace. In the film Jane dares criticize Rochester's lack of kindness for the child and speaks of his faults as if she were a judge; in this scene as in others screening a confrontation between master and "paid employee", the depth of the room is used to make Jane's mask-like face stand in the shadow of the dimly lit room, while Rochester is in the foreground with his back to us: the enunciative apparatus thus makes Jane address us at the same time as she is addressing Rochester, just as she shouts her hatred at Mrs Reed who is outside the frame to our left. However unlike the bright light which is used to give sharp relief to the child's features, in the Thornfield sequences of Jane's self assertive statements, she is mostly in a penumbra which makes her figure recede into the background, as if she too could haunt the house.

The chiaroscuro lighting which is also used to frame the "family" as they spend an evening together is very different from the stark lights on Blanche Ingram and the other guests during their stay. While they are framed as distinct from Thornfield Jane on the contrary is shot in a way suggesting it is her 'natural' home. When she makes her entrance as a veiled bride to be, the lateral light on her is particularly white and suggests she is something of a ghost, echoing Rochester's earlier remarks about her being an elf, or a fairy who would have cast a spell on his dog Pilot. Not unlike the mirrors and the windows which are also part of the setting in the Thornfield episodes, the veil conveys to the viewer a sense of her blindness which is shattered by the discovery of Bertha, a scene in which Jane literally lifts her veil to better see the stark truth.

The film transfers to the interior architecture of the "gothic" (*i.e.* Tudor ...) castle several premonitory clues: the haunted house motif is motivated by the gloomy rooms, the ill lit corridors, the sheets covering the furniture, as well as the Gytrash motif in Jane's first encounter with Rochester. The dog which plays the part is certainly not a Conan Doyle "Hound", but the way it is shot by the camera makes it ubiquitous and might suggest Rochester's mysterious double after all, despite the fact that the cliché of the love of the British for their dogs might also be felt as spoiling the effect, the dog itself being after all rather unthreatening on the whole.

The homely atmosphere that Mrs Fairfax establishes on Jane's first encounter with Thornfield nevertheless partly erases the haunted house cliché: for instance she shows Jane her room and insists that this is not a dream, but that they are quite real; her first welcome shows her standing among the various stage props connoting everyday ordinary life: she then turns round and points out a fire outside the frame on our left, whose light is visible on her face and hands. In the novel, she underscores the contrast between appearances and reality and shields Jane against the truth as long as she can, while in the film she is given a more likely role since it is suggested she herself does not know the truth, but only suspects there is something wrong: the first clue or hint the spectator is allowed to notice is underscored by a complex mirror composition as she is showing Rochester's room. We see Jane's full portrait encased as it were within the frame of a large mirror, on the right of the frame, while Mrs Fairfax's face is also reflected in a mirror—a small circular mirror—which provides a slight sense of the uncanny by the displacement of the speakers' voices outside the screen, or nearly so, while we only perceive their shadows in the mirrors. Besides we are confronting the huge latticed window at that moment and thus the mirror is in backlighting for us, which adds complexity to the already complicated visual composition.

Indeed mirrors and windows are given in the film their usual role to allow for the theme of the double, of empathy and even telepathy to appear in the screen narrative; while it is a mirror which is shown as the cause for Jane's terror in the red-room, mirrors also abound at Thornfield and later, as icons of her inner doubts and her struggle to free herself from the domination of her master, or of her sudden impulse to yield to his insisting courtship, or later her decision to leave her true family the Rivers to return to Thornfield. In that sequence, a frontal shot on Jane shows her inexpressive face with downcast eyes in a mirror connoting deep thought, and as she at length raises her eyes to a distant point in our own backs, her face gathers expression connoting her free and deliberate choice of casting herself again at Rochester's mercy while her freedom of choice is underscored—as in the novel—by her newly inherited wealth.

After staying with her cousins the Rivers, a stay which revolves around a sudden lapse in mystery or excitement of any sort, the mystery of her origin being elucidated along with her recognition as a legitimate heir by her uncle John from Madeira, Jane goes back to Thornfield and in the novel eventually settles at Ferndean.

In the film we attend the fire and subsequent destruction of the castle: this is visualized by long shots of the battlements with shrouds of smoke and Bertha's silhouette, then the camera cuts to a high angle shot on the yard with people running to and fro, and Rochester entering the tower door: the indoor scene is a setting of the ceiling and the last storey ablaze, in which first Grace Poole then Bertha fall to their death, as still shots on their bodies asserts, and a crash of the roof timber ensues which is edited with a loud cry so that we assume Rochester is trapped underneath. This scene Jane does not witness, as shots on her as she races to meet the oncoming Doncaster carriage and climbs inside despite Rochester racing in her pursuit on his horse. He then turns round to see that the castle has caught fire.

The succession of shots in these three sequences (DVD ch.14) which begins with a shot on Grace Poole looking through the window and Bertha escaping with two firebrands and setting fire to Jane's bridal dress in her deserted bed-chamber is devoted to speed of movement, abrupt changes in direction: Rochester rushes from the left of the screen to the right in hot pursuit, then from right to left as he goes back, as well as in angle: long shot and standard angle on the carriage moving out if sight, opposed to low angles on the castle and from the bottom of the staircase, contrasting with sharp high angles on the dead bodies below, all dramatize a general metamorphosis of appearances—the clouds of smoke rising from the battlements, ending in the fire red screen which echoes the red-room shot visualizing Jane's fainting fit which introduces the credits of the film. Jane's early motto 'to stay alive' to escape hell's fire is here transposed from a religious threat about life after death into a material reality.

In this respect the film becomes quite a stranger to the novel, in which the images of starvation, despair, and death convey the extreme limits of survival which she endures, Jane spends two nights on the moors (ch.28); Nature is first depicted as kindly, but shifts from summer warmth to a wet night, in parallel with her loneliness and weakening strength. In the film, the views of the Yorkshire landscape do not metamorphose into another form of torment for the heroine. While, in the novel, the descriptions of Nature are rife in these scenes, as if some kind of purifying ritual were necessary for her final emancipation from Rochester's black schemes of bigamy; the film speedily makes her go back to Gateshead (only one shot on the Doncaster stagecoach, this time coming at us) where her cousins Rivers now live and be rescued by them. Her symbolic reward in the novel necessitates the experience of a new place and a new form of independence as a school teacher, in which she again starts from scratch to rise to yet another emancipation, this time from religious missionary zeal; it is only when she has overcome these new ordeals that she is rewarded by the discovery of her inheritance and her real family, the Rivers themselves with whom she shares her wealth. In the film the symbolic significance of the ordeal of escape, or of discovering her true family, are far from being clear: rather, the heirloom is introduced as a kind of magic trick, the code of the marvellous jarring with the depiction of Jane's own coach and servants in a livery, wearing expensive velvet and silk clothes, a circular brown bonnet, as they cross the bridge to Thornfield. The camera then cuts to Mrs Fairfax wearing glasses, signifying the passing of time, while Pilot greets Jane and leads her to chat now looks very much like Rochester's cave: the darkness in which he is sitting suggests his blindness, while we discover his maimed face: one eye is quite closed and from the opposite angle his "good" eye is quite useless.

While Rochester's attempted bigamy, signifying Jane's rape since the wedding could not have been true, is in the novel an interesting re-writing of Pamela vs Clarissa's fates at the hand of their 'admirers', the film devotes a few shots to a choreography of mutual devotion, as Jane is first seen leaning over his prostrated figure, then kneeling in front of him and finally raising her eyes to his face as the camera tilts to a high angle over her kneeling posture as he rises: a single beam of light from a narrow window in the middle ground underlines the depth of field and suggests a by analogy a depth of feeling uniting the pair.

The necessary final shot on a pastoral landscape as Jane's voice over brings closure to the tale in a way which remains distinctly different from the effect in the novel; in the film it is restricted to the two characters' fate; in the novel the narrator's voice addresses us to tie up the remaining threads of the story regarding her cousins and little Adele who is rescued from a bad school and educated at home, enjoying "a sound English education" which corrects 'in a great measure her French defects' (ch.38); the final words celebrate "perfect concord", which is rewarded by the partial return of his eyesight and the birth of an heir, and her cousins' fate suited to each of their purposes; St John Rivers is the last character in this concluding chapter and religion in his case brings him fulfilment. In the matter-of-fact tone of the concluding chapter we are brought back from romanticism into a form of social ideology which does validate the Establishment since it erases all traces of necessary rebellion: what Jane has been able to conquer is both equality in her couple while they start on a master-servant relationship, and the capacity to find happiness in a family which is both her real one and a family grounded on personal affinities. In a less striking manner, the film concludes on a pastoral romance which becomes like a painting as the figures recede into the distance.

There remains to examine what public the film addresses, in the 1995s: it seems to me the film depends on different aims: the more obvious one is the TV spectator who can view the film together with his whole family: as the DVD back-cover reads: language is mild, there is no sex nor nudity, violence is infrequent, mild or akin to the horror genre, and the genre is the "period drama". This is a far cry from the reception of the novel in its own day, but such a difference cannot be accounted for by an emancipation of the audience from earlier principles; rather it relies on a shift in interest from a play upon our expectations to a satisfaction of these. As Richard Alleva writes[1], the opening scene of the book was a completely unknown scene of a fierce struggle between Jane and her elder tormentor in which she beats him into defeat, quite different from Dickens's Little Nell, though of course Oliver Twist does beat his tormentors until he is locked up; what the novel brought to its readership was a sense of difference, and this is certainly what Zeffirrelli's film will not do. One remains wondering whether any spectator viewing the film will ever feel a curiosity about reading the book; as for those who have read the book before viewing the film, it is probable they will seldom feel it necessary to view the film twice.

The culture issue which this film raises, however, is not to be lain at the door of the film-maker, but rather I would think results from a general trend to erase cultural boundaries with a view to responding to widely different cultural audiences, a choice which inevitably must lead to a dead end, since form and content cannot be severed and where form, be it narrative or otherwise, is deprived of its edge, *i.e.* its play on our expectations, content is bound to become lose and meaningless. While we can still be gripped by Jane's struggle for recognition and social integration in the novel, despite the beautiful cinematography and the performances of both Anna Paquin and Charlotte Gainsbourg in the film, we remain less than thrilled by the film on the whole.

---

1. Richard Alleva, June 1, 1996 *Commonweal*; the review is available on internet http://findarticles.com/articles ...

Reading list

Books on film analysis

BORDWELL, David and Kristin Thompson, *Film Art—An Introduction*, New-York: McGraw-Hill, (1979) 1997.

CHATMAN, Seymour, *Story and Discourse—Narrative Structure in Fiction and Film*, Ithaca and London: Cornell University Press, (1978), 1988.

HAYWARD, Susan, *Cinema Studies—The Key Concepts*, London: Routledge, (2000) 2003.

Articles

COSTA DE BEAUREGARD, R. « La femme dans *Jane Eyre* (1847) » Caliban XVII (1980), p. 57-67.

GAUTHIER, Guy, « Le cinématographe entre le monde et l'autre monde », Littérature et cinéma, *La Licorne*, Poitiers : 1993, p. 81-94.

Que devient la narration à la première personne lors de l'adaptation cinématographique de *Jane Eyre* par Franco Zeffirelli ?

Christine Evain

Dans le roman *Jane Eyre*, Charlotte Brontë adopte le « je » de l'autobiographie fictionnelle. Plusieurs éléments de la stratégie narrative visent à accroître la vivacité du récit ainsi que la proximité avec le lecteur — ce dernier étant d'ailleurs souvent sollicité pour évaluer situations et personnages : « *whether what followed was the effect of excitement the reader shall judge.* » (Chap. XXXV). L'immédiateté du récit est fréquemment renforcée par des sauts au présent et par le recours au monologue intérieur. Les métaphores exprimant sensations et impressions abondent — ce qui permet au lecteur d'associer des images aux paysages intérieurs des personnages. Ainsi, malgré le mode essentiellement rétrospectif du récit, le discours « s'émancipe [parfois] de l'autorité narrative pour se faire confession immédiate[1] ». La narratrice ne porte pas un regard omniscient sur l'ensemble du déroulement des événements, car elle préfère les « mettre en scène ». C'est au lecteur qu'il appartient de *voir* et de *ressentir*.

Que deviennent ces stratégies subtiles d'effets de proximité, de mise à contribution du lecteur et de révélations partielles dans l'adaptation cinématographique du roman de Charlotte Brontë ? En nous appuyant sur plusieurs ouvrages consacrés à l'adaptation cinématographique de la littérature, notamment *Screening the Novel* de Robert Giddings, Keith Selby et Chris Wensley, nous mettrons en lumière la transformation de la voix narratrice romanesque dans le film de Zeffirelli. La voix romanesque n'est pas entièrement occultée, mais sa place semble considérablement réduite. Le point de vue de la protagoniste nous est communiqué autrement : par plusieurs techniques audiovisuelles auxquelles nous proposons de nous intéresser.

Dans un premier temps, nous étudierons la correspondance entre la voix narrative du roman et la voix-off du film. L'alternance entre *mimesis* et *diegesis* dans le roman trouve son équivalent dans le film, malgré une transformation radicale qui débouche sur un nouvel équilibre. Nous nous tournerons ensuite vers les techniques de caméra subjective/objective, montages parallèles qui prennent le relais de la voix narrative et qui permettent de jouer entre ancrage énonciatif et effacement de cet ancrage.

---

1. Bertrandias, Bernadette, *Jane Eyre, Charlotte Brontë, La parole orpheline*, Paris : Ellipses, 2004, p. 26.

Nous terminerons par les décors, la musique et les « *cutaway scenes* », en explicitant le lien entre ces différentes ressources fréquemment employées dans le film et les points de vue de la narratrice et de la protagoniste. En comparant les stratégies romanesques et cinématographiques qui explicitent l'intériorité du personnage de Jane ainsi que sa narration, nous illustrerons le commentaire de George Linden : « *A successful adaptation of a novel should not be the book. Nor should it be a substitute for the book. If it is truly successful, it should be a work of art in its own right which excites the reader to go re-experience that work in another medium : the novel*[1] ».

La voix narrative

À quatre reprises dans le film (et à quatre reprises seulement), la voix-off de Jane adulte — que le spectateur rapproche de la voix narrative du roman — entre en scène, pour quelques secondes à peine. Pourquoi une telle discrétion de la voix-off ? Selon Robert Giddings, Keith Selby et Chris Wensley auteurs de *Screening the Novel,* pour les adaptations cinématographiques, il importe de limiter l'intrusion de la voix à la première personne, voire de l'éliminer tout à fait, afin de conserver l'intensité du vécu présenté par le cinéma. Cette logique de l'écran est en effet contraire à celle du roman où le récit à la première personne rend l'univers fictionnel davantage crédible et proche au lecteur :

> In the novel, first-person narration serves, amongst other things, to impress more immediately upon the reader a sense of the reality of the fictional world. But in a film, attempts at first-person narration come over all too often as clumsy, ostentatiously and even pretentiously artistic. The tradition in film-making is instead an implied third-person narrative, deeply subsumed by the unobtrusive use of technology—through editing, music, camera-angles and the like—and it is likely that this first-person narration is the most fundamental aspect of the novel's structure which will need changing in moving from novel to film[2].

Si le récit à la première personne est déconseillé aux cinéastes, pourquoi alors le conserver lors d'une adaptation cinématographique ? Nous pouvons supposer que ce choix correspond ici à un désir de fidélité à plusieurs éléments de la stratégie narrative romanesque — notamment, la présence d'un regard rétrospectif allant de l'enfance malheureuse de Jane à l'âge adulte

---

1. George Linden, "The Storied World", in Fred H. Marcus (ed.), *Film and Literature : Contrasts in Media* (New York : Chandler, 1971), p. 169.
2. Robert Giddings, Keith Selby, Chris Wensley *Screening the Novel,* Houndmills, Basingstoke, Hampshire and London : Macmillan, 1990, p. 79-80.

où s'ouvre la perspective d'un avenir heureux. En outre, dans le roman, la vision et la sensibilité de l'enfance persistent tout au long du récit. La présence de la voix-off au début du film permet également de renforcer ce lien qui n'est pourtant que suggéré.

Prenons successivement les quatre occurrences de la voix-off pour établir la fonction de chacune de ces intrusions. Le film *commence* avec la voix-off de Jane. Cette voix ne reprend aucune des paroles du roman, bien qu'elle en résume le propos :

> My parents died when I was very young. I was sent to live with my aunt Mrs Reed and her children at Gateshead. For nearly ten years I endured their unkindness and cruelty. They did not love me. I could not love them.

Cette affirmation extrêmement concise et sobre est aussitôt suivie de plusieurs scènes emblématiques montrant les malheurs de Jane chez sa tante Mrs Reed[1]. L'hostilité ressentie par la protagoniste du roman est résumée dès le préambule du film, dans la séquence qui précède le générique. Jane est alors rudoyée par ses cousins qui lui reprochent sa pauvreté (« *You have no money* »), puis elle est enfermée par sa tante dans la chambre rouge :

> Mrs Reed: You will stay here until morning!
> Jane: No, I cannot endure it!

Lorsque Jane se retrouve seule, une musique qu'on peut qualifier d'inquiétante et des effets de miroirs illustrent l'angoisse de la fillette. La voix-off, quant à elle, se tait. Il suffit de la juxtaposition de ces deux séquences — la première avec voix-off (sur une image de Gateshead) et la seconde sans voix-off : scènes de dispute et de punition — pour établir le rapprochement entre le point de vue de Jane adulte et la sensibilité de l'enfant. Dans les scènes qui suivront, les événements subis par Jane sont mis en scène dans l'immédiateté du présent.

Dans un premier temps, le spectateur apprend à connaître Jane enfant : elle est celle qui, comme dans le roman, répond effrontément à Brocklehurst et à Mrs Reed, affirmant d'une part qu'elle souhaite rester en bonne santé pour ne pas aller en Enfer, et d'autre part qu'elle n'est pas une menteuse puisqu'elle ose dire à Mrs Reed combien elle la déteste. Nous remarquerons que le film n'utilise pas le commentaire de la narratrice romanesque sur l'impossibilité de se révolter contre l'injustice du monde des adultes[2]. Pour inclure un tel

---

1. Ces malheurs, dans le roman, sont relatés dans les chapitres 1 à 4.
2. Jane (narratrice adulte, à la fin du chapitre 4) s'exclame : « *A child cannot quarrel with its elders, as I had done; cannot give its furious feelings uncontrolled play, as I had given mine, without experiencing afterwards the pang of remorse and the chill of reaction.* » Voir l'analyse de Bertrandias, p. 22.

commentaire, il eût fallu faire intervenir à nouveau la voix-off. Or le parti pris du film, nous l'avons vu, est de limiter les intrusions de cette voix.

Pendant un espace-temps qui couvre plusieurs années du récit — jusqu'au départ de Jane de Thornfield, la voix-off est totalement absente du film. Puis à nouveau, elle intervient à trois reprises, alors même que le spectateur commence à perdre de vue le fait que cette histoire nous est rapportée par Jane adulte. Cette manière dont la voix-off se fait oublier pour resurgir plus tard évoque la nature paradoxale du discours du roman de Charlotte Brontë. En effet, la critique a souvent souligné que le discours de *Jane Eyre* oscille entre *mimesis* et *diegesis* :

S'il est vrai que l'ensemble du récit est bien l'énoncé d'un discours attribuable à Jane adulte, il n'en reste pas moins que les autres voix s'y font entendre, notamment celle de Jane plus jeune, l'héroïne, et que de ce dédoublement découlent des effets de contrastes, de contrepoint, mais aussi des glissements, des incertitudes, voire des confusions. Situation de dialogisme narratif, orchestrée par le sujet d'écriture qui… semble chercher un point d'équilibre entre la maîtrise d'un récit bien agencé dans lequel l'énoncé est tenu à distance, et une adhésion au plus près à une expérience qui porte toute la force du désir[1]…

De même, nous l'avons vu, dans le film de Zeffirelli, le passage de la voix-off aux premières scènes du film qui mettent en scène le personnage de Jane enfant, fait entendre les deux voix distinctes de Jane adulte et enfant. Cependant, il n'y a là aucune confusion entre les deux. Les premières paroles de la voix-off suggèrent une entière maîtrise interprétative de la diégèse. En effet, la voix-off est celle d'une narratrice adulte qui affirme sans détour le manque d'amour dont elle a été victime ainsi que son incapacité à aimer ses bourreaux. La voix de Jane enfant est celle d'une fillette sensible et courageuse qui cultive droiture et honnêteté malgré les fausses accusations dont elle est accablée. La confusion des deux voix romanesques, mise en lumière par le commentaire de Bernadette Bertrandias trouve son équivalent non pas dans les paroles prononcées mais plutôt par le biais de prises de vue et jeux de regards sur lesquels nous reviendrons.

À trois autres reprises dans le film (et à trois reprises seulement), la voix-off entre à nouveau en scène. Deux fois, le recours à cette voix permet de passer rapidement sur plusieurs chapitres du roman : Jane, après l'échec de son mariage quitte Thornfied et erre sans but :

> With no direction in the world for my future, I travelled for many days. At last, prompted by old memories, I made my way back to Gateshead Hall and to the home of the parsons Mr Rivers who had once been most kind to me.

---
1. Bertrandias Bernadette, *op. cit.* p. 9.

Arrivée chez les Rivers, Jane tombe malade. Elle est soignée pendant plusieurs mois, jusqu'à son rétablissement, mais ses pensées se tournent sans cesse vers Thornfield et M. Rochester.

> As the months passed, my health recovered and my strength returned. The more I knew of Mrs Rivers and his sister, the better I liked them. Despite their generosity and kindness my thoughts were constantly drawn back to the past to places and people I could not forget.

Si ces deux interventions de la voix-off permettent de résumer efficacement plusieurs épisodes, ces résumés auraient pu s'effectuer par une autre technique cinématographique, comme celle des « *cutaway scenes* » abondamment utilisées dans ce film. Le recours à la voix-off sert plusieurs objectifs supplémentaires. Il sert ainsi à rappeler au spectateur le point de vue à partir duquel s'effectue la narration. Il permet également l'écho avec le début du film narré par cette même voix, faisant état des souffrances de Jane enfant. Par cet écho, l'impression de souffrance subie par une Jane maintenant adulte est renforcée. Enfin, la voix-off réintroduit ce principe de double voix que le spectateur risque de perdre de vue — c'est-à-dire la voix de la narratrice et celle du personnage mis en scène. Cette dualité est également soulignée par une technique de double regard (caméras subjective et objective) particulièrement exploitée dans la dernière partie du film.

Pour clore ce commentaire sur la voix-off, il nous reste à évoquer la scène finale où la narratrice fait part de son bonheur :

> And so I married him! Slowly but surely Edward recovered his sight and when our first-born was put into his arms he could see that our child had inherited his eyes, as they once were: large, brilliant and shining with life. We sent for Adèle and she now lives with us, beloved as if she were our own dear daughter. We are truly devoted my Edward and I! our hearts beat as one! Our happiness is complete.

Cette quatrième occurrence de la voix-off offre un effet de contraste avec les trois premières, tout en les rassemblant dans un « *happy ending* ». Au-delà de cet effet de contraste et d'unité, le bonheur évoqué est exprimé de manière assez sobre puisque le style, retenu, d'une langue victorienne est parfaitement imité. Plusieurs phrases de Charlotte Brontë sont reprises avec les modifications qui s'imposent (et évidemment l'élimination de « *Reader* » en tête de « *I married him!* »). Au-delà de la sobriété de la voix-off, totalement en accord avec la personnalité de la protagoniste, la musique et l'image viennent donner au dénouement une dimension parfaitement lyrique.

Si les quatre différentes occurrences de la voix-off permettent d'atteindre de multiples objectifs, l'emploi de cette voix n'est pas la seule technique à laquelle le cinéaste a recours pour traduire la stratégie narrative du roman. Nous nous tournons maintenant vers deux autres techniques qui contribuent fortement à établir un rapprochement entre l'original romanesque et son adaptation à l'écran.

Caméra subjective/objective et montages en parallèle

La première de ces deux techniques est la caméra subjective. Pour donner un exemple de l'emploi de cette technique, revenons sur la scène de Jane, enfant, enfermée dans la chambre rouge. La « caméra subjective », c'est-à-dire le champ cadré du point de vue du personnage qui est supposé regarder l'espace (en l'occurrence, Jane) traduit l'intériorité de cette dernière : le travelling à la fois horizontal et vertical de la « caméra subjective » produit l'effet d'un regard en délire et correspond à ce que la narratrice du roman confie au sujet de ses traumatismes précoces : l'enfant qu'elle était alors éprouvait un sentiment de panique proche de l'hallucination. Par la technique de la « caméra subjective », le spectateur est invité à vivre directement l'expérience traumatisante de l'enfant.

De même, l'expérience de Jane adulte nous est donnée en direct par un effet de la « caméra subjective » reposant sur le rôle du miroir. Ainsi, le jour de son mariage, Jane se contemple dans la glace de sa coiffeuse et paraît surprise de se trouver belle. Cette image fait écho à une autre utilisation du miroir antérieur à celle-ci : Jane apprend par Mrs Fairfax que Rochester est attiré par une certaine Miss Blanche, réputée de grande beauté. Complexée, Jane se regarde dans le miroir d'un couloir et le spectateur comprend, par l'expression même de la jeune femme, qu'elle se trouve laide. Ces deux utilisations du miroir permettent au spectateur de saisir l'intériorité du personnage qui passe de la tristesse à l'espoir. Il est intéressant de noter que le roman exploite de manière très différente la scène du regard de la mariée dans le miroir. La narratrice de Charlotte Brontë décrit son reflet : « *a robed and veiled figure so unlike my usual self* ». Selon le commentaire de Claire Bazin, le miroir joue un rôle tristement révélateur : « Jane ne devrait pas être la mariée dont elle porte les vêtements — qui semblent ne pas lui appartenir : « *the strange wraith-like apparel it contained* » — et elle a hâte de fuir cette image qui n'est pas la sienne, tentant d'échapper aux mains de Sophie, qui l'a contrainte à se regarder : 'I hurried from under her hands'[1] ». Malgré la simplification imposée par le mode cinématographique, le

---

1. Claire Bazin, *Jane Eyre, le pèlerin moderne*, Nantes : Éditions du Temps, 2005, p. 28.

recours à la caméra subjective dans le film de Zeffirelli permet de rendre de manière visuelle un état intérieur que la voix narrative romanesque explicite par le discours. Si le film laisse de côté l'inquiétude prémonitoire de la protagoniste de Charlotte Brontë, la scène cinématographique de la mariée devant son miroir traduit l'espoir du personnage à cet instant-là, sans doute éphémère. En effet, l'espoir nous est donné avec une intensité d'autant plus vive que l'on attend la suite : le spectateur se doute bien que le film n'est pas terminé (cet épisode se situe à plus d'une demi-heure de la fin) et donc que le moment du « *happy ending* » n'est pas encore venu. En effet, la scène se déroule à un moment clé de l'intrigue : Jane vient d'être rassurée sur le fait que Rochester n'est pas amoureux de Miss Ingram mais elle ne connaît pas encore l'impossibilité du mariage auquel elle se prépare. Ainsi, la caméra subjective souligne un moment de bonheur, mais permet également d'alerter le spectateur sur la déception qui se prépare.

À d'autres moments du film, la caméra subjective permet de suivre le regard des personnages (celui de Jane principalement, mais également celui de Mason, le soir où il passe la nuit à Thornfield). Cette technique traduit les intuitions aussi bien heureuses que malheureuses de Jane. Lorsque celle-ci arrive à Thornfield, son expression est inquiète : elle entre dans la cour et lève les yeux sur les remparts. Cette contre-plongée traduit son sentiment d'infériorité face à l'impressionnante architecture de Thornfield. De même, alors que, plusieurs scènes plus loin, Mrs Fairfax emmène Jane à sa chambre, cette dernière découvre les longs couloirs de la demeure. De nouveau, c'est par la caméra subjective que le spectateur comprend l'état intérieur de Jane. Les couloirs, progressivement embrassés par le regard de Jane, s'avèrent interminables et sombres. Cependant, Jane est bientôt réconfortée par sa chambre devant laquelle elle exprime son émerveillement ; et le lendemain, la visite avec Mrs Fairfax suscite chez Jane un tout autre regard. La technique de la caméra subjective permet alors au spectateur de découvrir le bonheur de Jane dans cette demeure baignée de lumière, principalement dans ce grand salon où Jane contemple le portrait de Rochester, enfant.

Si la caméra subjective intervient principalement lorsqu'il s'agit de décrire l'intériorité de la protagoniste par le regard qu'elle porte sur son entourage, la caméra « objective », quant à elle, se rapproche d'une narration omnisciente. L'alternance entre les deux fait écho à la double voix de la narration romanesque qui apparaît sous la forme de la voix-off au début du film. Cependant, le spectateur risque de perdre de vue la voix narrative de Jane adulte sitôt que la voix-off se tait, comme c'est le cas après le préambule et pendant les deux premiers tiers du film. Afin de restituer les identités propres à ces deux voix distinctes — narratrice et protagoniste — la technique du montage en parallèle intervient à plusieurs reprises dans le film.

Le montage en parallèle est un montage alterné de deux plans dans le but de les confronter et de leur attribuer des valeurs comparatives. En anglais, cette technique qui porte le nom de « *cross-cutting editing* » est définie plus précisément dans le dictionnaire spécialisé de Susan Hayward :

> Cross-cutting is limited as a term to the linking-up of two sets of action that are running concurrently and which are interdependent within the narrative. The term parallel editing has been used incorrectly to refer to the same effect, probably because it is a literal way of explaining the effect of cross-cutting: putting in parallel two contiguous events that are occurring at the same time but which are occurring in two different spaces[1].

Dans le film de Zeffirelli, cette technique est employée afin d'avertir le spectateur d'un danger imminent dont les protagonistes n'ont pas encore conscience. L'omniscience que cette stratégie implique s'apparente à celle de la narratrice de Charlotte Brontë.

Nous avons un exemple de montage en parallèle, lorsque Jane enfant demande à Helen si elle peut faire son portrait. Alors que cette dernière est en train de poser, après avoir enfreint le règlement en enlevant son bonnet, le plan suivant nous montre Mr Brocklehurst et Miss Scatcherd ensemble dans les escaliers, se dirigeant vers la salle d'étude du pensionnat. Ainsi le spectateur sait que les fillettes vont être surprises avant même que cela ne se produise. Cette même technique de montage en parallèle est utilisée, avec davantage d'insistance encore, à deux reprises. Alors que Jane s'apprête à épouser Rochester et que Mason et son avocat sont sur le point d'empêcher le mariage, nous observons une succession de six plans : 1) Jane en robe de mariée converse avec Rochester ; 2) Mason et son avocat descendent d'une calèche ; 3) Jane et Rochester sont dans la chapelle — vus de dos ; 4) Mason et son avocat sont dans la cour intérieure de Thornfield ; puis de nouveau 5), nous avons une vue de dos du couple Jane et Rochester, et c'est alors, au sixième plan, que Mason et son avocat viennent interrompre la cérémonie.

Une seconde série de montages en parallèle suivra, plus loin, lorsque Jane, après avoir découvert l'existence de Bertha, décidera de fuir Rochester. Quinze scènes se succèdent : Jane court vers la calèche ; Grace suit le départ de Jane de sa fenêtre et en oublie de surveiller Bertha qui se tourne vers le feu ; Jane s'engouffre dans la calèche ; Rochester suit sa bien-aimée et l'appelle avec désespoir ; Bertha enflamme la robe de mariée de Jane qui est posée sur le lit ; Jane est dans la calèche ; Rochester monte sur son cheval ; Les serviteurs appellent Mr Rochester ; le cheval de Mr Rochester se retourne ;

---

1. Hayward, Susan, *Key Concepts in Cinema Studies*, Routledge : London and New York : 1996, p. 78.

le château a pris feu ; Rochester à cheval découvre les flammes ; Jane, dans la calèche, fuit, le visage douloureux ; Rochester entend le cri de Bertha ; Bertha est sur les remparts ; Rochester court vers le feu…

Avec cette série de montages en parallèle où le spectateur suit à la fois le départ de Jane, la poursuite de Rochester et le déclenchement de l'incendie, l'intensité dramatique est à son comble (accentué ponctuellement par un effet a-synchronique au moment où retentit le cri de Bertha).

Si les techniques de caméra subjective dans le film de Zeffirelli sont particulièrement efficaces pour dire les appréhensions, les espoirs et les prémonitions des personnages, les montages en parallèle suscitent, quant à eux, une autre forme de participation du spectateur. Ce dernier est amené à embrasser un champ de compréhension de l'histoire qui dépasse celui des protagonistes et qui rejoint la vision plus complète d'un narrateur qui nous fait partager son regard rétrospectif sur les événements, tout en ménageant le plus grand suspense. Le recours ponctuel aux deux techniques cinématographiques étudiées ici permet un effet d'alternance chez le spectateur qui se situe tantôt dans la perspective des protagonistes tantôt dans celle du narrateur, et qui est invité tantôt à partager une émotion tantôt à évaluer une situation.

Décors, musique et cutaway scenes

Il existe également une autre série d'outils traduisant la complexité de la voix narrative romanesque. Il s'agit des décors, de la musique et des scènes dites « *cutaway scenes* ». En effet, l'ensemble de ces ressources constitue des relais de la voix narrative romanesque dans l'adaptation cinématographique, tant il est vrai que les éléments visuels et sonores sont porteurs de message. La puissance de la musique et des images est au cœur même de l'art cinématographique et permet, comme l'expliquent Robert Giddings, Keith Selby et Chris Wensley, de susciter la participation du spectateur :

> The screen image can establish diverse relationships between a variety of characters and objects which enable the viewer to make simultaneous judgements on the action and relationships shown; in addition, a great deal of information can be conveyed almost instantaneously by presenting a character or event against a background which can establish a complex of secondary information. The close shot of a character's face, by which meaning can be conveyed by the slightest movement, and the use of sound to emphasize, prepare or undercut the screen images are also features which can greatly enhance the narrative[1].

---

1. Robert Giddings, Keith Selby, Chris Wensley, *Screening the Novel*, Houndmills, Basingstoke, Hampshire and London : Macmillan, 1990, p. 20-21.

Le film de Zeffirelli illustre parfaitement ce commentaire, autant par les images de gros plans (sur les personnages principalement) que par des vues d'ensemble (paysages, éléments du décor, groupe de personnages, etc.). Pour commencer, plusieurs exemples de gros plans : lors de la première soirée de Mr Rochester, le mépris de Miss Blanche envers Jane est exprimé par quelques coups d'œil cruels. Les gros plans successifs sur les invités, sur Jane et sur Rochester permettent au spectateur de comprendre la mortification de Jane ainsi que le sentiment de supériorité qui habite Miss Blanche et sa mère.

Plus loin, lorsque Jane comprend que son mariage est impossible, la souffrance de Jane et de Rochester se lit sur leurs visages, notamment lors de leur dernier échange. La musique mélancolique autant que la séquence d'images elle-même — les plans se succèdent à un rythme de plus en plus rapide — traduisent le tourment du couple qui se sépare. L'alternance des plans permet d'éviter de figer les personnages dans une expression que l'on retrouve pourtant d'un plan à l'autre — Jane, toujours en souffrance, silencieuse au fond d'une calèche qui l'emmène loin de Thornfied ; Rochester, alarmé par le départ de sa bien-aimée.

Bien évidemment, il nous appartient, à nous spectateurs, de déduire de ces images l'état intérieur des personnages, et les éléments visuels et musicaux suscitent des émotions qui nous permettent de comprendre personnages et situations. Cette immédiateté n'est pas sans rapport avec la qualité scénique de la narration romanesque. En effet, la voix narrative romanesque commente longuement les différentes situations et il lui arrive fréquemment de leur donner la vivacité de la *mimesis* grâce à plusieurs techniques narratives mises en lumière par Bernadette Bertrandias : «… [Le roman] *Jane Eyre* cherche à se présenter comme une *mimesis*, une représentation qui s'efforce d'adhérer le plus étroitement possible à l'expérience vécue, comme lorsque les questions empreintes d'angoisse et de passion semblent sans réponse[1] ».

Parmi les composantes de la forme scénique, Bernadette Bertrandias note l'importance du dialogue et des « fragments de monologue intérieur qui privilégient la métaphore pour exprimer la sensation et l'impression[2] ». En outre, Bernadette Bertrandias remarque que « partout, on relève une technique modale propre à suggérer l'illusion mimétique ». En effet : « Chaque glissement temporel produit l'effet d'une actualisation dans laquelle le discours semble s'émanciper de l'autorité narrative pour se faire confession

---

1. Bertrandias, Bernadette, *Jane Eyre, Charlotte Brontë, La parole orpheline*, Paris : Ellipses, 2004, p. 25
2. *Ibidem.*

immédiate[1] ». L'exemple choisi pour illustrer ce point est celui du chapitre 27 où Jane, devant la frivolité de Miss Blanche, se tient en retrait et donne libre cours à ses pensées[2]. C'est précisément la scène à laquelle nous nous référions précédemment afin d'illustrer la puissance d'évocation d'un gros plan sur l'expression d'un visage.

Ainsi, l'image entre parfois en résonance (avec les techniques narratives romanesques). Le recours au langage métaphorique de la voix narratrice romanesque est fréquent du fait que le monologue intérieur privilégie cette forme d'expression. On remarque par exemple la récurrence des symboles de l'arbre et de la foudre qui le détruit. La scène finale du film reprend cette image à son compte, non seulement dans le discours de Rochester mais également lorsque le couple sort dans le jardin : leurs silhouettes se détachent devant un arbre immense représentant la solidité de leur amour. Malgré les transformations que s'autorise le cinéaste, les effets de résonance symboliques entre le roman et le film nous font penser aux commentaires du cinéaste D.W. Griffith, du romancier Joseph Conrad et du poète et critique Herbert Read, rapportés par Robert Giddings, Keith Selby et Chris Wensley dans *Screening the Novel* :

> The task I'm trying to achieve above all is to make you see', Griffith is reported to have said in 1913 when outlining his aims as a film-maker. Sixteen years earlier Conrad had stated: "My task... is by the power of the written word, to make you hear, to make you feel—it is before all, to make you see." To this, one might add Herbert Read's advice to writers in 1945: If you asked me to give you the most distinctive quality of good writing, I would give it to you in this one word: VISUAL. Reduce the art of writing to its fundamentals, and you come to this single aim: to convey images by means of words. But also to convey images. To make the mind see... That is a definition of good literature... it is also a definition of the ideal film[3].

---

1. *Ibidem*, p. 26.
2. I compared him with his guests ... "He is not to them what he is to me," I thought: "he is not of their kind. I believe he is of mine;—I am sure he is—I feel akin to him—I understand the language of his countenance and movements: though rank and wealth sever us widely, I have something in my brain and heart, in my blood and nerves, that assimilates me mentally to him. Did I say, a few days since, that I had nothing to do with him but to receive my salary at his hands? Did I forbid myself to think of him in any other light than as a paymaster? Blasphemy against nature! Every good, true, vigorous feeling I have gathers impulsively round him. I know I must conceal my sentiments: I must smother hope; I must remember that he cannot care much for me. For when I say that I am of his kind, I do not mean that I have his force to influence, and his spell to attract; I mean only that I have certain tastes and feelings in common with him. I must, then, repeat continually that we are for ever sundered:—and yet, while I breathe and think, I must love him." *Jane Eyre*, Chapitre 27.
3. Robert Giddings, Keith Selby, Chris Wensley, *Screening the Novel*, Houndmills, Basingstoke, Hampshire and London: Macmillan, 1990, p. 1.

Ainsi, s'il est vrai que le récit de la narratrice de Charlotte Brontë s'attache à nous faire *voir* (« *To make the mind see* »), les images du film de Zeffirelli s'appuient sur les métaphores de l'auteur pour la composition de scènes.

Si l'on s'intéresse à la puissance des tableaux et de la musique dans le film de Zeffirelli, on ne peut rester indifférent à l'insertion de nombreuses « *cutaway scenes* ». C'est cette dernière technique que nous souhaitons aborder maintenant. Le terme mérite d'être expliqué : les « *cutaway scenes* » sont des scènes ajoutées dans le déroulement du récit à des fins de transition. Plus précisément :

> In film, a cutaway is the interruption of a continuously-filmed action by inserting a view of something else. It is usually, though not always, followed by a cutback to the first shot.
> Method: Cutaways usually don't contribute any dramatic content of their own, but help the editor assemble a longer sequence. For this reason, editors choose cutaways related to the main action, such as another action or object in the same location...
> Usage: Probably its most common uses in dramatic films are to adjust the pace of the main action, to conceal the deletion of some unwanted part of the main shot, or to allow the joining of parts of two versions of that shot. For example, a scene may be improved by cutting a few frames out of an actor's pause; a brief view of some listener can help conceal the break[1].

Dans le film de Zeffirelli, nous remarquons que les « *cutaway scenes* » véhiculent une intensité dramatique qui s'écarte des définitions des dictionnaires cinématographiques[2]. Même dans leur utilisation la plus simple, les « *cutaway scenes* » relèvent d'un choix artistique minutieux permettant d'atteindre plusieurs objectifs allant au-delà de la fonction de transition. En effet, que ces scènes représentent des paysages ou des gros plans sur des visages, ou encore des plans d'ensemble sur une situation ou bien un groupe de personnages, les « *cutaway scenes* » remplissent de multiples fonctions. Elles permettent de réguler l'intrigue, d'évoquer le passage du temps, et, comme le suggère la définition ci-dessus, de camoufler des coupures dans l'intrigue romanesque. Par exemple, une vue de l'extérieur du pensionnat de Lowood dans une lumière crépusculaire, évoque une journée entière qui vient de s'écouler. Ce plan suit et précède une scène où

---

1. Définition de « Cutaway scenes » proposée par Wikipedia.
2. La définition de « Cutaway scenes » par Susan Hayward rejoint le commentaire de Wikipedia selon lequel ces scènes sont utilisées pour réaliser des transitions et non pas pour proposer un contenu dramatique spécifique. Hayward, Susan, *Key Concepts in Cinema Studies*, Routledge : London and New York, 1996, p. 61-62.

Jane enfant est condamnée à rester debout sur un tabouret, toute la journée. Lorsque la caméra revient vers l'intérieur du pensionnat, elle n'effectue pas directement un « *cutback* » sur Jane mais s'arrête un moment sur le groupe des pensionnaires rassemblés pour chanter. Ce détour contribue non seulement à marquer le passage du temps mais également à communiquer au spectateur l'atmosphère du pensionnat.

Deuxième exemple de « *cutaway scenes* » : les tableaux d'hiver. Ceux-ci interviennent à deux reprises, lorsque Jane enfant se lie d'amitié avec Helen Burns. La première séquence des tableaux d'hiver effectue la transition entre Miss Temple qui s'inquiète pour Helen atteinte d'une vilaine toux, et le lit vide d'Helen à côté de celui de Jane. Deux tableaux de paysages de neige accompagnés d'une musique mélancolique suggèrent le passage du temps mais également les rudes conditions de vie au pensionnat, et finalement le danger que court Helen que le spectateur sait malade. Une deuxième séquence de « *cutaway scenes* » intervient après l'épisode où Jane a rejoint Helen dans sa chambre de malade. Une succession de trois tableaux d'hiver (la neige qui tombe, une ruine sous la neige, puis, à nouveau, la neige qui tombe sur fond de ciel qui vire à l'orange) représente un espace-temps : une nuit entière que les fillettes passent enlacées dans le lit de Helen. Les symboles des trois tableaux évoquent le temps qui passe, le froid, la mort, mais également l'espoir de résurrection qu'Helen communique à Jane. Lorsque la caméra monte vers le ciel pour suivre à contre-courant le mouvement de la neige qui tombe, la lumière se fait plus forte, jusqu'à prendre une couleur orangée, irréelle faisant un écho visuel au paradis de Helen.

La puissance de ces images, comme beaucoup d'autres à valeur symbolique, n'est pas sans rappeler les nombreux recours au langage métaphorique de la voix narratrice romanesque que nous avons précédemment évoqués.

Un dernier aspect du fonctionnement des « *cutaway scenes* » mérite d'être observé. Parfois, nous nous trouvons en présence d'un enchaînement de tableaux qui, sans parole aucune, prend en charge une partie du récit. Ni la voix narrative, ni celle des personnages ne vient s'ajouter à la succession d'images. Qu'il s'agisse d'un incident ponctuel (un réveil nocturne) ou bien d'événements qui se prolongent (une maladie, une convalescence), les « *cutaway scenes* » se succèdent pour « raconter » une histoire. Il est parfois difficile de distinguer entre ces « *cutaway scenes* » et une scène sans paroles. Les deux catégories semblent se confondre. Par exemple, la scène où Jane et Rochester conversent (après la danse d'Adèle) est coupée par une image de Thornfield la nuit, puis par une autre image : celle d'une fenêtre qui claque, et enfin, la scène suivante montre Jane qui se lève, réveillée par le bruit. La séquence de ces trois scènes de transition précédant la scène de l'incendie est une histoire en elle-même[1] : le spectateur comprend l'étrangeté de l'ambiance dans laquelle Jane évolue, les bruits qui la réveillent la nuit, l'inquiétude qui la gagne à tel point qu'elle sort de sa chambre. Ainsi, à plusieurs reprises, le cinéaste ne se contente pas d'une seule « *cutaway scene* » ; il profite d'une première image pour en insérer une deuxième, voire une troisième, permettant ainsi d'atteindre un triple objectif : un saut temporel, le renforcement d'un message symbolique, et, éventuellement la prise en charge d'une partie de la narration.

Conclusion

Nous avons considéré tour à tour un ensemble de ressources qui constitue des relais de la voix narrative romanesque dans l'adaptation cinématographique. Nous nous sommes également interrogés sur les correspondances possibles entre deux formes artistiques, et stratégies narratives, distinctes. Une fidélité littérale à la voix narrative romanesque dans l'adaptation cinématographique qui consisterait à construire l'ensemble du scénario à partir du texte de Charlotte Brontë ne pourrait cadrer avec les impératifs de l'art cinématographique. Il est évident que l'adaptation exige de couper une grande partie du texte original (pour ne pas dire quasiment l'intégralité), et de procéder à de nombreuses adaptations de l'intrigue, des dialogues et des séquences narratives. Selon James Andrew Hall, il est dangereux de se refuser à effectuer des coupures franches et massives :

> The danger of an adapter being overawed by his subject matter is the same as that of a surgeon operating on a member of his own family: he may shrink form applying the knife deep enough[2].

Nous remarquons effectivement que si le couteau de Zeffirelli entaille profondément dans l'œuvre de Charlotte Brontë, c'est sans doute pour le plus grand profit de l'adaptation cinématographique. Et paradoxalement, ce parti pris de reprendre si peu du texte original et de réduire au maximum la prise en charge du récit par la voix-off participe à l'élaboration d'une stratégie plus vaste qui n'est pas sans rappeler certaines caractéristiques de la narration romanesque.

En effet la stratégie narrative du roman trouve son équivalent dans le film selon différentes stratégies qui font appel aux ressources visuelles

---

1. De même, nous voyons plusieurs autres séquence d'images sans paroles qui se présentent comme une succession de « cutaway scenes », racontent une histoire : par exemple, Jane en convalescence chez les Rivers, puis Jane en possession de son héritage (avant son retour à Thornfield), etc.
2. James Andrew Hall, "In Other Words" in *Communication and Media*, volume 1, n°1, October 1984, p. 17.

et sonores du cinéma que notre analyse souhaite mettre en lumière. Ces richesses se déploient avec l'aide d'une palette de techniques, allant de l'alternance caméra subjective/objective, aux montages parallèles en passant par l'insertion de « *cutaway scenes* ». En s'affranchissant du texte original, le cinéaste parvient à en restituer, parfois de manière totalement inattendue, un certain nombre de caractéristiques.

Différents éléments de la stratégie narrative brontéenne ressurgissent alors. Nous les résumons en quatre points : alternance entre autorité narrative et immédiateté de la *mimesis*, unité du récit, richesse de métaphores pour dépeindre l'intériorité des personnages et les situations, et enfin, participation active du lecteur devenu spectateur. C'est sur ce dernier point que nous concluons, tant il est vrai que cette participation semble importer à la narratrice du roman qui interpelle le lecteur une quarantaine de fois : « Reader... ». La participation requise se situe autant au niveau de l'émotion que de la réflexion. Elle consiste à *voir* selon Griffith, Conrad et Read : se laisser toucher par l'œuvre qu'elle soit romanesque ou cinématographique : « *[a work of art which] make[s] you hear, [which] make[s] you feel—[and] before all, [which] make[s] you see*[1] ».

Bibliographie

BAZIN, Claire, *Jane Eyre, le pèlerin moderne*, Nantes : Éditions du Temps, 2005.

BERTRANDIAS, Bernadette, *Jane Eyre, Charlotte Brontë, La parole orpheline*, Paris, Ellipses, 2004.

BRONTË, Charlotte, *Jane Eyre*. 1847, New York: The Modern Library, 2000.

GIDDINGS, Robert, Keith Selby, Chris Wensley, *Screening the Novel*, Houndmills, Basingstoke, Hampshire and London: Macmillan, 1990.

HALL, James Andrew, "In Other Words" *in Communication and Media*, volume 1, n°1, October 1984.

HAYWARD, Susan, *Key Concepts in Cinema Studies*, Routledge: London and New York, 1996.

LINDEN, George, "The Storied World", *in* Fred H. Marcus (ed.), *Film and Literature: Contrasts in Media* (New York: Chandler, 1971).

---

1. Robert Giddings, Keith Selby et Chris Wensley *Screening the Novel*, Houndmills, Basingstoke, Hampshire and London: Macmillan, 1990, p. 1.

Subject, sadness and portraiture in Franco Zeffirelli's *Jane Eyre*

> They came out of my head (Jane to Rochester).
> Remember, the shadows are as important as the light (Jane).
> I will have a portrait painted (Rochester to Jane).
> From the film

Eithne O'Neill

As the tale of a governess' struggle for a place in early Victorian society, the novel *Jane Eyre* would seem to provide the screen with attractive mainstream subject-matter. Enhanced by the charm of the costume-film and the cogency of plot, a first person subject perspective should prove less of a stumbling block for the 7th art than the interlocking narratives of the contemporaneous *Wuthering Heights*. Yet, it is the subjective account of Jane's Bildungsroman that is in danger of being swamped by cosy sentiment or lurid effects. Furthermore, two strange novelistic closures, the marriage of a plain Jane to a crusty, chastened father-figure, the deferred Liebestod that reunites Cathy and Heathcliff, dovetail into the "happy ending" of romantic fiction. As it is, Zeffirelli's 1996 well-crafted *Jane Eyre* incorporates Mrs Fairfax's warning: "All is not gold that glitters". Indeed, the melancholy woodwind, a tinkling piano tune, the magnificent, portrait-laden gloom of Haddon Hall, the pathetic fallacy of a lingering snow-flurry at Lowood, herald the nostalgic vein of the genre of literary adaptation.

On closer inspection, the Italian director's film is seen to pay tribute to Brontëan earnestness and to the heroine's moral stamina. Tawny and dun hues prevail in and around Gateshead, Lowood and Thornfield; the chiaroscuro of shrouded decors makes a more sombre impression than Stevenson's black and white expressionistic blend of Hollywood Gothic and Film Noir. A pastoral landscape crossed by a sun-dappled river, serene in a high angle shot, gives way to the overcast skies and "the craggy pass where the whole of life's stream will be broken up." Gravity, not buoyancy, is the keynote. Clinging about her, the sadness of her childhood draws Jane to Rochester, himself described, before appearing on screen, as troubled by "painful memories, best forgotten."

A distinguishing feature of *Jane Eyre* is the attention bestowed on the female protagonist as a portraitist and painter[1]. Far from being illustrative,

---

1. Stevenson's *Jane Eyre* dispenses entirely with the trope of painting and portraiture. The 1995 BBC *Jane Eyre*, showing a garish picture of the Miltonian cormorant, has a dismissive Rochester

or a drawing-room accomplishment, the trope of the subject as artist helps to characterize the heroine by opening up that inner space concordant with Romantic feeling. What elements of cinematographic direction come into play here? How does the image of a grave and gifted Jane bear on the mainspring of the action, the heroine's path to self-awareness?

Subject

For our purposes, the word subject has a triple facet and will involve the concept of subjectivity. Its immediate reference is the topic of the eponymous heroine, the film being also a Portrait of Jane. The transposition to screen of the fictional autobiography entails the appropriation of the subject's viewpoint by an ostensibly omniscient camera. Long and high angle shots, superimpositions, depth of field and dissolves sustain Zeffirelli's vision of place, period and dramatis personae. The "I" of the 1st person narrative[1] becomes "She", a formal shift affecting content, since it is in part from "her" reserve that the viewer infers Jane's inwardness.

However masterful, the camera stops short before the characters as they appear on the screen, where, it must be remembered, appearances do not deceive. Medium close shots and reverse angle shots denote response through facial expression and physical attitude. In addition, the switch from a subjective focus to objectivity, through the interstices of seeing and being seen, points to the structure and evolution of Jane's self. Of the novel, Starzyk writes: "…a divided self…is indicative of her process of development[2]". Symbolised by the transferral to a dramatic and optic mode, Jane's position may be seen, not as synonymous with, but as metonymic for, the split subject, Lacan's term for the alienated human condition. As for Rochester, his brooding persists, whereby "the lines of now habitual sadness marking his countenance" (ch.37) translate into a visual medium.

---

use the words of the novel: "Peculiar drawings for a school-girl". Romantic love as an exclusive slant on *Jane Eyre* is common to both these versions. For readings of the watercolours, see Bazin, « Portrait de l'artiste en jeune femme», *op. cit.*, p. 100-107, and J. Starsyk's "On the Significance of Pictures" in Bloom, *op. cit.*, p. 74-80, and his "The Gallery of Memory: the Pictorial in *Jane Eyre*." From Papers on Language and Literature, v.33, n° 3, Summer, 1997, and http://www.bnet.com/. Also Annette Tromley's, *The Cover of the Mask: The Autobiographers in Charlotte Brontë's Fiction*, British Columbia: U. of Victoria P., 1982; Alexander Christine and Sellars Jane, *The Art of the Brontës*, C.U.P., Cambridge, 1995.

1. Beaty refers to the novel's "double-voicedness", *op. cit.*, p. 79. Deleuze describes the subjective perceptive image as direct speech, the objective-perceptive as indirect speech, *op. cit.*, p. 104. The intersubjectivity of the gaze arises here, notably in the society scenes, beyond the scope of the present study. While Lacanian concepts as *sensus communis* serve our argument, a thorough-going psychoanalytical interpretation, either of the film's discourse, or of Jane's art, is not our aim.
2. *Op. cit.*, p. 79.

Secondly, the subject-matter is that of Jane's situation as an orphan singularly deprived of affection. "My parents died when I was very young": the rewritten incipit is heard over the stylised opening shot on the grayness of Gateshead/ Haworth Parsonage. It lays down as premiss the indissociability of identity and loss; this formative lack is subsumed for the film's actants under the absence of parental love. Via the compelling "I", a saddened child (Anna Paquin) gives vent to anger. Rebelliousness converges with subjectivity in the latter's acceptation as a constituent of the Romantic outlook. A spirit to be tamed, in Brocklehurst's words, this subjectivity is henceforth contained in Jane's silent ways. Medium close shots add up to that quality of inwardness embodied by Jane/Ms Gainsbourg. Nearer the surface, the subjectivity of the glowering master, played by William Hurt, prolongs the novel's assessment of himself: when fate wronged me, I had not the wisdom to remain cool. (ch.14)

Thirdly, the subject's "I" and "She" coincide in Jane's confrontation with herself. Informed by ethical imperative, her conflicts take place on complementary planes of filmic plot and discourse. The forward narrative of events, concentrated on Jane, seen by others, including the off screen spectator alone, is the outer space which contains the inner movement, as in the face-to-face scenes where the camera avails of close-ups and of mirrors. Dilemmas arise, the acceptance or refusal of marriage-offers, the resistance or giving in to a proposition deemed inappropriate. A matter of bigamy, hinging on the impediment of a "mad woman in the attic", to cite Gilbert and Gubar, this concerns the "still small voice which interprets the dictates of conscience." (ch.19) At once moral demand and melodramatic device, its Freudian connotations have been analysed, Stoneman reminds us, as "the normal…path through the Oedipal complex[1]".

At the same time, a battle goes on between the voices of reason, of established morals, and Jane's subjectivity understood as the innate sense of self, an aspect of personality channelled into her artistic activity. A portraitist, she also produces art sprung from fantasy. Coming out of her head, expressive of deep sentiment, this endeavour is beyond the reach of mere rationality. Responsible to herself alone, Jane's desire to paint is coextensive with her autonomous bent.

---

1. "The Brontë Myth", Patsy Stoneman, in *The Cambridge Companion to the Brontës, op. cit.*, p. 234.

The camera portrays its subject

Bazin states: «...Les héroïnes sont avant tout ...en quête d'une identité...[1]" Identifying deixis of the heroine is a filmic leitmotif. All point Jane out and name her, as she names herself, and as her off-screen uncle names her his legatee. A 10 year-old, Jane lowers her gaze in thought before maintaining: I am not a liar. Albeit a negation, the self-definition implies that the truth is what our subject wants, including a more distinctive self-image. A shot of her as pupil, at Helen's fresh grave, dissolves into the sequence of the adult woman, quaint, quiet, grave and simple, among the tombstones. Constantly in death's shadow, mournful grown-up Jane is signalled by the tolling church bell.

Out in the world, sadness is compounded by mystery and trauma. After the first fire, the camera dwells in a near still on Jane's face before she answers Grace Poole's pointed probe: "Perhaps you heard something?" A forward tracking shot reveals her mute traits on learning of Rochester's departure the day after he intimates his affection. Our Jane tends to keep herself to herself. Back lighting, the monochrome wash around the head, the framing within the frame as she beholds the countryside from the rectangle of the carriage pane, her marked shadow on the wall as she listens to the story of Adèle's origins, all emphasize Romantic pensivity. A highpoint of this pattern is the first shot of the sequence of silent communing through the window with off-screen Rochester, reminiscent of the painting "Woman at a Window" (1822) by the German Romantic artist, Caspar David Friedrich.

Bringing Jane, subject and viewer, together, the representational medium close-up is comparable in composition to the Western tradition of the painted portrait. Mirrors further the self-knowledge, and ours, of a woman who has been forcibly relieved of worldly vanity. Motherly and stern, Fairfax is shown in a round table mirror in Rochester's quarters which reflects a larger mirror into which Jane looks. The trope of someone holding up the mirror to the subject reoccurs when a maid leads the bedecked bride to her picture in a looking-glass. The ghost of a smile attests to her seeing herself as other. With regard to the written model, Starzyk says "existence...is a matter of finding a likeness attesting to essential equivalency with an other[2]." Small wonder that Jane, the film-heroine, should be on the look-out for likenesses that may send her "picture" back to her. On being apprised of the ability of one pretty Blanche to cheer up her master, Jane stops before a glass, and pronounces judgement: "You are a fool." Tripled in the bevelling around the glass, her mirrored image is, quite literally, biassed. However vital the

---

1. *Op. cit.*, p. 8.
2. *Op. cit.*, "On the Significance of Pictures", p. 77.

urge to see herself, should she believe that she is, once for all, thus defined, Jane errs. The subject as a fixed, whole "ego" is an imaginary, even illusory construction. As Blanche dismounts, Fairfax identifies her, whereupon the camera, after a forward tracking shot, scrutinizes Jane in an emphatic close-up.

Morally justified in being circumspect, Jane proves intuitive as to her rival; the incident of the deprecatory interjection is a step towards selfhood. Subsequently, a compassionate camera gazes into Bertha Mason's scared eyes. A more genuine sister-soul for Jane than Blanche? The diegetic counterpart of the mirrored "fool" is the shot of the bride before a full-length mirror wondering at her apparel, her appearance and her self. Here she comes to her "craggy pass." While what appears does not belie, no single image of Jane reflects her with absolute accuracy. Despite its partial view of its subject, the camera is right to dwell on a blind man whose internalized Jane is closer to reality.

Ekphrasis is rendered by two backdrops picturing, turn by turn, the solitary figures of Jane, exploring the grounds of Thornfield, and Rochester after her departure. Pinpointed by a high angle-shot, Jane walks by the river. Her surrounds bear the mark of the picturesque, theorized by William Gilpin, later combined with more romantic elements by the Norwich School of Painting. In sorrowful contemplation on the edge of a crag, Rochester's posture is akin to that of *The Wanderer above the Sea of Fog*, Caspar David Friedrich's painting, circa 1818. Wordsworth's "naked crag" and the verse "while on the naked ridge I hung alone" from the *Prelude*, his posthumous poem on the subject of inner growth, echo here.

The master's abandonment is in fact the greater. Gainsbourg's Jane recalls the novel's heroine: "The more solitary, the more friendless, the more unsustained I am, the more I will respect myself." (ch.27) While her silence may indicate a "heart full and eager to overflow", Jane upbraids her master for his moral blindness to his ward, on whom he projects his own unhappy youth. His rejoinder "Because her mother abandoned her!" signs a resonant subtext that applies to all the main characters. Zeffirelli's Rochester abides little chastening: the actor's interpretation underscores, not forcefulness or virility, but the vulnerabilty of an injured soul.

When leaving Lowood for Thornfield, from thence, heading into the unknown, Jane carries a portfolio of drawings, a signifier of what suits her best. Although initially indebted to book illustrations, her work, as Rochester intimates, testifies to her reflective powers and perseverance. An authoritative, efficient teacher, Jane's determination to master the requisite skill in art is corroborated by her moral mettle. Hence, Rochester's inquiry as to happiness is ignored. "We will be happy?" asks Adèle Varens uncertainly. "We shall work and be content", is the reply. When tempted by a too easy happiness, Jane seizes her portfolio and departs. Tenacity "of life" and tenacity of morals are one. Meanwhile, the act of sketching furnishes a dramatic link between the painterly direction of the film and the presentational diegesis of the portraitist and portraiture.

Portraiture

As a portraitist, Jane's first subject shown is Helen Burns, who considers her lucky to have a gift, thereby endowing her with a sense of her worth. As Adèle's drawing-mistress, at her little pupil's request, Jane sketches Monsieur's portrait for a keepsake. Prior to Rochester's coming on screen, his portrait touches the governess; that of his dead, estranged father dominates a series of scenes between master and governess. On the doomed wedding day, Rochester intends to have the bride's portrait painted for Adèle. Portraits of father and uncle turn up at the end.

Painting a portrait is a poetic task, as the lyrical extra-diegetic strains suggest when Jane bends over her sketch-pad beside Adèle. Again, of the novel Starzyk asserts that its verbal "portraiture" is occasioned by intense feeling. Through a characteristic compression of Brontë's text, portraiture is also seen here as an ethical activity: "You examine me, Miss Eyre." When Jane calls herself a fool, the feared self-delusion translates the text's: "Place the glass before you, and draw in chalk your own picture... Portrait of a Governess... disconnected, poor and plain". (ch.26) In fact, Ms Gainsbourg's make-over with the arched eyebrows and pointed chin, her oval face topped by the smoothed hair parted in the middle, is reminiscent of George Richmond's 1850 chalk portrait of Charlotte Brontë. In the light of a candle, Zeffirelli's Jane might have stepped out of a Georges de La Tour "Magdalen."

From reproductive figure to spoken metaphor: Rochester growls "When I look at Adèle, I see a miniature of her mother". Since Jane is at Aunt Reed's bedside, Adèle and Rochester, Jane's portrait of him in hand, grieve over the absent one in a triangular recomposition of the Family Portrait. Thanks to Jane's art and moral stance, the rapprochement between foster-father and child reflects too the function of the likenesses shown on the screen: art shows what is invisible, mourned for, even feared, but not forgotten.

"Let me see what my paid employee has been drawing in her sketch book": the master's disgruntlement at her having "caught him utterly", that is, divined his Achilles' heel, conveys his displeasure at his own resemblance which he tries to destroy. We identify with the subject's subject on overhearing, as he does, Jane's advice to Adèle: remember, the shadows are as important as the light. Through its triple repetition, the metaphor of light and shadow, standing for the mixture within each of us, and within our lives, is Zeffirelli's overt moral symbol. When tending to Mason, Jane is reflected in a wall-mirror as a black shadow, an administering angel or the Angel of Death. Its counter-image is the blur of the out-of-focus shot of Jane in white as Mason strikes his blow.

Moral subjectivity of art

The practice of her art reaffirms Jane's moral individuality. Self-taught, as she says to Helen, she requires no master. Examining her work, her employer irks the governess by insinuating: perhaps some master helped you? The novel's wording is germane to our thesis: "The subjects as I saw them...before I attempted to embody them, were striking, but my hand... had wrought out but a pale portrait of the thing I had conceived." (ch.13) On screen, creativity is underlined by a valiant effort to reproduce her imaginative art. Medium shots single out two of the three watercolours whose bistre wash favours shadowy hues. One is of a recumbent male bust, with closed eyes; the other, taken to be a figuration of the Evening Star, a woman's face with open gaze and slanting rays superimposed on a moorscape through which a river runs. The romantic and mystical tendencies of Blake and of John Martin's *The Last Man* may be implied.

"You have secured the shadow of your thought", says Brontë's Rochester of the trio; Hurt's Rochester sums them up with the comment: The thoughts are magical. Distinct from both the realistic sketched and painted portraits of the male Rochesters, and the picturesque of the diegesis, the drawings comprise a self-reflector of the Romantic theme of a solitary figure in the vastness. On the eve of Helen's death, Miss Temple says the pupils are blessed with intelligence and, the greatest blessing of all, independence of spirit. Instead of guessing at the symbolism of the watercolours, the film retains the artist's eternal dissatisfaction with his work. Jane's intention to pursue her endeavours, in the hope that "the bright furniture in her head" will improve, is concomitant with the subject as a moral entity. She expresses her anxiety at the inadequacy of her attempts to embody what Starzyk calls "shadowy forms or ideas housed in memory... The Tennysonian aspiration of pursuing an ever vanishing horizon informs her horizons[1]..." Her very shortcomings as an artist drive her on; what is missing spurs her desire. "I didn't have the skill to paint what was in my imagination. I always wanted to achieve more".

---

1. Starzky, *op. cit.*, "On the Significance of Pictures", p. 79 and "The Gallery of Memory: the Pictorial in *Jane Eyre*".

Conclusions

Jane visits Lowood graveyard, confirming by the film's circular structure the need to find the familiar face, the kindred spirit. "My thoughts were constantly drawn back to the past, the places and the people I could not forget.» In a reversal of fortune, portraits of her father and uncle, who loved her, are discovered. Then a superb close up wordlessly conjures up that "inward eye" whereby she decides to go back to Thornfield.

In idyllic Ferndean, conflict dissolves in a reconnecting with roots. Jane's suffering is at an end. Taken up with a game of happy families, will her personality be fulfilled? Subjection to stereotype cannot be (mis)taken for genuine acceptance of shadows and sadness. Neither ethical conviction, nor the subjectivity of the imagination, nor rebellion inspires the conclusion. In their stead, a fusional sympathy in the coming to roost of two hurt creatures wins the day. Žižek, following on Lacan, writes: "The shift from ego to subject, from the axis *ego-id* to the axis *subject-truth*, is synonymous with the emergence of the ethical dimension proper." He then quotes the stolen boat episode from Wordsworth's *Prelude* as providing the exact conditions for the emergence of that "inner space", the "genius, the impersonal force within me that turns me from individual into a subject, that is, an agent of the Truth ... man's ego does not cover all of our subjectivity, which can only emerge through a long process of individuation... against a background of psychic substance[1]." At this point in the conflict, Zeffirelli's refined attempt to show Jane's "substance", her artistic scope and her moral resolve, contrasting both with Rochester's self-centredness and his irresolution, falls short of the ideal. The subject Jane has given up on her desire.

Adorned with the bland "enchevêtrement végétal" of the New Gothic, referred to by Bazin[2], the penultimate portrait ushers in the final freeze-frame. Without depth of field, as gray as Gateshead, it is, as Stoneman says "frozen in the form of a conventional engraving[3]." For all the world a Valentine, or a petrified forest, it disempowers woman and man alike. Whereas Ms Brontë's writings juxtapose modes such as realism and romance[4] it is doubtful

---

1. P. 149-150, "The Unbearable Lightness of Being No-one", p. 147-199, Part 11, in *op. cit.*, *The Parallax View*. Slavoj Žižek, whose approach combines philosophy, Marxism, psychoanalysis and knowledge of the cinema, is here concerned with reinstating the subject as an impersonal agent of truth, relying on the idea of truth emanating from a *position* that lends it authority. He quotes as an example of the ego's entry into subjectivity, Shakespeare's Prospero at the end: "Now my charms are all o'er thrown, / And what strength I have is mine own". Seen in the light of a "direct inscription of subjectivity into reality", this corresponds with the subjectivity of desire.
2. Bazin, *op. cit.*, p. 56.
3. Stoneman, *op. cit.*, p. 226.
4. Wolstenholme suggests that a mutual deconstruction of modes is at work in the novel, *op. cit.*, p. 58.

that, in this conclusion, Romantic irony and subversion of wish fulfilment intervene; it is equally unlikely that the conscious decorativeness amounts to more than an unwitting self-reflector of the film's conclusion. Be that as it may, thanks to the marriage of two genres, that of the illustrated Victorian fairy-tale and that of romantic drama for the screen, Zeffirelli's lovers are caught for ever in the fronds of Ferndean.

Bibliography

BAZIN, Claire, *Jane Eyre, le pèlerin moderne*, Nantes : Éditions du Temps, 2005.
BEATY, Jerome, *Misreading Jane Eyre. A Postformalist Paradigm*, Ohio State University Press, Columbus, Ohio, 1996.
BLOOM, Harold, *Charlotte Brontë's* Jane Eyre, Infobase Publishing, Bloom's Literary Criticism, New York, 2007. http://chelseahouse.com.
Cambridge Companion to the Brontës, ed., Heather Glen, Cambridge University Press, 2002.
GILLES, Deleuze, *L'Image – Mouvement*. Cinéma 1, Paris, Minuit, 1983.
LACAN, Jacques, *L'Éthique de la psychanalyse*, Éditions du Seuil, 1986.
WOLSTENHOLME, Susan, *Gothic (Re)Visions*, State University of New York Press, 1993.
ŽIŽEK, Slavoj, *The Parallax View*, Cambridge, Mass, The MIT Press, 2006. See also *Das Unbehagen im Subjekt*, Vienna, Passagen Verlag, 1998, et *La Subjectivité à venir*, Ed. Frédéric Joly, Climats, 2004.

Cet obscur objet du désir, jeux d'ombres et de lumière dans *Jane Eyre*

Remember Adèle, the shadows are as important as the light
Jane Eyre, le film

Isabelle Van Peteghem-Tréard

Lorsque Franco Zeffirelli réalise en 1996 l'adaptation cinématographique du roman de Charlotte Brontë, il jouit d'une réputation de cinéaste shakespearien aux influences classiques. Le réalisateur de *La Mégère apprivoisée* (1967) débute dans la création de décors avant de devenir l'assistant de Visconti. Il s'agit avant tout d'un homme féru d'opéra et de théâtre qui transpose au cinéma une technique soignée de mise en scène dramaturgique lyrique. Souvent critiqué pour son approche peu innovante et très conventionnelle, Franco Zeffirelli a réalisé avec sa *Jane Eyre*, un film baroque dans lequel, comme Charlotte Gainsbourg-Jane Eyre le fait remarquer à son élève, l'ombre est souvent plus importante que la lumière.

Il y exploite et manipule les procédés narratifs du roman en transposant le récit rétrospectif de Jane Eyre, la narration homodiégétique, dans la fonction particulière de la fenêtre, du cadre dans le cadre qui diffuse une luminosité filtrée vers l'intérieur et permet une ouverture côté jardin, opposant ainsi sans cesse la dialectique du dedans et du dehors. Il inscrit son adaptation dans un univers baroque avec l'utilisation d'un décor shakespearien, d'une esthétique Renaissance, un monde de lumière tantôt contenue, tantôt jaillissante, et d'obscurité labyrinthique à Thornfield Hall.

Franco Zeffirelli choisit également de mettre en valeur la représentation, l'imaginaire, et plus précisément l'utilisation par Jane Eyre du dessin comme procédé métadramatique d'une représentation du monde, de l'Autre. La captation spéculaire à laquelle se livre l'héroïne est le pendant cinématographique de sa voix romanesque chez Charlotte Brontë. S'ajoute à la représentation graphique une mise en abyme supplémentaire par l'usage des miroirs dans le film qui interroge sur la vision en clair obscur de Jane Eyre. Son dédoublement entre narratrice et personnage se retrouve dans la version filmée par ces scènes où le personnage contemple son reflet.

Enfin, le film marque l'avènement de la lumière sur les ténèbres grâce à une progression du voilement au dévoilement du sujet féminin, au sens propre comme au sens figuré. Franco Zeffirelli filme le regard, fenêtre fondamentale sur le désir, sur cette lueur qui échappe aux personnages et qui permet au spectateur d'accéder à la passion intime des protagonistes, à l'émotion contenue par les corps, à l'incandescence.

Fenêtre sur jardin : une adaptation baroque

En effet pour le Baroque, l'apparence phénoménale voile un fond originaire qui la transcende. Elle n'est pas la vérité dernière des choses et ne saurait par suite fermer la voie à une explication en termes métaphysiques qui fournit une interpénétration en profondeur de la réalité. L'indifférenciation des données immédiates recèle en outre des éléments d'organisation qui ressortissent à une dimension supérieure. Le Baroque se refuse à reconnaître que l'essence même de l'univers soit réductible à son extériorité observable, que le principe ultime de l'être s'abolisse dans la loi du hasard (Knecht, 338).

C'est dans la contemplation active que le spectateur peut ressentir ces vides. Comme dans l'*Art de la Peinture* de Vermeer (vers 1665), le lecteur voit son regard bifurquer vers une extériorité virtuelle qui, pourtant, semble déjà s'actualiser dans l'œuvre. Le baroque cinématographique est à l'image de ce célèbre tableau de Vermeer ; une ouverture sur l'infini pratiquée entre deux réalités immédiates. (Begin, 33)

Parce qu'il est un dispositif de projection d'ombres, d'artifices, d'illusions, de mise en mouvement des images, le cinéma de Zeffirelli semble correspondre au désir profond du baroque de dépasser la représentation réaliste du monde pour accéder à la dimension de l'imaginaire, insistant sur les artifices d'un décor en trompe-l'œil. Le baroque exploite le dédoublement, la multiplication, l'anamorphose, le néant travesti et le vide déguisé en récit.

Metteur en scène et décorateur de théâtre et d'opéra, Zeffirelli signe donc ici un film à l'esthétique baroque, optant pour un univers Renaissance à Thornfield Hall et non Victorien comme pour Gateshead et Lowood. Il choisit la profondeur, le relief et un univers de boiseries sombres, d'espaces immenses écrasant les personnages, pétrifiant la demeure et ses occupants dans le passé d'une faute originelle. Les couloirs sont labyrinthiques, leur extrémité demeurant invisible, enfouie, refoulée, à l'instar du ça, du réservoir des pulsions. Thornfield Hall est une bâtisse élisabéthaine enveloppée dans un léger brouillard, nimbée d'une lumière diffuse qui semble surgir d'un monde onirique, lorsque Jane Eyre y parvient (0h25). La perspective en plongée et la vision panoramique permettent au spectateur de prendre conscience de l'étendue du domaine qui se détache dans le paysage et semble occuper tout le champ. La diligence, filmée en travelling arrière, amorce une descente pour atteindre la maison, et suit une route sinueuse qui évoque les méandres à parcourir avant d'atteindre son but. Zeffirelli montre ensuite l'arrivée de Jane, la demeure est filmée en contre-plongée, la frêle silhouette semble écrasée par cette masse hyperbolisée qui se dresse. Une porte énorme apparaît entre la gouvernante et Thornfield Hall. Mais il y a une petite ouverture dissimulée dans la grande porte et c'est par cette entrée enchâssée qu'un domestique sort la tête pour identifier la visiteuse, insistant sur un monde clos, dissimulé derrière son enceinte et dans lequel on ne pénètre pas facilement. Le regard de Jane est attiré vers le haut, donnant l'impression qu'elle est encerclée par la cour intérieure et les murs imposants. Son costume gris foncé attire l'œil du spectateur. En dépit de son apparente austérité, elle amène une présence, anime ce monde par son regard émerveillé. La pièce dans laquelle Jane est introduite est impressionnante par ses dimensions et son décor de tragédie shakespearienne. Le lieu semble figé, suspendu à l'instar de ce chandelier en forme de roue et de la ramure d'un cerf. Le cerf, symbole de la royauté et de la virilité, est ici réduit à l'état de trophée, suspendu par deux fois, d'abord sa tête entière, puis des bois nus. La poussière et la pétrification sont matérialisées par la luminosité filtrée du soleil qui parvient dans la pièce qui nimbe le lieu d'un sentiment irréel de conte de fées. Le vide est symbolisé par les fauteuils déserts, les racines et l'héritage sont représentés par les boiseries chargées et la tapisserie qui recouvrent les murs.

La lumière se fait plus chaude, le lieu plus accueillant lorsque Jane se retrouve en présence de Mrs Fairfax. La cheminée projette sur le visage des femmes une lueur douce et chaleureuse. La pièce est investie d'une présence féminine, maternelle, confirmée par le comportement nourricier de Mrs Fairfax qui va veiller sur Jane. Le rapprochement entre les deux femmes est souligné par le gros plan sur les visages qui insiste sur la communication établie, les sourires échangés.

L'utilisation baroque de la profondeur de champ vise moins l'idée que le choc émotionnel. Lorsque Zeffirelli filme le couloir qui mène de la chambre de Jane au *no-woman's land* situé à l'autre extrémité, l'utilisation de courtes et très courtes focales produit un espace très «profond», comme creusé, où tout s'offre à la perception d'un monde divisé, d'un abysse entre les deux univers, d'une frontière infranchissable. La luminosité claire de la chambre de Jane, le caractère immaculé de la pièce procurent un sentiment d'ordre et de quiétude qui contraste alors avec l'obscurité du couloir.

Fidèle à l'esthétique baroque du dédoublement, Zeffirelli commence par présenter le couloir, ce cordon ombilical qui mène de l'autre côté, vers l'obscurité terrifiante, magnifiée par le non dit de Mrs Fairfax et de son regard qui se perd vers ce lieu inaccessible. Ce sont les multiples paliers qui, dans le film, symbolisent le passage d'un monde à l'autre et la complexité du dédale. À la différence du roman, l'accès à la chambre de Bertha Rochester, au troisième étage, n'est pas dissimulé au fond d'une chambre par une tapisserie qui voile l'entrée, comme on le constate au chapitre 26 lorsque Rochester va lever le voile sur le mystère de Thornfield Hall.

> He lifted the hangings from the wall, uncovering the second door: this, too, he opened. In a room without a window, there burnt a fire, guarded by a high and strong fender, and a lamp suspended from the ceiling by a chain.
> *(Jane Eyre, p. 250)*

Zeffirelli préfèrera un accès plus rapide, moins complexe, moins imbriqué, donc plus visuel à la chambre de Bertha après l'échec du mariage avec Jane : l'escalier au fond du couloir mène à la porte de la chambre de Bertha (1h31). Ces choix elliptiques du cinéaste condensent l'action et intensifient la sensation de fulgurance et de violence passionnelle de la personnalité de Rochester. Il s'agit d'un personnage extrêmement sombre, piégé par son histoire.

La lumière fonctionne ainsi comme une instance narrative et véhicule émotion et subjectivité dans l'adaptation cinématographique. Les scènes nocturnes sont baignées d'une luminosité baroque qui accentue les ombres du foyer et des bougies sur les visages des personnages, et fait ressortir l'intensité des regards, alors que les pommettes semblent enfin se colorer du sang qui jaillit et circule. Rochester et Jane semblent alors animés, traversés par la pulsion de vie et la lumière se fait plus chaude, enveloppante. Les scènes diurnes en extérieur sont tournées le plus souvent dans une atmosphère brumeuse qui semble émaner de la terre, des collines verdoyantes, des vapeurs du cours d'eau qu'il faut traverser pour passer de l'autre côté du vallon et s'éloigner de Thornfield Hall. Au loin, une autre respiration exhale du paysage. Même en extérieur, la lumière naturelle semble filtrée, comme pour adapter à l'écran le processus de remémoration du roman.

Lors de la scène de la rencontre [0h37], Jane marche, traverse un cours d'eau et le plan large renforce la sensation d'isolement de la jeune femme dans la nature. Elle atteint les rives d'un autre monde, et les couleurs s'atténuent lentement pour être remplacées par un contraste qui met en valeur la pâleur du visage de la jeune femme : son visage éthéré va ainsi jaillir contre un fond en noir et blanc et se détacher sur un arrière plan formé par des rochers qui bloquent toute autre perspective, limite le champ de vision et capte l'attention de Rochester. Dans cette scène, la nature se fige et les deux personnages semblent alors transportés sur une scène de théâtre alors que le monde autour s'opacifie. Cette sensation de mise en scène dramaturgique statique pour filmer les échanges entre les personnages est assez récurrente dans le film.

Zeffirelli fait également le choix de remplacer la narratrice homodiégétique du roman en déplaçant le cadre narratif de la voix de l'héroïne et du filtre de sa mémoire subjective vers le motif de la fenêtre, du cadre dans le champ de vision. C'est par la fenêtre de la diligence que Jane aperçoit pour la première fois Thornfield Hall, et elle se cachera de cette ouverture lorsqu'elle fuira après le mariage avorté. La fenêtre ouvre sur une autre perspective, un plan général, un espace non clos qui est également celui de l'imaginaire et de la lumière extérieure qui pénètre dans les recoins les plus sombres de l'âme humaine et de la demeure. Les personnages sont fréquemment filmés depuis l'extérieur dans un mouvement vers l'intérieur qui s'amorce en contre-plongée, alors que leur regard se projette à l'extérieur, et qu'ils observent une scène qui se déroule en contrebas. Ils sont en hauteur, au-dessus de l'action. Ils sont filmés à travers des vitres à croisillons qui découpent l'horizon de l'intérieur, et ressemblent à des barreaux. Parfois, les fenêtres sont entrouvertes vers l'extérieur. Ils apparaissent comme des prisonniers dans leurs corps et dans le manoir alors que leur vision s'échappe, s'ouvre vers l'infini et ils sont ainsi dépeints comme des êtres divisés.

Gaston Bachelard, dans *La Poétique de l'espace*, définit ainsi la « dialectique du dehors et du dedans » :

> Si c'est l'être de l'homme que l'on veut déterminer, on n'est jamais sûr d'être plus près de soi en « rentrant » en soi-même, en allant vers le centre de la spirale ; souvent, c'est au cœur de l'être qu'est l'errance. Parfois, c'est en étant en dehors de soi que l'être expérimente des consistances. Parfois aussi, il est, pour ainsi dire, enfermé à l'extérieur. *(Bachelard, 194)*

Le spectateur se retrouve lui aussi à l'extérieur de Thornfield Hall, comme exclu de façon temporaire avant d'être réintégré au cœur de la scène. Il voit les personnages, puis, en contre-champ, il contemple la scène par leurs yeux. Après la scène en extérieur au cours de laquelle Jane dessine Rochester de profil, cette dissociation permet d'apercevoir, en contre-plongée, une main qui s'approche d'une fenêtre et une silhouette fantomatique qu'on distingue en haut du manoir, double spéculaire de Jane, située elle dans la cour, lorsque toutes deux regardent Rochester enfourcher son cheval et fuir loin de la gouvernante et des sentiments troubles qu'elle a éveillés en lui.

C'est également par la fenêtre que Jane Eyre va pouvoir contempler pour la première fois le visage parfait de Blanche Ingram, détailler son profil d'ange lumineux [1h02] et rentrer ensuite en elle-même, comme l'indique le mouvement de la caméra qui va zoomer en gros plan sur les yeux dévastés et les traits assombris de la jeune femme, opposant, comme Jane le fait elle-même mentalement, la beauté solaire de Blanche au physique austère et ordinaire de la gouvernante. L'arrivée de sa rivale va ramener Jane à la réalité, à sa place de domestique et d'exclue, et lorsqu'elle contemple avec Adèle les jeux de toute cette belle société dans le jardin, la rivière et la plongée sont là pour rappeler au spectateur qu'il y a ici un monde inaccessible. Figée, Jane est alors prisonnière du cadre de la fenêtre comme elle l'est de sa condition.

De retour à Gateshead dans la maison du pasteur et de sa sœur, une ultime scène de dédoublement hors du cadre se produit, proleptique de son inexorable retour à Thornfield Hall. Ici, ce qu'elle voit véritablement importe peu puisque son regard est en fait tourné vers l'intérieur, vers le passé et la ramène à ce qu'elle a fui. Ses yeux sont brillants de larmes, animés d'une passion intérieure qui jaillit au dehors. Son regard va vers la gauche, le passé, la nostalgie, puis s'abaisse et enfin s'oriente droit vers la caméra avant qu'une ellipse ne montre un équipage reprenant à vive allure la route de Thornfield Hall. Le regard se fait alors mise en scène d'une absence, de l'évanouissement qui résulte de cette traversée. Mais le conflit semble enfin résolu puisque Jane, cette fois, suit ce désir qui la pousse à sortir d'elle-même et à agir enfin. Elle n'est plus spectatrice mais devient maîtresse de son destin. Cependant, pour cet ultime voyage, alors que le maître est devenu aveugle, c'est elle qui, paradoxalement abdique également son pouvoir de représentation et sa dualité de créatrice, d'énonciatrice. Elle se laisse narrer, représenter alors qu'auparavant, elle choisissait elle-même de capter l'image de l'Autre, de le figer sur une page blanche, posant ainsi la dichotomie fondamentale entre regard et vision, entre image et représentation, que le film met en valeur grâce à la mise en abyme du dessin et du miroir.

Captation spéculaire et représentation

Franco Zeffirelli a transposé sur le fusain de Jane Eyre et son carton à dessins l'instance autofictionnelle de l'héroïne et son dédoublement structurel entre énonciatrice rétrospective (elle a trente ans lorsqu'elle compose ce récit) et personnage, entre activité et passivité, entre sujet et objet. Il a pour ce faire modifié des scènes du roman et en a ajouté une, cruciale dans le film, celle où Jane croque symboliquement le maître, s'approprie son image et inverse les rôles.

L'entretien dans le cabinet de Rochester sur l'éducation d'Adèle amène le maître à exiger de voir les productions de Jane. Ils sont dans ses appartements, il est neuf heures du soir et ils sont seuls, alors que dans le roman, ils sont chaperonnés par Mrs Fairfax et Adèle. Jane est assise sur le sofa, comme une petite fille qui attendrait sagement, les bras croisés, les instructions et les conseils paternels. Le maître est debout et observe, l'air mi-amusé, mi-condescendant. Un froncement de sourcils, un sourire en coin témoignent de sa curiosité. La gouvernante accède à cette requête impérieuse de dévoilement de son moi intime. Elle se donne ainsi à voir en lui permettant de partager son imaginaire et un certaine vision onirique du monde. La baie vitrée en arrière-plan qui laisse entrevoir l'autre aile du manoir dans la pénombre renforce le sentiment d'isolement des deux personnages, de rapprochement entre ces deux solitudes. Les mains de Rochester sur les dessins de Jane annoncent une autre intimité. Ses manières abruptes et son ton péremptoire rappellent l'ordre patriarcal victorien.

Le montage en champ-contrechamp permet de restituer la dynamique de l'échange qui se transforme en affrontement lorsque le maître sous-entend que sa gouvernante a probablement été aidée ou inspirée par un modèle. Jane se lève alors brusquement et s'impose comme son égale : elle n'est plus en position de subordonnée mais s'élève physiquement tout d'abord avant de se rapprocher et de tenter de mettre des mots sur ses intentions artistiques. Derrière la posture sarcastique du propriétaire de Thornfield Hall se cache un intérêt qui dépasse la relation entre maître et domestique car Rochester souligne ici la dualité fondamentale de Jane, entre son air austère, son apparence ordinaire et la richesse de son imagination qu'il qualifie d'ailleurs de magique. Comme à leur première rencontre lors de laquelle il s'était prétendu ensorcelé, Rochester insiste sur le pouvoir d'enchantement de la jeune femme :

> You may have insufficient technique, but the thoughts are magical *[le film, 0h43mn]*

Les peintures monochromes sont au nombre de trois, toutes terre de sienne brûlée. Dans le roman, il s'agit d'aquarelles aux multiples couleurs contrastées et il est intéressant de noter que Zeffirelli a, là encore, choisi d'accentuer l'ombre plutôt que de diluer l'attention du spectateur en produisant des esquisses en couleur. Ce qui marque Rochester dans l'œuvre de Charlotte Brontë est justement l'étrange lumière opaque qui rend les dessins à la fois clairs et mats. La luminosité éclaircit donc la vision du monde de la créatrice tout en brouillant les codes émotionnels puisque le *ça* est dévoilé, le réservoir des pulsions, alors que l'inconscient toujours se dérobe.

> As to the thoughts, they are elfish. These eyes in the Evening Star you must have seen in a dream. How could you make them look so clear, and yet not at all brilliant? For the planet above quells their rays. And what meaning in their solemn depth? And who taught you to paint wind? *(108)*

Les dessins sont filmés en plongée, adoptant l'angle de vue de Rochester. Dans le premier, au centre, un visage posé sur une ligne horizontale qui pourrait être un socle de pierre, semble endormi ou sans vie. Tout autour, un paysage chaotique et tourmenté de tourbillons, de masses sombres, de lignes brouillées évoque les rêves du dormeur. La violence externe contraste avec l'apparente sérénité du visage. Ce premier dessin dans le film ressemble en fait au troisième dans le roman. Le second est à peine entrevu et représente un paysage là encore onirique. Le dernier, le plus mystique, dépeint un paysage de collines traversé par un cours d'eau avec, dans les cieux le visage d'une femme qui regarde le monde depuis l'au-delà. Sa tête semble voilée d'un halo qui forme des lignes de lumières, des traits qui descendent vers la terre. Le visage voilé du modèle féminin annonce également le voile de mariée. Les deux esquisses témoignent de la division fondamentale du sujet humain dont ne subsiste que la tête, le corps se fondant dans le paysage. Pour des raisons d'intensité dramatique, le réalisateur a donc inversé l'ordre des dessins du roman pour terminer sur ce visage de femme qui émerge de son environnement, se détache du monde et contemple l'univers. L'identification avec l'héroïne est donc davantage soulignée dans cette mise en abyme de l'acte créatif, qu'il s'agisse de représentation narrative dans le livre, ou de représentation picturale dans le film.

Le scénario crée une scène nouvelle qui se déroule à l'extérieur, sur une terrasse ouvrant sur le jardin de Thornfield Hall. Adèle et Jane, situées en hauteur, observent Rochester. À la demande de la petite fille qui souhaite conserver une image de son tuteur lorsque celui-ci sera à nouveau parti, Jane croque au fusain le portrait de profil du maître. Elle délimite clairement les contours du visage, repasse sur le trait, l'épaissit, puis, ébouriffe la chevelure amenant désordre et mouvement à la représentation. Elle s'approprie peu à peu l'image de l'homme, capte les zones d'ombre, le tourment condensé dans les lignes d'un front soucieux. Rochester découvrant le dessin fronce les sourcils et s'assombrit à la vue de cette esquisse sommaire qui accentue son apparence chaotique. Il se sent pris (« You have me utterly ») et froisse le papier mais Adèle l'empêche de détruire le dessin.

Remember Adèle,
the shadows are as important as the light [0h48]

Déconcerté par cette remarque de Jane, il l'interroge sur cette théorie et l'entraîne avec lui sous le porche sombre pour émerger avec elle dans la lumière et se confier, attendant précisément un message lumineux d'espoir, de possible rédemption. Cet échange existe dans le roman mais il a lieu dans la salle à manger. Il marque le rapprochement des personnages et surtout, la demande formulée par Rochester qui attribue à nouveau à Jane un pouvoir de magicienne, de fée.

> Yes: does that leave hope for me?
> Hope of what, sir?
> Of my final re-transformation from India-rubber back to flesh? *(XIV, 113)*

Le film exploite également la présence du miroir et ses effets pour évoquer à la fois le dédoublement spéculaire et le phénomène de distorsion entre image et représentation, entre diégèse et narration. Jane est un être profondément divisé entre la richesse de son univers créatif, fantasmatique, et l'austérité de son apparence extérieure. On lui rappelle fréquemment son physique plutôt ingrat par rapport à ses cousines ou à Blanche Ingram.

La phase du miroir renvoie au phénomène de reconnaissance par *l'infans*, entre six et dix-huit mois, de son image dans le miroir. Contrairement au chimpanzé qui se détourne de l'image une fois qu'il en a compris l'inanité, le petit humain joue de façon jubilatoire en éprouvant les relations entre ses mouvements dans son environnement et leur reflet. L'enjeu majeur est celui de la reconnaissance de l'unité corporelle comme métaphorisation de l'unité de la vie psychique : l'image de l'enveloppe du corps devient pour l'enfant symbolique de lui-même. Cette limite corporelle, en apportant un cadrage, lui permet d'atteindre la compréhension de son existence. C'est sans doute pour cette raison que cette expérience est associée à de la jubilation. Vient ensuite la dimension de perte, de limitation, de solitude issue de la séparation avec la dyade imaginaire où mère et enfant ne font qu'un.

Le miroir inverse l'image et change la perspective. Il s'agit d'un outil particulièrement utile puisqu'il permet de représenter de façon graphique la division de l'être et le jeu des apparences. Il projette une autre lumière sur un personnage et amène une focalisation particulière, qui pourrait être le pendant du phénomène de focalisation en littérature, puisqu'il insiste sur la notion de perception. Il est à la fois symbole de la réalité extérieure et de ce qui échappe, donc d'une certaine vérité. Mais son utilisation plus baroque témoigne de la fonction magique du miroir, à l'instar d'une porte qui ouvrirait sur un autre monde, celui de l'imaginaire, des fantasmes, de l'illusion.

Dans les appartements de Rochester, lorsque Mrs Fairfax lui fait visiter la maison, Jane apparaît filmée en plan américain dans le miroir en pied, à droite du cadre (0h33), tandis que Mrs Fairfax, qui lui tourne le dos, a son reflet dédoublé, une fois dans le petit miroir ovale de la coiffeuse, puis dans le grand miroir. L'effet d'emboîtement et de duplication procure une sensation de profondeur. La lumière provient de la grande baie vitrée située à gauche. Les miroirs permettent ici de compléter la vision puisque l'on voit le visage de personnages vus de dos ou hors champ. C'est dans la psyché que le visage de Mrs Fairfax est mis en abyme lorsqu'elle regarde la gouvernante tandis que les regards en diagonale convergent pour se rejoindre au centre de l'écran, leurs visages clairs se détachant sur leurs tenues très sombres. C'est là que Jane découvre le portrait miniature de Rochester enfant avant d'entendre pour la première fois des cris étranges. Il est intéressant de noter que les deux femmes pénètrent ici dans l'univers intime du maître en son absence, et que Mrs Fairfax souligne la complexité de la personnalité de Rochester, la dualité fondamentale de son caractère, alors qu'elle-même se dédouble entre réalité physique et reflet dans le miroir. Mais l'utilisation des miroirs dans cette scène ne marque pas encore l'avènement de la fonction narcissique chez Jane Eyre. Celui-ci se produit lorsqu'elle prend conscience de cette image peu flatteuse d'elle-même qu'elle avait oubliée en se perdant dans le regard de Rochester.

Après l'incendie de la chambre du maître, le départ de celui-ci et la mention de la merveilleuse Blanche Ingram amènent l'héroïne à se regarder dans un miroir du couloir. La vision est multipliée, fragmentée, totale et unie au centre, puis partielle sur les angles en biseau de la glace, comme pour considérer tous les angles de la représentation de soi. Lors de ce processus de réflexivité, Jane est à la fois objet et sujet, profondément aliéné, objet d'étude et sujet analysant. Et quel que soit l'angle de vue, force est de constater que son image ne lui convient pas et qu'elle est prisonnière de ce cadre, de cette apparence en surface. Elle s'adresse alors à cet avatar vaniteux d'elle-même : « You're a fool ». [1h01] L'impact produit n'est donc pas jubilatoire mais s'apparente à une douloureuse épreuve de castration et à l'acceptation du principe de réalité. Piera Aulagnier a écrit que face à la solitude du miroir, de sa propre féminité, la femme ne peut découvrir que ce qui en serait la négation, le manque, et que le point nodal de la féminité était donc la tromperie. Le signifiant le plus caché l'affronte ainsi dans un premier temps au registre du trompe-l'œil, ici, l'apparence terne de Jane Eyre dissimule un diamant brut aux multiples facettes, lumineux en profondeur, ce que Rochester a immédiatement repéré et que la caméra de Zeffirelli dévoile.

Le miroir redouble donc le cadre de la caméra, et alors que la fenêtre ouvre sur l'extérieur, sur le monde avec lequel les personnages doivent composer, le miroir permet de pénétrer dans l'intimité de Jane Eyre, d'accomplir cette traversée des apparences pour s'attacher *in fine* à ce qui est fondamental dans toute représentation, qu'elle soit littéraire ou cinématographique : le regard.

Que la lumière soit : le dévoilement du sujet féminin

> Sir, it removed my veil from its gaunt head, rent it in two
> parts, and flinging both on the floor, trampled on them
> *(242)*

Lorsque, dans le film, Jane Eyre se contemple en tenue de mariée dans une nouvelle scène de miroir, pour cette cérémonie qui devrait lui donner un statut essentiel dans la société victorienne, celui d'épouse, son regard est lumineux. Elle ressemble à une créature éthérée vêtue de satin nacré, sortie tout droit d'un conte de fées. La luminosité filtrée diffuse une atmosphère irréelle à la scène, celle d'un rêve qui se réalise. C'est ainsi qu'elle apparaît à Rochester, descendant l'escalier comme un être fantomatique recouverte de ce voile qui masque sa chair et les nuances de ses expressions pour ne laisser filtrer qu'une image romanesque de bonheur et de quiétude, laquelle est renforcée par la bande-son des violons. Mais la satisfaction du désir des personnages repose sur une ambiguïté. Le voile de mariée vient ici précisément symboliser l'organisation du désir et du chaos de la passion par le mariage, le contrôle par la société, la régulation de la sexualité.

C'est au cours de la scène de révélation de la bigamie de Rochester et de la tromperie dont il a été victime par sa famille et les Mason, que Jane relève son voile pour contempler l'Autre femme prostrée contre la cheminée, celle qui a habité la maison tout ce temps, et qui a enfin un visage et un corps. Le mariage raté permet ainsi de lever le voile sur le secret de Thornfield Hall et de révéler au monde entier l'existence de l'épouse du maître qui refuse de se laisser enterrer vivante et témoigne de sa vitalité par cette torche phallique qu'elle brandit contre son mari. Elle est celle qui n'abdique jamais et qui, en ne restant pas au fond de la pièce, dans cette zone trouble, floue du champ de la caméra, jaillit au premier plan et capte à nouveau l'attention. Rochester subit donc dans cette scène une première castration puisqu'il échoue dans la réalisation de son désir de rédemption en s'appropriant une autre femme, une version positive qui pourrait opérer comme un antidote à sa première union.

L'union est donc interrompue et le voile est déchiré symboliquement par l'autre femme, l'épouse légitime de Rochester, celle dont les passions ne sauraient être domestiquées, l'incendiaire que l'on doit enfermer dans un grenier, le *ça* qui doit demeurer caché. Zeffirelli a considérablement modifié la scène du voile dans le film puisque, dans le roman, le voile est déchiré par Bertha au chapitre vingt-cinq lorsqu'elle rend visite à Jane la nuit précédant le mariage. Rochester va d'ailleurs prétendre qu'il s'agit d'un mauvais rêve de la jeune femme et qu'il s'agissait juste de Grace Poole. Le caractère fantomatique de Jane lorsqu'elle se contemple en tenue de mariée fait écho dans le roman à la visite de Bertha, à sa présence spectrale dans la chambre.

Dans le film, Bertha met le feu à la robe de mariée de Jane qui vient de partir en empruntant la diligence qui est apparue opportunément, tel un carrosse magique, au moment où elle quittait Thornfield Hall. Rochester tente de la poursuivre mais doit choisir symboliquement entre les deux femmes. Si près du but, l'objet de son désir se dérobe lorsqu'il décide de se retourner vers sa demeure pour sauver son épouse des flammes. C'est vers la gauche de l'écran qu'il dirige ses yeux puis son cheval. Tout comme Orphée, il commet l'erreur de regarder en arrière et il y perd l'être aimé et la vue.

Claire Bazin considère que Rochester, comme tous les héros des romans brontéens, possède un regard fascinant (Bazin, *La vision du mal*, 115), envoûtant. Il subira une seconde castration symbolique, un châtiment lorsqu'il sera frappé de cécité, condamné aux ténèbres pour son crime. Dès leur rencontre, c'est Jane qui amène la lumière et la possibilité d'une rédemption, d'une autre existence avec une femme à l'apparence fragile mais qui possède la force intérieure lui permettant de résister à la passion du maître. Il l'investit du pouvoir de désenvoûter le sort maléfique qui pèse sur sa demeure et donc sur sa lignée puisqu'il n'a pas d'héritier, quitte à devenir bigame et à enfreindre tous les codes moraux.

Jane revient à Thornfield Hall en héritière, en femme libre qui a cette fois renoncé aux tenues austères de son statut de gouvernante. C'est le chien *Pilot* qui la conduit à Rochester dans ce qui ressemble à une crypte. La scène est d'abord filmée en légère contre-plongée, magnifiant la silhouette de la jeune femme, donnant l'illusion que la voûte est extrêmement basse et que Rochester, en arrière-plan à droite de l'écran est écrasé, emprisonné dans un tombeau de pierre. Seul vestige de sa superbe passée, le siège sur lequel il est assis et dans lequel il semble condamné à attendre. Lorsque Jane l'embrasse enfin, la caméra filme cette fois en légère plongée, en plan moyen, replaçant les personnages dans leur cadre intime, la crypte se muant ainsi en temple protecteur, en coque maternelle, accentuant leur rapprochement.

« I will be your friend, your nurse, your companion » [1h47] : Jane Eyre affirme son désir par l'utilisation du modal « will », l'adjectif possessif « your » soudant linguistiquement cette volonté de lui appartenir ; elle sera unie d'une façon ou d'une autre à Rochester. Le montage en fondu-enchaîné fait passer de la crypte à l'image de l'arbre aux branches déployées, figure de continuité, transition en accord avec les paroles des personnages sur la symbolique de l'arbre terrassé qui va à nouveau reprendre force et vigueur. Jane Eyre et Edward Rochester sortent donc de l'intimité de leur sanctuaire pour émerger dans la douce lumière de la campagne anglaise, se promenant sous un arbre immense, la voix *off* de la jeune femme évoquant leur bonheur conjugal, la naissance des enfants et la rédemption du maître : « And so I married him ».

La dernière image les représente en plan général, au centre de l'écran, observant l'horizon et la rivière en contrebas. La lumière est douce, les couleurs semblent atténuées par un filtre qui brouille les contrastes pour ne conserver qu'une impression d'harmonie. L'image cinématographique se ferme sur une gravure, figeant l'histoire dans les temps immémoriaux de la création littéraire de Charlotte Brontë.

Conclusion

The unconventionality of the heroine and the tormented unscrupulousness of Rochester (whose near-bigamy may be immoral but is also an attempt to restore love and sanity to his life) shocked many of its first readers. That power to shock isn't in this movie. The years have subdued the impact of the novel, and this new rendering doesn't wash away the pleasant patina of a century-and-a-half's acceptance. Zeffirelli's Jane Eyre feels like an instant classic: smooth, confident of our approval, a little dull. (Alleva)

Jane Eyre est présentée comme une jeune femme sans grâce et au physique peu harmonieux. La lumière qui émane d'elle provient de son regard intense. Charlotte Gainsbourg correspond assez bien à la description que fait Charlotte Brontë de Jane Eyre. Le réalisateur a renforcé l'austérité des traits par une coiffure qui durcit le visage et des vêtements très sombres. Mais le jeu de l'actrice manque souvent de nuances et elle ne parvient pas à exprimer toute la complexité du personnage de Jane Eyre, cette incandescence qui lui échappe lorsqu'elle regarde Rochester. Le critique Richard Alleva se plaint même la monotonie de sa diction. Quant à William Hurt, son interprétation ne témoigne pas de la puissance virile du personnage du roman et sa présence sexuelle a été considérablement édulcorée dans l'adaptation. D'ailleurs, Franco Zeffirelli et son scénariste, Hugh Whitemore, n'ont pas adapté la scène dans laquelle Rochester, refusant de laisser partir Jane, explique qu'il pourrait la forcer pour la posséder toute entière (ch. 28) mais qu'il ne deviendrait que le maître de son corps, pas de son esprit. Cette extrême violence du personnage disparaît dans le film au profit d'une certaine vision statique du désir que seuls des effets cinématographiques assez classiques comme les gros plans sur des froncements de sourcil ou des couloirs sombres vont venir souligner. Richard Alleva explique qu'il manque à William Hurt, comme au film, un élément primordial du roman : le danger.

Orson Welles, dans la version de Robert Stevenson de 1944 campait un Rochester proche du poète maudit Lord Byron et correspondait donc davantage à la représentation que pourrait se faire le lecteur du roman, même si le jeu théâtral de l'interprète peut aujourd'hui agacer. Quant à la version de la BBC réalisée par Julian Amyes en 1983, elle se compose de cinq épisodes de cinquante minutes avec une volonté de fidélité au roman. Timothy Dalton et Zelah Clarke sont convaincants en Rochester et Jane Eyre, mais l'approche du désir reste plutôt figée, encore trop sage, même si leur relation apparaît plus fusionnelle, passionnée et donc plus crédible que le couple formé par William Hurt et Charlotte Gainsbourg. On peut déplorer également les différences physiques importantes entre Rochester et Timothy Dalton, décidemment trop élancé et trop distingué. Mais contrairement à Franco Zeffirelli, Julian Amyes conserve l'essence contestataire du roman original.

Le roman inscrit clairement l'avènement du sujet féminin, le passage du voilement du sujet au dévoilement, au sens propre comme au sens figuré. Jane Eyre s'impose en tant qu'héroïne féministe et cet aspect fait défaut au film qui insiste davantage sur la résolution du conflit, le passage de l'ombre à une lumière (plus tamisée que crue) que sur la liberté essentielle de l'esprit créatif de Jane Eyre. Le réalisateur évacue la force du *Bildungsroman*, ne s'intéressant pas au parcours initiatique de l'héroïne, au pèlerinage, mais privilégiant la destination finale, l'union enfin consacrée. Le *happy-ending* sur la voix sage de Charlotte Gainsbourg oblitère la petite voix malicieuse et toujours rebelle de l'héroïne de Charlotte Brontë et l'ambiguïté de la relation à l'Autre femme. Le printemps peut revenir sur Thornfield Hall après la mort de Bertha dont le prénom renvoie au diminutif germanique de *berht*, « brillant » et « illustre » (d'où l'anglais *bright*) et à l'ancienne divinité germanique *Berchta*, la dame blanche, déesse de la femme, de la fécondité et du destin qui présidait au solstice d'hiver et annonçait la mort. Bertha l'incendiaire, est réduite à une présence fantomatique dont l'éclat ne saurait être dévoilé par crainte de son incandescence. Le côté maléfique de la déesse est annihilé pour ne préserver que la puissance positive de la femme : Jane Eyre, héritière de la place d'épouse, fille symbolique de *Berchta*, donne la vie. L'obscur objet du désir, la folle enfermée dans le grenier, disparaît dans ce mouvement final de réconciliation et d'ordre restauré.

Bibliographie

ALLEVA, Richard, « *Jane Eyre-movie reviews* » Commonweal, June 1, 1996, page consultée le 16 juin 2008, http://findarticles.com/p/articles/mi_m1252/is_n11_v123/ai_18354485.

AULAGNIER-SPAIRANI, Paula, *Remarques sur la Féminité et ses Avatars – Le Désir et la Perversion*, Paris, Seuil, 1967.

BACHELARD, Gaston, *La Poétique de l'espace*, Paris, PUF, 1983.

BAZIN, Claire, *La vision du mal chez les sœurs Brontë*, Toulouse, P.U. du Mirail – Interlangues Littératures, 1995.

BEGIN, Richard, *Le cinéma d'une promenade baroque*, Cahiers du GERSE n° 3, Automne 2001, 21-34.

BERTRANDRIAS, Bernadette, *Jane Eyre – La parole orpheline*, Paris, Ellipses, 2004.

KNECHT, Herbert H., *La logique chez Leibnitz : Essais sur le rationalisme baroque*, Lausanne, L'Âge d'homme, 1981.

Place and Space in Franco Zeffirelli's *Jane Eyre* (1996)

Anne Paupe

The *Bildungsroman* plays a pivotal role in Charlotte Brontë's *Jane Eyre*. It structures the novel, which is divided into five sections, each corresponding to a stage in Jane's life and located in a different place designated by a symbolic name: Gateshead, Lowood, Thornfield, Moor House, and Ferndean[1]. Adapting this novel to the screen therefore means dealing in some way with this topographic and narrative structure, while of necessity condensing the novel's plotline into the screenplay of a film whose screen duration cannot exceed two hours. Additionally, the change from novel to film entails a new set of medium-specific potentials and constraints, many of which have to do with the apprehension of filmic space, that is, with the way in which viewers imagine the diegetic world and form ideas of the relationships between the concrete places (sets and locations) presented to them during a film's projection[2].

Pro-filmic elements such as sets, locations and costumes (and therefore also colours and textures) depend on *mise-en-scène* choices, while cinematography, through framing and camera movements, structures space inside each shot. Finally, editing choices, by joining one shot to the next, have repercussions on the interaction of off-screen and on-screen space, that is, on what is, or not, revealed to the viewer. Faced with an accumulation of visual, auditory, compositional and relational cues during a film's projection, viewers are incited to constantly reconstruct the spaces that are presented to them, arranging them into a world onto itself[3]. The purpose of this paper will be to provide a brief overview of this process in the case of Franco Zeffirelli's *Jane Eyre*, trying to answer the following questions: what are the various

---

1. In particular : Claire Bazin, *Jane Eyre, le pèlerin moderne*, Nantes : Éditions du Temps, 2005, p. 23-30 and Sharon Locy, "Travel and Space in Charlotte Brontë's *Jane Eyre*", *Pacific Coast Philology*, vol. 37, 2002, p. 105-121.
2. For a detailed conceptual framework on place and space in the cinema, see André Gardies, *L'Espace au cinema*, Paris, Méridiens Klincksieck, 1993, especially p. 59-161 on diegetic and narrative space. To put it in a nutshell, a place is a concrete object in the film (*objet locatif*), while space refers to the abstract notion viewers form of this place and of its relations to other places and to characters.
3. In the case of literary adaptations, viewers are also aware that this film-based world took its point of origin in a classic English novel which itself presented its readers with some cues (in this case, linguistic and narrative ones) that prompted them to imagine a coherent diegetic world, which somewhat complicates the matter by creating conflicting spatial and diegetic expectations.

places that structure the spaces of this film? What are the values attributed to each space? What, then, is the type of world one imagines while watching this film?

Overall Topography

Zeffirelli's film is divided into seven distinct, temporally continuous units, each located in a specific place. Contrary to Brontë's novel, the film only presents us with three main places, if we consider that St John Rivers' rectory is shown to be in the vicinity of Gateshead. Its topography could therefore be summarised in the following way:

Place	Main events
Gateshead 1	Jane's early childhood at the Reeds'
Lowood 1	Jane's education Jane's friend Helen dies
Thornfield 1	Jane's post as a governess Jane falls in love with Rochester Rochester seems attracted to Blanche Strange events occur, involving Grace Poole
Gateshead 2	Jane meets St John Rivers Jane forgives a dying Aunt Reed
Thornfield 2	Jane's aborted wedding with Rochester Bertha's existence is revealed
Gateshead 3 [Lowood 2] Gateshead 3	Jane flees She is taken in by the Rivers She goes back to Lowood, where she hears Rochester calling to her She stalls St John's proposal
Thornfield 3	Jane is united with blind Rochester They are married and have a son

Gateshead

Gateshead first appears in what seems to be a lithograph which slowly morphs into a moving image, as Jane's voice-over informs us of her situation as an orphan at the hands of Mrs Reed and her children. The film associates this view of Gateshead with the long term, through Jane's sentence: *"For nearly ten years I endured their unkindness and cruelty."* The long shot on the Hall, filmed frontally and from a slightly low angle, literally invades the frame, looming above us and trapping us into this place, all the more so as the camera then moves closer to the building's front. We then proceed to an *in medias res* presentation of one of Jane's quarrels with her cousins, after which Jane is punished and locked up in a (red) room for the night. The still frontality of the façade is contrasted with the violent agitation of the interior, the dark hues, fast editing and disorienting angles of the latter replacing the light colours and stillness of the former. This overall pre-credits sequence thus builds a sense both of imprisonment in a confined place, and of disorientation. Structurally, Gateshead so far has been constructed as a fake front that hides violent goings-on (Jane is hit by her aunt and cousins, she is thrown into the red-room and jolts against the mirror).

However, this sequence also prompts us to form a distanced impression of Gateshead. The use of the voice-over narration draws our attention to the film's status as an adaptation of a literary work (although the text proper was written by the screenplay writers), while the presentation of Gateshead in a lithograph further points to the literary space the narrative originates in, by suggesting a picture that might have been included in an illustrated edition of the novel[1]. The credits sequence, with its obligatory mention of the film as "based on the novel by Charlotte Brontë", further strengthens our awareness of the film as adaptation[2] and, to my mind, undermines the effect of the pre-credits sequence by keeping our minds on the interrelation between cinematic and literary spaces, instead of prompting us to focus on the spaces built by and within the film.

After the credits, our perception of Gateshead alters. Another wide shot of the Hall, taken slightly from the left, gives us a view of its setting [03:37 to 03:46[3]]. This shot seems to position the film in the generic context of costume dramas and "heritage" films, with their connotations of old-fashioned stateliness. Thus, the previous denunciation of appearances now conflicts with a sense that the filmmaker endorses part of the very discourse of grandeur he had seemed to debunk in the opening sequence. However, the post-credits segment also further develops the theme of Gateshead as a place for false appearances, by insisting on the Reeds' change in behaviour when Brocklehurst enters the room: the drawing-room is shown as a stage on which the Reeds display their accomplishments and good manners (offering tea and playing the piano) and on which Jane expectedly performs badly, thus justifying her being sent to Lowood. Finally, Mr Brocklehurst's arrival and the subsequent scene during which we understand that Jane is to go to a school administered by Brocklehurst, at Lowood, modifies

---

1. Later on in the film, we might begin to interpret this picture as one of Jane's sketches, and hence, as an example of her authority on the narrative.
2. The American title of the film was in fact *Charlotte Brontë's Jane Eyre*.
3. This mention in-between brackets corresponds to the time indicated by DVD players.

our understanding of Gateshead's function in the film's narrative: as the plot proper now seems to begin, we no longer see Gateshead as a place for long-lasting suffering, but a repellent, in Greimassian terms a sender in Jane's trajectory in life.

Our view of Gateshead is even more radically modified when Jane returns there years later. Gateshead is now associated with a more modest building that the dialogue then enables us to identify as Gateshead Rectory, where St John Rivers and his sister live[1]. The façade of Gateshead Hall, what with the rutted lane in the foreground, now does not seem as imposing as before [01:15:54]. Its stately interiors have been replaced by the dreary room in which Mrs Reed is dying. The previous verticality of Gateshead has been superseded by the horizontality of Mrs Reed's bed; her previous domineering stance has changed into vulnerability, which is stressed by the high angle chosen for the shots which show her from Jane's point of view [for instance 01:16:11]. Gateshead, of course, has also changed in relation to Jane: she has developed from an angry child into a more subdued adult. Jane's new psychological state, however, owing to the choice of having Charlotte Gainsbourg play the role with extreme restraint, is made clear by the change in our perception of space, instead as by obvious cues from either dialogue or facial expressions. The second episode in Gateshead, then, is used in the narrative to provide evidence of Jane's transformation.

Jane's second return to Gateshead, after her wedding with Rochester has been cancelled, presents many similarities with her first return: this segment of the film opens with similar wide shots on the front of the rectory [especially 01:37:54], and the filming of a weak Jane recovering from the events at Thornfield in her bed remind us in many ways of the scenes with her dying aunt, all the more so as the same subjects (namely Jane's family connections and her uncle in Madeira) are evoked in the dialogue. Moreover, Gateshead Parsonage is also connected with the other places which have been pivotal in Jane's life through the editing, as the segment on Jane's return to Lowood is inserted inside this sequence. Our perception of the topography of and values associated with Gateshead therefore evolves considerably during the film's projection. By bringing together cues that remind us of the various stages and places in Jane's life, this segment in Gateshead builds a sense that all these places are connected, thereby preparing us for the film's dénouement.

---

1. This, of course, is a significant change from the novel, where Jane hears about the bad fortune of the Reeds from Robert Leaven, Bessie's husband. In the film, the rectory has taken up the place occupied by the lodge in the novel.

Lowood

The treatment of Lowood enhances its continuity with Gateshead: the connection between the two places, indicated in the numerous references to the school during Mrs Reed's conversation with Mr Brocklehurst, is made visible by the views of the carriage taking Jane from one place to the other, as a match on movement and a dissolve link the shot of Jane and Brocklehurst walking away in the hall of Gateshead, with the carriage driving towards the horizon [08:02 to 08:04]. In addition, the establishing shot showing Lowood is first static, then the camera moves in towards the building, as it had done when introducing Gateshead to us [08:10 to 08:30]. This similar treatment draws our attention to the resemblances between the two places: both are places where punishment is arbitrary and where Jane is imprisoned. At Lowood, this is suggested by the uniforms worn by the girls, as well as by the symmetry and deep focus used for the many shots on the teaching room and the dormitory. Jane is displayed as a spectacle in both spaces—in Lowood, the outer room where she is made to stand on a stool forms a sort of proscenium for the teaching, thus further suggesting the notion of spectacle.

There are also significant differences between the two places: especially, Gateshead was associated with disorientation and fake order, while Lowood is a place for calm and discipline—hence, the slow long lateral tracking shots of lines of girls. Besides, Lowood also differs from Gateshead because segments underlining the harsh discipline alternate with others showing Jane's friendship with Helen. Here, the treatment of space does not seem very coherent: the Vermeerian light, costumes and compositions of the scenes showing Jane's (relative) felicity at Lowood undermine the film's efforts to associate this place with negative values[1]. Admittedly, Helen dies, but even her death seems to have been an occasion for the filmmaker to connect Lowood with connotations of maudlin sentimentality. The shots on snow-covered landscapes at night that precede Jane's visit to Helen's sick room [18:55 to 19:00] provide no new information on how cold it must be inside Lowood (this had been demonstrated previously when the girls had to break the ice on their wash-basins in the morning)—to the contrary, they seem to underline the prettiness of winter, and therefore are rather at odds with what follows. Similarly, the heavily symbolic shots of snow falling on ruins [21:56], followed by a craning shot in which the camera moves upwards, mimicking Helen's ascension to Heaven, also undermine the sense of narrative drama and create confusion as to the values associated with Lowood.

---

1. In his review of the film, Jean-Loup Bourget pointed out that, though Zeffirelli claimed to have taken his inspiration in Blake's work, the film was more reminiscent of Vermeer and Millais: cf. *Positif*, n° 425-426, July-August 1996, p. 142.

Finally, the sequence in the cemetery, as it is suffused with light and accompanied by rising extra-diegetic music when Jane turns into an adult, paradoxically seems to associate Lowood with peace, rather than with dreadful death: it is a place for communication with the past and for supernatural communion with the dead. The fact that neither Miss Scatcherd, not Mr Brocklehurst are shown in the graveyard sequence further highlights Lowood's final positive image, as does the fact that, unlike what happens in the novel, Miss Temple stays in Lowood, stating "it is God's will [she] is here."

When Jane returns to Lowood, we only see an outside view of the school in a wide shot, as the stagecoach drives past it. The hardships Jane suffered there are now shown as things of the past, especially as the gate, in the foreground, maintains Lowood at a safe distance [100:55] The treatment of Jane's subsequent visit to the cemetery mirrors her farewell scene mentioned above (and was probably shot at the same time): both scenes have the same lighting and show a similar shot of Helen's grave. The sense of permanence that was previously associated with Lowood is thus reinforced, while also serving a narrative function, as the graveyard is the place where Jane hears Rochester calling out to her. The graveyard's association with supernatural elements therefore takes a new turn, as it is now the place where Jane communicates with the living, aided by nature (the sound of the wind in the trees' branches becomes very audible when Jane raises her head, trying to locate the source of the voice she hears). This may also be seen as casting a premonitory light on Jane's final reunion with Rochester, hinting to his position in-between life and death.

Thornfield

Our first view of Thornfield, contrary to our initial discovery of Lowood, is not prepared by numerous allusions in the dialogue. The only cues we have to picture it in advance are Miss Temple's statement that Jane "should be starting a new life", and the voice-over reading of Mrs Fairfax's letter to Jane. Therefore, contrary to Gateshead and Lowood, it appears as a welcome change in Jane's life, and also as quite mysterious. Our first view of the Hall in a wide shot filmed from a high angle, encompassing it in its surroundings, makes it at first look much less imposing than Gateshead or even Lowood were [00:25:54]. Our first sense of the topography of Thornfield is that of a fairy-tale castle: it is a semi-enclosed space, separated from the outside world by a bridge, then a heavy door. We expect it to follow rules of its own, and Jane to perform the role of Prince Charming waking up

Sleeping Beauty[1]—which in a way turns out to be true (Joan Plowright, as Mrs Fairfax, especially looks and sounds like a fairy godmother).

A second characteristic of Thornfield, its size and internal complexity, becomes apparent as we discover the Hall, following in Jane's footsteps. As Mrs Fairfax leads Jane to her room, a strange grave sound in the soundtrack underlines the gloomy associations conveyed, in the dialogue, by Mrs Fairfax's referring to the rooms in the front as "so dreary and solitary and no one ever sleeps there. One would almost say, if there were a ghost at Thornfield Hall, that would be its haunt[2]." The next day, this opposition between light and dark is repeated, as the shots of Jane contemplating the landscape around the Hall [31:49 to 31:53] are followed by a high-angle shot on the staircase where Mrs Fairfax is leading Jane in her visit of Thornfield, which implies that there is a silent observer upstairs, watching their every move [31:54]. Thus, Thornfield, while remaining associated with fairy tales, is also gradually linked with the Gothic. The alternation between welcoming and scary places is then further reinforced by a similar high-angle shot on the stairs [32:10 to 32:14]. The gothic undertones are reinforced by the visit of Rochester's apartment, where Mrs Fairfax tells Jane about his troubled past, after which Jane hears shouts coming from above. While Mrs Fairfax tries to attribute these shouts to a servant, Grace Poole, the filming and editing contradict this by showing that the shouts seem to be coming from even higher in the house [35:02 to 35:23].

These gothic undertones are momentarily forgotten when the romance between Jane and Rochester develops. Their initial meeting on the rock-strewn moors expands our knowledge of Thornfield, locating the Hall in a barren, stage-like setting, and associating Rochester's character with the troubled psychology symbolized by the rocks scattered in the landscape. After this encounter, Thornfield becomes a place for observation, as Rochester, sitting by the fireside with his back to the camera, examines Jane [41:16; 42:00; 42:20], while Jane also observes him, as two reverse-angle shots show Rochester in the background and Jane in the foreground, with her back to us [41:24 and 42:07]. This process of mutual observation continues with Rochester's comments on Jane's sketches being followed by Jane's drawing a portrait of Rochester: here, pictorial space becomes a privileged way for each character to understand and be drawn to the other.

However, observation is further contaminated by frightening overtones. The presence of uncanny off-screen elements is repeatedly alluded to. For

---

1. This is reinforced by Rochester's lines after their first encounter ("When I saw you on the lane, I thought unaccountably of fairy tales, and I had half a mind to ask if you had bewitched my horse! I'm not sure yet."), which the script writers have taken almost *verbatim* from the novel.
2. However, one might argue that the hallway which leads to the front rooms (and to Bertha's room) does not look very frightening.

instance, after the portrait scene, in which Jane and Rochester come to an understanding of each other (with Rochester telling Jane that she is "not naturally austere anymore than [he is] naturally vicious"), we see Rochester galloping away [49:22 to 49:32]. This shot may be attributed to an omniscient observer; however, the following shot, which shows an indistinct figure coming to an upstairs window to look outside [49:33 to 49:37], cues us to read it as a point-of-view shot. The film, at this point, encourages us to understand that there is another silent observer on the upper floor with Grace Poole, as the film then cuts to a high-angle shot of a conversation between Jane and Mrs Fairfax on Rochester's character [49:38], then on to a shot of Grace's face, obviously listening in [50:09 to 50:11]—it does not seem possible for Grace to have been both looking outside and listening in. One might argue here that too many cues are given to the spectator as to Bertha's presence, thus undermining the gothic effect.

The interweaving of the gothic and the romantic themes are translated in spatial terms by the link between jealousy and silent observation. The romance, with its confrontation between Jane and Rochester, is furthered during the party scenes, which develop Jane's jealousy—for instance, upon hearing of Rochester's alleged attraction to Blanche Ingram, Jane is showed staring at herself in a mirror, whispering to herself "You're a fool" [61:19]. The contamination of the romance by the gothic becomes even more obvious when Jane takes up the role of the silent observer: the camera repeatedly zooms in on her face as she watches the guests from the main gallery [62:38 to 62:40; 62:42 to 62:44 and 62:45 to 62:53]. Jane's role as an observer is then developed when she is summoned to the main gallery in the evening: the camera shows her watching Blanche from the end of the room. Interestingly, in the subsequent scene when Rochester notices Jane's departure and catches up with her takes place in the stairs, Jane's point of view on Rochester is filmed from a high-angle in a shot, which is quite reminiscent of those previously attributed to the unknown presence upstairs [67:00]. That there is indeed a *silent observer* other than Jane is however made clear in the segment devoted to Mason's being stabbed at night, with high-angle shots on the doctor's carriage arriving at Thornfield [71:08 to 71:18] once again attributed to Grace's point of view [72:01 to 72:03].

After Jane comes back from Gateshead, the same pattern continues: when Rochester proposes, the romantic couple's association with horizontality is strengthened both by their conversation on equality, and by the flat layout of the garden. However, several elements contradict this feeling of happiness: of course, Mrs Fairfax's cautionary conversation with Jane, but also a shot in which Jane looks at herself in the mirror (which reminds us of the previous scene when she had heard of Rochester's association to Blanche), and, especially, the ominous verticality of the stairs in which the bride and groom meet just before the wedding. A high-angle shot of Rochester walking up the stairs [87:47 to [87:56], though not attributed to the unknown silent observer upstairs, confirms our sense that something is wrong.

Finally, after Bertha's existence has been revealed to Jane and to us, the only topographic and narrative solution in order to eliminate this ominous upstairs presence is to have Thornfield burnt and Rochester's first wife kill herself. Thus, the exaggerated verticality of Thornfield, as it was repeatedly shown as an obstacle to the romance, is eliminated. Our final views of Thornfield show us the low-ceilinged, vaulted room located somewhere on the ground floor of the Hall where Jane is reunited with Rochester: the choice of a low angle underlines the restricted space now allotted to Rochester, contrasting with his previous freedom of movement [104:54 to 105:09]. Thornfield itself almost disappears from the film: as Jane's voice-over narration is heard, the last image of the film shows the couple with their backs to us, looking at the countryside [108:09 to 108:29].

The film's final emphasis on the trees that stand on each side of the image in the foreground serves as a reminder of the previous segments when happiness had been associated with nature. In addition, this sequence creates a sense of the triumph of a balanced and controlled nature, all the more so as this last image follows the codes of classical paintings, as devised by Le Lorrain, with the trees forming a *coulisse* that guides our gaze towards the couple which stand in the middle ground, in centre frame. As this moving image gradually morphs into a lithograph, which parallels the beginning of the film, we are left with a sense of permanence and circularity, which finally inscribes the film within the static codes of classical storytelling, and not within the more perturbing codes of the Gothic.

By substituting only three main places to Brontë's five, co-writers Zeffirelli and Whitemore have created a topography in which Jane's process of maturation is more strongly linked to returning to places than was the case in Brontë's novel. The diegetic world built by the film is based on recurring shots of familiar places, which we are prompted to form new relationships to, following Jane, the main focaliser. Thus Gateshead, from a place for imprisonment and disorientation, becomes associated with Jane's reconciliation with her past, while Lowood, at first linked with arbitrary discipline, becomes the place where supernatural events occur, and Thornfield, formally the stage of a conflict between the horizontal space of romance and the vertical space of the gothic, is almost completely destroyed and superseded by pastoral landscapes. Finally, what seems to be at stake in the film is the erasure of excessive man-made places and their replacement by a balanced, man-controlled nature.

The terror and enchantment of colours in Franco Zeffirelli's *Jane Eyre*

What a bright spot of colour you have on each cheek!
and how strangely your eyes glitter! Are you well?
Charlotte Brontë, Jane Eyre[1]

Taïna Tuhkunen

In the conclusive chapter of her book *Jane Eyre, le Pèlerin Moderne*[2], Claire Bazin underlines the impossibility of a definitive response to Charlotte Brontë's novel. The multiple readings allowed by the text prove its capacity to remain open to new approaches and subsequent interpretations, despite its roots in the Victorian world. As Bazin demonstrates in her study, besides as a *bildungsroman* and a gothic novel, Brontë's text can be approached in a variety of ways, including through the angle of fairy tales.

Within the necessarily limited framework of my article, I would like to follow in Claire Bazin's thought-provoking footsteps to show how Franco Zeffirelli's 1996 screen adaptation of Charlotte Brontë's *Jane Eyre* works as a similar "offshoot" (*un rejeton*[3]) of Brontë's novel. Literally "shooting off" from a pre-existing center, the filmic reading of the *urtext* not only offers another example of the fecundity of Brontë's writing, but provides a clear illustration of the multiple ways screen adaptations participate in the process of rereading. Despite the obvious differences between the two media, Zeffirelli's movie remains merely *one* potential variant, one potential reading of the novel it is based upon.

According to the Canadian scholar Linda Hutcheon[4], a film adaptation is to be understood as something fundamentally hybrid, a complex operation involving not only the visual, the verbal as well as the aural and the kinetic. While a screened version of a literary text seems to focus primarily on the visual (setting, characters, background elements, props, lights, movement, colours, etc.), one should not ignore the film's specific capacity to appeal

---

1. Charlotte Brontë, *Jane Eyre*, London: Norton Critical Edition, 2000 (1847), p. 238.
2. Claire Bazin, *Jane Eyre, le pèlerin moderne*, Nantes : Éditions du Temps, 2005.
3. « "Les rejetons" de *Jane Eyre* viennent en témoigner, qui s'emparent de l'un(e) ou de l'autre des personnages du Ur-text pour lui écrire une (nouvelle) histoire, re-situer la marge au centre, refusant de laisser dormir un roman qui les tient toujours en éveil », Claire Bazin, *Jane Eyre, Le Pèlerin moderne*, op. cit., p. 124.
4. Linda Hutcheon claims that adaptation has always been a central mode of the story-telling imagination. Examining how adaptations work in a wide variety of fields from comic books to video game versions of fairy tales, she makes a distinction between the "single-track" literary text and the "multi-track" language of film, Linda Hutcheon, author of *A Theory of Adaptation*, London: Routledge, 2003.

concurrently to more than one sense. Although this kind of multisensory reliance naturally also marks literary texts, namely through synaesthesia, it could be argued that in the cinema the reader-spectator is even more exposed to simultaneous sensory perceptions.

The aim of this essay is to focus on Franco Zeffirelli's use of colours not as an element of decor, but as a means to support the narrative and structure the diegetic space of the film. We shall begin by observing how colours are endowed with a proleptic function and how they participate in the shaping of the characters—namely in the cinematic re/construction of the eponymous heroine. As Zeffirelli's limited palette is made to echo Brontë's literary portrayal of the "plain Jane", the emphasis on the heroine's plainness is contested, quite similarly, by Zeffirelli's filmic accentuation on strikingly warmer hues and more passionate tones that heighten the spectators' sensations and affects.

While chromatic variations perceptible in Zeffirelli's film remain a crucial supportive technique in the service of the narrative, the openly suggestive or more subtly allusive power of colours serves further purposes, namely when faced with the question of format. Owing to their often quite spectacular capacity to establish immediate links, colours—and chiefly the colour red—are worked onto the screen in such a way as to trigger chains of associations that make it possible to position Zeffirelli's cinematic rendition of Brontë's novel within more general systems of signs and, to some extent also within existing literary genres. At the same time, one is to bear in mind that colours remain part of a complex system of interrelated elements, and should not be analyzed separately from the other important modes of construction of a text or a film.

The present article does not pretend nor wish to "explain away" the chromatic polysemy underlying Zeffirelli's *Jane Eyre*, but strives instead to map the outlines of its colourful as well as bleaker, less explicit objects, spaces and processes. Before entering the Italian movie director's revisited Brontëan *topoï* it is, however, imperative to remind the reader-spectator that there are no definite, easy-to-apply colour codes. For, as frustrating as it may sound, when trying to understand the more implicit chromatic issues we cannot—as Michel Pastoureau, a French colour historian recalls—depend upon "transcultural truths about colours[1]". Rather than approaching them as a universal set of signs, colours are to be viewed within the context of each particular text and film. At the same time, as readers and spectators of *Jane Eyre*, we may consider ourselves as fortunate, for thanks to the successive screen adaptations of this English classic, we possess ample filmic material to try and understand the mysteries that lie beyond the enigmatic "red-room" where everything seems to begin.

---

1. « La couleur est d'abord un fait de société. Il n'y a pas de vérité transculturelle de la couleur », Michel Pastoureau, *Bleu : Histoire d'une couleur*, Paris : Éditions du Seuil, 2000, p. 5.

Grey dwellings and the dynamics of redness

Zeffirelli's *Jane Eyre* opens on a view of Gateshead Hall, the house of the Reed family. Like the November weather described in Brontë's text as "cold", "sombre" and "raw", the handsome dwelling imposes its grey façade, hardly capable of providing a cosy shelter for an orphaned child of ten, the age of the heroine at the beginning of the novel.

Gateshead [00:40] is the first one in a series of dismal buildings which Zeffirelli's Jane Eyre will be intimately connected with. Followed by Lowood charity school [08:14], Thornfield [25:57] and Moor House [97:55], Gateshead remains fundamental for it is the only one to include a "red-room", the *unheimlich*[1] chamber that keeps throbbing through the story. Set up against preliminary greyness, it foreshadows the subsequent, even uncannier "goblin's cell" (p.264) at Thornfield and anticipates the chromatic, musical as well as matrimonial harmony expressed at the end: "the pulsation of the heart that beats in our separate bosoms; consequently we are ever together", (p.384).

Bearing in mind the main constraint inherent to any screen adaptation of a novel—the total duration which should not exceed two hours for a feature film[2]—it is not surprising that Zeffirelli wastes no time introducing the basic adversarial relationships of Brontë's long novel in the form of contrasted colours. A few seconds are enough to expose the predicament of a girl clad in a grey and black-striped dress, pushed around brutally by three other children wearing reddish clothes in velvet and other fancier material, like their mother's. The chromatic continuity between the austere house front and the prisoner's outfit, matched up against the colours worn by the Reeds is the first illustration of Zeffirelli's colour system. Overlapping and interacting with, rather than duplicating Brontë's palette, Zeffirelli's range of colours is based on a restricted scheme as if to ensure their capacity to convey meaning. If in Brontë's text the colour red retains its crucial role as the foremost tone in painting a "picture of passion" (p.9), other hues and tints are brought into play to complement or, on the contrary, challenge the supremacy of the primary colour. Compared to Brontë's novel, Zeffirelli's film reveals a similar awareness of the colours' interrelatedness, their need of other colours which, just like foils in character construction, reinforce certain aspects and traits that might have been difficult to perceive otherwise.

---

1. The Freudian term *unheimlich* denoting something both alien and strangely familiar, can be employed here in its literal, dual sense of the German word, for Zeffirelli never presents Gateshead as a true "home" for Jane.
2. Franco Zeffirelli's film adaptation of *Jane Eyre* is 112 minutes long.

Both the novel and the movie set up visible links between the "red chamber" and the domestic and spiritual tormentors who try to deprive Jane, the unwanted outsider, of her autonomy and ardour. But neither Mrs Reed's "cold composed grey eye" (p.22) nor Mr Brocklehurst's "two inquisitive-looking grey eyes" (p.26) manage to "dye" her luminous, red-hot passion. The staging of what today might be viewed as a dysfunctioning family could have taken longer, but as every word and gesture cannot be transposed on screen, the filmmaker counts on the suggestive power of colours for the transposition to operate more fully.[1]

At the same time, Zeffirelli's chromatic strategy cannot be reduced to a series of time-saving devices. As his re/portrayal of the Brontëan protagonists underlines, colours—including the cold, dreary and gloomier tones the emblematic red is contrasted with[2]—provide the filmmaker with a hybrid and therefore extremely valuable system of signs for adapting a literary text into a film, itself a complex and hybrid artistic enterprise. During this process, various literary effects are inevitably "lost", despite the fact that the change of media, the crossing over from page to screen also sheds light on some of the modes of construction of the initial literary work. What is of interest here is the cinematic strategies used to try and counterbalance the impression of a "lack" or "deficiency" by offering (colourful as well as bleaker) instances which, in the best of cases, set off just as compelling interpretative and cogitative processes as the literary text.

Enchanted by the intricate chromatic system set up by Charlotte Brontë, the reader of *Jane Eyre* may regret what seems to stand out as a more restrained *praxis* of colours in Zeffirelli's movie. Brontë's "reds", "blues", "whites", "blacks", or even more plainly put (mere) "colours[3]" are rendered

---

1. Despite its power of chromatic condensation, Zeffirelli's film nevertheless gives the impression, especially in the latter part of the movie, that he lacked time and had to "rush through" some of the final scenes. This is particularly true concerning the character of St John Rivers whose rapid filmic portrayal fails to present him as a foil to Edward Rochester, thus reducing some of the ambivalence of the main male protagonist.
2. Faced with the common distinction between "warm" versus "cold" colours, we are to keep in mind that the perception of colours remains highly subjective and that colour symbolism is a culturally conditioned phenomenon. In other words, "warm hues" (red, orange, yellow and brown)—capable of inducing a variety of intense emotions such as anxiety, anger, revenge, desire and cheerfulness—as opposed to "colder tones" (blues, greens and greys) evoking not only a sense of serenity but of sadness and melancholy—may *seem* universal, but in fact vary significantly from one culture to another. Thus, due to its metaphoric and context-related character, the expression to "see red", for instance, cannot be translated literally into all other languages.
3. Brontë's text sometimes offers the mere word "colour" to involve the reader in character completion. In his own way, Zeffirelli seems to play with the capacity of the spectator's gaze to produce, to "fill in" the "missing" colours. Mr Rochester: "I have a past existence, a series of deeds, a colour of life to contemplate within my own breast" (p. 115; "[Blanche Ingram] giggled, and her colour rose." (p. 157); "While arranging my hair, I looked at my face in the glass, and felt it was no longer plain: there was hope in its aspect and life in its colour" (p. 219).

polyvalent and treacherous by their capacity to resonate with other colours and musical tones. What makes their particular interest is their ability to reveal the presence of hypotexts. One of these is *The Little Red Riding Hood*, underlined by the epigraph chosen for this article. Just as the young Jane who refutes the adjective "deceitful" used by Mr Brocklehurst about her demeanour and manners at Gateshead, both the novel and the film refute their "deceitfulness" while cunningly leading the reader-spectator to believe in the physical reality of colours.

Despite the occasional storybook or colouring book effect created by *Jane Eyre* and its screen adaptations, the colours used by Brontë and Zeffirelli remain a thorny problem. As Michel Pastoureau underlines in his interesting essay on the colour blue, the linguistic roots of the word "colour" draw our attention to its double, or probably even triple function. Related to the verb "*celare*"—to "conceal"—, a "colour" is not only something that reveals, but which hides, conceals or deceives[1]. Equipped with this definition as well as with Jane Eyre's own, clearly voiced metatextual reference to the literary creation's intrinsic dishonesty or "deceitfulness"—crucial, as we know, in creating the make-believe world of literature and cinema—we may enter the "red-room" at Gateshead Hall (or Hell) without falling into a "pit full of fire" (p.27).

Rendered "hellish" through other means, Zeffirelli's red-room scene—a mere half a minute sequence in the film—is not prefigured by the more protective, other red space behind the "red moreen curtain" (p.5) mentioned before Jane's confinement into the crimson jail. By omitting this first space that the young girl had managed to create within the oppressive limits of the Gateshead household, Zeffirelli seems to truncate the text and reduce the multiplicity of the Brontëan literary *topoï*. For it is the less blatant red space, the one hidden behind "scarlet drapery" (p.5) which the novelist chooses, significantly enough, to juxtapose with whiteness, another important colour in her text. A chamber of porosity rather than of perfect enclosure, it is made to reverberate with foreign place names, allowing the young girl to flee to the "bleak shores of Lapland, Siberia, Spitzbergen, Nova Zembla, Iceland, Greenland" (p.6) and other imaginary "reservoir[s] of frost and snow" and "death-white realms" (p.6) which end up forming a curious mirror image of Jane's own frozen, dreary existence[2]. In Zeffirelli's film, we encounter no such story-hungry young girls sitting "cross-legged like

---

1. « [L]a couleur c'est ce qui cache, ce qui dissimule, ce qui trompe », Michel Pastoureau, *Bleu : Histoire d'une couleur*, Paris : Éditions du Seuil, 2000, p. 42.
2. Regarding this passage, Claire Bazin notes the impression of osmosis between the exterior "landscape" and the inner "soulscape" : « Le paysage désolé et hostile conduit finalement Jane à savourer la contrainte de rester enfermée, "confinée" : "Son enfermement devient claustrophilie, vecteur et facteur d'équilibre". » Claire Bazin, *op. cit.*, p. 67.

a Turk" (p.5) or "shrined in double retirement" (p.5) behind red curtains, but the theatricality of the filmic depiction is quite as effective.

As we shall see, Zeffirelli's adaptation of *Jane Eyre* is marked by symptomatic returns, yet not necessarily impressive "comebacks" of the inaugural redness. Resuscitated on screen, the chromatic signifier of rage and pain, Eros and Thanatos, seems to challenge the capacity of any other colour or symbolic system to express the return of the repressed with as few means. Adopting different forms and hues, the colour red never loses its ability to catch the spectator's eye. Either a drooping bouquet of flowers [34:07], a flamboyant red tree [45:53], an isolated drab rose [46:50], a red and white chess game [41:28] or a series of red dresses none of which is worn by Jane Eyre, the "red things" shown by Zeffirelli confirm the optical illusion that deceives the viewer into thinking that the warm-coloured object is closer, and thus somehow more significant, than the cold-coloured one. At the same time, like in the old tale where a poor young boy abandoned in the forest makes his way back home by picking up the pebbles he had been dropping along the way, Zeffirelli seems to be guiding his spectators with more or less little red patches towards the construction of meaning.

At the end questions persist, however, as we wonder, for instance, to what extent Zeffirelli counts on the spectators' capacity to create coloured afterimages—of the kind that appear after staring at a coloured object before fixing one's eyes on an empty space. Some of the scenes seem indeed to have been neutralised, more or less deliberately, as for example the sequence around Richard Mason [70:38]—[71:50] marked by somewhat "mushy" blood. Whatever the case, instead of foregrounding Gothic and other more spectacular or melodramatic motifs, Zeffirelli tends to disregard some of the most readily available devices and effects—such as "foul German spectre[s]" (p.242) or other blood-sucking "Vampyre[s]" (p.242)—to kindle the visual memory of the "red-room" through less dramatic means.

Chromatic gothicisms

In Zeffirelli's film, as the young Jane Eyre[1] is pushed into the metaphorically inflamed "red-room", she is also tossed against a mirror by Mrs Reed, the abject aunt whom she will meet, years later, on the aunt's death bed—the same kind of central piece of furniture found in the first flamboyant bed chamber. The mirror does not break, but the movie audience will be exposed to a fragmented vision of the early redness.

---

1. Quite brilliantly interpreted by Anna Paquin who had already received due attention for her Oscar-winning performance in Jane Campion's *The Piano* (1993).

The shift in chromatic emphasis during the opening sequence of the film is telling, not merely in aesthetic but historical terms. Calling to mind the cheerless Victorian social reality with its workhouses and other "charity" institutions for those who, like Jane Eyre, were not protected by prosperous families or truly charitable souls, Zeffirelli selects colours most likely to epitomize 19th century England. Not only do we think of "bleak houses" in the Dickensian vein, but of brothels—the "closed houses" ("maisons closes") for "fallen women" which also mark the crimson-draped theatrical setting for the earthbound gestures acted out in the filmic "red-room". Once rejected behind the blood-red door—the kind many cultures read as an entrance into a brothel—Jane's uprising gains further meaning, especially when contrasted with the "angel of the house" figure which so profoundly affected the Victorian representations of femininity.

Another equally ostensible link between *Jane Eyre* and the peculiar institutions of the time is provided by the anxiety aroused by Helen Burns's red hair. As Zeffirelli's shooting of the sequence underlines [13:50]—[17:03] Helen's long reddish locks make her look dangerously attractive in the eyes of Mr Brocklehurst, the sinister moral guardian who in the various film adaptations of the novel is made to look like an executioner wishing to chop the girl's head off, before indulging himself with metonymically cutting off merely her hair. The fact that Helen later "burns", quite literally consumed by a bodily illness, reflects the black and white punitive logic of sacrifice embodied by Mr Brocklehurst, despite the touch of solidarity and womanly wit introduced into Zeffirelli's filmic rereading of the scene.

As the films examined by Russell Campbell in his book *Marked Women: Prostitutes and Prostitution in the Cinema* illustrate, the red-headed *fille de joie* is quite a common stock character in the cinema. What makes these "red-stained daughters" horrifying in the Victorian context is the way they render visible the complementarity of two parallel institutions: marriage and prostitution. The stigma of redness with its scandalous hints at women's carnal pleasure of the senses is also brought to view through the references to Céline Varens, Adèle Varens's mother, a free-minded opera singer who anticipates another paradigmatic figure, that of *femme fatale*. A scarlet woman of the French or more generally of the Latin type, Céline Varens should not, however, be mixed up with Jane Eyre's passionate insubordination. As Zeffirelli seems to be stressing by his use of fading colours during the closing sequence, despite the fervent initial tones of his movie, Carmen-like colours prove rapidly too foreign, too outlandish to portray the self-disciplined heroine of Charlotte Brontë's novel. By depriving, in his turn, Jane Eyre of her chromatic vehemence, Zeffirelli—quite capable of using vivid colours throughout his other films, such as *The Taming of the Shrew* (1967) and *Romeo and Juliet*

(1968)—ends up accentuating the specifically Victorian Englishness of Jane Eyre's passion. In other words, while recalling the dual function of redness, as something that both attracts and repels, appeals and warns, Brontë and Zeffirelli seem to be saying that cross-cultural (here literally "cross-channel") redness is something to be approached with nuance.

However, as the Gothic elements of *Jane Eyre* suggest, the exotic, non-English colours cannot be kept off the palette when rewriting a 19th century romance. Although ending up with what Zeffirelli presents as a reassuring fusion, a fairy-tale-like blending with the English countryside, the ultimately faded carnal colours remain an important component in the construction of Brontë's *bildungsroman*.

When reading *Jane Eyre's* densely metaphorical "red-room", we are to keep in mind not only the broader cultural context, but also the technical constraints that guided Zeffirelli's choice of cinematic strategies[1]. Despite or perhaps *owing to* the scene's extreme compression on screen, Zeffirelli's red-room reads like the first step into the ramified redness that structures the entire film. Many of the objects such as the great looking-glass mirroring the "vacant majesty of the bed" (p.11) are there, as well as the recognisably "strange little figure" (p.11) glancing at her reflected image, but everything is shown so rashly that individual objects seem to dissolve in what becomes mere swirling coloured motion. It is as if the sought after effect was precisely this: the impression of an impetuous movement, so effectively conveyed by the cinematic media[2].

The spectator is never offered a complete guided tour of the Brontëan fictitious locations, including the "tabernacle"-like bed (p.10). Just as the young heroine's collapsing on the floor can be viewed as an anticipatory sign, foretelling the final crumbling of Thornfield (and its other chamber of lunacy), the deliberately gothicised bed is merely one link in a chain of objects and events resonating through the film. Presented expeditiously in the opening sequence—the red bed, the large mirror and the other subliminal "things"—will indeed be rediscovered during later sequences, in order to make the spectator ponder over their embedded and interconnected meanings.

---

1. The other film directors having adapted *Jane Eyre* into a colour film seemed to encounter similar problems with the red-room sequence. At least two of them—Christy Cabanne (1934) and Delbert Mann (1970)—did not even attempt to shoot this particular scene; opting for the presentation of Jane's "tantrum" as a more or less accidental fall in her own room (Cabanne), or skipping the sequence by moving the story's *in medias res* beginning to a later moment in Jane's life (Mann). In his essay «The Cinematic Reconstruction of *Jane Eyre*», Jeffrey Sconce informs us how Robert Stevenson, in his 1944 black and white adaptation, condensed the scene by showing Jane locked in a small closet. Charlotte Brontë, *Jane Eyre*, op. cit., p. 519.
2. For a more complete analytical visit to Charlotte Brontë's "red-room", see chapter "L'art de l'enfance" in Claire Bazin's *Jane Eyre, le pèlerin moderne*, op. cit., p. 13-23.

At the end of the "red-room" sequence, the mirror which has ceased to reflect Jane's image is left swinging, a movement underlined by the deliberately unsteady camera movement. As the scene slowly fades into a suggestive background composition accompanying the opening credits, the girl's sharp gestures and inarticulate cries are replaced by soft-contoured, ameba-like reddish figures that evolve in an indeterminate dark space. Backed up by Alessio Vad and Claudio Capponi's slow-paced musical score, the sluggishly emerging and dissolving figures make the viewer think of floating foetuses, and the general impact is that of a regression to a primitive stage. Echoing Jane's narratorial comment at the end of chapter one: "Four hands were immediately laid upon me, and I was borne upstairs" (p.9), Zeffirelli's film thus provides its own, subjective interpretation of a re/birth, of the "very natal pang of the divine passion" (p.262) that cuts across Brontë's novel.

As often, when examining a film based upon a literary text, the movie maker seems to have focused on a fragment or a particular expression, reacting sometimes to only a few words that will back up the more general structure of the adaptation. In this case, the passage that appears to have caught the filmmaker's (or the scriptwriter's) eye is the textual instance where Jane can be quoted thinking: "I had to stem a rapid rush of retrospective thought before I quailed to the dismal present" (p.11). Quite similarly, Zeffirelli's film seems animated by the need to "stem", that is to stop and contain the flow of associations to avoid being overwhelmed by the character's reminiscences. Once again, Zeffirelli's filmwork interacts, yet selectively, with Brontë's text.

The impact created by these filmically perceptible "chromatic brontëifications" is sometimes quite explicitly gothic, for instance in the descriptions of the nameless "things" capable of penetrating the rooms at Thornfield: "When I think of the thing which flew at my throat this morning, hanging its black and scarlet visage over the nest of my dove, my blood curdles—" (p.264). Typically enough, even some of the less disquieting passages lay the emphasis on the excess of colour and the uncannily evolving body: "I had more colour and more flesh, more life, more vivacity, because I had brighter hopes and keener enjoyments" (p.133).

The absence of clear borders, a further gothic trait, is perceptible through the blurred outlines between the categories of women which ought not to mix, if viewed according to the Victorian normalcy code. Not only does the distinction between the marriageable and the unmarriageable become hazy, but also the dividing line between the sane and the insane. As for colours, Blanche Ingram may be the only one to wear a mixed colour (purple), yet what is more interesting is Zeffirelli's quasi-chromophobia when screening Brontë's eponymous heroine.

Backed up by the convincing performance of Charlotte Gainsbourg whose fine, low-key acting gives us a renewed Jane Eyre in a scrupulously black and white Victorian packaging, Zeffirelli's screen version strikes as «authentic», despite the «fundamental irreconciliability of the film and the novel as semiotic systems[1].» Especially when compared with the 1970 adaptation by Delbert Mann where Susannah York's Jane wears heavy make-up all through the film. Gainsbourg's Jane is unadorned, but not "plain" nor too simple to untangle. Although she is screened in a way that preserves some of the basic literary mystery, it is difficult for the bride and the bridal dress alone—no matter how ghost-like they are made to look—to replace the various references to the angelic and monstrous female figures that Brontë's Jane Eyre is not merely surrounded by, but actually «made out of». At the same time, the wedding gown with its layers and veils to be peeled off, does create undeniable links between Jane and Bertha, the madwoman haunting Jane's bridal bedroom, without disregarding Jane's own vaporous mother. In a somewhat similar manner, Zeffirelli's filmic portrayals lead us into successive discoveries through a screen-like, sometimes nearly skin-like surface. Provided a movie adaptation can be considered as a "filmic text", we could argue in favour of a palimpsestic effect as the hypotext's colours remain visible through the screen.

> I have a rosy sky, and a green flowery Eden in my brain[2].

As already suggested, in Charlotte Brontë's novel, the outbreak of colours is frequently presented as a sign of emergence of the repressed inner workings or "inward bleedings" of the speaking subject, including during Mr Rochester's declarations to Jane. In keeping with the already mentioned etymological roots pointing to the capacity of colours to reveal as well as to conceal, colours appear to compose a sign language of their own.

Interestingly enough, the narrator who introduces us to the chromatic dichotomies of *Jane Eyre* does not always master its grammar, being herself lost in translation:

> [Grace Poole] looked up, while I still gazed at her: no start, no increase or failure of colour betrayed emotion, consciousness of guilt, or fear of detection. She said "Good morning, Miss," in her usual phlegmatic and brief manner, and taking up another ring and more tape, went on with her sewing.

---

1. Jeffrey Sconce, «The Cinematic Reconstitution of *Jane Eyre*», *Jane Eyre, op. cit.*, p. 516.
2. Charlotte Brontë, *Jane Eyre, op. cit.*, p. 267.

"I will put her to some test," thought I: "Such absolute impenetrability is past comprehension." (p.130)

It would be fairly easy to claim that Zeffirelli's *Jane Eyre* is, as many other film adaptations based on well-known literary classics, merely "illustrative". In other words, rather than creating a system of its own, the adaptation would merely help elucidate the structure and the mode of functioning of the literary work, and thus provide a pleasurable experience, most likely with the "original text" in the back of the spectator's mind. While this certainly remains true, to a certain extent, let us look briefly into a few additional aspects of Zeffirelli's screenwork. Notably by focusing on his sober use of colours which seems to rely on the awareness of the cinema's both constructive and manipulative skills, as well as on the excesses and limits of those skills.

However tempting, we should of course not simply pick up the various chromatic effects scattered through Zeffirelli's film in an involuntary effort to "retell Jane Eyre's life in colours". The heroine's early existence may well be marked by primary redness, the later charity school years by blue tones, her down-to-earth encounter with Mr Rochester starting a new brown period, before the blissful closure under pinkish trees, but there is more to the united colours of Brontë and Zeffirelli than mere trauma, victimhood, world-wariness and final, unearthy love.

If the novel's colder tones provide the background canvas against which redness gains its meaningful radiance, Zeffirelli refrains just as knowingly from attractional or kitchy exploitation of colours. Preferring pallor to present the "colours of life" underlined by Edward Rochester, he shuns oversaturation which easily makes one think of fantasy cinema, or the kind of chromatic euphoria created by Technicolor movies. After the theatrical entry through the impressive antechambre, the subsequent use of colours tends to remain economical. Rather than visually exciting the spectator, though over-dramatisations and other "easy gothicisms", Zeffirelli's chromatic know-how is put to the service of a far less dazzling palette.

During this process, even if biblical overtones remain palpable, one is gained by the impression that Zeffirelli is working towards another "grammar of colours". The resulting language ends up including past abuses, while extending beyond the ritualistic colourings and the punitive logic represented by the "red-room". In recreating the chamber meant to humble and tame "unruly spirits", Zeffirelli is not inspired by any *one* existing system. Rather than relying on the logics and aesthetics of sacrifice, his own filmic brushwork tends to blur the boundaries between the biblical and the Gothic contrasts, the latter challenging, as we know, many of the less graceful dualities the

Victorian society. Once again, we are to acknowledge the impossibility of a stable, objective or "politically proper" *praxis* of colours.

The deliberate downplaying already perceived in the portrayal of the heroine is also true regarding the depiction of Mr Rochester. Matched against the 1983 BBC TV-miniseries with Timothy Dalton, or Robert Young's 1997 adaptation for television with Ciarán Hinds in the role of the even more patently Byronian, vociferous and tumultuous Rochester, Zeffirelli's reconstruction strikes with its less elaborate impetuosity. Recreating a series of characters imprisoned by the Victorian idea that sexuality is something to be repressed and concealed behind locked doors, Zeffirelli uses significantly lower colour contrasts whenever possible.

This chromatic sobriety may account for some of the criticism received by the film. William Hurt's unsophisticated Mr Rochester whom many of the spectators claim to have been disenchanted with is indeed very different from his predecessors. Viewed against the previous interpretations of the Brontëan master of Thornfield, rooted—not in fleshy colours or in a bi-chromy composed of green and red or red and gold—but in the more modest shades of rural England, the 1996 Mr Rochester recalls another deliberately downplayed hero: Joe Wright's Mr Darcy in the 2005 remake of Jane Austen's *Pride and Prejudice*. Both heroes seem to reflect the contemporary filmmakers' wish to review old heroes in a new, less heroic light in present-day "costume dramas".

There is a scene in Franco Zeffirelli's *Jane Eyre* which can be read as the filmmaker's more general statement regarding colours. During the sequence where Richard Mason is shown driven away from Thornfield in a horse-pulled carriage, the camera eye lingers on the red wheel of the vehicle [72:08]. The diegetic focus remains on the "madwoman"'s brother's body, but within the framework of the specific colour-code of the film, the spectator's gaze is almost automatically directed towards the red wheel. Together with its metafilmic rotation, its symbolism as a wheel of mis/fortune, the turning wheel may also bring to mind the common representation—in the form of a wheel—of the system of colours made up of primary colours (red, yellow and blue) from which all other colours are made by mixtures.

Much remains to be said about the workings of this "colour wheel" in *Jane Eyre*, and the processes set in motion. Not merely in the re/making of the story, but in more technical terms. Whatever the angle of approach—narrative, symbolic, technical, aesthetic or ethnic[1]—the impact of colours remains important in making the filmic illusions operate, in other words,

---

1. The crossing of the colour line, in a more ethnic sense of the expression, does not appear in Zeffirelli's *Jane Eyre* nor in the other filmic rereadings of the novel. However, bearing in mind Bertha Rochester's Creole background, the very absence of cross-bred colours (miscegenation)

in "bringing the film alive". It is to be hoped that the examples used in this article did not create the false impression that the question of colours is merely a matter of "getting the red patches right". The multiple ways in which the return of the—more or less repressed—redness appears in many other films proves that the question cannot be treated once and for all[1].

The end of Franco Zeffirelli's film is marked by other conventionally coded colours, as the increasingly rosier hues signal Jane's final return to Thornfield [1:43:53]. While placing the movie in a long line of romantic films pivoting around star-crossed lovers, the adaptation definitely downplays the previous contrasts between Jane and the master of the now ruined power house. Anticipating the well-expected love-conquers-all-finale, Thornfield's grey walls and surrounding landscape are literally overwhelmed by subtle rosy tones in a final proleptic twist. As the camera swivels upwards during the closing shot, the touches of pale pink tones reinforced by trees about to blossom bring the impression of completion conveyed by the heroine's final sentence: "Our happiness is complete".

Yet, as we have seen, the closing scene is not the only instant when the diegetic is supported by the chromatic in Zeffirelli's film. If the prevailing tones often mimic the fairy tale or the Gothic quality of Brontë's prose, the spectator is just as struck by the effect of a colouring-book, namely when the ultimate garden scene is transformed into a drawing (just as Gateshead was first converted into a moving picture from a storyboard-like illustration). What is noteworthy is the way the ultimate garden sequence brings the two major colours of Zeffirelli's palette into a final balance. Harmony is restored between the cold, steely greys and the passionate reds, the flamboyance which had repeatedly interrupted the narrative's chromatic chilliness.

Consequently, and despite the fixed final image, it is the impression of circularity created by the rotating colours that prevails until the end. Juxtaposed rather than set up against one another, cold and warm colours alternate and interact, until their final fading. At the same time, Gateshead greyness and Lowood blues seem to give way to warmer tones as the narrative revolves towards the ultimate encounter. Never merely descriptive, but constantly backing up the narrative, diegetic colours—or their successive outbursts and effacements—serve a further mimetic function as they reveal

---

may be understood as one of the "visual blanks" in the film's portrayal of the still very colonial England.

1. To name but a few examples, in Arthur Hiller's *Love Story* (1970), bright redness works as a signifier whose easy identification rapidly turns it into a dead metaphor, a mere Saint Valentine's card effect. Steven Spielberg's *Schindler's List* (1993) pinpoints a reddish figure, a young girl in the radically different space of a concentration camp. In other films, such as Hitchcock's *Marnie* (1964) or Stanley Kubrick's *The Shining* (1980), redness is inseparably involved with the repressed.

the filmmaker's own ambivalence towards pigments. Just as his recreated characters, Franco Zeffirelli seems both restrained and attracted to this (now) moving "picture of passion!" (p.9). Indeed, compared to the previous colour adaptations of *Jane Eyre*, none of them exhibits a similar desire to control the impact of colours. Preferring understatement rather than flashy Technicolor tones, fairy tale exuberance or gothic excess, Franco Zeffirelli's colours remain deliberately low key.—Yet at the same time, akin to litotes, they often tend to say "grey" when they actually mean "red".

Bibliography

AUMONT, Jacques, *Introduction à la couleur : des discours aux images*, Paris : Armand Colin, 1994.
BAZIN, Claire, *Jane Eyre, le pèlerin moderne*, Nantes : Éditions du Temps, 2005.
BRÉMOND, Elisabeth, *L'intelligence de la Couleur*, Paris : Albin Michel, 2002.
BRUSATIN, Manlio, *Histoire des couleurs*, Paris : Flammarion, 1986 (1983).
DICKENS, Charles, *Bleak House*, London: Penguin Classics, 2003 (1853).
HUTCHEON, Linda, *A Theory of Adaptation*, London: Routledge, 2003.
PASTOUREAU, Michel, *Bleu : Histoire d'une couleur,* Paris : Éditions du Seuil, 2000.

Désir et monotonie dans *Jane Eyre*[1]

Laurent Mellet

À plusieurs reprises dans le roman, Jane Eyre manifeste ses frustrations, ses souhaits et ses désirs. Jeune fille promise par sa tante à un destin de servitude et de lassitude, Jane devient une femme qui sait et ose les pouvoirs de la parole pour se construire et se définir. Au cœur de multiples monotonies (topographiques, esthétiques ou encore narratives), l'héroïne inscrit et revendique ses désirs. Aussi la régularité, la répétition et la langueur semblent-elles s'effacer pour laisser poindre la promesse de l'objet du désir, imaginé ou bien connu, vers lequel personnages et narration dans le roman de Brontë, puis corps et espace filmique dans l'adaptation de Zeffirelli, n'auront de cesse que de se diriger.

C'est en effet la question du corps et de l'identité, romanesque à plus d'un titre, que les dialectiques du désir et de la monotonie soulèvent dans *Jane Eyre* : entre mouvement vers l'autre et immobilité, entre contact charnel et tristesse du manque, la monotonie appelle le désir autant que le désir se heurtera aux limites du déterminisme et ne trouvera comme conclusion (heureuse ?) qu'une nouvelle monotonie mâtinée d'ennui. Ces deux notions peuvent surprendre car le désir est sourd et la monotonie contredite par l'enchaînement d'événements à la limite du vraisemblable. En quoi l'expérience de Jane est-elle pourtant celle du manque et du renoncement à travers les monotones enseignements et les furtives espérances du désir d'être désirée ?

Il faudra ici souligner la manière dont les monotonies mènent à la recherche de l'objet du désir et ainsi à l'éclosion du narratif ; démontrer ensuite que le désir, par les corps et les couleurs qu'il engendre, fonde une poétique de l'espace et du mouvement à même de combler le manque et d'en rompre la monotonie ; enfin, interroger la pertinence de ces concepts dans la réception esthétique des deux œuvres, peut-être informées par l'ultime désir de Jane, celui du monotone.

À la recherche d'un monotone objet du désir

« *It was a very grey day; a most opaque sky, "onding on snaw", canopied all* » (32) : dans *Jane Eyre*, les paysages sont le plus souvent ternes et laissent affleurer une topographie, romantique, du monotone et de l'uniforme, que

---

1. Nous avons délibérément traité cette question comme s'il s'agissait d'une « dissertation ».

le film évoque abondamment. Qu'il s'agisse de la première image et de sa lente matérialisation de Gateshead [0:50] ou de celles de l'hiver qui s'abat sur Lowood [18:51-19], la grisaille et la fadeur définissent visuellement les cadres de vie de la jeune héroïne autant qu'elles caractérisent les premiers choix esthétiques du film. Ceux-ci construisent, avec la lenteur du texte et l'insipidité, revendiquée comme telle, de Jane, une première déclinaison du monotone, qui contamine également l'écriture de l'espace intérieur. Lorsque Jane pénètre, à la suite de Brocklehurst, dans Lowood, l'image là encore est fade, triste et presque sale [8:40], puis c'est bien une autre uniformité que dessinent à l'écran les uniformes des pensionnaires [12], tel un équivalent plastique de la monotonie de la vie de Jane à Lowood. Monumental et souvent austère, l'espace dans Thornfield Hall est dans un premier temps tout aussi morne, et ce, même lorsque la scène se veut paisible (la leçon de piano à Adèle [42:39-43:02]), ou au contraire pleine de gaieté et de vie, comme lors de la première soirée dans la grande galerie [64-66:52] : décors, costumes, accessoires rivalisent de monotonie pour évoquer davantage les frustrations de Jane que les frivolités des invités de Rochester.

Le lieu ici se fait le reflet de l'âme, et de manière générale la monotonie de ces espaces extérieurs comme intérieurs accompagne, complète ou bien révèle celle du personnage de Jane, qui se construit dans la douleur et la mélancolie. Frêle et craintive, elle est aussi quelconque et sans charme, ce qui constitue l'un des enjeux de l'écriture : faire d'une jeune femme monotone et sans saveur l'héroïne de ce long roman. Le film est scrupuleusement fidèle à cette écriture, tout d'abord dans le choix de Charlotte Gainsbourg, qui apporte une discrétion et une modestie, mais une force et une élégance, bienvenues. La monotonie se décline visuellement pour écrire son personnage à l'écran : coiffures austères, visage blafard et placide, robes toujours noires (sauf pour son mariage et une fois devenue riche). C'est ainsi la monotonie du visage de Jane que la caméra traque cruellement avec un zoom avant progressif, en la contrastant avec la blondeur et le sourire éclatant de Blanche qui arrive à Thornfield [62:37-62:53].

Si l'apparence de Jane est monotone, son comportement est aussi perçu en ce sens par Rochester : « *you have the air of a little nonnette/nun; quaint, quiet, grave, and simple* » (roman 112) et [film 46:34]. Plus loin dans la scène du film, Rochester se fait plus caustique : « *Do you ever laugh, Miss Eyre? Never mind.* » [47:11] Il faut néanmoins préciser que son personnage fait lui aussi l'objet d'une présentation qui évoque tout autant les affres de la monotonie. Pour Mrs Fairfax : « *nothing striking, but you feel it when he speaks to you; you cannot be always sure whether he is in jest or earnest, whether he is pleased or the contrary* » (89). Une telle constance de caractère peut certes être louable. Si, dans la bouche de Mrs Fairfax, elle n'est pas un défaut, elle rappelle la régularité du monotone et dénonce un tempérament tout aussi peu approprié aux relations humaines que celui de Jane.

C'est contre ces premiers fonds monotones dans le film que surgit parfois la couleur et plus spécifiquement le rouge comme possible trace de l'émergence du désir, irruptions d'autant plus remarquables qu'elles s'inscrivent donc dans une esthétique généralement terne. Quelques passages peu significatifs conduisent pourtant à une première rupture de la monotonie visuelle du film : le générique d'ouverture et ses taches rougeâtres, qui intervient après la scène de la chambre rouge, très rapide et sans grande conséquence sur la tonalité du film, ou encore ces traces sporadiques dans le cadre et le décor (arbres, fleurs, tissus). Le rouge se fait alors évocation visuelle et sensible du désir, ou plutôt de l'objet du désir, voire davantage encore du besoin de Jane de rechercher un tel objet. Avant même le désir, c'est son objet que Jane évoque lorsqu'elle mentionne le rouge du feu, sa poupée et le besoin d'affection :

> and when the embers sank to a dull red, I […] sought shelter from cold and darkness in my crib. To this crib I always took my doll; human beings must love something, and in the dearth of worthier objects of affection, I contrived to find a pleasure in loving and cherishing a faded graven image *(23)*.

Il faut bien trouver un objet, sous-entend ici la narratrice, et c'est ce à quoi Jane s'emploiera. On croise ensuite d'autres « objets » rouges dans des contextes les associant au désir, comme le rossignol qu'entend chanter Rochester (215) ou le pourpre de l'habit de Rosamond Oliver (313). En outre, un objet connu, d'abord monotone, peut devenir désirable. Un tel glissement vers le désir se retrouvera ici dans l'absence de beauté de Jane et de Rochester (96-97, 113), puis dans la surexposition ponctuelle du corps de la première, lumineuse dans sa robe de mariée [88].

Jane alors devient l'objet, radieux, du désir de Rochester. Elle évoque souvent combien c'est là son désir essentiel, le désir d'être elle-même un objet du désir : « *Why could I never please?* » (12) ; « *if others don't love me, I would rather die than live—I cannot bear to be solitary and hated, Helen.* » (58) ; « *at eighteen most people with to please, and the conviction that they have not an exterior likely to second that desire brings anything but gratification.* » (78) Nous y reviendrons, il y a au cœur de ce désir le souhait d'une réversibilité complète de l'objet et du sentiment : « *It is as natural as that I should love those who show me affection* » (48) ; « *loving him, being loved by him* » (312).

Cette émergence du désir, à travers celle de la couleur dans la monotonie, permet encore celle de l'événement, puisque Jane désire tout autant trouver un objet que rompre la monotonie de son existence par le changement et l'action. Déjà son départ pour Lowood est placé sous de tels auspices (« *a change seemed near,—I desired and waited it in silence* » (22), puis c'est la rencontre de Rochester qui répond à ce désir d'événement (« *It is in vain to say human beings ought to be satisfied with tranquillity: they must have action; and they will make it if they cannot find it.* » (93) :

> The incident had occurred and was gone for me: [...] yet it marked with change one single hour of a monotonous life. [...] I did not like re-entering Thornfield. To pass its threshold was to return to stagnation *(98-99)*.

Ce même désir d'agir occupe l'esprit de Jane dans les dernières pages : « *I sincerely, deeply, fervently longed to do what was right* » (357). Enfin, les soirées données à Thornfield, sur fond de « *crimson curtain* » (14 comblent à leur tour ce désir de Jane et lui apparaissent telle une parenthèse bienvenue dans sa monotonie : « *Merry days were these at Thornfield Hall; and busy days too: how different from the first three months of stillness, monotony, and solitude I had passed beneath its roof!*» (154) Ce désir est donc ici gage d'aventure pour Jane autant que de sursaut narratif pour le lecteur. Corps et événement, parole et narration, s'écrivent dans une nouvelle dynamique que permet la prise de conscience par les protagonistes de leurs désirs.

Dans le roman Jane sait très vite trouver une voix et imposer sa parole (« *Speak I must* » (30). Aussi ose-t-elle affronter verbalement sa tante puis Bessie (34), ici forte d'un certain don pour la repartie (212), là choisissant un mode incantatoire pour libérer son désir (236). Si le film édulcore sensiblement la rébellion de Jane contre Mrs Reed, la direction d'acteurs choisit parfois d'accorder à son personnage une présence visuelle et un pouvoir de la voix qui véhiculent cette écriture. Lors de la scène du jardin, Jane est d'abord filmée de profil puis se tourne et s'avance vers Rochester et la caméra pour laisser affleurer ses émotions (« *yes,—and to speak* » (215) dans une voix moins monotone et plus sincère [83] (en outre, ici elle ne répond pas à l'injonction de Rochester de l'appeler Edward). De la même manière, lorsqu'elle lui reproche d'être trop dur avec Adèle, si c'est alors la voix de Rochester qui devient ponctuellement moins monotone (trahissant malheureusement un piètre jeu d'acteur ici), le corps masculin est d'abord de dos au premier plan, simple spectateur de Jane qui ose déjà s'affirmer par la parole [51:30]. Ainsi, désir et monotonie s'entrelacent progressivement pour écrire ou filmer les personnages de *Jane Eyre*. À la recherche d'un monotone objet du désir, Jane rompt la monotonie topographique mais aussi narrative. Une fois l'objet trouvé, comment subvertir davantage encore la monotonie de l'espace pour placer le corps au centre d'une nouvelle topographie du désir et lui permettre de combler le manque ?

Combler le vide : corps et couleurs

Le désir implique d'emblée le corps et ses sensations, subtilement et logiquement disséminées dans les premiers paragraphes du chapitre XXIII, scène du jardin. Les traces du désir se dessinent en affirmant la présence du corps et Zeffirelli, çà et là, filme une Jane Eyre souriante et plus épanouie (en arrivant à Thornfield, avec Adèle, lorsque Rochester la taquine au sujet de ses dessins, ou encore à son retour de Gateshead). Il n'est alors peut-être pas innocent que dans le film la couleur rouge soit de nouveau associée à cette renaissance corporelle par le désir, quand les mains de Jane saignent dans celles de son maître après qu'elle a vidé un vase de ses roses lors de l'incendie [57:48]. Dans le roman déjà, le rouge du désir est bien celui du corps avec la chambre rouge, matrice sexuelle combinant symboles phalliques (« *influx, stood out, spread, prominent* ») *et réceptacles* (« *largest chambers, tabernacle, festoons* » (10-11). Le corps ici renaît, comme l'analyse Claire Bazin autour de « *l'homophonie du "I was borne upstairs*[1]*"* » ('Borne': à la fois portée *et* née). C'est peut-être cette même association que l'on retrouve dans l'épisode des cheveux roux, que le film développe malgré la condensation de deux personnages en un, Helen Burns (condensation évoquant en outre la dimension pénitentielle du roman puisque ici c'est la fillette aux choquants cheveux rouges qui mourra). Ce sont bien la vanité et le désir féminins que Brocklehurst veut faire disparaître en coupant les boucles rousses d'Helen : avant et pendant les coups de ciseau fatals, Zeffirelli monte deux inserts sur les visages de Miss Temple et de Miss Scatcherd (qui fait un pas en arrière, comme menacée elle aussi dans sa propre féminité), et les deux femmes ont chacune une grimace ou un mouvement de tête pour exprimer leur compassion [16:44-17:04]. Violence d'une défloration rimant ici avec castration, ou bien répression du désir pour garantir une monotonie rassurante, cet instant est ironiquement suivi dans le film des mots réconfortants de Miss Temple pour les pensionnaires sur la condition féminine, alors que les deux fillettes ressemblent à deux garçons, telles deux futures nonnes aux cheveux coupés et aux désirs éteints. Le corps, le rouge et le désir sont ici à opposer clairement à la monotonie de cette condition féminine dans un contexte biblique et liturgique.

Un autre écho corporel du désir se laisse percevoir dans la récurrence chez Brontë de l'idée d'un visage à lire et à déchiffrer pour pénétrer l'âme de l'autre. « *To read my face, as if its features and lines were characters on a page.* » (302) : c'est bien ce qu'aura fait auparavant Rochester déguisé en diseuse de bonne aventure (169-172), ainsi que ce que Jane fait à son tour après leur premier baiser, lisant alors un visage rouge et agité (217). Cette lecture des

---

1. Bazin Claire, *Jane Eyre, le pèlerin moderne*, Nantes : Éditions du Temps, 2005, p. 15.

traces corporelles du désir est pourtant bouleversée par l'étonnante adéquation pour Jane, annonciatrice du dénouement, entre désir et cécité (« *He made me love him without looking at me.* » (149), de nouveau au cœur d'une réversibilité du désir et du regard (« *I had often been unwilling to look at my master, because I feared he could not be pleased at my look* (219). Aimer sans être regardée, et être aimée sans regarder : telle est l'autre dialectique du désir et du corps dans *Jane Eyre*, qui paradoxalement en reniant le corps l'érige en ultime objet du désir : « *a very delirium of desire to behold my Jane again. Yes: for her restoration I longed* » (373). Ainsi, cet aveu de Rochester (« *You are a beauty, in my eyes, and a beauty just after the desire of my heart* » (220) confirme cet aphorisme rapporté par la narratrice : « *Most true is it that "beauty is in the eye of the gazer."*» (149)

Le film illustre cette réversibilité inversée en jouant sur les regards vers le hors-champ, comme lorsque Rochester lance ce long regard énigmatique à Jane une fois cette dernière sortie du cadre [45:12]. Quand elle vient demander la permission de rejoindre sa tante mourante, Jane n'est pas filmée en contrechamp sur le regard de Rochester : le premier plan sur elle, lointaine et frêle sur un fond monotone, évoque la manière dont Blanche, filmée ensuite, la considère et la voit alors. Puis Rochester (dont le désir est peut-être, de nouveau, évoqué par les roses rouges à l'arrière-plan) la regarde, mais un raccord dans l'axe et dans le mouvement remplace le contrechamp attendu. Lorsque Jane prend la parole, elle est filmée comme auparavant, mais il s'agit là encore de la vision méprisante de Blanche, dont le regard est ensuite à l'image. [72:52-73:09]. Ainsi il n'est pas nécessaire que le regard de Rochester sur Jane apparaisse à l'écran, et la dialectique construite par Brontë est respectée—(s')aimer sans se regarder ou être regardé. D'autres passages l'évoqueront, comme lorsque Jane dessine le portrait de Rochester à son insu [46], ou encore quand elle semble regarder à la dérobée, sans être vue, donc, le corps allongé de Rochester dans la scène du jardin (regard aux connotations peut-être plus sexuelles qu'il n'y paraît, ce corps ici lascif venant de prononcer ces paroles : « *I've heard of a* position *that might suit you* » -[81:56], c'est moi qui souligne).

Ces jeux de regard *par* ou *sur* le corps construisent un nouveau lacis du désir que le film souligne en faisant de ces corps les agents du désir corrigeant par leurs déplacements la monotonie d'un double espace, le lieu et le cadre de l'image filmique. D'abord discrète et monotone, nous l'avons vu, Jane est souvent filmée comme faisant partie du décor, son corps aplati contre ce décor et sa monotonie alors soulignée par cette réification visuelle. Telle est la logique du film quand Jane découvre la chambre du maître et s'appuie contre la cheminée [33:24] ou lorsque son corps menu dans sa lugubre robe noire ne se détache quasiment pas dans le plan large sur le décor tout aussi monotone du salon de Rochester [43:25]. Lors de la soirée à Thornfield, un nouveau cadrage cruel traduit le mépris de Blanche et la transparence de Jane qu'on ne remarque pas : tandis que les mots de Blanche, plus agressifs encore que dans le roman, déclinent le motif de la monotonie (« *A governess? Yes I thought I saw someone with her just now. You can always tell a governess at first glance. They're plain, in a very special way.* »), Jane apparaît de profil, plus pâle et plus fade encore, contre des tentures et des tapis tout aussi peu attractifs [65:14].

À ces plans s'opposent nettement les nombreuses scènes dans lesquelles le corps de Jane est en mouvement, vecteur d'un désir désormais tendance, mouvement du sujet vers l'objet. Zeffirelli filme très souvent un décor statique par un plan fixe, décor et plan dans lesquels pénètre ensuite le corps du personnage. Malgré la fadeur de la scène de la chambre rouge à l'écran, ne peut-on pas y lire un premier exemple de ce mouvement du corps, ici en direction de lui-même et de ses propres désirs, lorsque Jane pénètre dans la chambre et dans le plan avec un hurlement tout en étant projetée contre le miroir [1:14] ? Par cette esthétique récurrente, Jane devenue adulte traversera souvent l'espace du plan pour oser y affirmer la présence de son corps : en arrivant aux portes de Thornfield, filmée en légère contre-plongée [26:26], puis dans les deux espaces intérieurs dans lesquels elle entre ensuite. Le lieu est d'abord à l'image, avant que n'y pénètre le corps de Jane. Le metteur en scène choisit le même procédé lorsque Jane rejoint Rochester à la toute fin du film : le bien triste et monotone espace dans lequel est assis Rochester est filmé en plan fixe puis Pilot et Jane entrent dans le plan par la gauche [105]. De nouveau Jane est filmée en contre-plongée, comme pour mieux signifier l'urgence du désir et l'affirmation de l'identité. Leur rencontre déjà était placée sous le signe de cette promesse de rupture de la monotonie par de tels déplacements corporels : filmée en gros plan, Jane sort du cadre pour aller rejoindre l'espace de Rochester à terre [37:37], puis à deux reprises, elle pénètre de nouveau dans le plan de Rochester [37:40-38].

Dans une économie spatiale du désir ici véritablement cinématographique, les corps quadrillent et perturbent la monotonie de l'espace filmique afin d'y inscrire leurs désirs. Ces plans vides dans lesquels s'écrit ensuite le désir en évoquent une autre logique : le désir est constitué par le manque et l'absence, que l'objet du désir est appelé à combler. Le corps s'érige alors comme objet pour emplir l'espace et le vide. Ce manque constitutif du désir est dans le roman associé à un déterminisme sclérosant. Malgré sa chevelure de feu, Helen Burns se sait condamnée par la maladie autant que victime de ses propres carences : « *By dying young, I shall escape great sufferings. I had not qualities or talents to make my way very well in the world; I should have been continually at fault.* » (69) Plus loin, Rochester évoquera à son tour une semblable conscience de ses propres condamnations au malheur (116). Dans le cas de Jane, la lucidité de ses monotonies physiques et de ses désirs démesurés illustre autant la nécessité du sentiment de manque pour qu'affleure le désir, qu'elle souligne les ambiguïtés d'un personnage en demi-teintes : « *I ever wished to look as well as I could, and to please as much as my want of beauty would permit.* » (84) Les manques structurent bien ici le désir, créé et entretenu, défini même, par leurs entraves. De manière significative, les désirs de Jane d'être plus belle et moins monotone sont alors fortement colorés de rouge : « *I sometimes regretted that I was not handsomer: I sometimes wished to have rosy cheeks, a straight nose, and small cherry mouth. [...] And why had I these aspirations and these regrets?* » (84) Le désir n'est pas souffrance, mais le sujet sait ses démesures.

Avant de poursuivre l'analyse de ces surgissements de la couleur, signalons un autre manque déterminant dans la construction du personnage. La « présence » obsédante de l'absence de Mr Reed dans la chambre rouge est souvent évoquée par la narratrice comme objet d'angoisse autant que moteur de désir : dans les premières pages, c'est un tel homme, ou bien un tel père, qui manque à Jane, ce qui explique à ses yeux la cruauté de sa tante. Il faut alors souligner l'ironie répétée par l'arrivée de Brocklehurst (the "*Coming Man*" (52), à Gateshead puis à Lowood, jamais l'homme que Jane désire tout à fait (mais peut-être n'est-il alors pas si insensé de trouver dans le portrait du père de Jane chez Zeffirelli une troublante ressemblance avec l'acteur incarnant Brocklehurst [99:37]). Ainsi le manque du père constitue-t-il peut-être le désir de l'homme, logique qui, sans entrer dans des considérations psychanalytiques, est bien celle du désir fondé sur un manque : on ne saurait désirer que ce que l'on n'a pas.

Dans le roman, la couleur, avant même le désir et le rouge, peut alors combler ces manques et ces creux autant que casser la monotonie. Les couleurs et l'éclat de la chambre de Jane à Thornfield sont un exemple d'une telle rupture de la monotonie visuelle associée aux désirs et aux attentes du personnage (83). La description élogieuse du visage de St John repose également sur une palette assez insolite ici (294), tout comme l'était, dans les grisailles de Lowood, le choix de la part d'Helen de caractériser ses institutrices par la couleur : « *The one with red cheeks is called Miss Smith [...]; the little one with black hair is Miss Scatcherd; and the one [...] with a yellow riband, is Madame Pierrot* » (43). Comme les pointes de rouge perturbaient les topographies monotones et (r)éveillaient le désir, cette émergence de la couleur permet de combler les monotonies visuelles de l'écriture.

Ce rouge que l'œuvre donne parfois à lire ou à voir est alors le plus souvent associé à Rochester, tel un signal du désir qui viendra rompre la monotonie, celle de l'existence de Jane et celle, définitoire, de l'œuvre.

« *He is not a happy man* », assure Mrs Fairfax avant de remarquer que les roses rouges de sa chambre sont fanées [34]. Après leur première rencontre fortuite, Jane est reçue dans les appartements du maître dans un bain de lumière rouge (« *ruddy shine* » (100), tandis que dans le film cette lumière se fait rapidement plus verdâtre à l'écran [41:40]. Malgré les sanguines de Jane (des aquarelles chez Brontë), ce sera de nouveau le cas dans la scène suivante [44:38], le film souffrant ici d'un faux-raccord esthétiquement bien fâcheux. C'est encore le rouge qui illumine la scène de leur troisième rencontre (« *the large fire was all red and clear; the purple curtains hung rich and ample* » (111) puis que choisira Rochester pour se déguiser en vieille femme. Les corps et les couleurs sont donc dans *Jane Eyre* ce qui permet au désir de prendre vie et de briser la monotonie. Pourtant le revirement central de l'intrigue peut être synonyme d'un échec ou d'une frustration du désir, dont la dynamique de rupture n'aura plus lieu d'être puisque personnages et narrations feront le dernier choix du monotone comme objet de leurs désirs.

Les lassitudes du désir ou la frustration mise en scène

Certaines apparitions du rouge dans le film ne sont en rien liées au désir et marquent au contraire un danger ou un rejet. Ainsi en est-il des robes rouges des deux filles de Mrs Reed dans la première scène ou encore lorsque la caméra monte au ciel avec Helen et que le ciel neigeux se fait rose-rouge [22]. Mais le rouge du danger est avant tout celui associé à Bertha et au feu, au sang de Mason, et auparavant à son arrivée à Thornfield avec cette lumière rouge de mauvais augure sur sa voiture [67:50]. À cet égard il ne faut pas oublier que si, dans le roman, Grace Poole est aussi masculine qu'effrayante aux yeux de Jane (« *a set, square-made figure, red-haired, and with a hard, plain face* » (91), elle est aussi, donc, rousse, étrange paradoxe de la féminité après nos analyses des cheveux tondus de Helen dans le film.

Puisque le rouge peut aussi être dangereux, le désir sera tu dans un refoulement qui annonce une nouvelle dialectique avec la monotonie, celle-ci s'apparentant à une régularité dont il faut bien se satisfaire. En dépit de ses aspirations et autres agitations de caractère (« *I shall be called discontented. I could not help it: the restlessness was in my nature; it agitated me to pain sometimes* » (93), Jane désire par-dessus tout une vie convenable et vertueuse : « *and above all things, I wished the result of my endeavours to be respectable, proper, en règle.* » (75) Suivant les traces d'Elizabeth Bennet dans *Pride and Prejudice*, elle sait se satisfaire d'un bonheur mesuré, comme lorsque Adèle, Mrs Fairfax et Sophie lui témoignent une affection plus ou moins modérée à son retour de Gateshead (209). Dans le film, cette satisfaction raisonnable transparaît lorsque Adèle demande si elles seront heureuses et que Jane lui répond : « *We shall work hard and we shall be content.* » [30:20]

Le monotone et le fade s'avèrent-ils en dernière analyse les véritables objets de son désir ? Lorsqu'elle est encore à Lowood, ces objets sont d'abord conçus tel un pis-aller : « *What do I want? A new place, in a new house, amongst new faces, under new circumstances: I want this because it is of no use wanting anything better.* » (73) Les voies de la sagesse tempèrent le désir, et il y a jusqu'au dénouement qui remette en perspective la satisfaction de l'héroïne. Jane et Rochester trouvent la question du mariage monotone (« *that monotonous theme* » (169), Jane ne désire pas le mariage (« *I don't care about being married.* » (371), et les couleurs, les corps et les désirs n'auraient alors tenté de subvertir les monotonies que pour mieux en assurer le retour victorieux. Le *happy end* n'est pas absolu, et malgré l'énergie de la voix de Jane dans ses dernières pages, il s'agira bien de savoir se contenter de son ultime choix. La dernière image du film, inscrivant, de manière assez artificielle, le couple réuni dans une ultime topographie de la sérénité, ne saurait dissiper tout à fait les vieux fantômes de l'ennui et de la monotonie.

Jane fut-elle victime d'une imagination trop débridée, impossible à réconcilier avec ce désir du monotone ? La deuxième page du livre met en abyme sa propre construction topographique puis narrative dans un passage annonciateur des principaux désirs de Jane : voir et faire (« *I longed for a power of vision which might overpass that limit; [...] I desired more of practical experience than I possessed* » (93). Ainsi l'incipit du roman met en scène Jane en train de lire et d'imaginer les topographies de ses premiers désirs pour échapper à la monotonie de Gateshead : « *Of these dead-white realms I formed an idea of my own* » (6). Puis l'image laisse affleurer l'événement et la narration : « *Each picture told a story* » (6). Ces lieux et ces histoires qui naissent de la lecture confèrent au roman un caractère métaréflexif qui permet de lire dans les écarts entre désir et monotonie la source du romanesque, mais aussi un questionnement du désir et de la monotonie du lecteur. La monotonie narrative de *Jane Eyre* est ainsi dans l'ellipse (« *During these eight years my life was uniform* » (71 ; « *October, November, December passed away.* » (94), autant que dans la répétition parfois pesante de l'intrigue (190).

Si cette monotonie narrative peut susciter le désir du lecteur d'imaginer et de visualiser à son tour lieux et événements, le film n'y répondra guère. Simple répétition monotone du roman, l'adaptation de Zeffirelli est sans désir aucun pour son histoire, pas plus que pour ses personnages. Il est, par exemple, significatif que l'incipit métaréflexif du roman soit absent du scénario. Pourtant le film sait jouer avec notre désir de spectateur de voir et de savoir, mettant en scène ce désir autant qu'une ultime monotonie source de frustration. Le zoom avant sur les corps qui se touchent enfin après l'incendie

[58:10] apparaît tel un contrepoint au choix esthétique récurrent de Zeffirelli d'ouvrir une scène en plan serré sur un accessoire avant d'élargir le champ : lors de la seconde rencontre dans le salon de Rochester [40:50], pour ouvrir la scène des sanguines [43:07], ou encore lorsqu'on apprête la future mariée dans sa chambre [87:21]. Ici les fluides mouvements de caméra répondent au désir de vision du spectateur (plus qu'à celui de Jane rappelé plus haut) et construisent une esthétique aussi gracieuse que surannée. Pourtant les portes de Thornfield se ferment souvent sur notre regard [31:42, 56:30, 69:33]. Les chambres de Jane, de Bertha puis de Mason ne s'offriront ici à aucun regard. Aussi la loi a-t-elle en dernier ressort raison du désir, cette même loi qui interdira le mariage de Jane et de Rochester. L'image reste bouchée et interdite, insupportable et frustrante de monotonie, ainsi que dans ces autres plans dans lesquels les personnages s'inscrivent platement contre un décor triste et obstrué — contre les rochers après la rencontre [38], contre une fenêtre grillagée [44:40], ou encore contre cet arbre (aux feuilles certes rouges) dans la scène du portrait [45:55]. Aussi l'adaptation ne rompt-elle que partiellement la monotonie narrative du roman et ne répond-elle que ponctuellement aux désirs du spectateur. Des désirs las de Jane aux désirs frustrés du destinataire des œuvres, la monotonie s'impose comme objet ou comme conclusion d'un désir qu'on ne saurait suffisamment tempérer.

Les espaces et les personnages monotones de *Jane Eyre* se colorent ainsi souvent de désir, dans le texte comme dans l'image, désir grâce auquel les corps se font plus charnels et plus libres. La recherche de l'objet et le désir d'être soi-même objet du désir créent l'événement et laissent entrevoir l'espoir de freiner une monotonie programmée. Cependant le parcours de Jane est aussi celui de l'acceptation du manque et d'un désir à demi étouffé, qui doit être différé pour être comblé. *Jane Eyre* affirmerait donc que si les logiques du désir sont nécessaires et salvatrices, c'est avant tout pour atteindre à une maturité qui saurait alléger, et faire accepter, la monotonie d'un choix de vie. St John craint que l'ambition de Jane ne la détourne de l'emploi qu'il lui a trouvé (302-303) : l'ambition de Jane est tout autre, celle du désir et de la sérénité. Jane ne désire pas l'aventure, fût-elle sentimentale et respectable. Le vrai désir de Jane, c'est le désir lui-même, c'est d'avoir du désir. Il s'agit donc bien d'un idéal tout aussi heuristique qu'esthétique. Brontë comme Zeffirelli n'ont d'autre objet que de faire naître notre désir, de le léser et de le ranimer pour « créer des attentes pour les combler[1] ». L'expérience peut lasser, mais Jane, en tant que narratrice, lectrice et spectatrice raisonnée d'elle-même, saura s'en satisfaire et goûter un équilibre, sans cesse à renouveler, entre privation et jouissance — ce même équilibre

---

1. Bresson, Robert, *Notes sur le cinématographe* (1975), Paris, Gallimard, 1995, p. 103.

qui définit les enjeux de la création romanesque et cinématographique, entre reproduction passive du monde et imagination colorée de nos désirs. Ce serait donc, en dernier lieu, la question de l'exigence que *Jane Eyre* pose à son héroïne ainsi qu'à son destinataire.

Bibliographie

BAZIN, Claire, *Jane Eyre, le pèlerin moderne*, Nantes : Éditions du Temps, 2005.
BRESSON, Robert, *Notes sur le cinématographe* (1975), Paris : Gallimard, 1995.

Visualizing the Gothic in *Jane Eyre*

Shannon Wells-Lassagne

The title of this article is willfully problematic: it suggests a relationship between vision, the Gothic genre, and the novel and film *Jane Eyre*. However, Brontë's novel is well-known for its mix of genres—to reduce it to the sole genre of the Gothic would undoubtedly be a betrayal of the spirit of the text; likewise, as Misha Kavka reminds us in her article "The Gothic on Screen", there is not a clear category of "Gothic film" (Hogle 209), and the Gothic is traditionally related not so much to what is seen, as to what cannot be seen (227). However, given the paradigmatic status of Brontë's novel for Gothic tropes like the monstrous feminine or the uncanny, and its strong use of visual imagery and ekphrasis, it seems crucial to the study of text and adaptation to examine the transposition of both the Gothic and the visual into the medium of film. We will therefore begin by sketching the relationship between the visual and the Gothic in the novel, before examining the extent to which these and other Gothic tropes are translated onto the screen. We will conclude by suggesting the generic hybridity of both novel and film.

Seeing Red: Gothic Vision in Brontë's Novel

Though the spectacular nature of the certain Gothic scenes is obvious (the crisis of the red-room, Rochester's burning bed, as well as the discovery and eventual death of Bertha Mason), our primary concern here will be the extent to which vision and the visual is associated with the Gothic, suggesting that for the author, the transgression inherent in representing the visual by the textual is similar to the Gothic form's fascination with the limits of representation (Hogle 212). The recurrence of vision, the exchange of glances, is obvious even upon a first perusal of Brontë's novel; it is not a coincidence that John Reed punishes Jane at the beginning of the novel for "that look you had in your eyes" (8), nor that Rochester as gypsy declares he will not read Jane's palm, but her eyes (171). Indeed, the gaze is repeatedly shown to be an important means of communication of characters' feelings or personalities (in keeping with Brontë's fascination with phrenology): thus Mrs Reed has an "eye of flint […] covered with its cold lid", echoing "her inexorable soul" (205). The gaze is repeatedly associated with language, making it central to the written text: the fact that the gaze allows characters to *read* one another suggests just how high a value the novelist places on vision. St John's comments to Jane are but one example: "He looked at me before he proceeded: indeed, he seemed leisurely to read my face, as if its features and lines were characters on a page. [...] 'I read it in your eye; it is not of that description which promises the maintenance of an even tenor in life.'" (302-303)

If such is the case, then, the association of language and vision also implies a relationship between vision and narrative power—after all, much has been made of the power implicit in Jane's first-person narrative; it is she who controls the discourse, the representation of events, and those who attempt to tell her story in her stead generally fare badly (as for instance Mrs Reed claiming Jane is a liar to Mr Brocklehurst, or later that she is dead to John Eyre, or Rochester who is constantly attempting to impose his vision of her, whether it be as a fairy or a saint). If characters can read the truth of one another in their eyes, then they have power over those they see, and the male gaze as practiced by both Rochester and St John suggests that seeing someone can mean taking free agency from them. To return to St John, his influence first exerts itself in the weight of his gaze, as when he first considers asking Jane to study Hindustani with him:

> [...] I happened to look his way: there I found myself under the influence of the ever-watchful blue eye. How long it had been searching me through and through, and over and over, I cannot tell: so keen was it, and yet so cold, I felt for the moment superstitious—as if I were sitting in a room with something uncanny. *(338)*

Here it seems it is power, and not beauty, that is in the eye of the beholder. Once St John has won Jane to his cause, the unhealthy influence he exerts is again described in visual terms, where his eye becomes her own, where she will see only as his gaze directs:

> He wanted to train me to an elevation I could never reach; it racked me hourly to aspire to the standards he uplifted. The thing was as impossible as to mould my irregular features to his correct and classic pattern, to give to my changeable green eyes the sea-blue tint and solemn lustre of his own. *(340)*

In keeping with the association between vision and communication, St John is also usurping Jane's narrative power—he is demanding that she "see things his way", literally through his eyes, something that Jane recognizes as an impossible task.

If the prevalence and the power of the gaze seems clear, then, its relationship to the Gothic may appear less so; however, if we look at the first St John passage (338), the vocabulary in fact suggests the Gothic. The dissociation of the eye from its owner ("*the* ever-watchful eye") as well as the highly evocative term "uncanny" and the power the eye has over its object, all of these suggest one of the best-known Gothic short stories, Edgar Allan Poe's "The Tell-Tale Heart" (1843), where a man is driven to extremes by the sinister eye of his neighbor. The fact that the second quote is immediately followed by a characterization of St John's influence as "thrall" (340) is not coincidental—clearly, the reader is meant to consider the gaze as supernatural.

Indeed, the male gaze so often derided in feminist theory is present, but it would be reductive to limit the characterization of the gaze to the male characters; even outside of her interaction with male authority figures, the protagonist longs for power of vision to overcome her own limitations (physical and otherwise):

> [...] then I longed for a power of vision that might overpass that limit [the skyline]; which might reach the busy world, towns, regions full of life I had heard of but never seen [...] the restlessness was in my nature [...] my sole relief was to walk along the corridor of the third story, backwards and forwards, safe in the silence and solitude of the spot and allow my mind's eye to dwell on whatever bright visions rose before it [...] and best of all, to open my inward ear to a tale that was never ended—a tale my imagination created, and narrated continuously [...] *(93)*

The remedy provided by vision, both real and imaginary, is insufficient, (and will soon be tested by the coming meeting with Rochester), but it is once again associated with discourse; the transition from the outer eye (seeing past the skyline) to the inner eye and its powers of imagination suggest that vision, like language, represent a means of freeing oneself from constraints, be they social, physical, or mental. Once again, the reader may be reminded of the characteristics of the Gothic, which deal repeatedly with transgression of boundaries and with excess (Botting 1). The link between images and narrative is even more explicit in young Jane's remarks upon studying her beloved Bewick's British Birds: "Each picture told a story; mysterious often to my undeveloped understanding and imperfect feelings, yet ever profoundly interesting: as interesting as the tales Bessie sometimes narrated on winter evenings [...]" (6-7)

The idea of inner musings and imaginative vision, of stories and pictures, brings to mind what is perhaps the most obvious example both of the visual in the novel and its relation to the Gothic, the long ekphrastic descriptions of Jane's own artwork. The descriptions are detailed and evocative, portraying not naturalistic landscapes or figures, but a series of surreal images, far removed from any idea of realism: "The third [watercolour] showed the pinnacle of an iceberg piercing a polar winter sky: a muster of northern light reared their dim lances, close serried, along the horizon. Throwing these into distance, rose, in the foreground, a head—a colossal head, inclined towards the iceberg, and resting against it." (107) Clearly the subject matter is not realistic, but fantastic, particularly given that the artist has never left the confines of Gateshead and Lowood, and the idea of piercing the winter sky and the horizon seem symbolic of Jane's own desire to see past the horizon of Thornfield. At the same time, the ice could suggest the recurrent images of fire and ice in the novel, passion and restraint, and thus be considered foreshadowing for Jane's upcoming struggle to resist the temptation of St John's cool demeanor and intellectual appeal, for example: as such, these uncanny works serve as a metaphor for the novel in which they appear, once again associating visual and verbal representation.

Nonetheless, Jane's comments on her own work make clear that her talent is not equal to her ambition: "As I saw them with the spiritual eye, before I had attempted to embody them, they were striking; but my hand would not second my fancy, and in each case it had wrought out but a pale portrait of the thing I had conceived." (107) This inability to translate the image onto the page suggests the other transposition central to our study—is Zeffirelli's film also "a pale portrait" of the thing Brontë conceived?

Gothic Heritage: A Contradiction in Terms?

If the intermediality implicit in the extensive descriptions of the visual and of visual art lends itself to the Gothic, then it would seem logical to look for these same Gothic elements in transposing the story from a literary medium to a visual one. While the Gothic elements in Brontë's novel have been well-documented, leaving us only to establish its visual nature, the Gothic elements in Zeffirelli's film are much more problematic. As such, I'd like to examine the presence of Gothic tropes as they appear in the film adaptation of *Jane Eyre*.

In her article "The Gothic on Screen", Kavka lists a certain number of visual codes typical of Gothic film: a house or castle on a hill, in the fog, a dark cemetery with bare branches, heavy wooden doors shutting without cause, high arched windows, deep shadows, and close-ups of mad, staring eyes (210). What is interesting in examining these stereotypical Gothic images is that they are all present, but subverted, in the Zeffirelli adaptation. Indeed, Thornfield is on a hill, but never in a fog; the cemetery where Helen Burns is buried is visited both by a young and an adult Jane, thus giving it a significance it lacks in the novel, where it is simply mentioned as existing—but the cemetery is always viewed in the bright sunlight; in the film, the heavy wooden door of Jane's room is unlatched and then closed again, but this happens without the notice of the heroine, and without consequence for the rest of the story; there are extended close-ups of Jane's eyes, notably as she is making her decision to either accept St John or return to Rochester, but they are calm, tranquil, not crazed. The recurrent emphasis on Jane's gaze, and the widespread use of close-ups, suggest that Zeffirelli is attempting to translate the importance of the visual to the screen[1].

The use of light and shadow is perhaps the most interesting subversion of Gothic tropes in the film: whereas the predecessor to Zeffirelli's adaptation, Stevenson's 1944 version of *Jane Eyre*, interpreted the text in terms of almost pure Gothic romance, and used techniques common to both German expressionism and film noir, particularly the use of high contrast lighting, in the 1996 version darkness basically only exists for Mason's arrival, the ball, and Rochester's proposal, none of which figure among the canonically Gothic episodes of the novel.

Otherwise the film is shot in almost ubiquitous bright light (sometimes bright sunshine) even when the scene supposedly takes place at night. This unsuccessful "day for night" technique is used to such an extent that it sometimes interferes with the spectator's suspension of disbelief. The phenomenon is all the more surprising because in his first and arguably best-known adaptation of an English classic, *Romeo and Juliet* (1968), Zeffirelli makes conspicuous use of shadow and light, notably in the party and balcony scenes. One might postulate that this contrast with the Stevenson adaptation is voluntary, that the director expressly chose to distinguish his version of the story from its predecessor.

If these telling details which evoke the Gothic are absent, it seems relevant to examine two of the most Gothic figures in the novel: the Byronic hero Mr Rochester, and the "madwoman in the attic", Bertha Mason. Bertha is the major Gothic figure in the novel, with her mysterious laughter echoing through Thornfield and her eventual destruction of the same. Brontë spares no expense in making the character as monstrous as possible:

> In the deep shade, at the further end of the room, a figure ran backwards and forwards. What it was, whether beast or human being, one could not, at first sight, tell: it grovelled, seemingly, on all fours; it snatched and growled like some strange wild animal: but it was covered with clothing; and a quantity of dark, grizzled hair, wild as a mane, hid its head and face. [...] She was a big woman, in stature almost equalling her husband, and corpulent besides: she showed virile force in the contest—more than once she almost throttled him, athletic as he was. *(250)*

---

1. Indeed, the male gaze that so oppresses Jane with St John is to find its equivalent in Brocklehurst's insistence on a normative gaze; though Brocklehurst's speech presenting Jane as a liar is partially cut in the film, the emphasis on vision is actually amplified: "Does everyone see this girl? [...] This girl, take a look at her, this girl is a liar!"

This bestial, masculine character in the film becomes a thin pale woman shivering before the fire, her white nightgown echoing the bridal gown Jane wears, and the parallel between the two women, of similar build and coloring, both listening passively to Rochester's diatribe about her madness is obvious.

When Rochester asks his audience to "look at the difference!", the task is not as clear-cut as it may appear. Granted, Bertha has a penchant for "spreading the warmth", and her passivity alternates with moments of violence, but these seem motivated by jealousy rather than any kind of uncontrollable inner rage. The vampiric qualities of Brontë's figure (who bites Mason) are conspicuously absent from the screen version of the character: she may still want to "drain his heart" (181), but her fangs aren't out—we are not told how she injures him.

Rochester's qualifications as a Gothic figure are also indisputable: he is strong, sinister, mysterious, intimidating, with a dark and twisted past. His love for Jane is also excessive, in the tradition of *Wuthering Heights'* Heathcliff, though sometimes cruel (in his "games" with Blanche Ingram) and violent (in his passionate restraint of Jane when she first mentions leaving Thornfield following their aborted wedding).

The film attenuates this extreme version of the male lead; William Hurt's sensitive portrayal seems to concentrate on Rochester's inner pain rather than his harsh demeanor; the taunting of Jane with stories of marriage to Blanche are minimized, thus reducing the strong sense in the novel of the character manipulating events, controlling all aspects of Jane's world, to which she has no choice but to submit, and whose only form of resistance or rebellion is the refusal to display her emotions. Here, as Lisa Hopkins comments,

> [...] we never have a sense of Mr Rochester as powerful or in control of events; after the fire, nothing but shyness or lack of self-confidence seems to hold him back from kissing Jane, which appears to be the outcome towards which the shot is inevitably leading, and he also clearly suggests genuine uncertainty over whether Jane will return to him from the deathbed of Mrs Reed. *(94)*

Indeed, this Rochester seems motivated by a desire to ascertain Jane's own feelings, while Brontë's character admits that he "feigned courtship of Miss Ingram, because [he] wished to render [Jane] as madly in love with him as [he] was with [her]; and [he] knew that jealousy would be the best ally [he] could call in for the furtherance of that aim" (224), once more showing his desire to exert power over her.

Likewise, the passionate nature of the Byronic character is much attenuated in the Zeffirelli version of the story; this Rochester is soft-spoken, rarely raising his voice, and even his anger at being thwarted in his marriage to

Jane is kept on a relatively even keel—he does not shout, but whispers despairingly the name of his brother-in-law come to inform the assembly of his previous marriage. Brontë's character has a very different reaction:

> His eye, as I have often said, was a black eye: it now had a tawny, nay a bloody light in its gloom; and his face flushed—olive cheek and hueless forehead received a glow, as from spreading, ascending heart-fire: and he stirred, lifted his strong arm—he could have struck Mason—dashed him on the church-floor—shocked by ruthless blow the breath from his body—but Mason shrank away, and cried faintly, "Good God!" Contempt fell cool on Mr Rochester—his passion died as if a blight had shrivelled it up [...] *(248)*

In the same vein, his violent insistence that Jane is not to leave him[1] is reduced on the screen to a plaintive cry after seeing her alight in a carriage: "Jane! Don't leave me!" Rochester thus becomes more passive and weak than does his literary counterpart, almost feminized.

The consequences of condensing the plot for a feature-length film also make for an interesting analysis of the film version of Rochester. The fact that Bertha setting Thornfield afire and Jane's escape happen simultaneously causes these two crises to be seen as parallels of one another (two women essentially cutting themselves off from the disastrous past, and more specifically from Rochester, because of the presence of the other woman), and reinforces the idea that Bertha is in a sense Jane's alter ego, a stance made famous by Gilbert and Gubar in *Madwoman in the Attic* (cf. 483-491). However, it also creates a choice for Rochester, a test of priorities: which is more important, the house and his mad wife, or his now ex-fiancée?

One might argue that the noble sacrifice that Rochester makes by choosing to attempt to save his beleaguered wife and let his beloved Jane go creates a very different character from Brontë's Rochester, who was willing to board up Thornfield and to force Jane to come with him despite her moral qualms, all in the name of his obsessive love, a character who claims that in leaving him, Jane leaves him to a life of ruin, decadence and vice. Again, this changed characterization of Rochester downplays the dark brooding nature of the Byronic hero, making him more palatable to modern audiences no doubt, who might find the original Rochester's fixation on Jane a little "unhealthy".

---

1. "His voice has hoarse; his look that of a man who is just about to burst an insufferable bond and plunge headlong into wild license. I saw that in another moment, and with one impetus of frenzy more, I should be able to do nothing with him. The present—the passing second of time, was all I had in which to control and restrain him: a movement of repulsion, flight, fear, would have sealed my doom,—and his." (258).

The explanation for the manner in which the film downplays or rejects the novel's Gothic qualities no doubt resides in the film's own generic concerns; while Brontë seemed to want to use Gothic tropes to heighten emotional responses to her work, Zeffirelli seems to want to present the film as the adaptation of a classic tale of romance, trading on the respectability of the novel to present a story echoing many romantic dramas. As such, the director seems to want to identify *Jane Eyre* with the heritage genre. Andrew Higson's definition of the phenomenon corresponds to Zeffirelli's interpretation of Brontë's text:

> These films are set in the past, telling stories of manners and proprieties, but also the often transgressive romantic entanglements of the upper and upper middle-class English, in carefully detailed and splendid period reconstructions. The luxurious country-house settings, the picturesque rolling green landscapes of southern England, the pleasures of period costume, and the canonical literary reference points are among the more frequently noted attractions of such films [...] *(1)*

These costume dramas, whose heyday seems to have been in the mid-1990s, with the plethora of Jane Austen adaptations and Merchant Ivory films, are characterized as privileging attention to period detail and picturesque images, emphasizing the romanticism of these stories set in a "simpler", more attractive past. As Mettinger and Rubik suggest, these are "tasteful, middlebrow period drama[s] with English setting and characters, having strong literary connections and an intense appeal for female viewers". As such, Zeffirelli's film suggests, the educated middle-class feminine audience the film was targeting would necessarily be more interested in the comforting vision of a romantic relationship, rather than the ultimately destabilized and destabilizing vision suggested by Brontë's hybrid text in general, and its more Gothic elements in particular. In fact when promoting the film, Zeffirelli emphasizes both the popularity (and therefore the profitability) of the novel, and its attraction for women, placing his film squarely in the realm of the heritage film industry: "I think it's such an incredible novel. It has never been out of print [...] and it's a cult novel. [...] In fact the book created a lot of opposition and people were stunned, but women grabbed that [feminist] message [...]" (Charlie Rose)

Indeed, the casting also reflects this desire to appeal to fans of the heritage genre; one of the things Lisa Hopkins notices about the Zeffirelli adaptation in her book *Screening the Gothic* is the casting overlap between this film and another contemporary heritage adaptation, the BBC production of Jane Austen's *Persuasion* that had come out the previous year (1995), with both

Amanda Root (Miss Temple) and Fiona Shaw (Mrs Reed) (90); character actors like John Wood (Mr Brocklehurst) and Joan Plowright (Mrs Fairfax) are well-known figures in these types of films. Indeed, Zeffirelli goes so far as to claim credit for the heritage film phenomenon: "If there was one who started this [Austen mania, adapting classics to the screen] it was me, in 1968, with *Romeo and Juliet*." (Charlie Rose)

It is perhaps symbolic of Zeffirelli's directorial choices that Haddon Hall, where the film was shot, is indeed a medieval structure, but the arrow slits more traditionally associated with Gothic architecture have been refitted with large windows, transforming the dark and gloomy atmosphere more common during the period into one (anachronistically) filled with light to suit more modern tastes. The question, of course, both for the Gothic architecture and the Gothic story, is whether this change in fact distorts the beauty of the structure as a whole.

Adulterated Gothic

Of course, as a reading of Brontë's novel makes clear, the novel is not a simple Gothic novel, if such a thing exists. As Victor Sage suggests in his introduction to *Modern Gothic: A Reader*, "[...] there is no point in thinking of the Gothic as 'pure': it is an apparent genre-badge which, the moment it is worn by a text, becomes an imperceptible catalyst, a transforming agent for other codes" (2) Indeed, if the Gothic is omnipresent in the novel, it is certainly not alone, and it is not necessarily to be taken at face value: it could be argued that the Gothic elements of the novel are often undercut, much as the mysterious gypsy persona gradually gives way to a recognition of a disguised and more realistic Rochester. Thus for example Blanche's flattery of Rochester, telling him of her fascination for pirates, gentleman-highwaymen, or ruffians, is an almost stereotypical depiction of the female attraction to Byronic figures (157)—the fact that the flattery is completely insincere can only undermine that supposed magnetism. Likewise, the very reversal of certain Gothic stereotypes in the novel seems to suggest that the genre does not remain untarnished: the plainness of both lovers is one example, while the attractiveness of Mason (who is described by the female Eshtons and Ingrams as "'a beautiful man' [...] 'a love of a creature'" 162), who is in fact cowardly and weak, seems to suggest a criticism of the often bland and passive, but handsome male suitors to be found in the classic Gothic novel.

If the novel's Gothic nature, then, is not without question, the film, which initially appears to reject wholesale all but the romantic aspects of the novel in order to conform to audience expectations, nonetheless contains some attenuated Gothic references, notably those which refer directly to the visual.

Thus for example the fact that Jane and Rochester initially meet not on a stile as in the book, but on a rocky outcropping, could be seen as an allusion to Penistone Crag where Heathcliff and Cathy meet in the 1939 William Wyler adaptation of *Wuthering Heights*; indeed the forelock and sideburns of William Hurt's Rochester may owe much to Olivier's Heathcliff rather than to Robert Stevenson's 1944 *Jane Eyre*.

Likewise, the esthetics of the film sometimes appear to allude to the work of Caspar David Friedrich; given that he is perhaps the best known Romantic Gothic painters, this would necessarily suggest the Gothic genre. Thus, while waiting for Jane's return from Gateshead, a static shot of Rochester, alone on a cliff overlooking a misty landscape suggests Friedrich's *The Wanderer*, while Jane's silent decision process in choosing between her two suitors seems to echo Friedrich's *Woman at the Window*, the vertical lines of the tree at right echoing that of the ship masts in the painting and the low-angle shot of a ruined Thornfield amid bare branches suggests *The Abbey in the Oak Wood*.

In addition to this, we could say that there are two shared concerns for both the heritage film and the Gothic genre that consequently figure in both novel and film. The first of these is the importance of setting. The Gothic genre has traditionally been known for its exotic locales (most famously the south of France in Anne Radcliffe's *The Mysteries of Udolpho*) and its emphasis on domestic space made uncanny. Brontë is of course a prime example of the association of buildings and their inhabitants: critics have alternately seen Thornfield as the incarnation of Rochester, whose injuries coincide with its destruction, and as the ego, superego, and id of the protagonist (notably with the latter manifested in the third-floor madwoman in the attic, raging at the cruelties perpetrated by Rochester on Jane). Likewise, the importance of landscape and monuments figures largely in the characteristics of the heritage genre, as evidenced by the long establishing shots showing Thornfield Hall and its surroundings at different seasons and the loving attention afforded to its sculpted wood interiors.

The importance of the feminine is also a consideration shared by the two genres: just as heritage films target a predominantly feminine audience, so the readership of Gothic novels was composed primarily of women. As such, the common denominator is of course the central female protagonist; it could be argued that Brontë's feminism is in fact a break with the classic Gothic heroine, "bravely" fainting in the face of adversity, but Zeffirelli's comments suggest that it is also a break from the traditional romance (*à la* Samuel Richardson's *Clarissa* or Emily Brontë):

> This woman Charlotte Brontë came up with—while her sister Emily was still writing those romantic stories where women had to die for love [...] she came up with a different portrait of a woman. Jane Eyre won't die, she will fight through life, and establish her ethics, and fall in love—that happens in the film too, in the novel—but on her own terms. *(Charlie Rose interview)*

Here Zeffirelli implies that what attracted him to the story was in part its subversion of more traditional romance through Jane's own feminist actions.

Indeed, the endings of both novel and film suggest that equality is necessary for a "happy ending"; Jane tells us, "I hold myself supremely blest—blest beyond what language can express; because I am my husband's life as fully as he is mine. No woman was ever nearer to her mate than I am; ever more absolutely bone of his bone and flesh of his flesh." (384) Zeffirelli expresses this desire for equality visually: the branches framing the embracing couple in the final shot of the film (flowering buds on her side, suggesting her youth, evergreens on his, suggesting that he is indeed still "green and vigorous" 378-379) are intertwined while creating a balanced structure for the *tableau*.

Nonetheless, though Zeffirelli and Brontë find some common ground, the excessive nature of the Gothic affords much to the novel's passionate love story—paradoxically it may very well be that Zeffirelli's decision to largely eliminate this aspect of the source text and stick faithfully to the romantic genre so dear to the heritage film in fact weakens the very plot and the poignancy of the relationship he hoped to emphasize.

Bibliography

BOTTING, Fred, *Gothic*, London: Routledge, 1996.
HIGSON, Andrew, *English Heritage, English Cinema: Costume Drama since 1980*, Oxford: OUP, 2003.
HOGLE, Jerold E., ed., *The Cambridge Companion to Gothic Fiction*, Cambridge: Cambridge UP, 2002.
HOPKINS, Lisa, *Screening the Gothic*, Austin: University of Texas Press, 2005.
RUBIK, Margarete and Mettinger Elke, *A Breath of Fresh Eyre: Intertextual and Intermedial Reworkings of Jane Eyre*, Amsterdam: Rodopi Publishers, 2007.
SAGE, Victor, Smith, Allan Lloyd, eds., *Modern Gothic: A Reader*, Manchester: Manchester UP, 1996.
STEVENSON, Robert, director, *Jane Eyre*, 20th Century Fox, 1944.
WYLER, William, director, *Wuthering Heights*, Samuel Goldwyn, 1939.
ZEFFIRELLI, Franco, director, *Romeo and Juliet*, BHE Films, 1968.
ZEFFIRELLI, Franco, interview with Charlie Rose, Charlie Rose, April 4th 1996, http://www.charlierose.com/guests/franco-zeffirelli.

Jane Eyre, le film de Franco Zeffirelli

I - Filmographie

A. Films

L'édition Norton annonce « six silent film versions or thirteen television or film adaptations » (p. 523). On peut citer pour mémoire trois versions antérieures à 1934 : en 1914, une production Whitman Features avec Lisbeth Blackstone ; en 1918, Select Pictures d'Edward José, avec Alice Brady et Elliott Dexter ; en 1921, film d'Hugo Ballin avec Mabel Ballin et produit par Ballin… On retiendra ensuite :

Jane Eyre, de Christy Cabanne, Monogram Pictures (USA), 1934, avec Virginia Bruce (Jane) et Colin Clive (Rochester), scénario d'Adele Comandini, 65 minutes. Version assez « adoucie » : « Jane returns to her blind lover and forces him to accept love ».

**Jane Eyre, de Robert Stevenson, 20th Century Fox, 1944, avec Orson Welles, Joan Fontaine et Sara Allgood. Scénario d'Aldous Huxley, Robert Stevenson et John Houseman. Attention : DVD Zone 1 (USA). 96 minutes. Bonus (Joseph McBride).

Jane Eyre, 1971, de Delbert Mann, avec Susannah York et George C. Scott, sur un scénario de Jack Pulman : « suite de grands moments tous égaux en importance »… « la mise en scène ne recherche en aucune manière à trouver des équivalences stylistiques » (Alain Garsault, *Positif*, n° 146, p. 86).

Jane Eyre, de Franco Zeffirelli, Miramax 1996, avec Charlotte Gainsbourg, William Hurt, Joan Plowright et Geraldine Chaplin. 112 minutes. DVD.

B. Télévision

Les visages des Rochester sont souvent plus connus que ceux de Jane… j'indique les rôles constitutifs de leur *persona*.

Jane Eyre, série « Studio One » (USA), le 12 XII 1949, de Franklin J. Schaffner, avec Charlton Heston (aka Ben Hur) et Mary Malone (environ une heure). Voir Norton p. 525.

Jane Eyre, série « Matinee Theatre », le 16 mai 1957, de Lamont Johnson, avec Patrick MacNee (aka John Steed) et Joan Elam (une heure).

*Jane Eyre, BBC 1973 avec Sorcha Cusach et Michael Jayston. Très apprécié en GB.

Jane Eyre, Julian Amyes, BBC Two, 1983, avec Zelah Clarke et Timothy Dalton (James Bond), 250 minutes ! DVD facile à trouver.

Jane Eyre, de Robert Young, 1997, avec Samantha Morton et Ciaran Hinds. Disponible. Adaptation de Kay Mellor.

Jane Eyre, BBC One, 2006, de Susanna White, avec Ruth Wilson et Toby Stephens. Scénario de Sandy Welch. DVD disponible (232 minutes).

Il est évidemment très recommandé de revoir le *Rebecca* d'Alfred Hitchcock (Selznick, 1940), avec Joan Fontaine (la Jane de 1944) et Laurence Olivier. Le roman de Daphné Du Maurier et le film doivent beaucoup à Charlotte Brontë et ils préfigurent l'écriture du film de 1944.

II – Bibliographie

Sur l'adaptation en général

L'ouvrage le plus lu reste celui de Brian McFarlane : *Novel to Film, an introduction to the Theory of Adaptation*, Oxford U.P, 1996, 280 p.

Plusieurs ouvrages sont des *anthologies* d'analyses d'adaptations spécifiques, mais une seule est consacrée à *Jane Eyre* :

« The Red and the Blue: Jane Eyre in the 1990s », Lisa Hopkins, in Deborah Cartmell, I.Q. Hunter, Heidi Kaye and Imelda Whelehan (eds.), *Classics in Film and Fiction*, London : Pluto Press, 2000. Il s'agit d'une comparaison entre le film TV de 1997 (avec Ciaran Hinds) et le Zeffirelli de 1996, qui en sort plutôt grandi.

En revanche, ils indiquent des pistes de recherche et des méthodes de travail.

Sarah Cardwell, *Adaptation revisited, Television and the classic novel*, Manchester U. Press, 2002, 232 p. (100 pages d'introduction).

Deborah Cartmell et Imelda Whelehan, *The Cambridge Companion to Literature on Screen*, Cambridge, 2007, 274 p.

Robert Giddings et Erica Sheen, *The Classic Novel, From page to screen*, Manchester U.P., 2000, 242 p.

James Naremore, *Film Adaptation*, London: The Athlone Press, 2000.

Geoffrey Wagner, *The Novel and the Cinema*, Rutherford : Farleigh Dickinson U. Press, 1975.

Les ouvrages en français (J-M Clerc ou M. Cacaud-Macaire) ont tendance à aborder des films … français. Mais l'étude d'André Gaudreault (*Du Littéraire au filmique*, Colin, 1999) offre une stimulante initiation à la théorie de la chose.

Sur Zeffirelli

Franco Zeffirelli, *The Autobiography of Franco Zeffirelli*, London : Weidenfeld and Nicolson, 1986, 360 pages.

Franco Zeffirelli, *Portrait d'un homme du siècle*, Paris : Pierre Belfond, 1986, 482 pages. Index utile. L'édition française comporte une longue liste des films (comme décorateur, puis comme réalisateur), des pièces de théâtre et, surtout, des 72 opéras mis en scène de 1953 à 1987 — parfois avec beaucoup de bonheur.

Attention : la biographie date de 1986 et n'évoque donc pas le film de 1996 !

Mary P. Wood, *Le Cinéma Italien*, G3J, 2005 (Original : Oxford). Brève notice page 53 qui débute ainsi : « Zeffirelli est un réalisateur très injurié pour ses opinions politiques de Droite et qui ne fut, principalement pour cette raison, jamais pris très au sérieux par les critiques ».

L'édition Norton reprend l'article de Jeffrey Sconce sur le film de 1944 paru dans *Wide Angle* en 1988 et offre un texte original de Donna Marie Nudd (p. 522). Article filmographique prometteur signalé en note (p. 523) mais il date de 1991. De même, l'auteur signale une étude à laquelle je n'ai pas pu avoir accès : Donna Marie Nudd, *Jane Eyre and What Adaptors Have Done to Her*, dissertation, University of Texas, 1989.

Les auteurs

Claire Bazin, ancienne élève de l'ENS Sèvres, est professeur de littérature anglaise et du Commonwealth à l'Université de Paris X – Nanterre. Elle a publié *La Vision du mal chez les sœurs Brontë* (PUM, 1995) et *Jane Eyre, le pèlerin moderne* (Éditions du Temps, 2005), ainsi que de nombreux articles sur le XIXe siècle (les Brontë, Mary Shelley, Bram Stoker) et la littérature néo-zélandaise (Janet Frame). Elle co-dirige le groupe de recherche FAAM (Femmes auteurs anglaises et américaines) à Paris X.

Stéphanie Bernard est agrégée d'anglais, maître de conférences à l'IUFM de l'Académie de Rouen. Elle a écrit une thèse sur Thomas Hardy et Joseph Conrad et publié plusieurs articles sur ces auteurs. Ses travaux de recherche portent notamment sur la modernité naissante à l'aube du XXe siècle, ainsi que sur la question d'une écriture féminine.

Laure Blanchemain, agrégée d'anglais et ancienne élève de l'ENS de Fontenay-Saint Cloud, est maître de conférences à l'Université de Limoges. Elle est l'auteur d'une thèse intitulée *L'imagination féminine dans les romans de Frances Burney* et d'articles sur les romans de Frances Burney et Jane Austen.

Charlotte Borie, agrégée d'anglais, prépare actuellement une thèse sur l'intériorité chez les sœurs Brontë et occupe les fonctions de Lectrice de français à St John's College, Cambridge. Elle est l'auteur d'articles sur les écrits épistolaires, romanesques ou poétiques de Charlotte et Emily Brontë, parus et à paraître dans les *Cahiers Victoriens et Edouardiens* et les *Brontë Studies*.

Laurent Bury, ancien élève de l'ENS-Ulm, est professeur à l'Université de Lyon II. Sa thèse, *Seductive Strategies in the Fiction of Anthony Trollope*, a été publiée en 2004 par Edwin Mellen. Il est l'auteur d'un livre consacré à *L'Orientalisme victorien* (Presses universitaires de Grenoble, à paraître), ainsi que de nombreux articles sur la littérature et l'art anglais au XIXe siècle. Il a traduit des textes de Byron, Trollope, Stevenson et Henry James. Chez Ellipses, il a coordonné des recueils consacrés à George Eliot, Thomas De Quincey et Jane Austen.

Nicole Cloarec est maître de conférences à l'Université de Rennes I et l'auteur d'une thèse sur les longs métrages de Peter Greenaway. Membre de la SERCIA, dont elle a organisé le congrès international en 2005 à Rennes II, elle a dirigé et publié deux volumes d'Actes chez Michel Houdiard (« *Le Cinéma en toutes lettres : jeux d'écritures à l'écran* ») et aux PUR (2007 et 2008). Nombreux articles dans *CinémAction* et *La Licorne*.

Raphaëlle Costa de Beauregard est agrégée d'anglais et professeur des universités. Titulaire d'un Doctorat d'État sur l'image à la Renaissance Elisabéthaine, publié en deux volumes, elle enseigne la littérature et le cinéma à l'Université Toulouse le Mirail ; elle a fondé la SERCIA en 1993, et publié de nombreux articles sur le cinéma américain et le cinéma britannique. Elle a organisé en septembre 2007 un Colloque SERCIA sur la couleur et le cinéma ; elle a dirigé et fait soutenir plusieurs thèses sur le cinéma.

Pascale Denance, professeur agrégé (PRAG) à l'Université de Nantes, est l'auteur d'une thèse intitulée : « I—"Tim"—and—Me! » : essai sur l'entrelacs des genres comme fondement fictionnel à une rhétorique du sujet. Étude d'un corpus transgénérique de la fin du XIXe siècle : *The Portrait of a Lady* de Henry James, *The Yellow Wallpaper* de Charlotte Perkins Gilman et une sélection de poèmes d'Emily Dickinson». Elle s'intéresse à la réécriture de la subjectivité et du genre au XIXe siècle, notamment chez Jane Austen, Charlotte Brontë, George Eliot, Henry James et Emily Dickinson.

Max Duperray, professeur à l'Université d'Aix-Marseille, spécialiste de la littérature gothique et fantastique, a publié notamment *Lecture de Frankenstein* (PU de Rennes, 1994), *Le Roman noir anglais dit Gothique* (Ellipses, 2000), *La Folie et la méthode : essai sur la déréalisation en littérature* (L'Harmattan, 2001), *Les Confessions de Thomas de Quincey* (Armand Colin, 2003) et, en collaboration avec Dominique Sipière, *Dracula* (Armand Colin, 2005), *Londres, promenade sous un ciel couvert* (Michel Houdiard, 2005). Il a dirigé récemment, avec Gilles Menegaldo et Dominique Sipière, *Éclats du Noir : Généricité et hybridation dans la littérature et le cinéma du monde anglophone* (Publications de l'Université de Provence, 2007).

Christine Evain, professeur agrégée à l'École Centrale de Nantes, est l'auteur de plusieurs articles en civilisation (l'industrie du livre aux États-Unis et au Canada) et en littérature (Atwood, Purdy, Gallant, Ishiguro, O'Connor, Ford Madox Ford, Steinbeck et Maugham). Elle a également édité et co-édité plusieurs ouvrages sur des auteurs et des éditeurs canadiens. Ayant soutenu sa thèse sur la poésie de Margaret Atwood, Christine Evain travaille depuis plusieurs années à la traduction d'une anthologie bilingue.

Jacqueline Fromonot, agrégée d'anglais, est maître de conférences à l'Université Paris VIII Saint-Denis. Auteur d'une thèse intitulée *Figures du mensonge dans le roman victorien (1847-1896)*, elle a publié de nombreux articles sur la littérature britannique du XIXe siècle, notamment sur des romans de C. Dickens, W.M. Thackeray, A. Trollope et G. Eliot, qu'elle étudie tout particulièrement d'un point de vue narratologique et stylistique. Elle est également membre de la Société Française d'Études Victoriennes et Edouardiennes (SFEVE).

Xavier Lachazette est l'auteur d'une thèse sur l'œuvre romanesque de Benjamin Disraeli. Agrégé, maître de conférences, il enseigne la littérature et la traduction à l'Université du Maine, au Mans. Ses deux domaines d'étude sont la représentation littéraire ou scientifique de la nature au XIXe siècle (Darwin, G. H. Lewes et Jane Austen, par exemple) et la nouvelle de langue anglaise (Ford, Millhauser, Bennett, du Maurier, Forster), notamment dans le cadre du pôle « Nouvelles » du CRILA, le Centre de recherches inter-langue angevin.

Catherine Lanone est professeur à l'Université de Toulouse II. Elle est l'auteur d'un livre consacré à Emily Brontë (Wuthering Heights *d'Emily Brontë : Un vent de sorcière*, Ellipses, 1999), et d'un ouvrage sur E.M. Forster. Elle a travaillé sur Graham Greene et a publié des articles sur Virginia Woolf, Thomas Hardy et les réécritures du gothique, notamment chez Mary Shelley, Emily Brontë, Charles Dickens ou Bram Stoker.

Laurent Mellet, agrégé d'anglais et docteur en littérature anglaise de l'Université de Paris III-Sorbonne Nouvelle, est maître de conférences à l'Université de Bourgogne. Il est l'auteur d'une thèse intitulée *L'œil et la voix dans l'œuvre romanesque de E. M. Forster et ses adaptations cinématographiques par James Ivory*. Également diplômé en études cinématographiques, il a publié de nombreux articles sur la littérature britannique des XXe et XXIe siècles et sur les enjeux théoriques et esthétiques de l'adaptation filmique.

Eithne O'Neill, membre du comité de rédaction de la Revue *Positif* depuis 1997, enseigne à Paris XIII. Auteur de *Stephen Frears* (Rivages, 1994), co-auteur avec Jean-Loup Bourget de *Lubitsch, la Satire romanesque* (Stock, 1988 et Flammarion, 1990), elle a signé de très nombreux articles, notamment sur « Les Couturiers français à Hollywood », « Le Thème de l'initiation chez Miyazaki » et « Le Travestisme au cinéma ».

Élise Ouvrard, agrégée d'anglais, est maître de conférences à Caen. Elle est l'auteur d'une thèse intitulée *Expériences pédagogique et salutaire dans les romans des sœurs Brontë : l'engagement féminin* (2006). Elle a déjà publié plusieurs articles sur les Brontë. Ses recherches concernent les romans des femmes écrivains britanniques du XIXe siècle et plus particulièrement la relation qu'ils entretiennent avec la société et les grands courants de pensée de l'époque.

Anne Paupe, ancienne élève de l'ENS Cachan et agrégée d'anglais, est maître de conférences à l'Université Paris XIII, où elle enseigne le cinéma et la littérature. Elle a soutenu en 2006 une thèse de doctorat intitulée « Le road movie : définitions, structures, antécédents et évolution », à Paris X-Nanterre, sous la direction de Francis Bordat. Elle s'intéresse aux genres cinématographiques américains, à la critique de cinéma aux États-Unis et à l'adaptation littéraire au cinéma.

Gilbert Pham-Thanh, agrégé d'anglais, est maître de conférences à l'Université Paris XIII. Il a soutenu une thèse intitulée *Du dandysme en Angleterre au XIXe siècle et de ses répercussions en France*, et poursuit son exploration des champs de l'esthétique, de l'élégance, des mœurs, du dandysme et de la définition de la masculinité, dans la littérature britannique du XIXe siècle. Il est aussi membre de la Société Française d'Etudes Victoriennes et Edouardiennes.

Laurence Talairach-Vielmas, agrégée d'anglais, est maître de conférences à l'Université de Toulouse-Le Mirail. Elle est spécialiste de littérature victorienne et l'auteur d'un ouvrage, *Moulding the Female Body in Victorian Fairy Tales and Sensation Novels* (Ashgate, 2007). Elle a récemment assuré la réédition d'un roman de Mary Elizabeth Braddon, *Thou Art the Man* (Valancourt Books, 2008). Elle termine actuellement un ouvrage, *Wilkie Collins, Medicine and the Gothic*, à paraître chez University of Wales Press.

Dominique Sipière est agrégé d'anglais et professeur des Universités à Paris X (Nanterre la Défense) où il anime le CICLAHO (Centre de recherches sur le cinéma classique hollywoodien). Président honoraire de la SERCIA, il a surtout publié à propos du cinéma d'Hitchcock, des films de gangsters et de *Dracula* (Armand Colin, 2005, avec Max Duperray). Direction d'ouvrages sur *Les Autres arts dans l'art du cinéma* (Presses Universitaires de Rennes, avec Alain Cohen, 2007) et sur *Éclats du Noir* (Presses Universitaires Provence, avec Max Duperray et Gilles Menegaldo, 2008). Il publie également *Jane Eyre, itinéraire d'une femme, du*